NICHOLAS MOLODOVSKY, C.F.A.
1898–1969

INVESTMENT VALUES
IN A DYNAMIC
WORLD
The Collected Papers
of Nicholas Molodovsky

Financial Analysis Series

INVESTMENT VALUES
IN A DYNAMIC
WORLD

The Collected Papers of Nicholas Molodovsky

NICHOLAS MOLODOVSKY, C.F.A.
M.A. in Economics   Harvard University
Doctor of Law   University of Paris

including

The Stock Valuator

by Nicholas Molodovsky and Catherine May

edited by **ROBERT D. MILNE, C.F.A.**

 1974

RICHARD D. IRWIN, INC.   Homewood, Illinois 60430
Irwin-Dorsey International   London, England WC2H 9NJ
Irwin-Dorsey Limited   Georgetown, Ontario L7G 4B3

First Printing, November 1974

ISBN 0-256-01608-9
Library of Congress Catalog Card No. 74–76454

Printed in the United States of America

To
Katharine McGee Molodovsky

The Financial Analysts Research Foundation
and Its Publications

1. The Financial Analysts Research Foundation is an autonomous charitable foundation, as defined by Section 501(c)(3) of the Internal Revenue Code. The Foundation seeks to improve the professional performance of financial analysts by fostering education, by stimulating the development of financial analysis through high quality research, and by facilitating the dissemination of such research to users and to the public. More specifically, the purposes and obligations of the Foundation are to commission basic studies (1) with respect to investment securities analysis, investment management, financial analysis, securities markets, and closely related areas that are not presently or adequately covered by the available literature, (2) that are directed toward the practical needs of the financial analyst and the portfolio manager, and (3) that are of some enduring value. Within the constraints of the above obligations, the Foundation cooperates with other organizations, such as The Financial Analysts Federation and The Institute of Chartered Financial Analysts, that to a substantial degree share mutual interests and objectives.

2. Several types of studies and publications are authorized:
   A. Studies based on existing knowledge or methodology which result in a different arrangement of the subject. Included in this category are papers that seek to broaden the understanding within the profession of financial analysis through reviewing, distilling, or synthesizing previously published theoretical research, empirical findings, and specialized literature;
   B. Studies that apply known techniques, methodology, and quantitative methods to problems of financial analysis;
   C. Studies that develop new approaches or new solutions to important problems existing in financial analysis;
   D. Pioneering and original research that discloses new theories, new relationships, or new knowledge that confirms, rejects, or extends existing theories and concepts in financial analysis. Ordinarily, such research is intended to improve the state of the art. The research findings may be supported by the collection or manipulation of empirical or descriptive data from primary sources, such as original records, field interviews, or surveys.

3. The views expressed in this book and in the other studies published by the Foundation are those of the authors and do not necessarily represent the official position of the Foundation, its Board of Trustees, or its staff. As a matter of policy, the Foundation has no official position with respect to specific practices in financial analysis.

4. The Foundation is indebted to the voluntary financial support of its institutional and individual sponsors by which this and other publications are made possible. As a 501(c)(3) foundation, contributions are welcomed from interested donors, including individuals, business organizations, institutions, estates, foundations, and others. Inquiries may be directed to:

> Executive Director
> The Financial Analysts Research Foundation
> University of Virginia, Post Office Box 3668
> Charlottesville, Virginia 22903
> (804) 977-6600

ix

Foreword

ONLY A FEW DAYS before he left for Mexico City, where he died, I had lunch with Nicholas Molodovsky at his favorite French restaurant in midtown Manhattan. After gently but authoritatively pointing me toward his favorite delicacies— his selection was no more random than was his investment philosophy—Nick settled down to discuss his plans for the future. Most of the conversation was about his proposed book on financial analysis, a study that was to be a synthesis of his writings over a period of some 40 years. It was his hope, expressed modestly, that the study would serve in some way as a beacon for financial analysts in preparing for their examination for the professional designation of Chartered Financial Analyst.

That topic had been considered for over a year and now Nick was actually rearranging his many obligations and responsibilities to free time for even more writing. "When I return from Mexico City," he said with customary gentle determination, "I would like to spend some quiet days with you in Charlottesville. I am doing some new research and my goal is to put down in systematic fashion the results of my studies and experience. Maybe this could be of benefit to the Institute in our efforts to develop a common body of knowledge for financial analysts."

This book, while lacking the imprimatur of Nicholas Molodovsky, does expose the reader to his considerable wisdom, his catholicity of interests and his abiding intellectual integrity. As such, this publication represents a significant accomplishment. The sifting and sorting, the weighing and evaluating, the studying and understanding, required the judgmental qualities of an individual exceptionally well-versed not only in technical financial intricacies but also of one sufficiently familiar with the person of the author to know when and how cold print should be invigorated with the enduring qualities of a man preeminent in his profession.

For several years after his death the Foundation Trustees explored the possibility of publishing a representative collection of Nick's writings. The desirability of such a project was never in question but the selection of an editor did require considerable reflection. Few possess the necessary vitalizing qualities of editorship. Many in the profession had the technical qualifications: many more the essential dedication. It was in the person of Robert Milne that the desired attributes coalesced. The book in your hands is tangible evidence of the wisdom of this choice.

Bob is a partner in the investment counseling firm of Boyd, Watterson & Co., in Cleveland. He received his undergraduate degree from Baldwin-Wallace College and his J.D. from Cleveland-Marshall Law School. After receiving the C.F.A. professional designation in 1966, he participated in various activities of the Institute which he presently serves as President and Trustee. Additionally, Bob is an Associate Editor of the *Financial Analysts Journal* and he is a member of the Editorial Board of *The C.F.A. Digest*. Several of his articles have appeared in the *Journal* in recent years, evidencing his abiding concern with the continuing education of the Financial Analyst.

Some time ago, the Molodovskys gave me a beautiful embossed bowl, since shattered. Deep memories do not always require physical embodiment but it is satisfying to have at hand this book, a lasting source of Nick's seminal influence.

C. Stewart Sheppard, *Dean*
Darden Graduate School of
Business Administration

University of Virginia

Preface

NICHOLAS MOLODOVSKY LED the profession of financial analysis out of an era of simple rules of thumb and instinctive responses into a more objective view of the complexities involved. His many articles not only brought their own luminescence to the topics involved, but also pointed out the possibilities of deriving valuable insights into the forces affecting investments when the simple rules of thumb were examined in depth. Other students were encouraged to explore the field, and their efforts provided the basis for still further advances —advances that are still continuing. This aspect of Molodovsky's work is directly documented in the assistance that he gave to many authors during his tenure as associate editor of what is now the *Financial Analysts Journal,* and especially during the last five years of his life which he spent as editor and publisher of that journal. The enormous change in the *Journal* under his leadership reflected his encouragement of the academic community and others to explore the field of financial analysis to seek out objective measurements of the forces at work. His own articles were among the most significant published to advance the state of the art of financial analysis.

At the time of his death in 1969 Molodovsky was working on two books. One was to comprise 16 chapters covering a wide variety of topics relating to common stocks and the economic forces influencing them. Some of these chapters had their genesis as articles written 10 or 20 years ago. He had not forgotten his earlier work, but rather had been keeping the articles in mind during the intervening years noting which evidence confirmed his initial views and which evidence indicated that modifications or elaborations were in order. Other chapters were completely new and still others never emerged from the idea stage. Ten of the 16 chapters were sufficiently advanced to be edited to serve as Part I of this volume. Several titles were considered by Molodovsky, and the editor selected *Investment Values in a Dynamic World* as the most appropriate description of the approach of this work. The material was mostly in draft form, and the published version includes about half of the material included by Molodovsky in his initial drafts.

In order to trace the development of Molodovsky's investment thinking, Part II of this volume consists of abstracts of his complete published work—45 articles written over a span of 42 years, in addition to two books. His published works were far too voluminous to reprint in full, and yet some knowledge of them is necessary in order to appreciate fully the flavor and the value of the contributions of this extraordinary man. The editor regrets that the abstracts merely hint at the delights of Molodovsky's prose and are rather brief summaries of the major points covered in the articles with no mention of the digressions and amplifications which comprise so much of the value of each article. While all of Molodovsky's work was of great value, making "contributions so powerful and effective so as to change the direction of the profession" (to use the terms of the Financial Analysts Federation Nicholas Molodovsky Award) his most significant works of entirely original nature contained both in Part I of this volume and in the articles abstracted in Part II are:

1. Reviews of the complexities of dividend and interest yields, destroying the complacent attitudes of most analysts who had been contented with the easy answers to the subject.
2. Reviews of the forces affecting price/earnings ratios, bringing new insights into the subject and forcing analysts to study them in greater depth.
3. Development of valuation studies in an objective manner to determine investment values for the leading stock market indexes and, more importantly, for individual stocks all of which grow at different rates. Molodovsky made many contributions to the theory of valuation of stocks by discounting their future earnings and dividends. He was the most influential leader in establishing this theory as an essential foundation of any investment portfolio.

The other book which Molodovsky was working on at the time of his death was a joint effort with his assistant, Catherine May at White, Weld & Co. Incorporated. After his death, Ms. May brought the book to completion, and it comprises Part III of this volume under the title *Value and Return via the Stock Valuator.* It is a continuation and refinement of their work in developing the theory of valuation of stocks by discounting their future earnings and dividends. As such it reflects their final effort in moving from an obscure theory into a practical approach that can be used by any investor. The most useful tables have been included in this volume, but others have been omitted because of space problems.

This volume would not have been possible without the generous support of Katharine McGee Molodovsky who donated the manuscripts and other materials used. Catherine May also generously assisted by donating her many, many hours of work on Part III for inclusion in this volume. White, Weld & Co. Incorporated, made a generous financial contribution towards the expenses involved in the project, in honor of their distinguished long-time associate Nicholas Molodovsky. Edmund A. Mennis, C.F.A., generously donated the proceeds from his Nicholas Molodovsky Award to the project.

The Institute of Chartered Financial Analysts and the Financial Analysts Research Foundation have been responsible for bringing this work to its published state. C. Stewart Sheppard, Dean of the Graduate School of Business Administration at the University of Virginia, was the initiator of the project and has carried forward his great interest throughout the gestation period. The current executive director of the Institute, W. Scott Bauman, C.F.A., and especially Robert H. Trent of the Institute have been of great assistance.

Nicholas Molodovsky would have wanted to acknowledge the assistance of the following who reviewed sections of his manuscript and made valued comments: Stan West and Norman C. Miller of the New York Stock Exchange; B. Alva Schooner, American Stock Exchange; Steven S. Anreder of *Barron's;* Gerhard Colm of the National Planning Association; Joseph Y. Jeanes, Jr. of Wilmington Trust Co.; Frank Salz, Gerhard Bry, M. F. M. Osborne of the U.S. Naval Research Laboratory; James H. Lorie, Eugene F. Fama, and Harry Roberts all of the University of Chicago; Benoit Mandelbrot of IBM; and Robert I. Cummin of the Fidelity Bank.

The editor wishes to thank Katharine McGee Molodovsky, Mrs. Charles A. Wood (Ludmilla Molodovsky Wood), and Victor Molodovsky for their great assistance with the biographical sketch. The editor would also like to thank the Editorial Review Committee of the Financial Analysts Research Foundation which supervised the project. The members of this committee were Frank E. Block of Model, Roland & Co., Inc.; John Fountain of White, Weld & Co. Incorporated; and Edmund A. Mennis of Security Pacific National Bank. Each of these was a long time valued friend of Nicholas Molodovsky and served on the editorial board of the *Financial Analysts Journal.* The editor also wishes to thank Jack Treynor, the current editor of the *Journal,* for reading Chapter 10. Most importantly he wishes to thank his partner, James F. O'Neill of Boyd, Watterson & Co., who read all of the manuscript and made many, many helpful suggestions.

October 1974   Robert D. Milne

Contents

Nicholas Molodovsky—A Personal Reminiscence

SOME YEARS AGO while attacking the roast beef at a dinner meeting of the *Financial Analysts Journal* editorial board, I idly asked Nick what he thought of the movie *Dr. Zhivago*. After a number of compliments on the many fine scenes, he noted that the film gave the erroneous impression that the revolutions in 1917 were bloodthirsty affairs. "The 1905 Revolution was full of violence, but the 1917 Revolutions were less violent. The revolutionaries tried hard to avoid unnecessary bloodshed. I remember it well. One evening near the end of the regime, another cadet and I were standing guard in front of the czar's Winter Palace in St. Petersburg. Because of the Great War, I had entered St. Vladimir Military Academy.

"We two 18-year-old cadets were alone at our post that night. A Red Army tank rolled into the square in front of us. We didn't know what to do. After a time, the other cadet picked up his rifle and began firing at the tank. I did the same. Naturally, the bullets simply bounced off the tank. The tank could have used its machine gun to kill both of us, but contented itself with showing its authority by slowly moving around the square and—after an eternity—withdrawing. This was typical. The Reds were trying to avoid unnecessary bloodshed."

One never knew what would emerge from a conversation with Nick. His education (a doctorate degree), extensive reading, and a life spent in the maelstroms of twentieth century history furnished the raw material that was burnished by a fine mind that could illumine and clarify any point under discussion. Whether it was an example from the ancient Greeks, a comment that day from an internationally prominent friend of Nick's, or even his school motto, the illustrations were to the point and were offered—as being of possible interest—in an almost apologetic manner. He never offended anyone; his erudition simply spilled out by accident. He was eager to listen to the ideas of others—and quick to grasp the essentials of well thought out concepts—and courteous when con-

1

fronted with half-baked ideas. His distinguished successor as Editor and Publisher of the *Financial Analysts Journal,* Jack Treynor, said: "Nick was the only 60-year-old I've met with the open-mindedness of a college student—ready, willing, and eager to consider any new theory on its terms no matter how revolutionary and contrary to orthodox thinking. . . . He was certainly the most brilliant man I've ever met in the investment world."

One always felt good being around Nick. The courtesy of the Old World gentleman was felt and appreciated by even the crusty, brash, and unlettered among his vast array of investment clients and associates. This was not a cloak that he donned; it was his real self. The ambience of the Harvard Club of New York, where he liked to hold his meetings—friendly, but dignified—was the essence of Nicholas Molodovsky. Frank Block, a former president of The Financial Analysts Federation and an associate editor of the *Financial Analysts Journal,* once said: "I don't know how he does it. It certainly isn't pressure. But after talking with Nick, you find yourself promising to undertake whatever job he has for you—even though you might hate it."

Nick's outstanding personal qualities, which made working with him such a joy, coupled with his unbelievably diligent work habits and professional accomplishments in developing and promoting new investment theories, brought the *Financial Analysts Journal* from a trade association publication with some signs of promise to its present position as the authoritative journal of the profession with a worldwide readership and reputation.

A brief sketch of the mileposts in his life would task the talents of a novelist; but to begin, he was born in St. Petersburg (now Leningrad) on November 28, 1898, according to the Gregorian calendar. His father, Privy Counsellor Michael Molodovsky, was chargé d'affaires for Grand Duke Nicholas Michaelovich, a grandson of Czar Nicholas I and a cousin of the reigning Czar Nicholas II. Grand Duke Nicholas had inherited his father's fortune and thousands of square miles of farmlands. As chargé d'affaires, Michael Molodovsky developed large business interests that made the Grand Duke the wealthiest member of the imperial family. The Molodovsky family lived in an apartment in the Grand Duke's palace. The Molodovskys also owned a house in St. Petersburg and a summer property. Alexandra Molodovsky presented her husband with four children—first Nicholas, then Victor, then Nataly, and finally Ludmilla.

Nicholas graduated in 1916 from the German college in St. Petersburg and in the normal course of events would have aspired to a career of service in the management of the Grand Duke's properties. However, World War I was in progress. The Molodovsky connections enabled Nicholas to be admitted to St. Vladimir Military Academy. After an accelerated course of a few months, he graduated as a lieutenant. During his time at the Academy, in July of 1917, his battalion was the only one that saved Kerensky's Provisional Government from the first attempt of the Communists to take over. As a lieutenant, Nicholas was among the officers who tried to resist the October (1917) Revolution of the Communists and then planned a coup to overthrow the Communists the following month. Their list of names came into the hands of the new government, and Nicholas, on the Grand Duke's insistence, left St. Petersburg the same night, under Victor's name and with his passport. He joined the White Armies that were fighting in the South of Russia.

His younger brother, Victor, and his two sisters were sent by their parents to the South in the care of their German governess. His father and mother stayed on in St. Petersburg to be with the Grand Duke until his imprisonment by the Reds. Nataly became an interpreter for the British Military Mission, and the brothers saw action in different units of the White Army. The South had to live through a series of revolutions, and at one time there were as many as 20 separate governments in Russia. The civil war lasted for three years. In 1920, Victor became a victim of the spotted typhus epidemic that was sweeping the South of Russia. Nicholas saved Victor's life by removing him from the hospital and evacuating him in a horse-drawn buggy from Rostov-on-the-Don the day it fell into Red hands. Nicholas then caught the typhus from his brother and almost died due to a complete lack of medical help. Finally, with an uncle's help, Nicholas was able to join his entire family, including Victor, two hours before the last boat left Novorossiisk on the Black Sea in December of 1920. The parents had previously rejoined their children, after the Grand Duke's death at the hands of Russia's new government.

When I asked Nick about this period, after some hesitation he replied as follows:

Our family, with many others, was interned on a small island near Constantinople. Nataly and I found jobs in town which permitted the family to supplement the miserable food allowance of the refugee kitchens. Our father soon left for Paris using his good pre-revolution connections. Some nine months later the whole family followed him to Paris. In Paris I found that the best way to get a job would be as a stenographer, so I went to school for a six weeks course in shorthand. Then I found a job as a stenographer with the Paris branch of the Equitable Trust Company of New York.

I was interested in continuing my education, but it was necessary to keep on working. I found out that it was possible to enroll in the law school of the University of Paris and not show up for class since no record of attendance was made. I bought the law books and bought copies of lecture notes from students who attended class and studied on my own. At the close of each academic term I appeared and took the examinations. In due course I received my degree as Doctor of Law. Victor and Ludmilla also earned their law degrees, and both became associated with the Paris branch of the distinguished Wall Street law firm of White & Case.

I continued working as a stenographer at the Equitable Trust Company branch, which was mostly engaged in selling American securities. The Equitable Trust had a special scholarship program for employees to undertake graduate study. I applied for this, and with a fortunate assist of $400 from Otto Kahn, I left for Harvard Law School in the fall of 1926. You are a lawyer, Bob, so you know how radically different the American and British common law is from the Napoleonic Code which I had studied in France. I was hopelessly confused, all alone in a strange country, and undernourished by trying to exist on the meager funds I had available. By Christmas Day I was in the hospital. The combination was too much for me.

Dean Pound of the Harvard Law School understood the problem and arranged for my transfer to the Economics Department of the Graduate School. This was something I could grasp, and I thoroughly enjoyed my studies. My first article [abstracted in Part II of this volume] was published in the *Quarterly Journal of Economics* in August of 1927. I received my Master of Arts degree and was offered a scholarship to continue my studies for the Ph.D. and to join the faculty. I felt that I had been neglecting my family long enough, leaving my brother and sisters the entire task of supporting our parents. Thus, I returned to Paris in 1928 joining Harris Forbes & Cie., which became an investment banking subsidiary of Chase Bank. My sister Nataly joined the firm and worked with me in preparing a great variety of studies for clients of the firm.

The banking reforms of the New Deal forced a separation of the investment banking subsidiaries. I became an officer of Quotations Facilities Corporation, a Transmitting Correspondent of White, Weld & Co. My business grew during the 1930s with emphasis on American securities. I published a number of articles [abstracted in Part II of this volume] and went back to the Sorbonne for additional study. My dissertation, *The Battle against the Farm Crisis in the United States*, was published in 1936.

International turmoil again was at work to uproot the Molodovskys. In 1939 it became necessary for Nick to move to the headquarters of White, Weld & Company in New York. I asked Nick if it was difficult to start over and build up a new circle of clients in the New World. "Actually, most of my Paris clients had preceded me to the U.S., so it wasn't too bad." Nick had made a lengthy stay in America during 1937 while working on his thesis on the U.S. farm crisis. Robert Heim of the Empire Trust Company was of special help to Nick, and while staying at the Heims', he met their sister-in-law, Katharine McGee. Ludmilla was also a friend of Kay McGee. When Nick returned to New York in 1939, he renewed his friendship with Kay, and they were later married at Kay's apartment on East 86th Street.

Kay already had a young daughter, and the Molodovskys had two more daughters—Elizabeth (usually called Lisa) in 1941 and Mary in 1945. The girls were baptized in the Russian Orthodox church. Kay had been brought up as a Baptist and thought that some other affiliation would be best for the religious training of the daughters. St. James Episcopal Church was not very far from the Molodovsky apartment, and both parents agreed that this would be a worthy compromise. Kay Molodovsky became quite active at St. James. For many years she has been on the staff—initially in charge of the church school and more recently involved in the financial affairs of the church. Nick attended St. James on occasion, but worshipped at the Russian Orthodox church at times of special significance.

Nick was devoted to his family, but did not interrupt his work habits often to spend unscheduled time with his daughters. Kay says, "He was always postponing pleasures to the future so that he could do the tasks of today." After his daughters were grown, he regretted not spending more time with them. He did enjoy the times spent with his family. The Russian stories of Krylov and the Fables of La Fontaine were part of Nick's heritage to the girls. For his part, he became acquainted with the literary glories embodied in Mother Goose. Nick really always wished to be a playwright, not a part of the investment world. He had written several plays in Paris. These literary efforts and those involved with the children were the background that enabled him to express his investment theories with the charm, wit, and clarity that encouraged his readers to persist in trying to understand the important concepts he had discovered.

Nick began to spend more and more evenings at home studying the basic concepts of investment philosophy and developing new theories. Many reports emerged, and in 1946 he published a book, *New Tools for Stock Market Analysis* (abstracted in Part II of this volume). Nick continued this regime of work and began to publish more in the *Financial Analysts Journal.* He became an associate editor and in 1964 was persuaded to assume the offices of Editor and Publisher. His work pattern then began each day at the Park Avenue branch of White, Weld & Company where he served his many investment clients until the stock market closed. At 4:00 P.M. he walked some blocks to the *Financial Analysts Journal's* office where he worked until 7:30. Then home for dinner followed by more work. Friday night was an off-duty night—usually involving a movie or other entertainment. It was back to work again for the weekends. Vacations were also spent reading extensively and working on his manuscripts.

This work load was too much—especially for Nick's high standards of thoroughness. He could not imagine abandoning his investment clients, and he could not leave the *Financial Analysts Journal.* He just kept pressing on and performing both occupations superlatively, at the expense of his health and his family. The Molodovsky girls grew up during these hectic years with Elizabeth graduating from Radcliffe and Yale Law School. She became a lawyer on the staff of the Human Resources Administration of the Commonwealth of Massachusetts. Mary excelled in the arts and as a dancer. She graduated from Radcliffe and undertook further studies at Columbia University. Nick's sister Nataly was involved in a serious automobile accident in 1951 and moved in with the Molodovskys until her death in 1957. By heroic efforts Nataly was able to go to work every day.

Nick's youngest sister, Ludmilla, had become associated with the Paris office of the distinguished New York law firm of White & Case. In 1937 she married Charles A. Wood, a graduate of the U.S. Naval Academy and Columbia Law School. The Woods were an old American establishment family. Charles and Ludmilla came to own the family business, Chas. S. Wood & Co., one of the largest privately owned insulation and acoustics concerns in the East, and the Insulation Realty Company. Nick was very close to both Ludmilla and her husband and became a director of their companies. Ludmilla served at Chas. S. Wood & Co. as executive vice president and for five years had to run the company alone, being one of the few women executives in the building trades. The Woods retired to Mexico, and when Mr. Wood died, Nick and Kay went to Mexico City to help Ludmilla with some of the estate problems. Shortly after his arrival Nick died of a heart attack on March 7, 1969.

It is impossible to summarize his many contributions to the profession of financial analysis. His importance may be noted by pointing out that the highest award of The Financial Analysts Federation is the Nicholas Molodovsky Award. This award by the profession is given only every few years when a recipient is found to be worthy of the requirement that he has "made contributions so powerful and effective as to change the direction of the profession or lift it to higher standards of accomplishment." Nick was the first recipient of the award. He changed the direction of the profession with the stream of articles abstracted in Part II of this volume. He discovered the theory of valuation of stocks by discounting their future earnings and dividends and turned it from a theoretical and obscure theory into a practical and widely known approach. His assistant, Catherine May, worked at White, Weld & Company with him for over 17 years in preparing tables and charts, as well as giving other assistance in turning these theories into practical working tools. His persistence with article after article brought these concepts home to the practical working financial analyst.

His unique personality and his articles drew new authors to prepare articles for the *Financial Analysts Journal* and completely revolutionized the quality of this journal to inform the practicing analyst about the latest developments in investment theory and practice. He revolutionized the profession and was a prime mover in developing material for The Institute of Chartered Financial Analysts. When the Institute began its program of certifying analysts who passed rigorous examinations, Nick enrolled in the program on the same basis as anyone else, even though he was in his 60s and a theoretician of outstanding ability and renown. He completed his studies in the other aspects of financial analysis in which he was not directly involved and passed the examination with flying colors. His final work which is embodied in this volume should add lustre to a career unparalleled in the investment world.

Robert D. Milne, C.F.A.

Part I
Common Stocks

Introduction to Chapters 1–4

BOOKS on investments generally start out discussing stocks and bonds as if they were entities with a life of their own—completely independent from the economic, political, and sociological forces shaping the courses of the corporations that issued them. Molodovsky realized that he could not hope to compress all economic history into a chapter or two. Rather, he begins his work with a chapter outlining a few of the most significant events in the development of the business corporation over the centuries. Molodovsky gives his views as to the validity of several of the most important theories that have been formulated to explain the development of the modern business corporation. Chapter 1 is meant as an hors d'oeuvre to stimulate the reader's appetite so that he will delve into the extensive literature on the subject.

Chapters 2 and 3 discuss some of the problems inherent in constructing an index to measure stock prices and how the most important modern stock market indexes have attempted to solve these difficulties. Molodovsky began his interest in this area while working with a number of authors who prepared a series of articles on stock market indexes in the *Financial Analysts Journal* in 1966 and 1967. It did not start out to be a series. The first article encouraged another author to write the second article, which caused a third author to respond, and so forth. The discussion in these chapters is not of theoretical interest only. The practical investor will see which types of investment portfolio philosophy perform better than the more scientific stock market indexes and which perform less well over time.

Chapter 4 illustrates the value of understanding the economic forces at work in an industry. Failure to recognize what changes are taking place will result in missed investment opportunities if the changes are for the better—or losses if the changes are for the worse. Molodovsky completed this chapter in 1963, and his analyses of the economic forces at work in the automobile and steel industries have held up well in the years that have elapsed since then.

1

The Business Corporation

What history tells us about the forces which have shaped the corporations of today

ARTHUR DEWING remarks that "all corporations are in a very true sense business corporations, whether organized for profit or philanthropic purposes."[1] Philanthropic corporations such as our large universities and foundations may have large funds at their disposal and may receive and expend large sums of money, yet they cannot offer for sale any stock issued by their respective institutions. They have none. In the eyes of the law and the Internal Revenue Service, these are nonprofit organizations whether incorporated or not.

A good working characteristic of a business corporation is the presence or absence of capital stock. When the Lord brought forth Heaven and Earth, stocks and bonds were not part of his creation. They were and continue to be supplied by business corporations chartered for the purpose of making profits.

A FLASHBACK

The origins of business corporations antedate recorded history. The cultures of Sumeria and Akkadia indicate the existence of more or less definite and articulate trading agreements or associations among groups of merchants before 2000 B.C. These mutual trading agreements were publicly acknowledged—whether or not they received an explicit stamp of approval by the ruling monarch. They were the remote antecedents of present-day great business corporations.

---

[1] Arthur Stone Dewing, *The Financial Policy of Corporations*, 5th ed., vol. 1 (New York: The Ronald Press Co., 1953), p. 20, fn. jj.

11

THE JOINT STOCK COMPANIES

Limiting ourselves to Anglo-Saxon experience, and sidestepping noncommercial corporate bodies, it may be noted that great need for sharing risks was felt quite early in navigation and overseas trade. At first, such sharing took place by way of one-venture partnerships, of which the senior partner was a powerful merchant with a well-developed central administration. He could run many such enterprises simultaneously or in succession, usually specializing in a single foreign area or a single product with which he was particularly familiar. The senior partner contributed the largest share of the venture capital and collected the largest share of the profits. The success of many of these ventures led to the development of more permanent trading associations which were capable of outlasting not only one single voyage but also the single human life of the senior partner. The most successful of such English joint stock companies was the East India Company. It was formed in 1559, chartered in 1600, and sent out its first trading fleet in 1601. In 1607 came the Virginia Company, in 1620 the Plymouth Company, and in 1629 the Massachusetts Bay Company.

The wealth brought back by many trading companies must have made the crown feel that it should not miss an opportunity for partaking in this prosperity. A doctrine evolved in English law that a separate and distinct legal personality of a trading company was a fiction that could be created only by a grant of the sovereign. This doctrine was extended to all collective bodies even beyond the realm of commerce. The concession of a fraction of the state's sovereignty was particularly valuable when a monopoly was involved. The state had the privilege of determining the beneficiaries of the charter grant and of the prerogatives extended to them. Kings and politicians could subscribe to large blocks of shares and conveniently forget about paying for them.

Joint stock companies gained a firm foothold in India and achieved the colonization of America. Nothing succeeds like success. This hackneyed phrase, however, had little application to the colonization companies. Even by trying hard, most of them did not succeed in business. Unlike India, there was nobody to trade with in the new colonies. The enterprise was hazardous and costly in lives and property. The settlers had trouble enough to survive and could neither enrich themselves nor repay their stockholders. All lost money. Managements were replaced and companies reorganized. Yet more companies were being formed to launch new ventures. Even the old unsuccessful companies, still struggling to keep afloat, were able to receive some influx of fresh blood. Brave men and scum, brought in by dragnets, went to replace those who had died. The lure of profit and religious frustration at home motivated those who went of their own free will. Hope, faith, sweat, and blood were bringing forth, with painful setbacks, a great new country.

Like most human institutions, corporations were gaining a place in the history of economic civilization by the skin of their teeth and through a long chain of alternating success and failure. Sometimes, hope yielded to illusion. This happened in the case of the South Sea Company, which was formed in 1711, 100 years after the East India Company was reorganized to give it a more flexible capitalization.

The South Sea Bubble

The South Sea Company was created for the purpose of strengthening public credit.[2] It undertook to provide the funds for the pay of the army and the navy as well as to take care of the interest on a portion of England's unfunded debt. As a consideration for carrying such considerable financial obligations, the company was to receive a 6 percent interest on certain specific duties received by the government. It also received the monopoly of trading in the South Seas (i.e., in the Pacific Ocean), from which the company took its name.

During the first decade of its existence, the new company was doing well. The country was enjoying great prosperity. The general affluence was rising; many ventures brought financial success; an increasing number of people were becoming rich. The speculative spirit was mounting; the foam of rising paper profits began to becloud realistic visibility.

Some audacious and not disinterested politicians and financiers sought to harness speculative gains while lightening the burden of the national debt. In 1720, the King recommended to the Commons legislation to that effect. The debts of the English State were estimated at £30,981,712. It was proposed to fund them all into one. The South Sea Company offered to take them over. It was willing to make an immediate payment of £3,500,000 as well as pay on the amount of the debts an annual interest of 5 percent for seven years and 4 percent thereafter. This offer made an impression not only on the government but on the Bank of England as well. The Bank's governor and company felt that their institution was being pushed into the background and tried to outbid the South Sea Company. Violent debates raged in Parliament for several months. Fortunately for the Bank of England, it lost out. The South Sea Company was given the royal assent. When dissolving Parliament in June 1720, the King congratulated the two houses on having set the liquidation of the national debt on a firm basis without violation of the public faith.

The South Sea Company began offering, at frequent intervals, subscription lists to its shares at ever rising prices. Four million shares were subscribed. Some of the directors were made baronets for their great services.

Between the fall of 1719 and April 1720, when the assent law was passed, the South Sea Company shares rose from £126, which was itself a new high, to £310. Six weeks later, they were selling at £500. Early in June, they were

---

[2] A. Andreades, *History of the Bank of England, 1640 to 1903*, 2d ed. (London: P. S. King, 1924), pp. 128 ff. Our account of the South Sea Bubble episode is based on Andreades. The sources used by him seem to antecede those of Walter Bagehot's "Lombard Street."

quoted £890 a share. At the end of that month, the price had reached £2,000. The air was thick with rumors of the acquisition by the company of distant and invaluable markets and of discovery of fabulous mines and hidden treasures.

The mass illusion was spreading. Companies were being organized for various purposes ranging from the legitimate to the absurd. The real aim, of course, was to enrich the promoters. One project aimed to discover perpetual motion; another to import large jackasses from Spain; perhaps the most ingenious proposal was to found a company "for carrying on an undertaking of great advantage which shall in due time be revealed." Each subscriber was to deposit two guineas, in return for which he would subsequently receive a 100-guinea share, and would then be informed of the nature of the project. In five hours, the promoter had collected £2,000 with which he decamped the same day. This super-boom could not outlast the faith in a continued rise of share prices.

In a way, the South Sea Company became its own executioner. In 1719, Parliament had passed the Bubble Act prohibiting the formation of companies without a charter. Urged by Walpole, the King issued on June 11, 1720, a proclamation against mischievous and dangerous undertakings presuming to act as corporate bodies or raising stocks or shares without legal authority. The following day, Parliament passed an act dissolving them. Alarmed by the proliferation of new companies, some of which could become potential rivals, the South Sea Company obtained on July 12 a writ from the Lord of Justice which enforced their dissolution.

In the price collapse that followed, the shares of the South Sea Company were not spared. By the end of September 1720, they dropped to £175 versus £2,000 at the end of June. The panic brought an economic calamity which transcended national boundaries.

The Bubble Act had been devised to protect the shareholders as well as the general public. It ruled that joint stock companies should be not only chartered but also operated under state authority. It was repealed one hundred years later, in 1825, without having served its protective purpose at the time of the greatest need.

The Aftermath

The experience of the South Sea Bubble was not soon forgotten. It took time to outlive it and to place it in the perspective of a warning inscribed into historical annals. Joint stock companies fell into ill repute. The formation of new corporate business ventures was meeting with distrust.

The feeling of investment caution crossed the Atlantic. Even in the early post-colonial times, corporate charters could not be secured in the United States except through a special act passed by a state legislature. The creation of each charter required a separate act. In England, a charter had to be bestowed by the crown. In America, the sovereign powers of the various states served as the crown's successors.

This practice was abandoned with the adoption by most states, in the 1830s, of general incorporation laws. This led to the disappearance of controls of corporate promotions. The corporate charters or, as some states came to call them, the Certificates or the Articles of Incorporation, were no longer discussed in detail by legislators intent to protect the interests of shareholders, creditors, and the public; they were buried with indifferent silence in the archives of the departments of state. The mere filing of an application became equivalent to incorporation.

Another corporate legal document, the bylaws, provides the detailed administrative rules concerning corporate management and procedure. The purpose of the charter is to delineate the nature of the business in which the corporation may engage. In the absence of legislative checks, the promoters tended to draw ever widening circles of permissible corporate activities and managerial functions.

THE LEVER OF LIMITED LIABILITY

The gigantic strides made by the American corporate economy throughout the nineteenth century drew their energy from two forces above others. One was technological. It consisted of the appearance of mechanically powered machinery which expanded the horizons of manufacturing production. The other force was of an intangible nature. It manifested itself by applying on a vast scale the ancient discovery of limited liability, thereby gaining access to unlimited resources of capital. This invisible force blended well with the capitalistic system of industrial organization. Without it, the scale of operations demanded by the new technology could not have been financed by the savings of individuals. The greatest incentive of public corporate stock ownership is its limited liability. Financially, it is the core of the economics of the corporate system.

Members of business associations, partnerships, and owners of individual enterprises are liable without limitation, with rare exceptions. This is not true with corporate stock, although before the banking reforms of the 1930s, bank stocks were an exception with double liability being the usual situation and occasionally unlimited liability.

Taussig mentions the case of the City of Glasgow Bank, which failed in 1878, leaving hundreds of small shareholders in Scotland ruined because each found himself liable for the bank's debts without limit.

> Probably few of them were clearly aware of this possibility when they became owners of their shares. The general practice of strict incorporation and consequent limitation of liability had put them off their guard. If experiences like theirs were frequent, it would not be possible to gather the capital for large enterprises by contributions from many scattered individuals.[3]

---

[3] F. W. Taussig, *Principles of Economics*, 3d ed., vol. 1 (New York: Macmillan, 1926), p. 84.

The combination of the forces of the industrial revolution and of limited liability created a multiplier of promotional capital. The early promoters were strong and able men, more distinguished by the ambition for wealth and power than by sensitivity of moral fiber. A blacksmith would make machines from designs possibly stolen abroad by his employer and a new manufacturing enterprise was born. But the promoter's will for growth could not be satisfied unless he could attract the public's money to his venture. This enabled him to liberate at least some of his original capital and use it, by successively repeating the process, to forge an industrial complex.

Between 1800 and 1820, some 550 manufacturing companies were incorporated in eight states, Massachusetts and New York being far in the lead. But soon the acceleration of investment became tremendous.

> From 1820 to 1860 the growth was from $50 million to almost an even billion dollars. The output of factories grew even more rapidly than did investments, in some industries the annual gross production exceeding the total of capital involved.[4]

The country's industrial development made strong demands on financial resources. When efforts were made to pull a vast continent together by transportation more efficient than the horse and wagon, American capital was scarce. Many railroad promoters had to seek financing in London.

European investors became early attracted to American railroad securities. The height of financing the construction of railroads by foreign capital was probably reached soon after the discovery of gold in California in 1849. Until the early 1890s, many American railroad systems were financed abroad, or powerful foreign investment interests helped their expansion. Even the panic of 1873 was only a temporary killjoy. But the previous successful placing of so much American paper abroad had deep effects on the sequence of developments during the crisis of 1893 and the years that followed.

The acuteness of the 1893 panic itself was accentuated by foreign liquidation of American bonds and stocks reaching hundreds of millions of dollars. It brought a severe collapse of prices. Two years went by before improving business brought renewed foreign buying of American railroad securities. It helped to finance an adverse balance of trade. The economic recovery in this country contined to rise, blossoming out into great prosperity by 1898. Within the next few years most of the foreign-held American railroad securities were repurchased from abroad.[5] Thenceforth, the strength of American capital markets had no need to lean on foreign lenders and investors.

Still, the memory of their ventures into America continued to linger in European financial circles. It was not extinguished even by the Great Depression when one third of Class I railroads were swallowed by receiverships. London brokers

---

[4] Fred Albert Shannon, *Economic History of the People of the United States* (New York: Macmillan, 1934), pp. 251–52.

[5] William F. Ripley, *Railroads, Finance & Organization* (New York and London: Longmans, Green & Co., 1927), pp. 6–7.

and Amsterdam bankers preserved an extraordinary curiosity and an amazing knowledge about the financial structure of American railroads even when they became bankrupt. Investments made in securities of American railroads in reorganizations were later liquidated with great profit. But at the end of World War II, investment interest in rails was largely played out, both at home and abroad. War brought in its wake many fascinating innovations. Investors veered to emerging new horizons.

SEPARATION OF OWNERSHIP AND CONTROL

Limited liability paved the way for unrestricted growth of the size of a single corporate enterprise. American business history is full of examples of corporations which grew into giants out of a small original investment by the founder and a few relatives or friends. The founder's equity, whether contributed out of previously accumulated or newly borrowed funds, represented, as a rule, the largest ownership share and placed him in undisputed position of proprietorship and managerial control. The dominating position of the original entrepreneur often passed to his direct descendants creating a reigning dynasty of owners. There was no cleavage between ownership and control. The interests of the enterprise were equated with those of the owners who were responsible to no outsiders. Whether the fortunes of the enterprise rose, fluctuated with the business tides, or deteriorated through inept management or misfortune, the owners were the principal beneficiaries or victims. Indirectly, the fate of their employees was, of course, affected, as were the consumers of the products they manufactured and the finances of the creditors.

Things were different, however, in the case of publicly-owned corporations. The managements were responsible to shareholders who owned the property and to the directors whom the stockholders had appointed as their representatives for the supervision of the property. So long as the stockholders remained relatively few and owned substantial numbers of shares, the responsibility of the management was effective and real. Yet with the passage of time the numbers of stockholders tended to grow, while their holdings of stock were being splintered. With the appearance and expansion of organized security markets, increasing opportunities for tempting investments were calling for diversification rather than concentration of stock ownership. The relative merits of numerous balance sheets and income statements could be compared.

The gradual loosening and the eventual virtual disappearance of the ties between the managers and the owners of incorporated property raised justified fears of the effects produced by absentee ownership. The fierce energy of a ruthless entrepreneur, battling for ever larger personal profits, could not be expected to be matched by hired handlers of assets whose owners were becoming increasingly dispersed. There was even a greater danger than a flabby and ineffective mismanagement. A conflict of interests could arise between the anonymous stockholders and those managers who were bent to derive above all—and to the largest extent possible—personal benefits from positions of strength which could be rendered self-perpetuating.

Many books have been written—and continue to be published—on the subject of what became known as the "managerial revolution." The most influential single work dealing with the broad aspects of the social, legal, and economic significance of the new corporate economy made its appearance during the Great Depression under the title of *The Modern Corporation and Private Property* by Berle and Means.[6] They emphasized that the transfer of a large proportion of the country's industrial wealth from individual ownership to that of large, publicly-financed corporations had deeply affected the economic bases of modern civilization. The divorce of ownership of these quasi-public corporations from actual control was resulting in a new form of economic organization of society.

In fact, Berle and Means believed that the corporation had already transcended the boundaries of a business organization and was in the process of becoming a social institution rivaling the power of the state. They thought that the future might see the corporation successfully competing on equal terms with the state and possibly even superseding it as the dominant factor of social organization.[7]

Berle and Means felt deeply that the era of individually-owned private enterprises, which had lasted for 300 years and had succeeded medieval feudalism, was being in turn replaced by an economic and social organization financed by vast aggregates of anonymous capital removed from the actual control and ruled, instead, by a small managerial group.

In retrospect, it is clear that their findings and projections were overstated. Two different economic and social aspects are intermingled in the picture painted by Berle and Means. They equated their significance. Yet, in reality, while interrelated on the surface, they have no identical implications. These two factors are:

1.   A wide diffusion and liquidity of certificates of ownership.
2.   Control of economic power.

The first condition is inherent in the existence of a fully developed capitalistic system endowed with organized security markets. The diffusion of ownership has progressed even far beyond the situation that existed when Berle and Means wrote their book. Many giant proprietorships, such as Ford Motor, have become publicly owned.

Berle and Means studied the nature of the voting control of the 200 largest nonfinancial corporations in 1929, and their study has been brought more up to date by another author who reviewed the situation as it stood in 1963.[8] The results can be summarized as follows:

[6] Adolf A. Berle, Jr. and Gardiner C. Means, *The Modern Corporation and Private Property* (New York: Macmillan, 1933).

[7] Ibid., p. 357.

[8] Robert J. Larner, "Ownership and Control in the 200 Largest Nonfinancial Corporations, 1929 and 1963," *The American Economic Review*, vol. 52, no. 4 (September 1966).

	1929	1963
Management control.......................	44%	85%
Control by a strong minority interest	23	9
Majority or private ownership................	11	
Other	22	6
	100%	100%

On a statistical basis, therefore, management is in control since no other group owns sufficient stock to dictate to management. Yet, the device of using managerial control as a residual pool of economic power containing all corporations that are not clearly situated within some other area of control does not impress us as felicitous in logic. The concept of control, as well as its factual presence, is subtle and complex. Sometimes a combination of bankers and others represented on the boards actually direct the policies of the corporations, even though on a statistical basis management is in complete control. Corporate power is an elusive subject, difficult to define or measure.

We encounter yet another complexity of life which is inadequately reflected by the terms we use in this context. "Managerial revolution," "managerial control"—and other variations on this theme—imply the existence of management as an entity. Outside of rare cases in which a member (or a group) of the top management is simultaneously the corporation's controlling stockholder, management not infrequently resembles more a bunch of watchful scorpions guardedly crawling up an organization chart than a Sunday procession of vestrymen in striped pants marching the money collections up to the altar.

This comparison is manifestly unfair. It is used to dramatize a point.

Who are, in fact, the members of the managerial class? They are American citizens—often of humble descent—to whom professional business management became, by choice or accident, a career. The top echelons are filled, as a rule, by a process of competitive selection of the fittest.

It may be stated, in fact, that the corporate system has evolved into a strong yet beneficial sector of the American economy. Instead of exploiting the consumers, it offers them abundance and quality. Far from repressing individual ability and initiative, it opens to all comers countless and varied opportunities for building personal success and wealth. The old French saying that every soldier carries in his pack a field marshal's baton has never been truer. Nor has the corporate system enslaved labor; it now deals with unions on the basis of negotiated contracts whose terms, more often than not, are close to labor's writing its own ticket. The managerial class issues no commands to constitutional powers, but stands before them in awe. It has to take into its stride so much competition, so many limitations and controls, that the enrichment it has brought to American life is a noteworthy and remarkable achievement.

It is true nevertheless that rivalries inside executive suites do not contribute to monolithic decision making. No men are more closely watched by their own associates than top management members, unless, to repeat, they happen to control the company's stock. Decisions are the joint product of men standing high on ever more vulnerable corporate rungs. And, in turn, they draw on the cumulative wisdom and experience of technological expertise and talent. The latter play varying roles in different corporations, and the numbers of technical people employed depend on the nature of each company's operations. However, the complexity of corporate organization, and its numerous checks and balances, do not drown out the decisive voice of the chief executive. The final decision and, in particular, its timing, come from his mind. When the decision is far-reaching in technological significance and capital involved, the chief's intuition lays on the line both the corporate future and his own career. Yet by emerging from such a strong understructure, the odds in favor of the venture are usually higher than its risks. Only infrequently does it happen that a business leader suffers from a temperamental compulsion to gallop on white Napoleonic steeds. Luck willing, he may remain firmly in the saddle for years. Yet the fall is preordained.

"Managerial revolution" is a romantic term. Four decades ago, Berle and Means envisioned a society ruled by financial princes. To be sure, some successful financiers and industrialists have accumulated personal fortunes of a princely size. Their influx has swelled the ranks of men of great wealth and the numbers of palatial estates and residences, racing horse stables, polo ponies, private yachts, and wall-to-wall Karakul carpets. Rembrandts and Picassos have found new walls, lined by precious furniture. Shelves in sumptuous libraries display rows of beautifully bound rare books whose contents are less familiar to the host than those of his favorite cocktail or the aroma of his Cuban cigar imported via London. Private jets, twice as many automobiles of the finest makes as there are family members, dogs with much longer pedigrees than their masters' and of rarer breeds, staffs of highly trained servants, fine jewels on the mansion's hostess, a more receptive Social Register—all this adds to the pleasures of living of the very rich. Soon they are taken for granted. Glamor fades from the worldly goods. It is more important to ask what they have added to the possessor's economic power. To answer this question, let us leave the luxurious establishments of the most successful members of the managerial class. They are not necessarily typical. Not all men are overwhelmed by money cloudbursts. There are people of simpler tastes and stronger propensity for social giving. Yet before abandoning wealth as a trail to power, let us climb the Olympus all the way and take a peek at the gods.

There are not many men either in this country or overseas whose net worth approaches or exceeds a billion dollars. What does the extent of their economic power mean in precise, concrete, specific terms? It is clear that they can own vast aggregates of commercial and industrial properties as well as, for pure enjoyment and pleasure, residences of the type described above. They can employ many men in personal service or for industrial work. Outside of thriller movies and books, we have no knowledge of personal wealth devoted to corruption and crime, except by Mafia members. In their circles, power is a true goal, as it was for Stalin and Hitler for not dissimilar reasons.

It was not in personal abuses of wealth that Berle and Means and other writers saw a menace to society, but in the dominion over large areas of production and distribution of goods by managements not accountable to property owners. They did not seem to realize that no managerial revolution ever took place. It was an unavoidable transition, an evolution brought about by the country's economic growth.

The growth of demand opened up opportunities for new entrepreneurs and for the broadening of activities of those already profitably engaged. A successful entrepreneur who was enlarging his plant or was expanding his business geographically, especially with entry into unrelated industries, was bound to dilute his energies and attention. The bigger his industrial complex became, the thinner was the actual control he could effectively exercise over the growing number of his enterprises. Even if he retained full, or majority, equity ownership over them all, after inevitable borrowing or equity financing, it became imperative to hire general assistants and local managers to develop the new ventures and oversee the going concerns.

Undoubtedly, nothing of an alarming or reprehensible nature would have been observed by any agencies protecting the public interest in seeing the owner delegate administrative powers to hired personnel. In fact, if he had not done so, he would have acted with improvidence and neglect. At some point, the stretching of operating management would have gone too far. The connecting link between ownership and control would have suddenly snapped.

The much lamented separation of ownership and control marked in reality a giant forward step in the development of corporate economy. Growth would have been unthinkable without it. It represented an inevitable branching out and the most valuable practical application of the principle of limited liability. Without the latter, as without the separation of ownership and control, and without the creation and development of organized security markets, there could be no economic progress.

A *reductio ad absurdum* can demonstrate the fallacy of ownership of an unlimited number of enterprises without surrender of control. While the form is different, the situation is the same when a chain of enterprises of varying sizes is replaced by a few corporate giants. Assume, for argument's sake, that the entire American industry of today is fully and indivisibly owned by a single individual, Godo. There is no separation between ownership and control: Godo owns and manages all the enterprises in the land. It is an obvious impossibility, both financial and physical. It is equally obvious that the only workable solution is the one which was historically and naturally developed by the modern corporate economy. Even in the Soviet communist state, Godo has to appoint managers. In the capitalist system, collective stock ownership by individuals replaces Godo's communist proprietorship.

A man worth a billion is poor compared to Godo's total hypothetical wealth which, translated into real terms, is the wealth of this country at large. A billionaire's total economic power can control only a small section of industry. The joy dispensed by yachts and palazzos is ephemeral. Unless he discovers happiness in working and giving, or can attain the country's highest political office, which comes nearest to power over fellow men, Godo will shrivel up and die from loneliness and boredom.

Perhaps the clearest result of the separation of ownership and control has been the creation of a new profession. Graduate schools of business have joined on the campus those of medicine, architecture, engineering, and law. The hierarchy of success and financial reward forms many echelons in all professional fields. The pride of achievement, a scholar's fame, an artist's glory, social ambition, political power are placed by many above dollars and cents. A Nobel prize may be coveted more than a huge fortune. A businessman, Harold S. Geneen, has remarked that one may work for money at first, but later—and much harder—for pride. Semon Knudsen was surely not motivated by money in switching from General Motors to Ford, and later taking on the responsibilities of White Motor.

MANAGERS AND STOCKHOLDERS

The plurality of motivations and the variety of their mixes in different men necessarily creates a conflict of interests between managements and stockholders which no system of options and incentives can cure. The stockholder's interest in a corporation has one dimension only: the financial return. An ambitious executive's relation to his corporate employer is more complex.

There exists an abundant academic literature which examines in detail, and from many points of view, the functions of the corporate executives and the roles played by them in the fields of competition and monopoly, as well as the effects of their pursuits of personal enrichment and of less tangible aims, such as promotion and status. They all affect the welfare and the allocation of resources of the corporations under their management, their stockholders, and society at large. The simple concept that the only goal of all managements is to maximize corporate profits does not appear to provide a full or accurate answer.

Despite the fact that maximization of profits may not always be the overriding objective of management, an excellence of performance is still its best line of defense. If it falters, the dormant dichotomy between managers and stockholders may degenerate into an open rift.

An incapable management cannot endure. The wide publicity given to financial statements makes poor results visible to all. If their own board of directors will not dislodge the chief executive officer and his associates responsible for mediocre figures, outsiders will step in. Groups will be formed to acquire enough stock to vote the inefficient out, if sound analysis reveals that the assets can be put to better use. This is particularly true in the case of relatively small firms. The cash takeover device can be used, among its other objectives, to attain this goal.

The top managements of large and *successful* corporations are more securely entrenched. Through the mechanism of proxies, which they can usually put together in sufficient numbers to assure a majority vote, managements with only nominal personal holdings of stock can remain in control year after year. It takes unusual determination and large funds to force them out. The simplest way for a stockholder who has doubts concerning the company's future outlook is to sell the stock, unless he has prohibitive capital gains. A proxy contest makes sense only when a powerful group intends to take over the management. The challenger must be prepared to meet a heavy cost, which, in the case of a struggle for the control of a major corporation, can run into millions of dollars. Still, many proxy fights have taken place, not infrequently ousting established managements, for better or worse.

There exists another method to attack the management. This is the derivative suit. It is an indirect attack. A minority stockholder can bring suit in the name of the corporation itself to repair any damage that the corporation could have sued to redress. This is a difficult action to undertake. It is subject to various court-imposed requirements which were introduced because of many previous abuses. However, some individual lawyers have achieved distinction and fortune in this specialized field.

INSTITUTIONAL INVESTORS

A fairly recent book expresses the hope that effective control of management policies could be exercised by large institutional investors.[9]

Berle and Means could not foresee that the fragmentation of stock ownership into small pieces would be reversed by the appearance in the economic and stock market arena of institutional investors. Through the liberalization of investment statutes that controlled them, they made an inconspicuous entrance. Their power has been rapidly growing, transforming the vision of the future that appeared to the disturbed view of Berle and Means.

> A market populated by elephants trading among pygmies cannot be run by rules designed for competition among equals. . . . The institutions, it is argued, are in the position of dominant stockholders and, as such, have a duty to scrutinize the actions of management. . . .[10]

Once again we are plunged into a difficult problem, but in a different type of world. So far, institutional investors have preferred selling the stocks of companies with whose managements they are no longer impressed.

The reluctance of institutional investors to engage in proxy struggles is due to legal and practical reasons. Above all, they are trained as financial analysts, not in the management of corporations operating in numerous and varied indus-

---

[9] Daniel Jay Baum and Ned B. Styles, *The Silent Partners: Institutional Investors and Corporate Control* (Syracuse, N.Y.: Syracuse University Press, 1965).

[10] Ibid., from the Introduction by Father Harbrecht.

trial fields. Social questions of corporate responsibility are becoming a concern for institutional investors. This should not preclude, however, prior to selling, informal conferences between institutional investors and the managements of corporations whose professional performance is being questioned.

This route appears now to be increasingly followed. The feeling seems to be growing among the institutions themselves, as well as stock exchanges and supervisory bodies, that a greater participation by institutional investors in discussions with corporate managements whose stocks they control, sometimes to an important extent, could render a real public service. Some investment fund managers are fairly outspoken in their views on this delicate problem and on the kind of action they recommend and take. Yet reticence is the more general rule. It is at least of interest to note that a powerful proprietorship interest in corporate enterprises is again becoming an important fact of life after it had practically vanished from the economic scene.

While it is still in a state of flux, the institutionalization of investments in common stocks will certainly contribute in some measure to further dissipation of the fear that corporate managers will rule the modern industrial society. This fear had been long overblown out of its true proportions with reality. Much more vital and far-reaching are the questions posed by the role played by business corporations in the economic concentration of industry.

2

Measuring the Market

BEFORE turning to some of the more complex aspects of the relations between stock prices and corporate earnings, it is necessary first to examine the statistical apparatus for measuring stock prices. There is a great dispersion of stock price changes. Figure 2.1 shows the dispersion of stock prices for some of the 200 largest American nonfinancial corporations for the 12-year period 1953 to 1965. Even if the seven stocks with the sharpest gains are ignored, as well as the one downward slip, the remaining range of price changes still extends between practically zero and 1,000 percent. Such a tremendous range would not be very helpful for comparative purposes if we tried to study changes in stock prices in relation to changes in other economic factors.

Yet, in order to make meaningful comparisons with other economic factors, a way must be found to express the heterogeneous experience of individual stocks by a single figure which could legitimately represent the average behavior of stocks. Prices of individual common stocks do not fluctuate in swings of equal amplitude, nor even necessarily in the same direction. Is it possible to construct a meaningful common measure representative of their dissimilar action? This difficulty also applies to efforts to measure other types of price changes. As Irving Fisher expressed it:

> Most people have at least a rudimentary idea of a "high cost of living" or of a "low level of prices," but usually very little idea of how the height of the high cost or the lowness of the low level is to be measured. . . . There would be no difficulty in such measurement . . . if all prices moved up in perfect unison or down in perfect unison. But since, in actual fact, the prices of different articles move very differently, we must employ some sort of compromise or average of their divergent movements.[1]

This difficulty applies to stock prices as well. In fact, it is greater than in the case of most commodities. Commodities may remain substantially unchanged

---

[1] Irving Fisher, *The Making of Index Numbers*, 3d ed., rev. (Boston and New York: Houghton Mifflin Co., 1927), p. 2.

FIGURE 2.1
Stock Price Changes—200 Largest Corporations

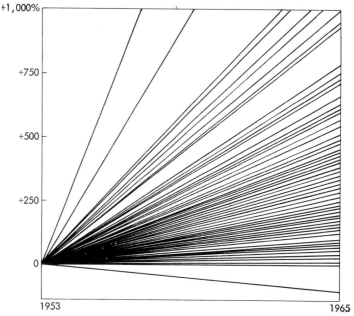

through years and centuries as a result of fixed units of measurement and well-defined grading standards. The concept of a stock price is in a different logical category. A stock is essentially a claim on the earnings and dividends of a corporation, and these are in a constant state of flux. Corporations are always changing, and thus the nature of a share of stock is similarly changing. This problem of measuring change will underlie much of the contents of this book. For the time being, we shall limit ourselves to considering stocks as commodities and will review the attempts of early students to construct indexes to measure the height of the stock market. In Chapter 3, we will discuss the basic statistical assumptions which are used in the more widely accepted modern stock market indexes.

The first stock market measure was published on July 3, 1884, in a daily financial news sheet brought out by Dow Jones & Company. It consisted of 11 active representative stocks, 9 of which were railroad issues. Delaware & Hudson was eventually added to the list of the Dow Jones averages, bringing the total to 12 stocks. When *The Wall Street Journal* began appearing on July 8, 1889, it continued to print the same stock average.

It was not until *The Wall Street Journal* was rounding out the seventh year of its existence that an average was inaugurated which was composed of industrial stocks alone. The Dow-Jones Industrial Average (DJIA) was born in May, 1896.

It also consisted of 12 stocks. From among the present 30 DJIA stocks, only General Electric and American Brands were in the original group of 12. Nor did they remain permanently thereafter in the DJIA. They have been eliminated and reinstated during the intervening years, reflecting the ebb and flow of industrial life.

The DJIA was enlarged to 20 stocks in 1916. Not until 1928 did the composition of the Average reach the present number of 30 stocks, which number remained unchanged ever since. However, only slightly more than half the stocks included in the 1928 list of 30 components still remain in the Average.

As noted, the DJIA numbered 12 stocks in 1896. It may seem an inordinately small sample. Yet, for a long time, the number of publicly traded stocks was quite limited and reliable records of their quotations were even more so. Their numbers grew slowly.

An indication of how few issues had an active market is the following table:

TABLE 2.1
Issues Trading at Least Once a Month on the New York
Stock Exchange

	Railroad Stocks	Other Stocks
1870	42	10
1880	57	7
1884	80	16
1896	85	36

While the total number of industrial issues quoted on the New York Stock Exchange was quite small in these years, the rapid industrial growth then under way resulted in the following gains in the number of listed issues:

TABLE 2.2
Issues Listed on the New York Stock Exchange

	Railroad Stocks	Other Stocks
1900	177	185
1910	175	251
1920	173	509
1930	160	1,133

When the number of stocks in the Dow-Jones Industrial Average was increased to 30 in 1928, it may have already become, in terms of number of issues, a small and perhaps unrepresentative sample of the entire industrial list quoted on the Exchange. Yet, this observation does not hold if the comparisons are made in terms of the respective dollar values of the total list and of the Dow-Jones sample. According to one study, the 30 DJIA stocks consistently accounted for between 30 percent and 36 percent of the total market value of all stocks listed on the New York Stock Exchange during the 20 years 1946–1965.[2] The same study comments further:

> The DJIA is also well balanced in providing representation in most of the major sectors of American industry. There are ten companies supplying daily necessities to the consumer, three automotive issues, four chemicals, three oils, and ten capital goods companies. In most cases an industry is represented by its largest company. In summary, apart from the individual preferences that any analyst would have, the 30 DJIA stocks appear to represent a sound cross-section of mature, blue chip stocks.

Industrial life is in a state of constant change. The 12 stocks which compose the original Dow-Jones Industrial Average would, in the case of most of them, no longer be very representative of present realities. They included such issues as American Cotton Oil, Chicago Gas, Distilling & Cattle Feeding, and Tennessee Coal and Iron. Other glories of the past such as Standard Rope and Twine, Pacific Mail, Central Leather, Famous Players Lasky, and Victor Talking Machine have had their day. But as the drama of economic life unfolded, other components replaced them. This process of substitution has never ceased. As recently as 1959, four important stocks, American Smelting, Corn Products, National Distillers, and National Steel, were politely let out of the house and had to concede the floor to Alcoa, Anaconda, Owens-Illinois, and Swift.

These substitutions aim to reflect more accurately the current industrial scene. Whether they always succeed may be questioned. No scientific rigor or statistical industrial classification guides the departures and the arrivals. Nor are they the result of periodic revisions or any formal and systematic procedure. They stem from the general business experience and judgment of a small and changing group of men. Since 1939 substitutions have been made on only two occasions. The financial editor of *The Wall Street Journal* is the Average's watchdog. When he feels that a change in the Average's composition is in order, he writes a detailed memorandum to the management of Dow Jones & Company outlining the suggested substitutions. The president and such other officers as he may call in make the decision.

IBM was taken out of the Average on March 14, 1939. This was not done out of prescience of its future market action. Simply, it was selling only a few times each month and was adding or dropping a score of points between each trade, thereby distorting the Average. The elimination of IBM was a stroke of luck, because the Average might otherwise have risen to perhaps twice its current level. However, in fairness to the compilers of the index, it is unlikely that IBM would have survived for a much longer time as a component. The proved astute business sense of the Average's makers would have undoubtedly caused a substitution at an appropriate moment.

---

[2] Robert D. Milne, "The Dow-Jones Industrial Average Reexamined," *Financial Analysts Journal*, vol. 22, no. 6: 83–88 (November–December 1966).

In 1939, IBM was replaced by American Tel. & Tel. This stock could not be used in the Dow Utility Average since its high price at that time would have completely outweighed the other stocks in this Average. The propriety of American Tel. & Tel.'s being included in an average of industrial stocks has been questioned, from time to time, by financial writers, and it has been considered by the insiders at Dow Jones & Company. Yet, so far the latter have felt that American Tel. & Tel.'s ownership of Western Electric justifies its presence in the DJIA as a representative of the telephone business.

ADJUSTING FOR SPLITS OF STOCKS IN THE DJIA

As already mentioned, the number of stocks in the DJIA has remained at 30 since 1928. However, while the number of components remained the same, stock splits continued to take place. If they had not been made, most American investors would have been transformed into buyers of odd lots. For example, if General Motors common had never been split, it would be selling for $10,200 per share instead of the $85 per share prevailing at the time of this writing.

Before 1928, the method of adjusting for splits in any of the DJIA stocks was direct and simple. If a stock was split 2-for-1, the following day its price was multiplied by two. (A similar procedure was followed in the case of substitutions by applying to the price of the new stock the appropriate factor.)

Since 1928 a rather unusual method has been used, a method not employed in any other index that this writer is aware of. This method is a changing divisor method. We shall illustrate it by a hypothetical example. The average is computed by totaling the market price of the 30 stocks included in the index and (originally) dividing the total by 30 to give the average price of a share. However, if we assume that the average is 100 and that stock A, also selling at 100, splits 2-for-1, the adjustment will be made as follows:

TABLE 2.3

	Day before Split	*To Adjust for Split*
Total for 29 stocks	2,900	2,900
Stock A	100	50
Total for 30 stocks	3,000	2,950
Divisor	30	29.5
DJIA	100	100

Thus, every time a stock splits, the divisor is reduced in order to adjust for the split (or large stock dividend). The effect of numerous stock splits over the years had reduced the divisor to 1.661 at the start of 1973.

The main criticism of this method is that it reduces the importance of any stock which splits. In our hypothetical example, stock A accounted for 100/3,000 or 3.3 percent of the DJIA prior to its split, but only 50/2,950 or 1.7 percent of the index after its split. The difference in its weight is distributed among the other 29 stocks in the DJIA which did not split—and they therefore become more important in determining the future movements of the DJIA.

The net effect of using the changing divisor is to diminish the weight of those stocks which advance fastest in price and are therefore split, and to increase the weight in the DJIA of the slower moving stocks. The question of the presence or absence of bias in the DJIA introduced by the method of a changing divisor has been vigorously discussed pro and con in the pages of the *Financial Analysts Journal.* We refer interested readers to this debate.[3]

In addition to a possible bias, the Dow-Jones Industrial Average has been accused of other sins as well. The growth of the stocks comprising the DJIA over its 77-year history has resulted in a very high index value. When investors follow changes in the DJIA, they actually look at the fluctuations of stock prices through a powerful magnifying glass.

In watching the swings in the DJIA figures, it is psychologically difficult to remain constantly conscious of the fact that they represent nothing but point changes of an index. Even in the minds of professional observers, these point changes are instinctively related to dollars and cents. This mental difficulty of dissociating index points from their real money effects can produce an emotional impact on buying and selling decisions. In fact, changes in the DJIA are frequently expressed in terms of dollars and cents. Many brokers would be more likely to tell their clients that the market was down on a given day by $18 than that the DJIA had declined 18 points. In fact, the name of the average would probably not even be mentioned. The ingrained habit of its use is so great that most people would have to make an effort to think in other terms.

An 18-point change in the DJIA is equivalent to just about a one dollar average change in the price of each of its component stocks. This is because the current divisor of the total prices of the stocks in the DJIA is 1.661 instead of 30. A movement up or down of 18 points in a single day makes a strong impression on participants or bystanders. Yet a corresponding dollar result is not as significant. For the DJIA itself, an 18-point change in one session, when the index stands at 1,000, is a 1.8 percent change. It is a substantial change, occurring only a few times each year.

Personally, the author enjoys the magnifying effect of the DJIA. It changes nothing in practical results, but makes life seem less drab. He recognizes, however, that this is not a very civic feeling. He has been watching the tape daily for over three decades, and has painstakingly dissected the structure of all indexes. He recognizes that the effect might be quite different on a nonprofessional, especially if he is a neophyte or if nature has endowed him with a sensitive and vulnerable nervous system.

Various "cures" have been suggested for the DJIA. The most common is to "split" the Average 10:1. This would merely amount to shifting the decimal point

---

[3] See the *Financial Analysts Journal,* vol. 22, no. 6 and vol. 23, nos. 1, 2, and 3.

one place to the left. Dow Jones & Company do not feel that the suggestion is constructive. George Shea, the former financial editor of *The Wall Street Journal,* has even expressed the opinion that any tampering with the DJIA would merely lead its countless followers to reconstruct it themselves on the old basis. This view is not without support from existing evidence. *The Wall Street Journal* has been for some years reporting in each issue on its very first page changes in all the Dow-Jones indexes, not only in points, but also in percentages of change from the preceding session. From the author's observations, nobody pays the slightest attention.

One of the distinguished financial journalists had conducted for some time on the pages of a well-known New York evening paper, which unfortunately is no longer in existence, an intensive campaign for a reform of the DJIA. As a "public service," he even began reporting in his column the DJIA in dollars and cents as well as in points. His main contention was, however, that what was really needed was an electronically calculated hourly index of all listed stocks—and not just of 30 industrial leaders. While not as a direct result of his urging, the New York Stock Exchange introduced such an index in 1965 and it is gaining wide acceptance. This index and other stock market indexes will be described in the next chapter. It will be interesting to see which index will be the ultimate winner, if any, among the proliferating measures of stock market action. Dow Jones & Company will undoubtedly continue to publish the DJIA which appears every half hour on its well-established and widespread communications system, the broad tape of its news ticker. The DJIA is also computed electronically on the various stock price computer terminals available in virtually every brokerage office. A good indicator of public acceptance of the various stock market indexes is the way most television news programs refer to the day's stock market action in approximately the following terms: "The stock market declined 2.93 points today as measured by the Dow-Jones Industrial Average on 17 million shares; while the price of an average share was off 44 cents according to the New York Stock Exchange Index."

3

Modern Stock Market Indexes

To BEGIN our review of modern stock market indexes, we shall consider the mechanics of constructing an index. There are two basic decisions to be reached in the construction of any stock market index:

1. The stocks which should be included.
2. How much weight should be given to each stock in the index.

The methods for calculating various types of indexes have numerous technical problems, and this chapter will concern itself with the general approach in each type and leave a more rigorous explanation to the textbooks.[1] The two series of stock market indexes most widely followed (apart from the Dow-Jones Averages) are those prepared by Standard & Poor's Corporation and by the New York Stock Exchange. Both of these series are in the category described by mathematical statisticians as weighted aggregative price index numbers.

To simplify our discussion of the subject, let us assume that there are only two stocks traded and that we are interested in preparing a measure of their price fluctuations as indicated in Table 3.1.

TABLE 3.1
Stock Prices and Shares Outstanding

	Prices			Shares Outstanding (millions)	
12/31	*U.S. Steel*	*Xerox**		*U.S. Steel*	*Xerox**
1960.	75.50	5.06		54.03	56.11
1961.	78.50	10.72		54.11	56.66
1962.	43.62	10.55		54.11	58.40
1963.	53.12	28.53		54.12	61.02
1964.	51.00	32.88		54.13	61.56
1965.	52.25	67.33		54.14	63.36
1966.	36.88	65.83		54.14	64.12
1967.	40.75	101.00		54.14	65.91
1968.	42.88	89.16		54.15	67.31
1969.	33.75	105.75		54.17	77.90
1970.	23.62	86.50		54.17	78.32
1971.	30.25	125.25		54.17	78.53
1972.	30.50	149.25			

* Adjusted for a 5–1 split in 1964 and a 3–1 split in 1969; two rights offerings ignored.

---

[1] See texts such as D. A. S. Fraser, *Statistics: An Introduction* (New York: John Wiley & Sons, 1958), and F. E. Croxton and Dudley J. Cowden, *Practical Business Statistics* (New York: Prentice-Hall, 1960).

Weighted aggregative price indexes attempt to measure what is happening to the total market value of stocks held by all investors as a whole. To illustrate, Table 3.2 indicates the change in market value during 1961.

TABLE 3.2
A Weighted Aggregative Price Index for 1961

	12/31/60	12/31/60		12/31/61	
	Shares (millions)	*Price*	*Value (millions)*	*Price*	*Value (millions)*
U.S. Steel	54.03	$75.50	$4,079	$78.50	$4,241
Xerox	56.11	5.06	284	10.72	602
			$4,363		$4,843

$$1961 \text{ index} = \frac{\$4,843 \text{ million}}{\$4,363 \text{ million}} = 111.0\%; \text{ index} = 111.0 \ (1960 = 100)$$

Thus, while U.S. Steel rose only 4 percent in price during 1961 and Xerox rose 112 percent, U.S. Steel was so much larger in terms of market value that its 4 percent increase amounted to $162 million ($4,241 million − $4,079 million) or about half as much as the $318 million increase in market value for Xerox ($602 million − $284 million). The weighted aggregative indexes such as the Standard & Poor's indexes and the New York Stock Exchange's indexes therefore provide an exact expression as to what happened to market values as represented by the combined holdings of all investors. This weighting method is continually changing as the relative importance of individual stocks grows or declines. Table 3.3 shows how this method would be applied in 1972 to our two-stock index.

TABLE 3.3
A Weighted Aggregative Price Index for 1972

	12/31/71	12/31/71		12/31/72	
	Shares (millions)	*Price*	*Value (millions)*	*Price*	*Value (millions)*
U.S. Steel	54.17	30.25	$ 1,639	30.50	$ 1,652
Xerox	78.53	125.25	9,836	149.25	11,721
			$11,475		$13,373

$$1972 \text{ index} = \frac{\$13,373 \text{ million}}{\$11,475 \text{ million}} = 116.5\%; \text{ index} = 116.5 \ (1971 = 100)$$

In 1972, Xerox accounted for the bulk of the increase in market value, and thus the 16.5 percent change in the index was mostly the result of the 19.2 percent increase recorded by Xerox, and the nominal .8 percent gain by U.S. Steel did not hold the index back to any great extent.

The principle of weighting stock price indexes by market values is still not universally accepted. Modern financial literature counts many proponents of the view that stock price measures should be constructed with each issue being given equal weight. These proponents note that while the weighted aggregative indexes give an accurate representation for the stock market as a whole, they do not reflect the experience of the average investment portfolio. For example, an investor in 1960 would not buy 14 times as much U.S. Steel as Xerox—and yet that is the ratio assumed by the weighted aggregative price indexes. In its stead, some propose the use of an arithmetic average with all stocks being given equal importance in the base years. Table 3.4 indicates the ease with which such an index can be calculated.

TABLE 3.4
An Arithmetic Mean Price Index

	12/31/60 Price	Shares	Market Value
U.S. Steel.................	75.50	.6623	$ 50.00
Xerox....................	5.06	9.8853	50.00
		Index =	100.00

	12/31/72 Price	Shares	Market Value
U.S. Steel.................	30.50	.6623	$ 20.20
Xerox....................	149.25	9.8853	1,475.39
		Index =	1,495.59

As indicated in Table 3.4, the more successful stocks will dominate such an index after a number of years of growth. Since this type of index really doesn't accurately reflect the position of a normal investment portfolio, others have advocated using a geometric mean for a stock price index. This type of index is computed by finding the antilogarithm of the arithmetic mean of the logarithms of the stocks included in the index. More important than the mechanics involved is the basic concept that this type of index keeps the dollar investment in each stock constant by, in effect, selling off portions of all stocks showing above-average gains and reinvesting the proceeds in the underachievers in the index. This does not represent typical investment portfolio management either, so the search still continues for the perfect measure of the stock market.[2]

Some indexes—most notably the Dow-Jones Averages discussed in the preceding chapter—are based upon methods adopted for the convenience of their makers. These have little or no justification for their pattern of construction. Figure 3.1 illustrates the results of the three major types of indexes based upon our two-stock sample. Table 3.5 indicates the weighting proportions used in each method.

---

[2] Paul H. Cootner, "Stock Market Indexes—Fallacies and Illusions," *The Commercial and Financial Chronicle* (September 29, 1966).

FIGURE 3.1
Stock Price Indexes—U.S. Steel and Xerox

Index: 1960 = 100

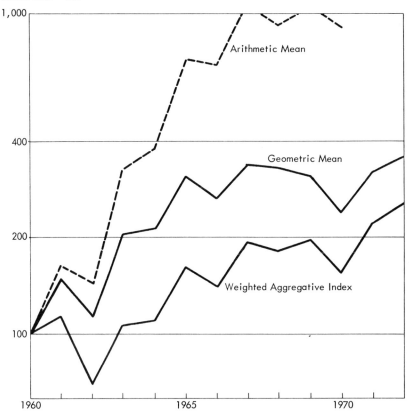

TABLE 3.5
Relative Weighting in Different Indexes

	1960 Weights (percent)		1972 Weights (percent)	
	U.S. Steel	*Xerox*	*U.S. Steel*	*Xerox*
Weighted aggregative.........	93%	7%	12%	88%
Arithmetic mean	50	50	1	99
Geometric mean.............	50	50	50	50

Before proceeding to a somewhat more complete discussion of the most generally useful series of indexes—the family of Standard & Poor's indexes—we shall summarize in an oversimplified Table 3.6 a general classification of some of the more widely followed modern stock market indexes.

Articles on some of these indexes can be located by referring to footnote 3 to this chapter.

TABLE 3.6
Modern Stock Price Indexes

Weighted Aggregative Indexes		
New York Stock Exchange	Composite	All stocks listed on NYSE
	Industrials	All industrials listed on NYSE
	Utilities, etc.	All utilities, etc.
Standard & Poor's	500 Composite	500 Large issues comprising 90 percent of the value of all shares on the NYSE
	425 Industrial	425 Industrials, included in composite
Moody's	200 Composite	
	125 Industrials	
Arithmetic Mean		
Indicator Digest		All stocks listed on NYSE
Geometric Mean		
Value Line Composite		1,400 widely held stocks
Unique Methods		
Dow-Jones Industrials		30 mature blue chip stocks
American Stock Exchange Index		All stocks listed on that exchange
Fisher Rate of Return Index		All stocks listed on NYSE

We are trying to cover in this chapter a reasonably detailed general introduction to the major problems attempted to be solved by modern stock market indexes. Yet we can make no claim of presenting an exhaustive treatise. A thorough student of stock market measures will need to consult a vast and growing literature, especially in the form of increasingly learned articles on the subject appearing in the pages of economic and statistical journals. He will do well to begin his research by consulting both the Introduction and Appendix I to the Cowles Commission Monograph #3, "Common Stock Indexes." He will find in the Appendix abundant material dealing with United States and Foreign Common Stock Indexes. Some of these indexes are no longer in existence and their study is primarily of historical interest. But the serious scholar will also find in this source an account of the origin and gradual development of some of the measures of stock prices which continue to dominate the practical work of financial analysts. When their study is pursued in depth, it may lead to perplexing and startling questions rather than easy answers. Our brief case history of

---

[3] Alfred D. Cowles, 3d and associates, *Common Stock Indexes*, 2d ed. (Bloomington, Ind.: Principia Press, Inc., 1939).

W. L. Crum's efforts to build a satisfactory stock market measure illustrates the types of statistical techniques and thinking that are relevant to the construction of measurements of trends and levels of the stock market.[4] Even simple averages raise intertemporal problems. Complex index numbers can reach high sophistication and still leave unanswered the question of what they succeed in measuring.

STANDARD & POOR'S INDEXES

In 1939, the Cowles Commission for Research in Economics published, for the period 1871–1938,[5] monthly indexes of common stock prices, earnings and dividends, as well as of their principal interrelations—yields and e/p ratios—for 69 industry groups and combinations of groups. It originally planned to take its indexes back to a still earlier period. But, as was already shown in the preceding chapter, a survey revealed appalling scarcity or even absence of data.

To extend its indexes into the future, the Cowles Commission spliced its indexes to those of Standard Statistics Company, now Standard & Poor's Corporation.

The process of splicing created a discrepancy between the original Cowles Commission indexes, which were not continued beyond 1939 and the extension of the present S&P composite "500" index into the past. The discrepancy exists for the years 1926–1938. When the Cowles Commission was preparing for the eventual splicing, the "500" index did not exist. Beginning with 1926, the Cowles Commission used the weekly stock price indexes of Standard Statistics. Back in 1923, Standard Statistics constructed a stock price index of 233 stocks derived from 26 subgroup indexes of leading industrial groups. These indexes were based on 1926 = 100. This base was subsequently shifted by Standard Statistics to the average of the period 1935–1939 = 100. When Standard & Poor's revised its indexes in 1957, and enlarged its composite index to 500 stocks, it changed its base period to 1941–1943 = 10. This base period was selected because the resulting composite index then came very close to the price in dollars and cents of the average price of all common stocks listed on the NYSE at that time. This average price in 1957 was about $41 and the average level of the S&P Industrials was 47.63. The closeness of this relationship no longer exists. The index value of the "500" is now over twice as high as the price of the average share on the Exchange as a result of splits and stock dividends in the intervening years.

We shall revert forthwith to the construction of the present S&P indexes, as revised in 1957. For the sake of accuracy of historical comparisons, we would like, however, to note the reason why a careful student will find, for the years 1926–1938, a discrepancy between the Cowles Commission stock price indexes (1926 = 100) and the S&P series (1941–1943 = 10).

---

[4] Nicholas Molodovsky, "Building a Stock Market Measure—A Case Story," *Financial Analysts Journal*, vol. 23, no. 3: 43–46 (May–June 1967).

[5] Cowles and associates, *Common Stock Indexes.*

In addition to the weekly indexes originated by the Standard Statistics Company, Standard & Poor's Corporation was computing daily, prior to 1957, a composite index of 90 common stocks and of its constituent indexes of 50 industrials, 20 rails, and 20 utilities. On March 1, 1957, when S&P expanded their daily indexes to cover 500 stocks, they abandoned the earlier series which had been used by the Cowles Commission. At that time they chose their series of 90 stocks to reconstruct the past because they considered this series adequately representative of the market. An additional consideration was that they had daily observations of this series, and comparison data of earnings and dividends based on it.

Thus discrepancies between the Cowles Commission and S&P stock price indexes for the period 1926–1938 are due entirely to the difference in sample. Standard & Poor's are satisfied that during this period their composite index of 90 stocks accurately measured stock price behavior. We might add that their enlarged composite of 500 stocks and the Cowles Commission all-stock indexes must have come increasingly nearer to representing the general market, subject to the validity of the weighting method used, which all these indexes had in common.

Under the S&P method, which this statistical organization has used consistently since the introduction of the old Standard Statistics indexes, each component stock is weighted so that it will influence the index in proportion to the respective total dollar market value of all the outstanding shares of the same company. This weighting principle had also been used by the Cowles Commission. The SEC used the same weighting method for its own index, before its discontinuance in 1964. Thus, the total market value of a company's outstanding stock determines the relative importance of the stock in the index.

The formula adopted by Standard & Poor's for the construction of its index is a modified Paasche formula, defined as a base weighted aggregative expressed in relatives with the average value for the base period (1941–1943) = 10.

We shall spare the readers a reproduction of the formula. It varies mostly in details from the methods outlined in Tables 3.2 and 3.3 since their construction is essentially governed by the same statistical needs. Yet it should be noted that the original base value, as determined by the formula, is not immutable. An adjustment must be made in the base period value when the weighting factors themselves are changed. As a net result, the index number reflects only fluctuations in current market values, absorbing within its structure all changes due to stock dividends, split-ups, rights, consolidations, and acquisitions as well as additions of new stocks or disappearances of others from among listed stocks.

Standard & Poor's composite index of 500 stocks consists of three other composite indexes: 425 industrials, 50 utilities, and 25 rails. In addition, S&P has broken down its 500 composite into 93 individual groups. It also computes four supplementary group series: Capital Goods Companies, Consumer Goods, High Grade Common Stocks, and Low-Priced Common Stocks. Also, for the more recently developed industries, indexes have been computed for Savings and

Loan Associations, Cosmetics, Trucking, Discount Stores, and Vending Machines. These new indexes are expressed in terms of various recent base periods and are not included in the S&P series of 500 stocks. Besides these new indexes, S&P also has some older indexes which do not enter into the 500 composite group. These are indexes of Bank Stocks, Investment Companies, and Insurance Companies.

The four main composite indexes are computed, thanks to electronic computers and input feeders, at five-minute intervals. They are not published, but S&P maintains a record of them. Hourly indexes are published in the Daily News section of S&P's Corporation Records and daily high-low and closing indexes appear in many newspapers as well as other publications of Standard & Poor's. The American Stock Exchange's ticker carries the hourly S&P indexes, and the electronic quotation services also carry them.

We will close this chapter by noting that serious scholars will find an Appendix at the end of this chapter which includes some rather difficult to locate statistics covering many decades of price ranges, earnings, and dividends for the Dow-Jones Industrials and the Standard & Poor's 500. Figure 3.2 traces the longer term price records of the DJIA and the S&P index, which indicates that both measures follow the same general course most of the time, with some instances in which the peculiarities of the construction of the DJIA have led it astray for a while.

FIGURE 3.2
Dow-Jones Industrial Average and the Standard & Poor's 500—Yearly Means

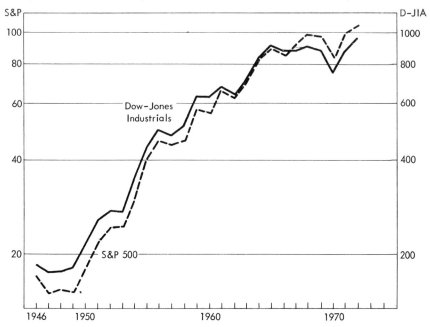

APPENDIX TO CHAPTER 3

Dow-Jones Industrial Average

Year	High	Low	Close	Earnings	Cash	Dividends Including Stock
1973	1051.70	788.31	850.86	86.17	35.33	
1972	1036.27	889.15	1020.02	67.11	32.27	
1971	950.82	797.97	890.20	55.09	30.86	
1970	842.00	631.16	838.92	51.02	31.53	
1969	968.85	769.93	800.36	57.02	32.29	33.90
1968	985.21	825.13	943.75	57.89	31.34	31.34
1967	943.08	786.41	905.11	53.87	29.84	30.19
1966	995.15	744.32	785.69	57.68	30.11	31.89
1965	969.26	840.59	969.26	53.67	28.17	28.61
1964	891.71	766.08	874.13	46.43	25.38	31.24
1963	767.21	646.79	762.95	41.21	23.20	23.41
1962	726.01	535.76	652.10	36.43	22.09	23.30
1961	734.91	610.25	731.14	31.91	21.28	22.71
1960	685.47	566.05	615.89	32.21	20.46	21.36
1959	679.36	574.46	679.36	34.31	19.38	20.74
1958	583.65	436.89	583.65	27.95	19.00	20.00
1957	520.77	419.79	435.69	36.08	20.27	21.61
1956	521.05	462.35	499.47	33.34	19.72	22.99
1955	488.40	388.20	488.40	35.78	18.73	21.58
1954	404.39	279.87	404.39	28.18	16.96	17.47
1953	293.79	255.49	280.90	27.23		16.11
1952	292.00	256.35	291.90	24.78		15.43
1951	276.37	238.99	269.23	26.59		16.34
1950	235.47	196.81	235.41	30.70		16.13
1949	200.52	161.60	200.13	23.54		12.79
1948	193.16	165.39	177.30	23.07		11.50
1947	186.85	163.21	181.16	18.80		9.21
1946	212.50	163.12	177.20	13.63		7.50
1945	195.82	151.35	192.91	10.56		6.69
1944	152.53	134.22	152.32	10.07	6.40	6.57
1943	145.82	119.26	135.89	9.74	6.50	6.30
1942	119.71	92.92	119.40	9.22	6.50	6.40
1941	133.59	106.34	110.96	11.64	7.50	7.59
1940	152.80	111.84	131.13	10.92	7.05	7.06
1939	155.92	121.44	150.24	9.11	6.30	6.11
1938	158.41	98.95	154.76	6.01	4.84	4.98
1937	194.40	113.64	120.85	11.49	8.15	8.78
1936	184.90	143.11	179.90	10.07	7.07	7.05
1935	148.44	96.71	144.13	6.34	4.12	4.55
1934	110.74	85.51	104.04	3.91	3.28	3.66

Dow-Jones Industrial Average (continued)

Year	High	Low	Close	Earnings	Cash	Including Stock
					Dividends	
1933	108.67	50.16	99.90	2.11	3.03	3.40
1932	88.78	41.22	59.93	(.51)	4.09	4.62
1931	194.36	73.79	77.90	4.09	6.73	8.40
1930	294.07	157.71	164.58	11.02	7.44	11.13
1929	381.17	198.69	248.48	19.94	7.06	12.75
1928	300.00	191.33	300.00	15.36	5.92	
1927	202.40	152.73	202.40	13.18	5.54	
1926	166.64	135.20	157.20	14.44	6.35	
1925	159.39	115.00	156.66	13.54	4.17	
1924	120.51	88.33	120.51	10.52	4.27	
1923	105.38	85.76	95.52	11.38	3.94	
1922	103.43	78.59	98.73	8.20	3.38	
1921	81.50	63.90	81.10	–0–	2.96	
1920	109.88	66.75	71.95	6.74	3.44	
1919	119.62	79.15	107.23	13.77	4.07	
1918	89.07	73.38	82.20	16.18	5.64	
1917	99.18	65.95	74.38	21.90	5.63	
1916	110.15	84.96	95.00	18.62	4.27	
1915	99.21	54.22	99.15	10.59	2.20	
1914	83.43	53.17	54.58			
1913	88.57	72.11	78.78			
1912	94.15	80.15	87.87			
1911	87.06	72.94	81.68			
1910	93.34	73.62	81.36			
1909	100.53	79.91	99.05			
1908	87.67	58.62	86.15			
1907	96.37	53.00	58.75			
1906	103.00	85.15	94.35			
1905	96.56	68.76	96.20			
1904	73.23	46.41	69.61			
1903	67.70	42.15	49.11			
1902	68.44	59.57	64.29			
1901	77.08	61.52	64.56			
1900	71.04	52.96	70.71			
1899	77.61	60.41	66.08			
1898	60.97	42.00	60.52			
1897	55.82	38.49	49.41			

Sources: Dow Jones & Co., except: cash dividends 1954–1958, The Value Line Survey; earnings and dividends 1915–1928 and cash dividends 1929–1944, Benjamin Graham, *Commercial & Financial Chronicle* (10/18/45).

Standard & Poor's 500 Index

Year	High	Low	Close	Earnings	Dividend
1973	120.24	92.16	97.55	8.11	3.38
1972	119.12	101.67	118.05	6.42	3.15
1971	104.77	90.16	102.09	5.70	3.07
1970	93.46	69.29	92.15	5.13	3.14
1969	106.16	89.20	92.06	5.78	3.16
1968	108.37	87.72	103.86	5.76	3.07
1967	97.59	80.38	96.47	5.33	2.92
1966	94.06	73.20	80.33	5.55	2.87
1965	92.63	81.60	92.43	5.19	2.72
1964	86.28	75.43	84.75	4.55	2.50
1963	75.02	62.69	75.02	4.02	2.28
1962	71.13	52.32	63.10	3.67	2.13
1961	72.64	57.57	71.55	3.19	2.02
1960	60.39	52.30	58.11	3.27	1.95
1959	60.71	53.58	59.89	3.39	1.83
1958	55.21	40.33	55.21	2.89	1.75
1957	49.13	38.98	39.99	3.37	1.79
1956	49.74	43.11	46.67	3.41	1.74
1955	46.41	34.58	45.48	3.62	1.64
1954	35.98	24.80	35.98	2.77	1.54
1953	26.66	22.71	24.81	2.51	1.45
1952	26.59	23.09	26.57	2.40	1.41
1951	23.85	20.69	23.77	2.44	1.41
1950	20.43	16.65	20.41	2.84	1.47
1949	16.79	13.55	16.76	2.32	1.14
1948	17.06	13.84	15.20	2.29	.93
1947	16.20	13.71	15.30	1.61	.84
1946	19.25	14.12	15.30	1.06	.71
1945	17.68	13.21	17.36	.96	.66
1944	13.29	11.56	13.28	.93	.64
1943	12.64	9.84	11.67	.94	.61
1942	9.77	7.47	9.77	1.03	.59
1941	10.86	8.37	8.69	1.16	.71
1940	12.77	8.99	10.58	1.05	.67
1939	13.23	10.18	12.49	.90	.62
1938	13.79	8.50	13.21	.64	.51
1937	18.68	10.17	10.55	1.13	.80
1936	17.69	13.40	17.18	1.02	.72
1935	13.46	8.06	13.43	.76	.47
1934	11.82	8.36	9.50	.49	.45
1933	12.20	5.53	10.10	.44	.44
1932	9.31	4.40	6.89	.41	.50
1931	18.17	7.72	8.12	.61	.82
1930	25.92	14.44	15.34	.97	.98
1929	31.92	17.66	21.45	1.61	.97
1928	24.35	16.95	24.35	1.38	.85
1927	17.71	13.18	17.66	1.11	.77
1926	13.66	10.93	13.49	1.24	.69

Source: Standard & Poor's Corporation.

4

Economic Insight

THE GROWING SPECIALIZATION so evident in medicine, law, engineering, and other professions is likely to become more strongly marked in investment analysis also. Much training and experience are needed for a meaningful selection of significant facts from the welter of an industry's activities, or even those of a single corporation. The need of expert qualifications is still greater for accurately interpreting and adjusting the reported figures of past and current profits, as well as projecting them into the reasonably visible future.

A different kind of skill is required to use effectively such facts, estimates, and interpretations for appraisals of values. It seems probable that, as time goes on, the delineation between the functions of economic scholars, students of stock market trends, analysts of corporate data, and appraisers of stock values will become more sharply defined.

No single individual can accumulate an adequate store of information about the technologies of all the different enterprises in various industries, about the markets for their products, and the characteristics of their respective managements to be able to form competent judgment on the prospects of all individual stocks. Their diversities are so great that rarely can expert knowledge be reached beyond a handful of companies.

In evaluating the prospects for a stock, one should read the reports of expert security analysts in that area to see if the essential economic forces in operation are clearly perceived by the analyst and that they are in line with his recommendations. The complexities and difficulties of financial analysis are present at all times. They are magnified in periods of economic change. The investor must be aware of the significance of the changes and how far they are likely to reach. Case sketches from the postwar history of two major industries—motors and steels—may illustrate the point.

43

GM IN FINANCIAL LITERATURE

John Burr Williams estimated GM's earning power for the eleven years 1926–1936 at $3.52 per share. Williams pointed out that this period contained the results of four good, four bad, and three fair years of general industrial activity. He therefore assumed that it constituted a fair sample and was willing to project the period's annual average as GM's future normal earnings.[1] Adjusting for the 1950 and 1955 splits of GM common, GM's prewar normal annual earning power amounted, on this basis, to about 60 cents per share after taxes.

Being subject to excess profits taxes, GM's wartime reported earnings remained well within the prewar range. The wartime earnings trend was in line with the 1926–1936 average computed by Williams.

In 1946, with the disappearance of military orders, GM's per share earnings plunged to the level of the depression year 1933, as shown on Figure 4.1. But, within four years, a fabulous lift of a thousand percentage points took GM's per share annual earnings from 30 cents to $3.00. Financial analysts were stunned by this explosion. They ascribed the fantastic earnings rise to a temporary bulge of pent-up demand. Even in 1949, when the violent upward breakout was already an accomplished fact, the probability of the company's earning power remaining at the new level did not seem sufficiently convincing.

This skepticism with respect to earnings could not fail to become reflected in the stock's price expectations. Analysts could not forget that, prior to 1950, GM's price, in terms of the present twice-split stock, rarely exceeded 10. To pay a higher price had proved unwise. This is apparent from Figure 4.1.

The caution of financial analysts was shared by statistical "services." In March, 1949, a leading service reported that earnings for that year would not differ materially from the $1.62 of 1948. By August, it realized that a new peak was coming and forecast earnings of about $1.80 on the present adjusted basis. Earnings reached $2.44. In 1950, GM's net rose to $3.12 per share. But a few weeks before the close of 1949, statistical organizations were advising that keener competition pointed to a decline in the following year. Not until June did they foresee a "small" gain, while in fact a rise of 28 percent was realized. Writing in the 1949 Fourth Quarter issue of *The Analysts Journal*, GM's economist, Rufus S. Tucker, could see little prospect for 1950 domestic passenger car sales exceeding 85 percent of their 1949 total. GM's own 1950 sales were 132 percent of 1949. In May, 1951, the "services" expected GM's earnings to fall sharply; by August they projected 92 cents a share for 1951. The actual figure turned out to be $1.88.

The forecasts of the years that followed lost nothing of their prophetic touch. But the advisory services began to acquire the habit of thinking of probable increases in GM annual sales in billions. Their new boldness was still being outdistanced by events. In May, 1953, they were estimating that sales would

---

[1] John Burr Williams, *The Theory of Investment Value* (Cambridge, Mass.: Harvard University Press, 1938), p. 400.

FIGURE 4.1
General Motors Common Stock

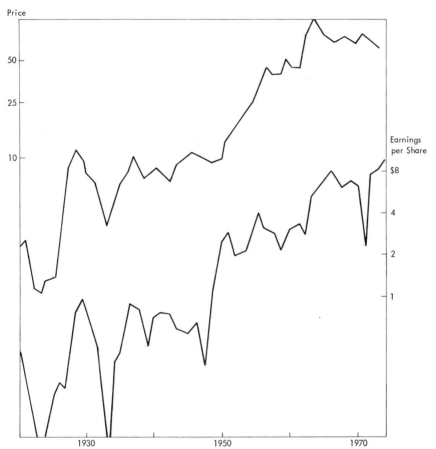

make another billion dollar jump to $8,500 million and that, generally, annual sales in the mid 1950s would average $8 billion. Sales in 1953, 1954, and 1955 were respectively, in millions, $10,028, $9,824 and $12,443.

By the time this astounding tidal wave was approaching its crest, investment services and financial writers started to rationalize the phenomenon. The outlandish creature began to be caressed as a domestic pet. Its further healthy growth was being bravely predicted. Many happy returns were yet to come of larger and larger sales.

Motor stocks were being welcomed to the rapidly increasing family of growth equities. Not only were their earnings, subject to mild interruptions, to continue to rise, but the stock market was likely to capitalize them in the future with more and more generous multipliers.

To account for what had already taken place, and why it was offering such a brilliant promise for the future, persuasive reasons were suddenly not lacking. Two factors seemed to stand out: the automobile had ceased to be a toy of the rich and had become a necessity for the masses; and this collective buyer could afford many more cars because of a wider distribution of purchasing power and availability of credit.

These reasons, however, were not actually new. Henry Ford had felt too that the motor car possessed potentialities as a mass product; proving his point, he created an industry and acquired some personal financial well-being. As to the car makers' ability to make good use of consumer credit, GM had commissioned, long ago, in 1927, a famous economist to write a treatise on the subject. The two volumes produced by the professor and his assistants were presented with fanfare at a gala dinner.[2]

Even more subtle reasons of a psychological nature, such as the power of obsolescence to set off resonant vibrations of human instincts, and the significance of the automobile as a symbol of economic victory and personal freedom, could not have been described more eloquently than was done, still in the thirties, by Mead and Grodinsky.[3]

NATURE OF FORECASTING ERRORS

There would have been no point in recounting the projections which proved so wrong in GM's case for the stale satisfaction of showing that no one can read the future.

In the words of an eminent authority:

> The outstanding fact is the extreme precariousness of the basis of knowledge on which our estimates of prospective yield have to be made. Our knowledge of the factors which will govern the yield of an investment some years hence is usually very slight and often negligible. If we speak frankly, we have to admit that our basis of knowledge for estimating the yield ten years hence of a railway, a copper mine, a textile factory, the goodwill of a patent medicine, an Atlantic liner, a building in the city of London amounts to little and sometimes to nothing; or even five years hence. In fact, those who seriously attempt to make any such estimate are often so much in the minority that their behavior does not govern the market.[4]

But in this particular case, the differences between forecasts and reality were monumental. They lasted for many years, and all unanimously and consistently underestimated the magnitudes of even the nearest realizations. Invariably, projections fell so widely short of the targets that they seemed to reveal the existence of a common cause producing this uniformity of errors. A force whose potential

---

[2] Edwin A. R. A. Seligman, *The Economics of Installment Selling* (New York: Harper Publishing Co., 1927).

[3] Edward Sherwood Mead and Julius Grodinsky, *The Ebb and Flow of Investment Values* (New York: Appleton-Century, 1939), p. 20.

[4] John Maynard Keynes, *The General Theory of Employment, Interest and Money* (New York: Harcourt, Brace & Co., 1935), pp. 149–50.

was apparently not fully realized seems to have been carrying the postwar expansion of the American economy far beyond the most optimistic expectations.

And yet there was no lack of faith on the part of investors, nor of the management of General Motors—once the fears of an immediate postwar depression were dissipated—that economic progress should be substantial.

At the close of World War II, the automobile industry was well aware of the accumulated deferred demand. But it was struggling with shortages of materials. In the annual report for 1948, GM still expressed regret for its inability to fill all orders promptly. Not until the second quarter of 1949 was the more than three-year log jam for shortages of steel finally broken. And this problem was soon to plague the industry again at the time of Korea.

In its 1949 report, GM's management stated that the potential market for new cars had been permanently expanded. It pointed to the country's growth and to the increase of the numbers of family units in the medium and higher income groups. More people could afford to buy new cars than before the war. GM's report indicated that the company had shown considerable foresight: "Even before the end of the war in 1945 General Motors recognized that the demand for its automobiles and other products would pose a production problem that could not be solved with its prewar facilities. Accordingly, a postwar program was developed to meet this production challenge."

GM was mobilizing to provide an adequate supply. The errors were made in underestimating demand. They were due to lack of recognition of the causal effect on consumer demand of the tremendous increase in the stock of money.

THE CURIOUS CASE OF THE STEEL STOCKS

Not always do financial analysts err on the side of conservatism and caution. They underestimated the postwar demand for automobiles. More recently, in the case of another basic industry, many analysts and investors became overly enthusiastic.

On October 22, 1959, Charles M. White, board chairman of the Republic Steel Corporation, gave an address before the National Association of Investment Companies. In his talk he painted a glowing picture of steel industry's outlook:

> All signs point to a record year for 1960. We anticipate that Gross National Product will reach well over the half trillion dollar mark—probably around $515 billion. As for steel, the situation looks extremely promising. Automobiles and capital goods, for example, are on the rise, with a probable production of around seven million passenger cars, and capital expenditures near $37 billion. Steel consumption of other industries will be up with the possible exception of construction. Add in a sizable amount of steel to restore inventories of steel users to good working levels in 1960, and a reasonable estimate of steel ingot production would be a new record between 120 and 130 million tons. This is a gratifying prospect, but it is only a step in the upward trend of our economy if we keep our wits about us.[5]

---

[5] *The Commercial and Financial Chronicle* (October 29, 1959).

At the end of 1959, many financial analysts shared the steel industry's rosy view of its 1960 outlook. It had become a habit to think and say nothing but the best about the steels. The industry's early "scrape and scrabble" days mentioned by Mr. White in his address had been long since forgotten except by teachers of economic history. Even the "prince and pauper" or "boom and bust" era seemed to belong to the past. The steel industry was apparently becoming less exposed to cyclical influences.

As 1960 bowed in, steel's prospects seemed brilliant. The longest strike in the industry's history, lasting 116 days, had just been settled. 1960 production was expected by some experienced observers to reach an all-time high of 130 to 135 million tons, equivalent to an operating rate of close to 90 percent of capacity. New earnings records were confidently anticipated, and a number of dividend increases and stock splits appeared to be in the cards.

Table 4.1 indicates 1960 per share earnings estimates for ten well-known

TABLE 4.1
Earnings and Price Ranges of 10 Selected Stocks

	Earnings			Market Prices		
	Early 1960 Estimates	Actual 1960 Earnings	% Actual Below Estimates	1/4/60 High	1960 Low	% Price Decline
Allegheny Ludlum.....	$ 3.50	$2.25	36%	$ 56½	$32¼	43%
Armco Steel	6.90	4.76	31	77½	57	26
Bethlehem Steel	5.30	2.52	52	57¼	37¼	35
Granite City	4.00	2.59	35	37½	30	20
Inland Steel..........	4.70	2.68	43	50	36½	27
Jones & Laughlin......	9.00	4.04	55	89¾	49¾	45
National Steel........	5.00	2.77	45	49⅛	34	31
Republic Steel........	8.00	3.36	58	78¾	48½	38
U.S. Steel	8.70	5.16	41	103	69¼	33
Youngstown S. & T. ...	16.50	7.38	55	138½	84½	39

steels, as they were projected by representative steel industry analysts at the inception of that year and adjusted for subsequent 1960 stock splits. The table also shows the actual 1960 earnings and compares the highs of January 4, 1960, the year's first stock market session, with the subsequent 1960 lows of the same stocks.

The earnings estimates in Table 4.1 were high. In most instances they were quite a bit higher than the peaks reached by the respective companies during the industry's most prosperous years, 1955–1957. However, the wage settlement which had been just imposed on the industry seemed to call for a price increase of at least $8 per ton. The estimates shown were, therefore, on the conservative side, reflecting as they did only a $5 per ton increase operative for just the last six months of the year.

Toward the end of February, 1960, when stock prices were already speeding down the slide of a cyclical recession and the descent of steel stocks in particular was gaining momentum, a leading brokerage firm had the following comments:

> Another instance of current business not coming up to earlier exuberant expectations, and one of considerable impact on the prevailing sentiment in the stock market, is steel. . . . We see no reason as yet to change our estimate of actual consumption. This would leave 1960 steel production in the neighborhood of 125 million tons, respectable even if related to stated capacity of 148.6 millions tons, and even closer to optimal operations if it is realized that part of the theoretical capacity is represented by superannuated and obsolescent and hence high-cost equipment. Moreover, one should not forget how successful the industry has been in improving its profitability by modernizing its plant, changing its product-mix, strengthening the stability of its price structure and lowering breakeven points; witness the operating experience in recessionary 1958. . . . We do not know how much longer the present unsettled state of the stock market is going to last, nor where exactly it will carry the averages. . . . Withal, steel shares at ten times or less of current earning power appear quite reasonable.

With few exceptions, expert opinion continued to remain favorable to steel stocks, and to the market, throughout most of the first half of 1960.

Between May, when the business cycle reached its reference peak, and October, which marked the low of the cycle of stock prices, the Dow-Jones Industrials dropped 100 points. Steel production also fell drastically. During this period, the estimates of 1960 steel company earnings underwent belated changes.

The 1960 projections of steel industry's earnings were as grossly wrong as the postwar estimates of automobile manufacturers' profits. But they erred in the opposite direction. Instead of falling widely short of the mark, they overshot reality by a huge margin.

Such poor vision by so many people of developments so near at hand may have been due, in part, to insufficient understanding of the nature of business cycles—and to lack of familiarity with tools designed for coping with them, imperfect as they are. This failure was compounded by a misreading of the significance of changes in the steel industry as well as those of the structural characteristics of the economy at large.

POSTWAR TRENDS IN THE STEEL INDUSTRY

A steel industry expert, Lillian B. Green, executive assistant to the board chairman of Granite City Steel, examined in detail, and over a long period, the relative cyclical action of indexes of steel ingot and industrial production and compared shipments of heavy and light steel mill products.[6] She concluded that analysis of production trends and of changes in type of product both denied that the steel industry was much more cyclical than the economy as a whole.

"The steel industry, too, has its growth factor," said Miss Green. "It should

---

[6] Lillian B. Green, "Facts and Fiction Behind Price-Earnings Ratios of the Steel Stocks," *The Analysts Journal*, vol. 13, no. 4: 35–42 (August 1957).

be noted that per capita steel consumption has been increasing at the rate of approximately 2 percent per year in the past ten years and is currently at approximately 1400 pounds. If projected increases in population are anywhere near correct, the steel industry will again be pushing capacity sometime in the next several years. By 1965, the steel industry should be short of capacity."

That steel was already a growth industry was contended by another authority. In August, 1956, a well-known financial analyst submitted in a professional journal facts and figures illustrating that the earnings per share of U.S. Steel, Bethlehem Steel, and Republic Steel had recorded a greater percentage increase from 1939 through 1955 than had duPont, Dow Chemical, Monsanto, Union Carbide, Minnesota Mining, Alcoa, and Minneapolis-Honeywell. He also showed that 1939 was not a "freak" year, but that similar relative comparisons would result if 1945, 1947, or 1950 were taken as the base years. The conclusion was that, in the only kind of growth which really matters, namely, the growth in earnings per share, the leaders of the steel industry ranked extremely high as compared to the performance of a recognized list of "growth stocks."

This analyst's conviction was so strong that he followed up his 1956 article by another study in May, 1959. He concluded that future growth in earnings per share should produce substantial capital gains for the holders of good steel stocks.

In retrospect, it seems clear that by 1959 the steel industry had reached the end of the road of its postwar prosperity. Steel prices had remained stable since the summer of 1958. The industry was hoping that the efficiency newly built into its plants should suffice to absorb the added wage costs. But after the protracted strike of 1959 and its costly settlement, price increases seemed to have become inevitable. Yet none followed. They were prevented by increased capacity both at home and abroad and the development of new products by other industries.

The first study to recognize the changing investment climate of the steel industry was a penetrating article published in August, 1959, by Edmund A. Mennis, at that time director of research of Wellington Management Company. Dr. Mennis recognized that, since World War II, steel stocks had been gaining increasing favor among discerning investors and analysts because of growing earnings and dividends and less violent cyclical fluctuations which had been characteristic of the prewar period. This resulted in a rising level of capitalizers that the market was willing to apply to the earnings of steel stocks.

"This improvement in steel earnings and dividends," said Mennis, "has not been brought about by any spectacular growth in demand for steel products. It is the result, rather, of internal cost control and efficiencies in operations of the steel companies, and more importantly the establishment of a pricing structure in steel products that has more than compensated for increased costs and has not been subject to the same erratic fluctuations as steel demand."

After passing in review the more recent developments in the steel industry, Mennis concluded that "the capital-gains potentials of the past decade, based on an upward revaluation of the industry by the investing public, were largely completed."[7]

The August, 1959, article by Mennis was a condensed version of a study he had completed for the Wellington Fund organization in early May, 1959. It offers a remarkable demonstration of economic insight.

FIGURE 4.2
A Ton of Steel (cost of employment and price)

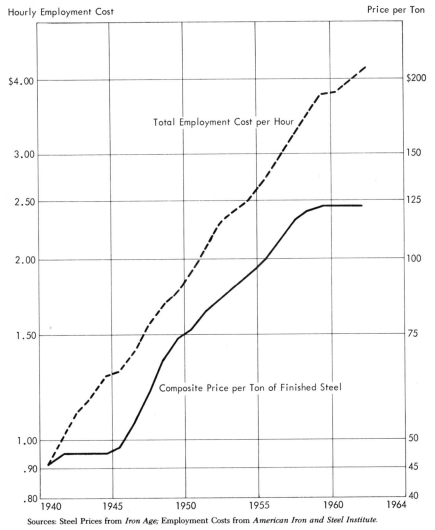

Sources: Steel Prices from *Iron Age*; Employment Costs from *American Iron and Steel Institute.*

---

[7] Edmund A. Mennis, "A Reappraisal of the Steel Industry," *The Analysts Journal,* vol. 15, no. 4: 15–23 (August 1959).

One of the findings of the Mennis study was the effect of the pricing structure on the industry's profits.

Released by the war's end, steel prices started climbing in 1946. Figure 4.2 shows, beginning with 1940, steel industry's average annual data of total employment cost per hour and price per net ton of finished steel, as published by the American Iron and Steel Institute.

Between 1945 and 1959, hourly employment cost (including pensions, insurance, supplemental unemployment benefits, and social security) rose 190 percent and steel price per ton—153 percent. Since 1959 wage costs kept mounting, while product prices stood still. When prices were still chasing wages, their average annual rise during this period was respectively 7.92 percent for employment costs versus 6.85 percent for prices.

Like Mennis, some other financial analysts saw the situation in a clear light. In the last quarter of 1959, a brokerage firm published a study entitled "The Steels: A Minority View." It denied that steel was a true growth industry. It pointed out—and supported its finding by persuasive statistics—that the growth in earnings of recent years appeared to have come primarily from the leverage of higher selling prices on per-share results. Unit volume had increased only moderately. The writer felt that to argue price increases were forced on the industry by increased labor costs may be true, although it hardly bolstered the investment appeal of steel stocks.

"PHASE B"

The great expansion of expenditures of the early postwar period slowed down during the middle fifties. Peaks of the previously rising curves of production of consumers' and producers' durable goods began forming a ridge. By 1955 the automobile industry had made, in the United States alone, 48,508,037 passenger cars since 1947. In 1946 the total number of privately-owned passenger automobiles in this country was 28,100,188. A similar situation prevailed for many other consumer durables. Rates of spending, production and employment could not be sustained at such a rhythm. A sluggish sideways movement and pressure on profit margins came in the wake of the boom.

The decrease in the rates of growth was gradual and did not affect all forms of economic activity at the same time. Subject to intervening cyclical fluctuations, construction of plants, as well as purchasing and leasing of industrial equipment, continued to rise through 1957. Then it peaked out. Residential construction began to subside two years after that. The persistence of the same phenomenon through so many different manifestations left little doubt that the general lassitude of the private durable sector was a basic development.

The steel industry could no longer pass on to consumers most of the cost increases and fill the gap by raising productivity financed by higher prices. The price of steel slipped out of the industry's hands. Greater influences were reinforced concrete, aluminum, and foreign steel, the latter's impact being stronger than the modest tonnage imported would suggest. Foreign quotations had to be matched or compromised.

All industry had to make the adjustment to a different competitive environment and to new cost-price relations brought by the end of postwar inflation.

Economic necessity had dictated the steel industry's decisions both in pursuing and in terminating its price-raising policy. Plant modernization had become vital and it had to be financed internally. Steel companies were afraid to increase their indebtedness, having already come close to defaulting on their debt structures during the depression. And their equities were weak, offering inadequate return on invested capital and selling at such low prices in the stock market—with relation to their book values—as to make them unsuitable for new stock offerings.

Narrowing the steel industry's case to that of U.S. Steel Corporation, it seemed clear that, in complete contrast to General Motors, the company was losing ground in terms of its share of the industry's shipments. Its 1962 cash flow was one-half of the 1957 figure. After paying dividends, the company had practically no income left available for reinvestment. The management had underestimated the demand for lighter steel and was paying a heavy price for this error. U.S. Steel was receding within an industry which, instead of growing, was itself retrogressing.

Yet the big national issue was growth. It had been given high priority in Senator Kennedy's presidential campaign. To restrain inflation and to promote growth in real terms had been his major commitment. This objective transcended economics, being essential for freedom's survival in a grim struggle. And growth had bogged down.

Financial analysts are not professionally involved in politics or business. They can survey the scene as objective observers. If it was difficult for them, in this impassive role, to gain clear economic insight into the events unfolding before them, how much more trying was this task for the actors of the drama facing operational compulsions.

In industry's camp, big steel was used to the role of an unassailable leader in size, efficiency, and earnings. It had the widest geographical spread. Its product diversification reached well beyond steel operations and imparted to it an unsurpassed competitive advantage as well as the industry's widest margin of profit. But recently its sales and profit margins had begun to show a negative performance. The image of its prestige within the industry was fading. To reassert its leadership, big steel's management arose as the champion of the industry's most important cause: generation of sufficient internal funds for the preservation and modernization of plant and equipment.

The function of business managers is the maximization of the firm's profits. Subject to good neighborly relations, a consciousness of social solidarity, and patriotic duty in times of national emergencies, the major goal of industrial leadership is the growth of net earnings. It is a legitimate and necessary social role. A *Fortune* article, featuring Bethlehem Steel, opened with a forthright statement of the company's controller: "We're not in business to make steel, we're not in business to build ships, we're not in business to erect buildings. We're in business to make money."

The driving force was such that it blurred the economic insight of big steel's executive committee. In a period of economic readjustment it tried to buck the trend by raising prices. In so doing, it overstepped the thin blue line dividing reality and illusion.

THE VISIT

Late one April afternoon Alice, illusion's child, was peering through a window of the presidential study. She was hoping to catch a glimpse of Caroline's smiling face. Instead she perceived the solemn mien of Roger Blough who was being ushered in. When the visitor left, her dismay and anger were small compared to the president's.

A conflict between the government and the steel industry was not new in itself; nor was the government always the winner. In 1949, President Truman bluntly threatened the industry with quite a big stick. He asked Congress for legislation authorizing the government to build new steel capacity in case the industry would not promptly expand its facilities to take care of the then existing steel shortage. The first postwar recession which developed that year took care of the shortages and created overcapacity.

In 1952, Mr. Truman even tried to seize the industry. The Korean War was still in progress and uninterrupted production of steel was needed for national defense. Yet the Supreme Court held that the president had exceeded his powers. As a result, and after a seven-weeks' strike, the steel industry gained a considerably higher price rise than had been offered by the Wage Board.

Legally, Mr. Blough did not bind the corporation to hold the price line when the new labor pact had been signed just a few days before his visit. But his tacit agreement could be implied from the surrounding circumstances. The labor contract signed on April 6, 1962, did hold the wage increases down. Yet U.S. Steel felt that it still had no choice except to lift prices.

Mr. Blough's sudden visit catapulted with incredible force the price of a ton of steel into the center of the national arena. It is hardly doubtful that John F. Kennedy viewed the presidency in power terms. And since his actions had an immediate effect on the sources of his power, a strong action on his part could have been anticipated in the face of Roger Blough's challenge.

RELATIVE ACTION OF STEEL STOCKS

Mr. Blough did not succeed in making steel price increases stick in April, 1962. Nor did the president's victory result in a resumption of economic growth. The net effect of the collision between government and business was a stock market panic.

Investors' confidence was unquestionably shaken by the sequence of events and utterances following Blough's visit. We should not, however, as has been

FIGURE 4.3
Relative Action of Steel Stocks

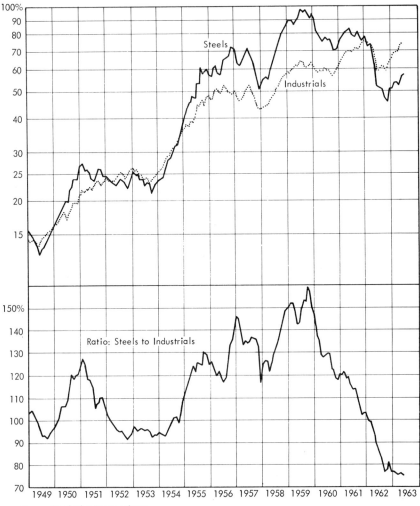

Source: Standard & Poor's indexes.

done, ascribe to it the sole responsibility for destroying an economic dam and precipitating cascades of falling stock prices. It triggered them in time and it intensified their extent and violence. The market's cycle had run from accumulation—through overspeculation—to distribution. Moreover, numerous stocks were flagrantly overpriced in terms of their investment values. Finally, various stock groups had already been engaged for some time in private bear markets of their own. For steel stocks this had been the case for close to three years. This is illustrated by Figure 4.3.

An intriguing aspect of Figure 4.3 is that the relative weakness of steel stocks was manifest already when the majority opinion was still extremely bullish. Apparently, this loudly voiced enthusiasm had little influence on the more reticent sellers.

LOOKING FORWARD

To reduce to its barest essentials the working of a system of predominantly free enterprise and markets, we may think of it in terms of forces building up or destroying profitability. A satisfactory relation between selling price and production cost is a prerequisite. And demand must exist to make product sales possible. Money and credit, if available, make demand effective.

Of the two major industries we have been using for doodling our vignettes, one has been restored to prosperity and growth. The outlook for steel is more complex. Technological innovations are helping to boost productivity and moderate the effects of wage hikes, but demand continues to expand at less than a 2 percent annual rate and foreign competition from even more efficient overseas plants successfully captures an increasing share of the market.

Turning to the economy as a whole (in this chapter written in 1963), the assumption is not far-fetched that the American economy has been building a springboard for a new dynamic phase. Industry's productivity has been rising. During the current cyclical expansion, output per man-hour has been advancing at a rate almost double the long-term average. The upwards trends of GNP and of industrial production suggest that business is emerging from a sideways movement and lifting itself off a plateau. A real breakthrough seems to be in the making in capital spending. While it is not expected to be of boom proportions, it should carry plant and equipment outlays well above the flat level which has prevailed since 1957.

The combined effect of these and other constructive factors will propel the economy upwards. But how vigorous can its progress be? The financial analysts will be hard pressed, as always, to keep up with changing economic developments. Yet, a sound understanding of the economic forces affecting a company's markets and operations is essential if the analyst is to awaken to opportunities presenting themselves and to avoid the disasters lurking ahead.

Introduction to Chapters 5–7

THESE CHAPTERS constitute Molodovsky's final reflections on some of his work which contributed greatly to the advancement of the art of financial analysis in 1953. Chapter 5 examines the price-earnings ratio and demolishes the complacency of investors who had thought that the simplicity with which the price-earnings ratio is calculated meant that the ratio behaved in a simple manner. In reality, the price-earnings ratio is full of complexities. Two facts stand out. First, no relation exists between price-earnings ratios and the levels or trends of stock prices. Secondly, the relationship assumed by some to exist between stock prices and price-earnings ratios in reality links changes in price-earnings ratios to cyclical fluctuations in earnings. The revisions made in the 1953 article were extensive, but did not require modification of the points originally covered.

Chapter 6 represents an extensive revision of a 1953 article whch developed a theory of price-earnings ratios. The preceding chapter had indicated the complex and ever-changing relations of the two factors that determine the price-earnings ratio. In this chapter a way out of the complexities is offered. Use of a moving average to determine earning power is found to simplify the situation into a practical method for determining whether the stock market is too high, too low, or just about right in its relationship to average earning power. The 1953 article had an enormous impact on investment thinking at that time, and it has worked out well during the two decades which have elapsed since then.

Chapter 7's title, "The Many Aspects of Yields," accurately indicates that this is an examination in depth of the complexities of yields. Not only yields on common stocks are considered, but also bond yields and yields on real estate and other types of investments. The chapter is an outgrowth of a speech delivered at the 1962 annual meeting of the American Statistical Association. Countless published studies and private memoranda were painstakingly assembled in this country and in Europe. Chapter 7 distills the most significant of the many contributions made over the decades to the understanding of yields and yield relationships as well as presenting Molodovsky's synthesis of this complex topic.

5

Some Aspects of Price-Earnings Ratios

THE PRICE-EARNINGS RATIO is the most common yardstick for comparing the relative attractiveness of individual stocks, or stock groups, and for appraising whether the general market is relatively high or low.

Financial literature abounds with discussions of price-earnings ratios. Countless articles have treated this subject. Few books dealing with stocks fail to consider it. In a representative volume written some thirty years ago, its author claims that "this whole question of the price-earnings ratio is perhaps the most significant one in relation to stock market analysis."[1]

Modern writers are just as interested in price-earnings ratios as were their predecessors. According to an authoritative manual: "The main purpose of calculating earnings per share, aside from indicating dividend protection, is to permit a ready comparison with the current market price. The resultant 'price-earnings ratio' is a concept that the working analyst will have to deal with extensively."[2]

Even more frequently than in formal studies, the price-earnings ratio is used in the ceaseless torrent of informal written and verbal comment accompanying daily stock trading. The simplicity and convenience of this yardstick are so great that its use is extremely widespread.

Unfortunately, the most important characteristic of the price-earnings ratio is that it is an expression of a relation between two different factors which are not homogeneous.

We cannot attach the same economic meaning to all identical numerical values of the ratio. The relative magnitudes of the numerator and the denomina-

---

[1] R. W. Schwacker, *Stock Market Theory and Practice* (New York: B. C. Forbes Publishing Co., 1930), p. 406.

[2] Benjamin Graham, David L. Dodd, and Sidney Cottle, *Security Analysis: Principles and Techniques*, 4th ed. (New York: McGraw-Hill, 1962), p. 229.

tor may often be more significant than the ratio itself. Before using the ratio, it should be ascertained whether it is not rooted in arithmetic rather than economics. If we analyze identical ratios, we shall find on many occasions entirely different economic relations governing corporate earnings and stock prices.

Moreover, price-earnings ratios differ not only from company to company and industry to industry, but also from period to period.

It is not always realized that these two variants of price-earnings ratios are not identical. In the first case, the ratio is used for comparing different stocks with one another. In the second, it compares the same stocks, or an average presumably representing the general market, with themselves in order to discover the significance of changes brought about by passage of time.

A BRIDGE INTO THE FUTURE

The first variant places different stocks or stock groups on a common denominator. It expresses their prices in terms of earnings. When the earnings of different stocks are divided into their respective prices, it becomes apparent that they do not command the same multipliers. Variety, not uniformity, of price-earnings ratios is usual.

> When the student compiles a large assortment of price-earnings ratios, he is likely to be bewildered by their diversity and inconsistency. Since many stocks cover a wide price range within a single year, this would mean that their ratios will vary correspondingly in that year. The average annual ratio for nearly every stock is likely to be different in one year than in another. Finally, the ratio of different stocks when observed at the same moment could readily range from less than seven times to more than 70 times current earnings.
> It seems almost impossible to make any degree of order out of this chaos.[3]

Varying prices are paid for one dollar of earnings of different companies. The reason for the existence of such discrepancies lies in the fact that investment is a disposition for the future. Even though price-earnings ratios are usually based on current earnings, they indicate the market's estimate of probable future earnings.

This variant of the ratios is concerned with valuation. It attempts to transcribe the different growth rates of projected future earnings into differences in the levels of capitalizers applicable to current earnings.

Through constant observation and comparison, analysts evolve rule-of-thumb multipliers which represent pragmatically acceptable capitalizers for stocks belonging to different representative industries. The higher the typical rate of annual earnings growth of the industrial group to which a stock belongs, and the longer this growth can prevail, the higher will be the earnings multiplier assigned to the stock by the market. It would be a destructive procedure to try to find

---

[3] Graham, Dodd, and Cottle, *Security Analysis: Principles and Techniques*, p. 230.

a normal capitalizer for all stocks by averaging, for instance, their individual multipliers. This would wash out their most important personal characteristics—the rates of their respective earnings growth. The point was already made in the essay dealing with measuring the market.

The existence of a high price-earnings ratio reflects the judgment of investors that the profits currently earned by the company in question are low compared to its projected future earning power.

Similarly, when a stock has a low price-earnings ratio, it expresses the opinion of buyers and sellers that the current earnings of that corporation are higher than its expected future representative earnings level.

The very purpose of using price-earnings ratios as a means of comparing the relative values of individual stocks or stock groups is to have them reflect the relation of current earnings to future earnings. Otherwise, all stocks showing identical current earnings would have the same multipliers. And they do when facing a similar future. But similarity is not a basic law of economic life. The April, 1956, issue of *The Exchange*, a monthly magazine published by the New York Stock Exchange, compared price-earnings ratios of forty companies and found that they ranged from approximately 8.5 times current earnings for Bethlehem Steel and Republic Steel, whose earnings had made new records, to 137.5 times for Avco Manufacturing, whose earnings were lower than in the preceding year.

Since the purpose of the price-earnings ratio, when it is used in comparing different stocks to one another, is to measure the ascertainable present in terms of the estimated future, and because future prospects of individual corporations vary greatly, the ratios of individual stocks must cover a wide range. In fact, if such were not the case, there would not be much point in computing them.

In financial history, there have existed only a few periods during which price-earnings ratios have shown any great measure of constancy. One of the longest originated about the turn of the century and lasted until the outbreak of World War I. Many leading stocks were then frequently selling in the market at stable multipliers of about ten times earnings. This was due to the combined effect of coincidental conditions.

Stock prices and corporate earnings were then moving in closely related swings. Their respective changes from year to year were proportionate to each other. For this reason, price-earnings ratios moved sideways or changed little, remaining for years at a time within a very narrow zone.

Many leading stocks in those days were selling to yield 6 percent, while their average dividend payments amounted to 60 percent of earnings. It is clear that a stock earning $1 per share and paying a 60-cent dividend must sell at $10 to yield 6 percent. And at that price it would sell at ten times earnings.

The simultaneous existence of this double condition gave birth to a belief that ten times earnings is a normal price-earnings ratio. This conviction was born from observable facts, and a theoretical background was furnished by the assertion that 6 percent represented an economically justified return on invested capital.

The assumption of the existence in fact, and of the validity in theory, of constant price-earnings ratios became so strongly entrenched that, even several decades after such a relationship ceased to exist, it still found a reflection in financial manuals. Among the rank and file of investors and traders, the impression still lingers that ten times earnings is a pretty good rule of thumb for the valuation of common stocks. Such is the power of folklore and legend. The old forms are gone. On the historical rocks we do find imprints of their former existence. We live in a different era. But some of us dwell under the delusion that dinosaurs are crowding our planet.

THE RATIO IN MOTION

When earnings remain stable, a constant capitalizer makes sense. But the multiplier should reflect expected changes in earnings.

For those who believe that ten times earnings, or some other fixed multiple, represents a normal level for the price-earnings ratio, it is quite consistent with their thinking to reach the conclusion that those stocks whose ratios stand well below normal are cheap and therefore should be held or bought, and that stocks whose ratios are high should be avoided or sold.

It takes an almost imperceptible shift from this line of reasoning to transplant us into a different set of relationships. All it needs is to introduce the element of time into the comparisons. The transition seems natural from the idea that, if stocks endowed with low price-earnings ratios are cheap, the total stock market itself becomes cheap when its price-earnings ratio falls below an estimated normal. And that, conversely, when price-earnings ratios rise above the average level of their usual fluctuations, stocks become overpriced. This may further imply that in hard times price-earnings ratios are low, but that in periods of prosperity, and particularly around the tops of bull markets, they can reach great heights.

Probably the clearest and most practical way to bring the historical relations between prices and price-earnings ratios into sharper focus is to look at Figure 5.1 which covers the Standard & Poor's 500 Index over the century-long period 1871–1971.

The general impression from Figure 5.1 is that there is no sustained correlation between prices and price-earnings ratios. It cannot be said that price-earnings ratios tend to be high at market tops or low at market bottoms. The price-earnings ratios at the various turning points of stock prices are intermixed. They offer little basis for judgment as to whether the market is high or low.

Nor can it even be said that there existed a marked tendency on the part of price-earnings ratios to rise in bull markets and to accompany bear markets in their fall. To be sure, we find a rising trend of both price-earnings ratios and stocks from 1923 to 1929, and from 1953 to 1961. But, with a similar consistency and much more dramatically, price-earnings ratios were declining during the last five years of the bull market ending in 1937, and in the bull market ending in early 1969.

FIGURE 5.1
Stock Prices, Earnings, and Price-Earnings (P/E) Ratios

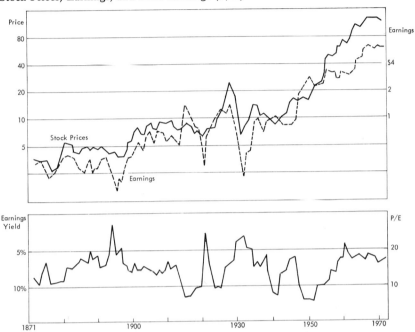

The lack of correlation between prices and ratios becomes particularly striking when we observe the range covered by prices within the same relatively limited zone, such as the 13 to 17 times earnings. Within these relatively narrow limits, stock prices are widely dispersed and encompass both bull market peaks and bear market bottoms. (The average price-earnings ratio for the century was 14.0.)

While there is no ironclad pattern in the general structure of the diagram, the price-earnings ratios tend to cluster in the middle or "temperate" zone, and the "tropical" zone of the highest ratios is dominated by years of economic and market recessions. The "arctic" region of the lowest ratios has less clearly marked characteristics, but many war or rearmament years are in it, reflecting, most likely, the extreme uncertainty of the earnings outlook.

Figure 5.1 conveys the impression that price-earnings ratios have a greater relation to underlying economic conditions than to any particular level of stock prices.

If, for instance, we follow on the chart the scale of price-earnings ratios, instead of that of prices, the rise between 1927 and 1929 is small. But between 1929 and 1931, which saw a decline in stock prices commensurate to its rise during the preceding three years, the price-earnings ratio was lifted substantially. It indicated the passage from prosperity into depression.

A short period of stability in the decade prior to the outbreak of World War

I offers a striking contrast to the era that followed. Punctuated by wars and revolutions, it spans an economic range from depressions to booms. These two economic extremes produce in turn extremes in price-earnings ratios. Strange as it may seem, periods of peak prosperity brought the lowest price-earnings ratios, while their greatest heights were reached during depressions.

A CLOSER VIEW

To what extent has the validity of Figure 5.1 been weakened by the use of annual data? They average out and may neutralize the fluctuations in stock prices. Steep rises and deep declines sometimes take place during the same year. Summarization in a single figure obliterates them. In terms of the Dow-Jones Industrials, the annual mean price for 1970 was 736; but during the first half of the year the DJIA collapsed to 631 before beginning its recovery which reached 839 at the year-end. This illustration is not unique. On the contrary, many stock market tops and bottoms have been characterized by sharp V formations—sometimes within the confines of a single year.

The writer has published elsewhere his investigations into a closer examination of the fluctuations of price-earnings ratios during the course of the year.[4] These included examination of the trends of quarterly earnings related to monthly prices of stocks, with attention being given to determining whether the stock market was anticipating changes in earnings before they took place. The results were inconclusive—although there was some evidence to indicate that the stock market did anticipate the earnings level to be reached in the next six months, rather than simply reflecting earnings progress reported to date. While much of the results achieved may be inconclusive, the concept of using a price-earnings ratio over a shorter time span and using current and expected earnings is a sound concept that may in time bring forth fruits through the efforts of further studies.

THE CONCEPT OF CURRENT EARNINGS

Monthly data should be adequate for our purpose. But they do not exist for earnings. We have to create them.

Until relatively recently, many corporations did not publish income statements for periods shorter than their fiscal years. In numerous cases, sound accounting reasons, connected with the nature of the company's business, militated against too frequent a publication of earnings. Other companies disliked divulging them for reasons of policy.

After World War I, the New York Stock Exchange began a campaign insisting on the filing of quarterly reports by listed domestic companies. At first, the effort to induce corporations to sign agreements to file quarterly statements was a slow

---

[4] Nicholas Molodovsky, "Some Aspects of Price-Earnings Ratios," *The Analysts Journal*, vol. 9, no. 3: 65–78 (May 1953).

and gradual process. By now, the majority of domestic companies have obligated themselves to do so. As a result, some existing price indexes do have, for the more recent periods, corresponding quarterly earnings figures. Standard & Poor's has published quarterly earnings for their indexes since 1935.

Obviously, if price-earnings ratios are based not on monthly mean prices but on full annual earnings of either the preceding or the current year, or even quarterly figures, their monthly changes are less significant. Monthly fluctuations of the ratio will follow exactly and exclusively the movements of price. This must be so because the ratio is a ratio. The price index would change from month to month. It would, nevertheless, each month be divided by the same earnings figure. Furthermore, the transition from December of one year to January of the next year would see very radical changes because, with rare exceptions, earnings will not remain unchanged from year to year. Yet, neither the rate of earnings nor the price-earnings ratios, that is the multipliers with which investors are capitalizing earnings, change drastically between 12:00 midnight, December 31, and 12:01 A.M., January 1.

When earnings figures appear they are already relatively stale. A certain delay must inevitably occur between the completion of a fiscal period and the publication of the report. Even with quarterly earnings, several weeks and sometimes more than a month elapse between the quarter's closing date and the appearance of the figures. In the meantime, the flow of earnings—or deficits—continues unabated. Investors and speculators are keenly following and constantly appraising the direction as well as the intensity of this flow.

Like many other financial concepts, such as the rate of interest or the dividend yield, earnings are usually related to an annual basis. Even when quarterly figures are used, they are, as a rule, either annualized or taken as part of 12-month moving totals. The latter procedure offers the advantage of smoothing out seasonal variations which, in some industries, can be quite marked. It also dissolves non-recurrent bulges or deficiencies and special accounting adjustments.

However, while the concept of earnings is related to an annual base, the actual earnings that most forcibly impress themselves on investors' minds are just as current as the prices themselves. They may be thought of, or expressed, in terms of annual earnings rates on a per-share basis. But they are not earnings for the 12 months ended last December, nor ending at the date when the books were closed for the latest quarter. They are at least partly projected. They represent a fusion between the earnings of the immediate past and those of the immediate future, with the present serving as the connecting link.

Statistically, this should mean that the most sensible way of confronting monthly average prices with earnings is by using figures for a full year ending six months hence. Earnings for the last six months of this period would then represent projected or estimated earnings. On a historical chart, annual earnings figures could be centered at the midpoint of the year instead of at its end. When quarterly earnings figures are available, they may be advanced by two quarters. By interconnecting such annual or quarterly plottings we obtain on the chart graphic interpolations of twelve months' earnings to correspond to each monthly average price. As a further refinement, we can spot them in the middle of each monthly space. The resulting ratios would be the nearest approximation of current price-earnings ratios.

This method does not imply that the majority of investors can always accurately estimate earnings six months ahead. Often they will be wide of the mark. But they are aware of the general trend and accordingly adjust their investment ideas to earnings expectations which thus become integrated into records of the already available knowledge with which the projections then form one continuous flow.

SOME CONCLUSIONS

If we look once more at Figure 5.1 plotting the movements of price-earnings ratios, prices, and earnings for the last century, we shall find long periods during which price-earnings ratios and prices had no visible relation to each other. Periods occur when these two factors do move together, as they did during the more recent times, especially during the 1950s and early 1960s. It is then possible, however, to attribute this concurrence to outside factors and to suggest that changes in price-earnings ratios were not governed by a different capitalization of earnings. Earnings contributed little during this period to the process of stock price formation. It was their temporary paralysis that caused parallel movements of price-earnings ratios and stock prices.

In the turning areas of business cycles, changes in price-earnings ratios are likely to be the result of a time lag in the movements of stock prices and earnings. Both factors are among the economic series most sensitive to cyclical influences. Both are classified among the leading indicators by the National Bureau of Economic Research, as will be shown in Chapter 8. Yet, their respective peaks and troughs may be reached months apart. This was what had happened many times and confused many investors.

Even during the middle phase of an expansion or contraction, when earnings and prices move in the same direction, their relative rates of advance or decline often differ markedly because of the cyclical time lag, or other reason, causing changes in price-earnings ratios. Such shifts can be baffling to those who would always like to interpret the ratios as deliberately applied capitalizers.

Our charts reveal, on the other hand, that throughout this long and extremely varied period, rich in great military and political events, in social and economic transformations, during which several of the most impressive bull and bear markets in American history unfolded their dramatic sequences, there has persisted almost unfailingly a directly inverse relationship between earnings and price-earnings ratios.

In this study, we set out on a search to discover how closely price-earnings ratios follow the fluctuations of stock prices. We found that their relationship is at best erratic and that even when it exists it is coincidental rather than linked together by cause and effect. On the contrary, the inverse relation between price-earnings ratios and earnings recurs with great regularity. With rare exceptions, the curves of earnings and price-earnings ratios not only move in opposite directions but also reach the opposite poles of their turning points with perfect simultaneous timing.

Two facts stand out as a result of our survey. First, no relation exists between price-earnings ratios and the levels or trends of stock prices. There are no typical ratios to correspond to any particular price strata.

The formation of stock prices is a complex subject. Among its many aspects are the relations between stock prices and dividends, stock yields and interest rates, and stock prices and earnings. They have all to be examined before it is possible to arrive at a well-rounded investment theory.

As a step toward this goal, the main point of this chapter was to establish that the relationship allegedly existing between stock prices and price-earnings ratios in reality links the latter to corporate earnings. In fact, several principles governing it yield themselves to precise formulation. They lead to the very heart of the economics of stock prices.

6

A Theory of Price-Earnings Ratios

THE PRICE-EARNINGS RATIO has become the most popular yardstick in financial analysis because it seems so bewitchingly simple.

Nevertheless, as the preceding chapter suggests, the ratios are not foolproof. Their apparent simplicity may be a booby trap. It camouflages complex and ever-changing relations of two factors that are in constant flux and quite frequently unrelated.

IMPORTANCE OF ADEQUATE CONCEPTS

The story of price-earnings ratios is not unlike that of phlogiston. According to chemistry textbooks, two centuries ago a German scientist "explained" burning by a chemical fluid he dubbed phlogiston, "the thing that makes things burn." Everything flammable, he claimed, contained some phlogiston. When it burned, the phlogiston escaped, causing crackling, sparks, flames, and smoke.

While phlogiston presumably accounted for some of the aspects of burning, it led to many difficulties and contradictions until the discovery of oxygen. Not only could burning then be understood, but Lavoisier's experiments soon laid the foundation of modern chemistry.

False as were the ideas about what happened in burning, ores were smelted into metals and fashioned into tools, ornaments, and weapons for thousands of years before Lavoisier was born. And several decades elapsed before his teachings were accepted even by his fellow chemists. Men of affairs—if they heard about him at all—must have considered him a stodgy egghead, an insufferable bore. In their practical work they could get along quite well without dull theorizing. Yet clearer concepts led to technological advances that would have been unthinkable without them.

We agree that a stock's earning power is an important determinant of its market value. But it must offer a broad base and cannot be portrayed by photoflash snapshots of fleeting current earnings.

The concept of estimated earning power is in line with theoretical teaching and decisions of the courts. Yet, to establish its validity in the specialized economics of common stock prices, it should be capable of meeting two important tests.

First, to have operational significance, the earning power concept must be capable of serving as a foundation for a consistent theory of price-earnings ratios. Such a theory must provide an adequate and unequivocal explanation of the functioning of these multipliers.

Second, if a satisfactory theory of the significance of earning power for the formation of stock values can be developed, it should itself be submitted to an empirical test of concurrence between theory and practice.

A HYPOTHETICAL DIAGRAM

Earning power is essentially an average. It contains within itself high earnings as well as low. Therefore, when current earnings rise above the estimated earning power, they should be capitalized by the application of a lower multiple; when they fall below such an estimate, the multiplier should be higher than if it were used for capitalizing earning power itself.

The principles underlying the relation between earnings and price-earnings ratios can be illustrated by a simple diagram, Figure 6.1. The solid line in the lower part of the diagram indicates estimated earning power, while the solid line in the upper portion of the figure indicates the hypothetical price which is assumed to be ten times estimated earning power.

Weaving around estimated earning power are the fluctuating annual earnings depicted by a broken line. The middle section of Figure 6.1 depicts the price-earnings ratio. When current earnings fall below the level of estimated earning power, the price-earnings ratio rises since our hypothetical price is related to estimated earning power, not to actual current earnings. Similarly, when current earnings are at a cyclical peak in excess of estimated earning power, the price-earnings ratio drops to a low.

In other words, compared with current earnings, the highest relative price is theoretically paid for a stock at the depth of a depression. And, if at that time earnings are transformed into deficits, i.e., if they become negative, any price paid to buy them, no matter how fractionally small, is by comparison infinitely large. In such cases, the price-earnings ratio rises to infinity.

This suggests the existence of a mode of capitalization of current earnings governing the changes of price-earnings ratios. It may be called the principle of compensation and discount. It applies not only when current earnings are lower than estimated earning power, but also when the opposite condition exists. At such a time, the greater the upward deviation of current earnings from the representative earning power—the wider the spread between them—the lower the price-earnings ratio will have to plunge in order to discount the rise of current earnings above a longer term measure of earning power.

There is a time when both current earnings and price-earnings ratios are "in

FIGURE 6.1
Hypothetical Stock Price-Earnings, and Price-Earnings Ratio

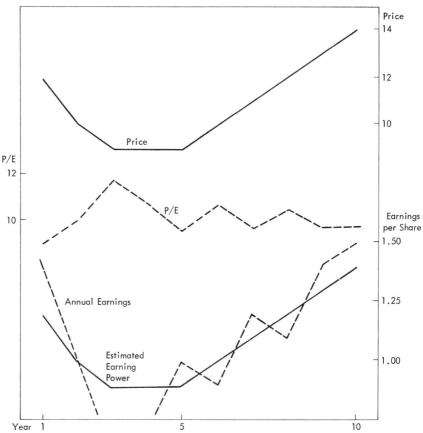

neutral." This occurs when current earnings equal estimated earning power. Then there is no need for either compensation or discount of current earnings. The level of this "horizon" indicates the magnitude of the multiplier used by investors for the capitalization of earning power.

A STILL COMES TO LIFE

This mechanism of price-earnings ratios discussed above may be named, for short, the compensating principle. It is necessary to examine the evidence in order to see if there is any validity to this theory. Figure 6.1 used hypothetical figures both for earnings and for prices in order to state the theory as simply as possible. It is now time to test the theory in the light of real events.

Figure 6.2 illustrates 40 years in the history of the Dow-Jones Industrial

FIGURE 6.2
Earnings and Price-Earnings Ratios—DJIA

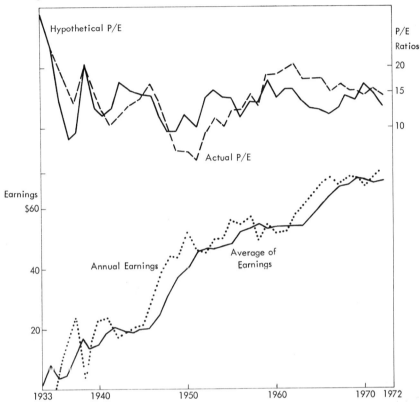

Average—the period from 1933 to 1972. At the bottom of Figure 6.2 is depicted the annual earnings of the DJIA as a dotted line, while the solid line represents an exponentially smoothed average of the DJIA's earnings.[1] This exponentially smoothed average represents the estimated earning power of the DJIA. The average price-earnings ratio for the 40 years was 15.25, so the hypothetical price each year would be 15.25 times the estimated earning power as calculated by the exponentially smoothed average. However, actual earnings move above and below the average earning power, and thus at the top of Figure 6.2 is a solid line representing the hypothetical price-earnings ratio for each of the 40 years. This is calculated by dividing the hypothetical price by the actual earnings for that year. The dashed line depicts the actual price-earnings ratio for each year, calculated by dividing the average price for the DJIA each year by the actual earnings for that year.

---

[1] An alpha of .4 was used as the smoothing constant.

Later on in this chapter, Figure 6.3 will illustrate the price orbit of the DJIA which is merely our hypothetical capitalization of estimated earning power by a multiplier of 15.25 times. The reader might note whether or not this would provide the investor with a sound basis for taking action to buy stocks when opportunities are especially favorable and also to avoid temptation when investment sentiment is particularly exuberant.

Moving back to Figure 6.2 and our examination of price-earnings ratios, we note that the exponentially smoothed average of earnings has been moving upwards fairly steadily during the 40-year period. True, there were several periods of plateaus—the controlled years of World War II, the immediate post-Korea years, and the years 1965–1971. While year-to-year earnings can move rather dramatically, there have been no significant declines in the exponentially smoothed average of earnings. Thus, this would appear to be a reliable measure of earning power for the mature industrial giants which comprise the Dow-Jones Industrial Average.

Earnings on the DJIA peaked in 1929 at $19.94—a level not reached again until 1948. They collapsed to $11.02 in 1930, then to $4.09 in 1931, and a deficit of $0.51 in 1932. Although the DJIA dropped nearly 90 percent from the 1929 peak to the 1932 low, the price-earnings ratio moved up to infinity since earnings had vanished and a deficit was recorded. As Figure 6.2 illustrates, earnings broke out into the black in 1933, the first year on our chart, and advanced sharply through 1937. There was a 48 percent collapse in earnings for 1938, but war clouds from Europe and other measures enabled a good recovery in 1939 followed by the conditions of World War II when demand exceeded capacity; however, controls and excess profits taxes kept net income from expanding.

The hypothetical price-earnings ratio made wide swings in this period fluctuating from 38.5 in 1933 down to a low of 9.0 in 1936 as earnings recovered; followed by an upward swing to 23.2 in 1938 before settling to more normal levels during World War II when actual earnings closely approximated the plateau of estimated earning power. The reader will note how closely the actual price-earnings ratio followed the convolutions of the hypothetical price-earnings ratio. True there were some differences, but the movements were closely related.

It is unnecessary to continue a year-by-year account of the action appearing in Figure 6.2. It unfolds its own story. There is no absolute identity between actual price-earnings ratios and the hypothetical ratios, but they follow similar courses. During the immediate postwar years the actual price-earnings ratios were below the hypothetical ratios because of the general undervaluation of the stock market in those years, while actual price-earnings ratios were above the hypothetical ratios during a good part of the 1960s, reflecting generally optimistic valuations then prevailing. But even during these periods of digression, the general nature of upswings and downswings in both series tended to occur at the same time.

The point of Figure 6.2 is that life does follow the theory expounded and that the theory was derived from real life. The precise contours of the curves of all the factors and the details of the timing of their swings will be different in each individual case. But the function of the price-earnings ratio as a link between current earnings and representative earning power will prevail at all times.

AN HISTORICAL PERSPECTIVE

The hypothetical diagram of Figure 6.1, as well as the 40-year diagram of Figure 6.2, have certain limitations. It is conceivable that they apply only to these periods and not as a general case of universal applicability. This writer has examined elsewhere the track of hypothetical price-earnings ratios and actual price-earnings ratios for the Standard & Poor's 500 index.[2] The relationship between the hypothetical and the actual was good in all periods studied. When one considers the number of theories solemnly set forth which have a coefficient of determination explaining only 10 to 20 percent of the actual fluctuations, the following relationships between the hypothetical and actual price-earnings ratios is most impressive:

	r^2
1880–1894	84.0%
1894–1914	47.4
1914–1937	64.4
1936–1951	75.1

MOVING AVERAGES AS A MEASURE OF EARNING POWER

The agreeable concurrence of theory and practice continues as we examine the concept of using a moving average as a measure of earning power. Any moving average of past earnings is not an accurate measure of corporate earning power. It is too crude a device to serve as a fully convincing appraisal of the complex subject of fundamental earning power. Yet it has the merit of being simple, even when using exponential smoothing, and it is not devoid of statistical justification. This was recognized by Benjamin Graham in a 1945 article: "Although, in theory, it is only expected future earnings that are to be capitalized, in practice there is a strong tendency to accept past average earnings as the best guide for the future."[3]

It is clear, however, that an average of past performance can be accepted only as a point of departure. It has to be adjusted continually. When corporate earnings are subjected to violent fluctuations within short spans of years, the application of a moving average will create distortions in the trend of earning power which it is supposed to measure.

---

[2] Nicholas Molodovsky, "Stock Prices and Current Earnings," *The Analysts Journal*, vol. 11, no. 4: 83–94 (August 1955).

[3] Benjamin Graham, *The Commercial and Financial Chronicle* (October 18, 1945).

Despite these objections, the exponentially smoothed curves of earnings for the Dow-Jones Industrials or the Standard & Poor's 500 indexes have functioned quite well as measures of the demonstrated earning power of these indicators. When examining the record of one company only, moving averages cannot do the job adequately. A more complex study of the factors involved is essential.

MARKET VALUE

In a later section of this book, we shall study the nature as well as the methods of computing moving investment values which are independent of price and which represent the equivalent of today's worth of the income-producing wealth that they contain. They are economic entities quite different from actual market values which are determined by the best judgment of investors as to a stock's current fair price. But even in this limited sense, market value cannot be derived from the mere knowledge of the current price and current earnings. It is an expression of the capitalization by investors of a stock's estimated normal earning power. Current earnings fluctuate around earning power, and current prices fluctuate around market value.

Current prices and current earnings are volatile. They are sensitive to many influences—real or illusional—and can move rapidly, sometimes in divergent directions. If one divides the current price of a stock by its current earnings, the resulting ratio will not very frequently coincide with the multiplier which a sensible investor would deem appropriate for the capitalization of earning power that produces a stock's normal market value. It is by comparing the "normal" price-earnings multiplier to the actual ratio that judgment may be exercised about the desirability of a particular stock. An understanding of the nature of market value and a sound approach to price-earnings ratios are, therefore, essential prerequisites to the more basic appraisal of moving investment values.

The size of the market's own capitalizer depends not on present earnings alone, to which it is generally applied, but on estimated future earnings as well. If earnings are expected to grow, the market will place a higher multiplier on current earnings. By changing multipliers, the market, i.e., the investors and speculators who comprise it, differentiate between stocks with different earnings prospects. Even in the case of the same stock, its market capitalizer will change when the evidence becomes convincing that the rate of growth in its earnings is changing.

Despite its shortcomings, this sketchy review has hopefully established the validity of the concept of capitalized earning power as an operational expression of value in the stock market. When current earnings get out of line with estimated earning power, changes in price-earnings ratios compensate for the deviations.

Many advanced concepts of price-earnings ratios have been developed over the years. References to some of the more interesting ones are to be found in

FIGURE 6.3
Dow-Jones Industrial Average

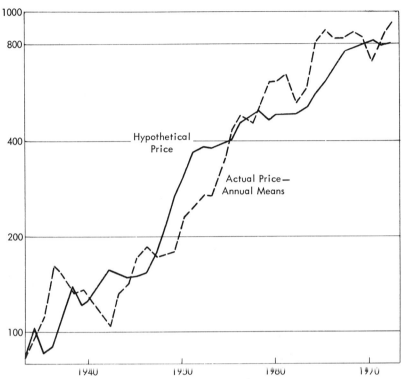

footnote 4 to this chapter. However, we will simply conclude with Figure 6.3 which traces the hypothetical orbit of the Dow-Jones Industrial Average during the 40 years 1933–1972 using a 15.25 price to exponentially smoothed earnings, as well as the average price of the index each year. We shall leave it to the reader as to whether or not there is a "built-in gyroscope" which in time brings the actual course of the market back to the hypothetical orbit.

4 Ralph A. Bing, "Survey of Practitioners' Stock Evaluation Methods," *Financial Analysts Journal,* Vol. 27, No. 3: 55–60 (May 1971); Nicholas Molodovsky. "Recent Studies of P/E Ratios," *Financial Analysts Journal,* Vol. 23, No. 3: 101–8 (May 1967).

7

The Many Aspects of Yields

NEXT TO price-earnings ratios, various yield relations are widely used by many financial analysts as measures of the soundness of the market's level. Most frequently relied on are common stock yields themselves, and the ratios of stock yields to bond yields. Applying another variant, the Cleveland Trust Company computes stocks as multiples of dividends and publishes charts of this indicator in its *Business Bulletin*.

It has been observed that periods preceding turning points of rising markets, when dividends are high but an exuberant confidence lifts the prices of stocks to peak levels, are marked by very low stock yields. The reverse is true of periods when ebbing confidence places a low valuation on dividends. Certain conclusions may be drawn from such observations.

> An examination of the All Stock monthly index for yield expectations shows that four times in the last 68 years, the expected yield has dropped below 3 percent. These were in February–March–April, 1899, April, 1901, August–September, 1929, and July, 1933. Each of these four periods was a favorable one for the sale of stocks, since in each case lower prices developed in the next year. There have also been three cases where yield expectations rose above 8 percent. These occurred in October, 1873, October–November–December, 1917, and April–May–June– July, 1932. In each of these three instances stock prices averaged higher in subsequent 12 months. It would thus appear that, when average yields are below 3 percent, stocks are priced too high, and when average yields are above 8 percent, stock prices are too low.[1]

The practical value of these findings is, however, quite limited. In the course of 1871–1938, the period covered by the Cowles Commission study, the upper and lower boundaries which it singled out were reached only a few times. Twenty-eight years elapsed between the second and the third recurrence of the lower limit; and 44 and 15 years separated the second from the first and the third from

---

[1] Cowles, and associates, *Common Stock Indexes*, pp. 46–57.

the second appearance of the upper. Furthermore, and paradoxically, yields were low also in periods when they could not possibly be regarded as warning signals. In some part of every year between 1932 and 1940, yields of industrial stocks were lower than at the bull market peak of 1937.

This has led other analysts to narrow the range of average yields serving as indicators of turning points of stock prices. Many seemed to feel that when average stock yields drop below 4 percent, and especially when they begin to approach the 3 percent level, stocks are already skating on thin ice; when stocks yield on the average over 6 percent, and particularly when their average yields exceed 7 percent, common stocks in general are in a buying area. With respect to the ratio of stock yields to bond yields, it is usually considered that when this ratio falls below 1.3, it flashes a danger signal. The higher the ratio, the safer are stock purchases. The validity of these various indicators of turning points is open to serious question.

SOME ILLUSTRATIONS

For quite a long time, stock yields have been declining while bond yields were rising. They have been moving so long in such appallingly "wrong" directions that by 1958 the average stock yield dropped below the average yield on corporate bonds. Some analysts called this differential "the reverse yield gap" and saw in it a financial revolution. If we disregard the purchasing power risk, which is a characteristic of fixed income securities, even the best among equities carry a larger degree of investment uncertainty than certificates of indebtedness, especially when the latter are bonds of the highest grade. It is a logical thought that in order to compensate the investor for accepting the greater risk of holding common stocks, he should enjoy a richer return from his investment. During most of the 1930s and 1940s, the ratio of stock yields to bond yields was appropriately high—the return on equities being larger and, at times, two or three times as large as the return on high-grade corporate bonds.

But, since the 1950s, an irreverent note began creeping into this eminently proper picture. By 1955, the ratio of the two yields dropped below the level it had formed at the tops of the two preceding bull markets—those of 1946 and 1937—and yet no reversal of stock prices took place. A few years later, the ratio was already below the point marking the ill-fated peak of 1929. Yet still no disaster followed. As it happened—and this was downright embarrassing—a bull market was born in October, 1960, when the ratio of stock yields to bond yields was close to the lowest point it had registered since the beginning of this century.

The curtain of the drama rises on the inception of the stock market's postwar advance. While the upward movement of stock prices was progressing, with cyclical interruptions, from its 1949 low to exalted heights, stock yields were shrinking. Far from losing their shirts and being, on the contrary, ever more luxuriously outfitted by their haberdasher brokers, investors were feeling, nevertheless, after every additional purchase, an increasingly uncomfortable tightness around their necks. Each vigorous upward push of stocks made it more difficult to find "sanforized" yield material offering new buyers preshrunk current income from their stocks.

Dividends were increasing too, but not at the same rate as the prices of common stocks. The fastest postwar advance in annual dividend payments took place between 1945 and 1950. Then their engine stalled for several years. When it got going again, it did so at a much reduced speed, contrasting sadly with the joyful flight of stock prices.

Stock yields are a ratio of dividends to prices. When dividends—standing in the numerator—increase at a stingy rate, while the price denominator is quite generously enlarged, the ratio falls.

THE VOICE OF HISTORY

In the light of the century-long historical perspective offered by Figure 7.1, what are the observations that may be noted?

The lower panel of Figure 7.1 shows that, until the beginning of this century, stock yields remained often below the yields on bonds. In fact, the curve of bond yields could almost serve as a trend line—or at least as a guideline—for the wider fluctuations of stock yields for the first sixty years through 1931. There is visible

FIGURE 7.1
Stock Prices, Yields, and Bond Yields

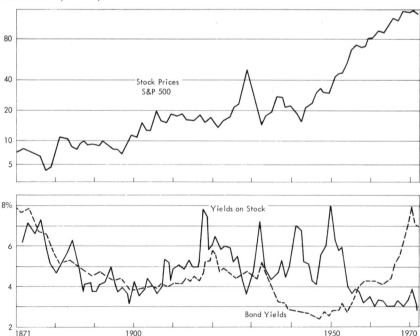

also an occasional inverse relation between the peaks and troughs of stock prices and stock yields. But this inverse relationship was irregular and had no specific numerical characteristics.

The bull market which began just before the turn of the century witnessed, at its inception, the lowest stock yields in recorded statistical annals prior to 1959. And the 1919–1921 bear market, which was much more severe than it may look on Figure 7.1, was underway when stock yields were high. We may also stress once more that stock yields were often below the yields of bonds. Investors were apparently sufficiently smart to realize the constructive implications for equity values of growing corporate earnings and this, surprisingly enough, without the benefit of ever having read Edgar Lawrence Smith's *Common Stocks as Long-Term Investments*[2] or, still more frustratingly, this author's articles on this subject in the *Financial Analysts Journal*.

THE GREAT DISRUPTION OF YIELDS

As we look at Figure 7.1 the wide gulf which developed since the middle of the 1930s, completely separating stock and bond yields for a period of 20 years, stands out as a unique occurrence strangely isolated from the entire previous experience.

It is probably fair to say that for the first 60 years of the period covered by Figure 7.1, stock yields and bond yields showed a propensity to travel in the same direction. What brought about their separation in the 1930s?

Yields on high grade bonds dropped from 5.3 percent in 1932 to 4.3 percent only two years later. This trend continued until a low of 2.6 percent was reached in 1946, only half the 1932 level. This rapid descent of bond yields was caused at first by the depression. Subsequently, bond yields were pinned down by the money and credit policies of World War II. Bond yields became managed, while stock yields remained free.

Yields on the highest grade corporate bonds remained below the 3 percent level for many years—as long as interest rates remained artificially "pegged" by the Federal Reserve Board. The gap between bond yields and current returns on stocks was widened between 1946 and 1949 by a decline in stock prices and increased dividend payments.

By 1949, the deep undervaluation of stocks in the face of sharply rising earnings and dividends, and the enforcement of a cheap money policy, were a combination of factors quite adequate in themselves to originate a bull market. Its potential thrust was boosted by events which were to gain a cumulative and lasting effect on the demand-supply relations of common stocks.

Bond yields came back to life when a free money market was re-established in 1951. The rapid decline in stock yields beginning in the early 1950s coincided

---

[2] Edgar Lawrence Smith, *Common Stocks as Long-Term Investments* (New York: The Macmillan Co., 1924).

with changes instituted in the investment laws of the key state of New York. Life insurance companies and savings banks were permitted to invest in common stocks. Even more important were the changes permitting bank trusts and pension funds to invest much more heavily in stocks. The dynamic impact of pension fund and bank trust buying began to make itself felt. The flowering of investment companies shifted more investment demand toward equities.

The numbers of private stockholders and the means at their command also grew. All these developments swelled the demand for stocks which were already being driven upward by the momentum of the bull market and their undervaluation. Yet no corresponding increase in their supply took place. Capital gains taxes, a more favorable tax treatment of bond issues, and depreciation policies, limited the offers of stocks to the anxiously bidding buyers.

Perhaps equally telling as the shift in the demand and supply equation was a change in the philosophy of stock investment due to the growth stock concept. The advantages of seeking growth through purchases of stocks became widely accepted in the late 1920s, but the popularity of all stocks was soon undermined by the depression. In the 1950s, interest in growth stocks reawakened. At first, private investors were the principal purchasers of growth stock. Yet, this philosophy is infinitely more suited to the policies of "immortal" institutions. Any initial small stock yield, with dividends growing even at a slow rate, is bound to exceed, at some point, the rate of return from fixed income securities.

EUROPEAN EXPERIENCE

European and particularly French experience with government and private financing through bond issues is relevant to our investigation of relative stock and bond yields. It goes full circle. From the ashes of complete collapse of investors' confidence in bonds as an instrument of savings and source of stable income, bonds were restored to an important role by means of special clauses designed to shore up the purchasing power of the money of payment.

As an investment medium, bonds held in Europe an undisputed primacy prior to World War I. In France, the holders of *rentes* (i.e., of government bonds), the most typical of which were perpetuities, became known as *rentiers*. And this term gradually acquired the more general meaning designating any person living from unearned income. The fate of European *rentiers* was a sad one. For generations they financed the industrial development, as well as the armaments of their own and foreign countries, only to witness the substance of their savings go up in the smoke of revolutions and inflations. The bond certificates with their sheaves of pretty coupons—carefully preserved under mattresses or in strong boxes—became completely worthless. But, before this happened, bonds were held in high esteem.

As a rule, European economists share the belief that prior to World War I, stock yields were consistently higher than bond yields in all the principal international financial centers, including New York. They seem satisfied to rationalize this assumed spread in respective returns via the usual argument of corresponding risk differential. But the statistical bases of their findings are slight.

According to Otto Donner, stock yields in Europe showed a remarkably constant relation to bond yields from 1870 until World War I.[3] The level of stock yields in Germany held about 1.5 percent above the yields on high grade bonds; in France, the gap was not so wide—about 0.75 percent. For England, his comparison of bond yields is made with shares issued by Investment Trusts. From 1890 to 1913, they had an average current return of 5.35 percent, as against 2.98 percent from British Consols.

In getting these figures, Donner used such indexes as he could find. There were none too many, nor were they homogeneous. The source material enumerated in his footnotes—at least in respect to yields—is a statistical tossed salad.

This pleasing picture of stocks providing for half a century higher returns than bonds—whether it existed in real life or only in some statistical figures—did not survive the political and economic havoc which descended on most European countries after the end of World War I. The flight from the currency into assets offering more solid value such as real estate or sound foreign money, and other islands of financial salvation from the mounting flood of paper, destroyed the value of bonds and rendered bond yields quite meaningless. In several European countries, in the years between the two world wars, periods of monetary stability have been brief and intermittent. They could not restore confidence in promises to pay sums of money in legal tender. Being certificates of ownership, stocks stood closer to tangible assets, and investors were anxious to reach for them, bidding up their prices, while the prices of bonds remained depressed. Stocks began yielding less than bonds.

GOLD CLAUSE IN AMERICAN LAW

The depreciating purchasing power of the return from a fixed income security may become, during an inflationary period, a force tending to lift bond yields and depress bond prices. Figure 7.2 illustrates the ravages of inflation in reducing the investor's true return as measured in terms of constant purchasing power. Many methods have been used over the years to protect the creditor and the financial structure at large against the risk of a depreciation of the money of payment stipulated in the contract. The gold clause is the most typical device of such protective agreements. In most countries, the courts adopted a nominalistic attitude towards the money of payment and pronounced gold clauses illegal as undermining the foundation of national currency. But in this country, several decisions rendered by the Supreme Court of the United States in the years immediately following the Civil War, despite the fact that the economy was drowning in depreciated "greenbacks," proclaimed the validity of the clause in private contracts whether it was tied to gold coin or gold value.

---

[3] Otto Donner, *Die Kursbildung am Aktienmarkt* (Berlin, 1934).

FIGURE 7.2
Bond Yields and Inflation in the Consumer Price Index

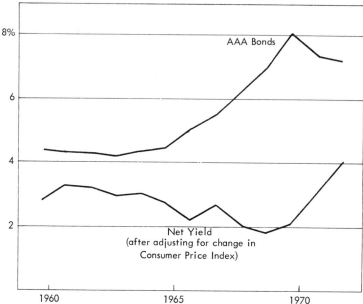

In the case of its own debt, the federal government went even further than the Supreme Court did in the matter of private contracts. The latter were considered payable in legal tender in the absence of a clause stipulating a specific money of payment.

At the close of the Civil War, the federal government saw itself in a very difficult financial situation. It was, therefore, proposed to effect the redemption of the public debt in depreciated currency. There existed no objection of a legal nature, notes being legal tender and the very large majority of securities issued by the government containing no clause stipulating the reimbursement of the principal in gold or in any other sound currency.

There was persistent agitation in favor of paying in paper money. But finally the thesis of payment in gold was victorious. In 1869, a law was passed forcing the government to pay obligations issued by the United States in gold coin or its equivalent. In spite of the inevitability of heavy charges and the very grave difficulties of the hour, it was declared that national honor required the public debt to be paid in gold to the last dollar.

Desirous of conferring henceforth to its credit a character of unquestioned strength, the government included a gold clause in each of its loans floated during and after World War I. The clause was phrased in terms of absolute precision, stipulating that principal and interest were payable in gold dollars of the weight and fineness of the date of issue.

In fact, the gold clause was so well safeguarded by American law that this protection finally defeated its own purpose. It became universally used, as a matter of course, in all bond issues. All dollar bonds issued by the federal government, the states, the municipalities, and other public bodies, as well as by private corporations, contained a clause of payment in gold coin. When the country went off the gold standard in 1933, a general economic collapse would have followed if the gold clause had been enforced. There was only one way to resolve the conflict between the letter of the law and national economic survival. In cases which reached the Supreme Court in February, 1935, and in March, 1937, the Court held that the gold clause interfered with the constitutional power of Congress to regulate currency in amount of face value of the contract. The gold clause in American law was dead.

Its demise caused no catastrophes. It is remarkable that following the disruption of two world wars the massive process of saving and investing through fixed interest obligations has survived unimpaired in the United States and was only temporarily damaged in England and the rest of the Western world. The conversion gadgets have come and gone. The success of Eurobonds has demonstrated the regained strength of the European money markets.

VIEW FROM MOUNTAIN'S TOP

Before abandoning the subject of the money of payment, we shall use a passage from a scholarly work comparing the relative impact of depreciating currency on stock and bond yields.

In a doctoral dissertation, "Le Rendement des Placements," running in excess of 500 pages, and presented at the University of Louvain in 1943, G. Van de Velde reviewed the history and the economics of yields throughout the entire range of investments—from land to common stocks—for the period 1865–1939. Mr. Van de Velde's study was limited to Belgian experience only. However, its implications transcend its political frontiers. They are typical for Western Europe. It helps to realize the vastness of the subject, its many ramifications, the great variety of assets producing investment returns, as well as the wide range of the returns themselves.

This study uses a unique approach. It investigates long-term returns on investments expressed in stable money. It adjusts for the cyclical fluctuations of yields and for changes in purchasing power of the monetary unit. We translate from page 215 a passage containing one of its findings:

> In comparing stock yields with bond yields, we observe that even during a period of monetary stability, the return from stocks has greater regularity. The spreads between highs and lows are more moderate. *In the long run this investment is therefore less speculative than the others* in the sense that after completion of a full economic cycle, the monetary value of a stock portfolio seems to approach closer its point of departure than bonds or perpetuities. . . . This is as it should be because the value of stocks has a certain relation to reality, while the value of a bond is

much more conventional. The value of a stock is related to that of the enterprise it represents. . . . But nothing similar exists for the bonds whose value is bound to the monetary unit; the value of the latter is conventional and, besides, once the bond is issued, the creditor is immutably bound by the terms under which the loan has been issued, even if they no longer have any contact with reality. On the contrary, the debtor has usually the right to free himself by redeeming the loan.

OTHER TYPES OF YIELDS

A look from a mountain into the valley of past experience can be instructive. It helps to see the landmarks in a truer perspective. And it offers a wider horizon. The close-up attention of this chapter is focused on stock and bond yields. But there comes into our field of vision, while we still stand aloft, many other types of returns from investments. They are all of interest and importance. We shall merely list them *pro forma* as part of an overall panorama.

There exist, indeed, numerous investment possibilities outside of stocks and bonds. Real estate—whether it is approached on an individual basis or through the more recent real estate investment trust—is itself a major field. And beyond it lie various other types of investment or speculation. Some are highly specialized. When investors leave the more familiar hunting grounds, they begin to form noncompeting groups. They are mostly led to them out of particular backgrounds, by unusual experience or training, or a chain of circumstances bringing them into the inner circle of an exceptionally gifted leader.

While all investments influence one another, their interconnecting pipelines are not wide in diameter, have many curves and grades and few compressor stations. In the long run, yields from similar assets tend to level out. But it can be a slow process and, in the meantime, we encounter premiums and discounts even in the case of theoretically related returns.

EARNINGS YIELDS

The yields we have been discussing so far represent actual payments of money. But there exists one so-called "yield" which is not a payment at all. It lies in hiding, so to speak, between stock prices and stock yields. From this secreted position it wields considerable power by its bearing on the complex problem of cost of equity capital. We refer to "earnings yield." They may be found graphically depicted in the bottom panel of Figure 7.3.

Developed by the Federal Power Commission, the cost of capital theory of the rate of return originated in the famous 1952 decisions in the Northern Natural Gas and Colorado Interstate cases. Originally, the cost of money was measured by the interest and dividends that investors were willing to accept as a return on their capital. But dividends can be reduced or omitted. This is not the case with the earnings yields.

However, whether a single price-earnings ratio is used, or many of them are

FIGURE 7.3
Stock Prices, Earnings, and Price-Earnings Ratios

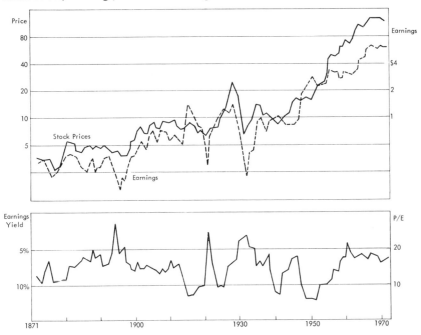

averaged covering a period of years, such ratios can have a meaning only under conditions of earnings stability. Both for theoretical and practical considerations discussed by us in connection with price-earnings ratios, their reciprocals, i.e., earnings yields, have also to be transcribed, after taking into account projected rates of earnings growth, into more valid terms. We shall tackle this problem in the pages that still lie ahead.

THOSE DYNAMIC EARNINGS

Of the three principal stock market factors—prices, earnings, and dividends —earnings are the most dynamic. Compared to them, stock prices are relatively stable, while dividends are still more tame. Stock prices and stock yields frequently move in opposite directions. Their divergence is more pronounced than that of stock prices and dividend yields. In other words, changes in stock prices tend to dominate—and often to account for all of the change in stock yields, in the short run.

Over the long run, however, earnings dominate the picture with stock prices following along—or sometimes leading the way. The earnings yield fluctuations which are volatile in the short run, do not have any especial longer term trend. Perhaps it would be well to note at this point that the earnings yield is the reciprocal of the price-earnings ratio. For example, a 10 percent earnings yield is equivalent to a price-earnings ratio of 10, a 5 percent earnings yield is equivalent to a price-earnings ratio of 20, and so forth. A price-earnings ratio or an earnings yield is a meaningless measure when applied solely to current earnings. This is because earnings fluctuate greatly in the short run.

To reach this "finding" we do not have to dive into great depths of theoretical analysis. So often we heard—especially in the later 1960s—that stock prices were too high simply because they had been rising while earnings were falling off. Yet where should we cast the anchor of comparison? Why not begin with 1932? And if it is claimed that this is an exceptional case, let's grant a generous ten years' grace. Let's begin with 1942 and use that year as the point of departure in studying Figure 7.3. The year 1942 saw a 6 percent earnings yield—nearly equivalent to a price-earnings ratio of 17 times. In examining Figure 7.3, this appears to be a fairly normal capitalization ratio.

BACK TO THE WORKBENCH

Descending from the mountain, we are taking with us some wide angle views. They should help us to perceive more clearly the relations of stock and bond yields.

> Investors have a wide range of yields from which to choose when making commitments these days. . . . The spread between bond yields and stock yields is unusually wide. . . . As time goes on, people who are partly or wholly dependent on their savings for living expenses are more and more pressed for income. . . . A man who has saved $100,000 finds it hard to be satisfied with a return of $2,000 or $2,500 a year, and is tempted to transfer an increasing part of his funds into equities. He could secure $6,500 now by making the transfer complete.

We trust he did! The above quotation is taken from an investment review dated December, 1949. At that time, the DJIA was around 200. His capital would have increased more than four times and he would have enjoyed a vastly increased income from his investments.

But now he stands at the other end of the rainbow. And while he cannot hope to ride back to its crest again and quadruple his capital by reverting to bonds, he considers the switch for the sake of preserving his funds. He could considerably enlarge the income from his investments and even make it at least partially tax exempt. He hesitates, having heard a lot about inflation and the weakening position of the dollar. From experience, he knows that money does not buy as much as it used to. He has some other dollar assets: insurance, some savings, and some social security payments when he is ready to retire.

Mulling the situation over, he recalls that the decision of switching back into bonds had been pressed upon him by well-meaning advisers for the last 15 years. But, in the meantime, the income spread between the returns from stocks and bonds has become wide enough to make the temptation to benefit from it an almost irresistible force.

Yet business is good and seems to be improving. The budgetary deficits are mounting. Stocks are supposed to protect against inflation. Their latest weakness scared him somewhat. He sold a few stocks at the worst possible moment, using the proceeds to buy some bonds. He is glad that he did not sell more, now that stocks are recovering and bonds have declined. He knows nothing about the economics of stock and bond yields. But his instinctive shrewdness makes him feel that pretty soon he might resolve all these doubts and indecisions by rolling his money into two bundles of about equal size—half stocks and half bonds.

We envy the simplicity of his common sense decision and shall not trouble his peace of mind by sending him a copy of this book. But financial analysis, once embraced as a profession, is not easy to give up. We shall drag out our blueprints and shall pour over them again and suffer through every nook and cranny of their design for financial living.

BOND YIELDS

Yields of high-grade bonds measure long term interest. It is an economic factor of the highest order. As long as the soundness of the money of payment is not in doubt, values of all fixed income-producing assets vary inversely with changes in interest rates. The higher the prevailing rate of interest, the smaller the multiplier applicable to a given return for estimating the amount of capital necessary to produce it. When interest rates rise, a relative smaller capital produces the same income as before the rise. Rising interest rates tend to lower values, and declining interest rates to lift them.

According to an old established theory, changes in interest rates are determined by the intensity of demand by borrowers and the supply of funds available for lending. The typical changes in the demand and supply equation of money occur in response to cyclical fluctuations in business and to policy action of monetary authorities.

Cyclically, interest rates are affected by the profitability of industry. When profits are mounting, business enterprises seek additional capital, and their cumulative demand pushes interest rates up.

Since higher interest rates, through their inverse relation to income-producing assets, tend to cause stock prices to decline, rising earnings—by stimulating interest—have in the later stages of cyclical expansions conflicting effects on stock prices. Their direct effect is to push prices up. Indirectly, by lifting interest rates, rising earnings have a dampening effect on stock prices in the final phase of a cyclical expansion.

At first, the tendency toward declining stock prices brought about by the rise in interest rates is more than offset by the continued growth of earnings. In other words, the rise in interest rates then acts merely as a brake on the further rise of stock prices. It is not yet able to reverse their upward trend. But interest rates react upon the economic environment in which they were born. The interest rate is a derivative factor only as far as the profits of yesterday are concerned; it is itself a determinant of the profits of tomorrow. Higher interest rates ultimately bring lower earnings.

In sum: The conflicting influences of earnings and interest rates on the trends of stock prices are rooted in earnings. The growing profitability of industry—a phase of the rising tide of the cycle—becomes reflected in higher equity prices. But through a slow and subtle process it contains within itself its own countermeasure—its stimulating effect on the interest rate. Many other economic factors also carry within themselves opposing forces of propulsion and regression, revealing the fundamental balance of economic life. They themselves reverse the very trends they originate.

AN EXPERT'S VIEWS

Interest rates also reveal more lasting trends than fluctuations caused by business cycles or passing incidents. A long-term history of American high-grade bond prices and bond yields since the 1870s may be gained from the monumental work of Sidney Homer.[4] His views may be summarized as follows:

1. Bond yields are dominated by long-term secular trends. Since the beginning of this century, financial history has witnessed a bear market in bond prices between 1900 and 1920; a bull market lasting from 1920 to 1946; and, finally, a great bear market from 1946 on, which may or may not have reached its ultimate depths in the demoralized bond markets of 1974. These secular trends are not rhythmic; their time spans vary greatly, and their course is unsettled by business cycles.

2. The long-term trends of bond yields have been largely determined by the alternations of war and peace.

3. The catalyst between the political environment and interest rate trends is the trend in wholesale commodity prices. They usually coincide. However, the influence of commodity prices on bond yields is not secular only, but cyclical as well. It is often difficult to separate these respective influences.

UNRELATED SERIES

The review of the main trends of stock and bond yields over a century-long period points up the differences in their economic natures and in the mechanisms of their directional changes. It is probably safer to use them as separate economic guides than to try to draw conclusions from their confrontation. And, needless

---

[4] Sidney Homer, *A History of Interest Rates* (New Brunswick, N.J.: Rutgers University Press, 1963).

to say, each time both yields must be carefully disentangled and read in the light of the meaning of the action of their underlying forces.

Another reason for caution was pointed out in a letter to the author by the late Jules I. Bogen, Professor of Finance of New York University:

> Qualitative questions raised by a comparison of bond and stock yields in the 19th century are frightening. In an era when substantially all earnings were paid out as dividends, dividend yields meant something quite different from what they do when only half of earnings are paid out on the average, and that after a very large depreciation allowance and heavy research outlays. There is no practical way to allow for such qualitative factors in yield indices, but they are vital to an interpretation of yield comparisons going back so many years.

In addition to these various pragmatic considerations, there also exist strong theoretical reasons throwing considerable doubt on the validity of using stock yields and their ratios to the yields on bonds as indicators of impending trend changes in stock prices.

We can scarcely hope to reach reliable conclusions concerning the state and outlook of the stock market by drawing them from comparison of factors whose very natures are different.

STOCK YIELDS AND STOCK VALUES

Do so-called stock yields, i.e., current returns from common stocks, then have no meaning at all? They do.

They are a basic point of departure for measuring the total return from dividends. Such an overall effective yield—including not only the current return but future payments as well—could be legitimately compared with bond yields because it also introduces the factor of time which is an essential ingredient of all investment concepts. This is the road toward appraising investment values.

During the five years elapsed between 1896, when Charles H. Dow devised the Dow-Jones Industrial (and Rail) Averages, and his death in 1902, Dow often referred in his editorials in *The Wall Street Journal,* of which he was a founder, to stock values. Regardless of temporary fluctuations in stock prices, he felt that values were the determining factor in the long run. He believed that values were measurable by the return to the investor.

The idea was sound. But as in the case of many another pioneer, Dow's tools were primitive. The number of stocks in the original averages was small. All his observations were made from a narrow base and over a short period. If he had lived longer he might have come to realize that values cannot be meaningful if they consider the present only; they should discount the future as well.

On the basis of such observations as he had been able to accumulate, Dow thought that when a stock sells at a price which returns only about 3.5 percent on the investment, it is "obviously" dear, unless there existed some special reason for supporting so high a price. We referred to similar concepts at the outset of this chapter.

Some present-day Dow theorists continue to be faithful to the founder's concept of value. Not very long ago, a well-known follower of *The Theory* related that after studying the action of the DJIA from 1920 onwards, he found that it would be advisable to begin selling stocks when the average yield on the Dow-Jones Industrials recedes to the 3.5 percent area and to accumulate them when the average yield on the Dow-Jones Industrials rises above the 6 percent level.

The date on which these remarks were published in a financial periodical happened to stand in the midst of the earliest swirling weeks of a bull market that was just getting under way. Yet, under Dow's measures of value, stocks should have been sold.

This example shows again how unreliable such comparisons are. The basic idea behind them—the search for investment values—is correct. But an adequate technique is lacking. Perhaps the weakest point in trying to use current yields for appraising stock values is the fact that they depend so much on the action of stock prices themselves whose validity they set out to measure.

We must be able to determine an overall "effective yield" before we can make a significant appraisal of a stock's investment value. As in the case of bond yields, the effective yield is that rate of discount which will equate the sum of present values of future payments with current price. It reinstates the essential factor of time in the appraisal of common stocks. We shall discuss this more fully in Part III of this volume.

Introduction to Chapters 8–10

THESE CHAPTERS were prepared solely for this volume to provide a basic review and introduction to three areas which are essential for a sound understanding of investments. They do not contain original contributions by Molodovsky. His preferences as to conflicting theories are spelled out well. Ones that he regarded as frivolous are ignored or quickly brushed aside. These chapters are not the last word on these complex topics, and the reader is encouraged to delve further into the literature in these areas.

Chapter 8 discusses the fundamental importance of being aware of the nation's economic policy. Economic policy greatly influences both the nation's corporations and the securities markets. Brief overviews are given as to how the nation's economic policy is carried into effect. The Federal Reserve is in control of the determination of monetary policy and is responsible for its implementation. The federal government determines what fiscal policy should be followed and this is carried into effect by the federal government's policies with respect to taxation and spending.

Chapter 9 discusses business cycles and their relationship to the securities markets. The investor with a strong grasp of what course the economy is likely to take as a result of fiscal and monetary policies will be in a better position to plan his own investment program soundly and effectively.

Chapter 10 is an introduction to a topic which originated in the academic community and which has given rise to considerable uneasiness in the investment world. The topic is the random walk—that is, do stock prices simply wander around in a random fashion unrelated to any fundamental factors? Over long periods of time, stock prices obviously relate to earning power and dividends as is so well demonstrated earlier in this book, notably in Chapter 6. Over shorter periods of time, the random walk theory has been the best explanation put forth to date. There are many important lessons to be learned from the random walk theoreticians, and this chapter is an introduction to them.

8

Economic Policy

IN THE PRECEDING CHAPTERS we have observed that while investment values, dividends, and earnings are interrelated, they often respond, as do stock prices also, to the influence of many other factors, which thereby affect the outcome of investments in common stocks. Among them we noted the state of confidence, business cycles, and the rates of change in the money supply. This chapter will review the monetary and fiscal aspects of investments. Money and credit are managed by the Federal Reserve Board whose members are appointed by the President. The President himself, assisted by the Secretary of the Treasury and the Council of Economic Advisers, proposes legislation involving fiscal policy and is in direct charge of actual expenditures. These fiscal measures, together with money and credit policies, form the government's economic policy.

Gogol's postmaster in *The Inspector General* arrived at an understanding of the functioning of the universe using his own mental powers only. His "common sense answers" little resembled those of Laplace and Newton. Unless an investor is an economist by profession, he can easily fall into the same predicament. Our survey will necessarily be brief. Yet if some of the more technical details of the nature of credit and money, the banking system, and the elements of fiscal policy may not be directly relevant to investment decisions, they will be useful for a clear understanding of the inner functioning of the mechanisms which determine, at least partially, investment results.

The monetary policy of this country is determined by a quasi-governmental agency, the Board of Governors of the Federal Reserve System, theoretically independent, but in reality, subject to fierce and relentless pressures from the executive and legislative branches of government, not to mention public opinion. The Federal Reserve Board should have the qualities of courage, diplomacy, technical knowledge, and economic vision if it is to succeed in directing the destinies of monetary policy. As events have shown, monetary policy has been the dominant factor of economic policy in this country. While no board composed of mortal men can have perfect economic foresight, the Federal Reserve

Board has made a significant contribution to the economic well-being of our nation.

THE STRUCTURE OF CREDIT

Countless scholars have contributed to the theory of money and banking over the centuries. The following descriptions of the monetary system are simplifications of fairly complicated mechanisms which leave out many of the refinements. The interested reader can refer to any of a number of texts to obtain a more complete presentation.[1]

Savings banks and savings and loan associations do not create credit. A savings bank merely uses the savings deposits of its clients to make loans. The fundamental nature of the dollars deposited and the dollars lent out are not changed.

The situation is completely different with commercial banks. Centuries ago when the first banks began to accept deposits as an accommodation, they found out that under normal conditions withdrawals from the bank would amount to only a fraction of deposits. Thus the banks did not need to keep all the deposits idle and unproductive, but could use a large proportion of these deposits to turn a profit by making loans. The borrower would be given a demand deposit in the amount of the loan against which he would write checks. The businesses and organizations in the community which received the checks would probably not require payment in cash, but would prefer to add them to their own accounts at the bank. At this point the original depositor has a demand deposit equal to his original deposit and the various businesses who supplied the borrower now have increased their demand deposits to the extent of the loan. The total of demand deposits has been doubled; the bank has created credit. The chain could continue with new loans creating new deposits, and increasing the loan interest income of the bank.

The practice of commercial banks was aimed at making profits; the creation of transferable demand deposits was the result. The larger the proportion of deposits loaned out, the greater profits were. However, there are continuous withdrawals from banks even under normal business conditions, and by experience banks learned that they should carry some reserves to provide for partial withdrawals. These could be currency reserves or accounts with other banks.

To lend with safety, banks found it necessary from time to time to seek outside help when withdrawals against their liabilities exceeded the average and especially when demands on them to pay suddenly swelled to an extent straining their full resources. When such demands reach emergency proportions, banks will all fend for themselves. In self-defense, they would have to call loans, thereby contracting economic activity, sometimes to the extent of causing a general business recession and even a financial panic. In this country, during the crises of 1873, 1893, 1907,

---

[1] See texts such as: Lester V. Chandler, *The Economics of Money and Banking*, 4th ed. (New York: Harper & Row, 1964).

and 1932, many banks had to suspend payments. A lender of last resort, a central bank, is needed to protect the banking system from the danger of periodic breakdowns. It can also perform other useful functions connected with money transactions. Such guardian angel institutions have existed in Europe for a long time—the Bank of England being established in 1694 and the Bank of France being founded in 1800. The present central banking system in the United States came into being just before World War I.

The title of the Federal Reserve Act, signed by President Wilson in 1913, describes its intended functions: "An Act to provide for the establishment of Federal reserve banks, to furnish an elastic currency, to afford means of rediscounting commercial paper, to establish a more effective supervision of banking in the United States, and for other purposes."

President Wilson, his advisers, and the Congress which designed the Act had no clear vision that, in addition to the aims described, they were creating a powerful monetary engine.

THE FEDERAL RESERVE SYSTEM

The first few years following its creation were spent by the "Fed" (as it is frequently called for short in money circles) on constructing and perfecting the mechanism of its internal organization. One of the early measures was to lower the legal reserve requirements of member banks which, in the absence of a central bank, were high. National banks had been required by law to keep up to 25 percent of their deposits in reserve accounts with other banks, but there were no uniform regulations as to the location and financial solvency of the banks where the reserves were to be kept. Since 1917, all reserves of national banks and other banks that are members of the Federal Reserve System have been kept at a Federal Reserve bank.

We shall sketch only briefly the many turbulent events which have added to the Federal Reserve System's experience and financial know-how. World War I produced financial needs which could not be met by orthodox financing methods. The Federal Reserve was willing to make loans to banks to carry Liberty Bonds at lower interest rates than the coupons on the Liberty Bonds. Thus, the Treasury Department was able to sell sufficient Liberty Bonds to finance the war—some to true investors and some to the banking system. During the postwar boom the Fed warned the banks and the public of the risks of speculative credit expansion and took what steps it could. The Fed was not listened to and the bubble burst in 1920, followed by a short, but severe, depression. The Fed used its resources in helping the recovery and before long the major boom of the 1920s developed. When the speculative aspects returned, the Fed again tried to warn the nation, but its resources were not equal to the task, and the general exuberance of the times prevailed over the Fed's conservative financial philosophy. During the 1930s the Fed returned to the job of helping to encourage an economic recovery. The long-due banking reforms gave added powers to the Fed.

Money and credit were supplied freely in an effort to restore prosperity. When World War II broke out, the Fed became once more primarily concerned with patriotic duties: financing the war and protecting the market prices of the bond issues comprising the enormously enlarged national debt. Even after the war ended, it continued this emphasis and did little to combat the inflation which took hold after price controls were lifted. Finally, in 1951 an accord with the Treasury Department ended its obligation to support the prices of U.S. government securities, and the Fed was now free to move against price inflation. The theme of the last two decades has been to discourage inflation by tightening credit during business expansions, followed by a return to more easy money and credit conditions during recessions.

EXPANSION AND CONTRACTION OF DEPOSITS

A banking system in which the required legal reserves represent only a small proportion of demand deposits has great leverage. Reserve requirements are varied from time to time and differ according to various classifications of banks. In late 1972 the nation's larger banks were required to hold reserves of 17.5 percent against their demand deposits, a 3 percent reserve against savings accounts, and a 5 percent reserve against other time deposits.

The 17.5 percent reserve against demand deposits is equivalent to a multiplier of credit expansion of approximately six times. This figure is the "upside-down" relation, i.e., the reciprocal of 100/17.5. Conceptually, all the member banks of the Federal Reserve System may be grouped together and viewed as a single commercial bank leaning on the total reserves of a single central bank, represented by the twelve Federal Reserve banks. When this single commercial bank receives or creates a new demand deposit, it must increase its reserve account at the central bank by an amount equivalent to 17.5 percent of the new deposit liability. The remaining funds can be used by it for making new loans or for investing in other earning assets such as U.S. government bonds or tax-free state and municipal bonds. If the bank makes another loan and thereby creates another demand deposit, once more it must send 17.5 percent of this to the central bank. Eventually six dollars of loans can be made for the one dollar reserve added to the account at the Federal Reserve bank.

The bank's management is simply striving to make its customers happy by granting them loans. Bond investments also provide added profits, and whatever the mix between loans and investments the bank's management selects, the additional supply of money which banks as a whole can put to productive use, is approximately six times as large as the newly acquired reserves. Economic necessity will compel the banking system to use the reserves fully, as otherwise some of the available funds will remain unemployed and unproductive. This multiplier of six times will remain in effect as long as the legal reserve requirements continue at the 17.5 percent level and so long as none of the deposits are withdrawn.

This leverage works both ways, of course. Should the bank's reserves contract, it must restore them. In so doing, it brings down deposits to a level determined by the same multiplier of six. The bank will have to call loans or sell earning assets to reduce its deposits to an amount consistent with reserve requirements. Otherwise, its reserve position at the central bank will become deficient.

TRADING IN FEDERAL FUNDS

When commercial banks have insufficient funds for meeting credit demands made upon them, or when their required reserves at their regional Federal Reserve bank are deficient, they may borrow from the Reserve bank at the prevailing rate—termed the "discount rate"—upon furnishing collateral which usually consists of U.S. government bonds. This is termed borrowing at the "discount window." If such loans exceed 15 days, a penalty of an additional 2 percent is imposed. The discount window is a privilege, not a right guaranteed to the member banks.

Because of the penalty and the unwillingness of the Fed to provide funds at the discount window for extended periods, a system has developed over the years which enables member banks to borrow reserves from other banks with excess reserves in their accounts at the Federal Reserve bank serving their district. This borrowing and lending of reserves is termed the Federal Funds market. It is comprehensive and efficiently organized. Without going into the mechanics of the Federal Funds market, we shall simply note that this has largely replaced direct borrowings from the Federal Reserve banks. In the early years of the Federal Reserve System, direct borrowings were the rule and thus the Federal Reserve was able to make its monetary policy felt through changes involving restrictions on member bank borrowings and the "rediscount rate," which is the interest rate charged.

OPEN MARKET POLICY

When the Federal Reserve System began operations, the 12 regional Federal Reserve banks used a portion of the funds deposited with them to buy U.S. government securities and thereby earn interest. It was observed that as the Federal Reserve banks were acquiring government securities, member banks were reducing their borrowings from the Reserve banks. The inflow of funds into the open market resulting from the payments made by the Federal Reserve was used by the member banks to repay their loans from the Federal Reserve banks.

A little later, when the Reserve banks liquidated the government securities purchased by them, this led to a shortage of funds in the commercial banking system. Commercial banks returned to the discount windows of the Reserve banks to borrow money. Clearly, a link existed between the Federal Reserve operations in government securities and the money flow in the open market.

In its May, 1923, monthly Review, the Federal Reserve Board stated that the timing and amounts of open market investments by the Reserve banks should be governed with primary regard to the accommodation of commerce and business and to the effect of such purchases and sales on the general credit situation.

The realization of the hidden power of open market operations as a tool of monetary action developed gradually through experience. Reference was also made to the Bank of England which had found it expedient to contract business credit by the sale of British government securities. The Bank of England found that such an action on its part had a multiplier effect because the Bank was the foundation of the entire credit structure.

The importance of this monetary tool was recognized in 1933 by the formation of the Federal Reserve Open Market Committee. The committee consists of the 7 members of the Federal Reserve Board and 5 of the 12 presidents of Federal Reserve banks. The five presidents serve on a rotating basis, except the president of the Federal Reserve Bank of New York who has permanent status.

The Fed's open market operations are the most powerful lever of its monetary policy. Basically, open market policy consists of selling or buying a predetermined package of government securities, thereby withdrawing from the economy or injecting into it a desired amount of purchasing power. Because of many diverse influences making themselves felt in the money market in varying combinations and changing degrees of pressure at different times, the Fed's open market policy is a never ending flow of study, decisions, and action coming from the highest echelons of its hierarchy.

As already indicated, a fractional reserve central banking system, in which the required legal reserves represent only a fraction of demand deposits, has great leverage through a built-in multiplier and divisor of credit expansion and contraction. This is true not only when commercial member banks extend loans to their own customers, but also when they engage in securities transactions with the Federal Reserve banks.

Should the Open Market Committee decide to increase the potential bank credit to the extent of approximately $6 billion, it would need to buy only $1 billion of government bonds. This action would increase the cash reserves of the banking system by $1 billion, which when used as a reserve would support $6 billion of deposits. At the start of 1973, total reserves available to support private nonbank deposits, or RPD's as they are known, amounted to approximately $29 billion and supported $200 billion in demand deposits.

The process would be reversed if the Fed decided to tighten credit by instructing the Open Market Committee to sell a certain amount of the Fed's holdings of government securities. The effective cancellation of credit would carry the same divisor as the multiplier in the case of expansion.

THE FED'S MONETARY POLICY IN ACTION

The Fed has other tools at its command and does not hesitate to use them when it deems them appropriate. Changes in reserve requirements or in the ways of calculating reserves have the same multiplier effect as in open market operations. Other elements at the Fed's command are of lesser importance.

In evaluating Federal Reserve policy, it is essential to keep in mind that while the Fed can effectively contract credit when the resources of the banking system are fully employed, it can only lay the groundwork for credit expansion. Business conditions are the final arbiter of credit use. Potential borrowers may be reluctant to take advantage of cheaper or more abundant credit. In this instance, credit expansion would be delayed until borrowers began to use the easier credit provided by Federal Reserve actions.

Four business recessions have taken place during the last two decades—in 1953, 1957, 1960, and 1970. In each case, the Fed did not remain a passive onlooker. It acted to enlarge the reserves of the banking system and made credit more abundant and thereby cheaper. The timing of the results varied with then prevailing business conditions, but the Fed's actions proved to be beneficial. The 1958 rebound was so rapid that the Fed was led to early anti-inflationary measures. These may have hastened the oncoming of another recession, which ended early in 1961. The ensuing recovery was the longest in American economic history, benefiting from both a milder monetary policy and an expansionary fiscal policy. Inflation returned, balance of payments problems arose, and the Fed's restrictive policies combined with a deflationary fiscal policy played a large part in the ensuing recession. The recovery which began in 1971 is continuing and is being aided by a relatively mild monetary policy.

The Fed has been criticized in some quarters for making sharp swings in the past which subsequently proved to be too drastic. For the foreseeable future, the Fed is likely to be more moderate in its application of monetary policy, allowing the money supply to grow at about the same rate as the economy as a whole.

FISCAL POLICY AND THE INVESTMENT MULTIPLIER

The concept that a government might have a fiscal policy that would affect the well-being of the economy is a fairly recent idea. The world was made conscious of this concept by a book which had great impact on both theoretical economic thinking and practical financial policy—*The General Theory of Employment, Interest and Money* by John Maynard Keynes, published in 1935.[2] Keynes provided the theory which explained why an economy could, under some conditions, stagnate at a low level of output with little hope of a return to prosperity until investment outlays began to increase significantly.

When Keynes, like all economists, discusses investment, he has in mind durable assets such as plant and equipment which enlarge the productive stock of the economy. Keynes stated his conclusion as follows:

> We can now carry this line of thought a stage further. For in given circumstances a definite ratio, to be called the *Multiplier*, can be established between

[2] Keynes, *General Theory* (New York: Harcourt, Brace & Co., 1935).

income and investment and, subject to certain simplifications, between the total employment and the employment directly employed on investment (which we shall call the *primary employment*). This further step is an integral part of our theory of employment, since it establishes a precise relationship, given the propensity to consume, between aggregate employment and income and the rate of investment.[3]

After giving due credit for the introduction of the concept of the multiplier to R. F. Kahn, Keynes proceeds with its integration into his theory. He demonstrates how an increment of output will have to be divided between consumption and investment. We shall not reproduce his mathematical proof. But in plain English he tells us that when there is an increment of aggregate investment, income will increase by a greater number, which is the product of the multiplier times the increment of investment. The investment multiplier is an indicator of the amount of increase in national income that will result from a given increase in investment spending.

The multiplier effect of changes in investment spending results from a chain reaction much like the process of bank credit expansion. The amount spent on new investment will pass in diminishing fractions from hand to hand, increasing incomes. Some of this increase will be saved and some spent on extra consumption. The amounts spent on consumption will depend on the desire to consume. The percentage that will be saved will determine the investment multiplier, just as the Federal Reserve's required reserve ratio limits the expansion or contraction of credit. However, the motivation to consume rather than save varies. It will not produce a fixed multiplier factor like the ratio of required reserves. The propensity to consume extra income stemming from new investment changes with business conditions and also with relative affluence. At some point, expansion will yield to contraction and incomes in general will tend to decline.

Another way to describe this process is to note that income not spent on consumption is saved and, directly or indirectly, invested in the stock of productive facilities. The amounts that people spend on consumption go to the merchants and, through them, to producers. Middlemen and manufacturers are also consumers in their own right. The initial extra consumption from new investment is thus multiplied many times. Since the economic circuit never closes, but continues as life goes on, new consumption creates new investment which, in turn, gives rise to more consumption and more investment in a ceaseless stream. The intensity of this circuit varies with the cyclical fluctuations of business which alter the relations between economic growth and stability.

While the economic process is continuous, though of varying strength, the investment multiplier may be considered a child of production. Production initiates economic activity, builds wealth, and creates incomes. Sunning oneself under a palm tree and knocking down a coconut for subsistence does not contribute to economic welfare and progress. Herein lies a major difference between underdeveloped and industrial nations.

[3] Ibid., p. 113.

FISCAL POLICY

It is beyond the scope of this chapter to do more than dip briefly into Keynes's great work. Consequently, we shall content ourselves with the statement that when investment by the private sector of the economy is stagnating at a level which keeps the economy operating well below capacity, increased government budget deficits will work somewhat in the same fashion as the investment multiplier in boosting total spending with a multiplier effect. Keynes wrote to George Bernard Shaw that he expected his book published in 1935 to "largely revolutionize—not I suppose at once, but in the course of the next ten years—the way the world thinks about economic problems."[4] His timing was just about perfect.

The date of February 20, 1946, marked an important event shaping the future destinies of the American people. On that day, President Truman signed the Employment Act passed by the Congress. It stated that the government must ensure a national economic environment conducive to employment of all citizens. The federal government was given the duty to create and safeguard conditions providing employment opportunities for those able, willing, and seeking to work.

The new act did not express just a pious intent; it meant business. Those who have missed reading the Economic Reports of the President, which are transmitted to the Congress early each year, are likely to be astounded by the characteristics of the environment in which we live, and which shapes the values of their investments, unless they are well versed in the new economics.

The major part of the President's Economic Report to the Congress consists of the Annual Report of the Council of Economic Advisers. President Johnson's Council's report for 1965 ran to 145 pages of text plus 120 pages of tables. Its keynote statement is contained in the Introduction:

> In 1964, the United States passed a watershed in economic policy. After lengthy debate, this country boldly reduced taxes to accelerate expansion and reduce unemployment. The effects were immediate and telling. A mild expansion—which might soon have lapsed into tired decline—picked up its pace, and at year end showed every sign of long and vigorous life. . . .
>
> A new era for economic policy is at hand. A wide consensus of responsible opinion now recognizes that Federal fiscal policy must be geared to keep the economy moving ahead.[5]

The Keynesian revolution became bipartisan as illustrated by President Nixon's Council's 1973 report stating:

> The path of the economy . . . calls for slowing down the rise of money GNP, which was about 11 percent during 1972, to about 9 percent during 1973 and to a steady rate less than that thereafter. This desired shift to a slower rate of increase of money GNP would be assisted by a shift of the budget—from a position in which

---

[4] Quoted in Robert L. Heilbroner, *The Worldly Philosophers* (New York: Simon and Schuster, 1953), p. 259.

[5] *Economic Report of the President* (Washington, D.C.: U.S. Government Printing Office, January 1965).

the unified budget would be in deficit at full employment to a position in which it would be in balance at full employment. In fact, the strength of the private demand forces in the economy, described below, argues that this shift in the budget position is essential to avoid an inflationary pace of expansion.[6]

Many economists contributed to the flowering of economic thinking during the last four decades. The Nobel prizewinner Kuznets' work helped lead to the development of statistics to measure economic activity. Governments today expend large sums to compile voluminous statistics detailing all aspects of economic activity. The availability of economic statistics lead to the development of new and more penetrating concepts of economic realities. Modern economists make no empty boasts when they claim to possess new understanding as well as better tools. To be sure, there is no unanimity among them. There are many disagreements among the various groups. But few claim a monopoly of the truth.

Our discussion has been kept on an elementary plane. It can be summed up by noting that the Employment Act of 1946 gives the federal government the duty to maintain a prosperous economy with ample employment opportunities for all, while the theoretical and practical insights into the workings of monetary and fiscal policy have provided the government with the tools for achieving prosperity. Despite this progress, there are still many, many unsolved problems including such major ones as inflation, the balance of international payments, and the inability to "fine tune" fiscal and monetary policy to keep the economy on a steady growth trend rather than a growth trend interrupted by even relatively short recessions and periods of overenthusiastic booms.

---

[6] *Economic Report of the President* (Washington, D.C.: U.S. Government Printing Office, January 1973).

9

Cycles and Indicators

IF PROSPECTIVE INVESTORS could consult today quotation sheets of a year hence —or even those of tomorrow—and have this privilege extended to them indefinitely in the future, they would travel a much smoother road to riches. Being denied this advantage, they have to grope, as best they can, in the uncertain darkness. One of the largest stumbling blocks on their way is the relation of business cycles to future fluctuations of stock prices.

In the July 27, 1946, issue, *The New Yorker* brought out in its own inimitable fashion the helplessness of investors and their advisors in this respect. In an Alan Dunn cartoon picturing a Wall Street office, a lady client instructs her broker to take all her money out of stocks and buy bonds "just before the next depression."

Whatever her knowledge of economics, the lady's instinct was unerring. Stock prices were approaching an important peak. We trust the broker did advise her to sell the stocks at once and repurchased them three years later.

The relation between short-term movements in business and in stock prices is too loose and uncertain to make the former eligible for forecasting. Many short-term oscillations of the market originate in unexpected events or sudden changes in sentiment. They are random. Shrewd observers may sense them, but they cannot be forecast through a study of prevailing conditions.

Figure 9.1 shows the cyclical movements in stock prices and business since World War II, as classified by the National Bureau of Economic Research. The shaded areas on the chart show periods of cyclical recessions; the expansions occupy the clear spaces between them. From peak to peak, or from trough to trough, complete cycles are of a duration lasting from roughly two to approximately five years. As may be noted on the chart, the turning points of stock prices precede the changes of business conditions as a general rule. The cyclical fluctuations of stock prices weave around the slowly rising long-term, or so-called secular, trend line. Stock prices, earnings, and dividends are not the only economic factors which are subject to cyclical phases of expansions and contractions. All economic

FIGURE 9.1
Stock Prices and Business Cycles (Recessions Shaded)

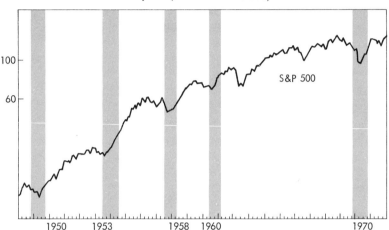

time series are affected by them, whether they represent a single specific activity or large aggregates, including the sum of them all, Gross National Product.

Cyclical fluctuations in business have sufficient affinity to those in stock prices to justify a search for the nature and sequence of their relations. Their duration and amplitude are such that they can seriously affect the financial welfare of investors.

At one time many believed that long-term trends alone were of concern to investors, that the rising secular trend of stock prices was an automatic safeguard for their holdings. Edgar Lawrence Smith's famous study *Common Stocks as Long Term Investments* contributed in no small measure to this belief. It translated the remarkable growth in the American economy into a "law of increasing stock values and income return." According to this "law," over a period of years the principal value of a well-diversified holding of the common stocks of representative corporations in essential industries tends to increase in accordance with the operation of compound interest and "may be relied upon over a term of years to pay an average income return on such increasing values of something more than the average current rate of commercial paper."[1]

Smith's evidence consisted of twelve statistical tests of results obtained by investing identical amounts in high-grade bonds and in common stocks selected at random. The tests covered varying periods, averaging about twenty years, between 1866 and 1922. Smith later expanded the scope of his research, and other financial writers have since carried his tests and similar statistical comparisons into periods close to our own times.

---

[1] Edgar Lawrence Smith, *Common Stocks as Long Term Investments* (New York: Macmillan, 1924), p. 79.

Smith indicated several reasons why common stocks should prove more profitable long-term investments than bonds. For one thing, they represent claims on the entire residual corporate earning power, which tends to increase with the country's growth. The "human factor" of management and the persistent historical erosion of the value of the monetary unit should also be taken into account. But for Smith the main cause was the one embodied in his "law": the compounding effect of reinvested corporate earnings. Stock values grow at approximately the rate at which earnings are reinvested. By paying out less in dividends than they earn, companies gradually build up their net worth, or book value. Modigliani and Miller regard retained earnings as equivalent to a fully subscribed, preemptive issue of common stock.[2]

It is not our purpose to discuss in this chapter the merits and frailties of Smith's analysis, which became known as "the common stock theory" and received exceptionally wide publicity. This has been done abundantly by many writers.[3] Suffice it to note that the theory helped to implant the common stock idea in the consciousness of the public. It served to justify to many their purchases of common stocks. And since common stocks were declared to be sound long-term investments, temporary interruptions of their upward trend could be disregarded with impunity. "No doubt the 'common stock theory' gave even to the downright speculator the feeling that his actions were based upon the solid rock of scientific finding."[4]

This blissful dream was disrupted by the cruel awakening of 1929 and the ensuing long depression. The severity of the punishment impressed upon many investors the grave consequences cyclical fluctuations in business may have for the values and prices of common stocks.

The reminder was long overdue. The protracted bull market of the 1920s and the emergence of the "new era" philosophy had tended to make the public forget, just at the time it should have been especially watchful, that cyclical downturns in business and finance are inevitable. They had forgotten the harsh but brief lesson of 1921. During the two decades preceding World War I most economic factors had been exceedingly stable, with a marked long-term upward trend. Nevertheless, bonds and mortgages practically monopolized the attention of investors. Common stocks were held in such low esteem that for many decades they sold at about three-quarters of their value as measured by the return to the investor. Since then the social and economic currents had been undermining this stability. But the fact that the 1926–1927 business recession had no effect on stock prices, and a belated wave of optimism, hid the changes that were building up cycles marked by wider amplitudes of fluctuation.

---

[2] Franco Modigliani and Merton Miller, "The Cost of Capital, Corporation Finance, and the Theory of Investment," *American Economic Review*, vol. 48, no. 3: 261–97 (June 1958).

[3] See in particular: Chelcie C. Bosland, *The Common Stock Theory of Investment: Its Development and Significance* (New York: The Ronald Press, 1937); Cowles, and associates, *Common Stock Indexes*, pp. 40–50; Graham, Dodd and Cottle, *Security Analysis*, p. 48.

[4] Bosland, *Common Stock Theory of Investment*, p. 4.

After the costly experience of the 1929 collapse, investors intensified their efforts to catch cyclical turns. This is not easy. While all business cycles bear a certain family resemblance, each is unique, never repeated.

It is true that conditions prevailing in each cyclical phase tend to generate the next phase, revealing the existence of internal causation. But knowledge of this fact does not help us to determine in advance the particular chain of circumstances that will bring about a turning point, nor does it always allow us to locate its causes even when the effects are already visible. The particular combination of stresses among economic processes that cause the expansion phase of one cycle to degenerate into recession may not be repeated in other cycles. The peculiarities of each cycle rule out the possibility of precisely timing cyclical turns through comparison with the past. However, "there is a pronounced tendency towards repetition in the relations among the movements of activities in successive business cycles."[5] Could not, therefore, the current movements of some individual economic factors such as interest rates, dividends, and earnings— the chief ingredients of stock values and stock prices, and also the main underlying trends of business activity itself such as production, commodity prices, money, and credit—serve to forecast movements in stock prices? Chapter 4 has shown what changes in economic conditions can do to stock prices.

Any student of cycles must begin with the great work done to measure economic factors in an objective manner, led by the National Bureau of Economic Research established in 1918 with Wesley C. Mitchell as its first director of research. Mitchell and his successor, Arthur F. Burns, devoted considerable time to the study of business cycles. Others have joined in the research effort over the years and today the student of business cycles is admirably served by the monthly publication of the Department of Commerce entitled *Business Cycle Developments* and familiarly known among economists as BCD. It contains hundreds of charts and the statistical tables on which they are based. Many analytical measures are presented, keeping the reader up to the "state of the art" in the analysis of business cycles.

STOCK PRICES AND INTEREST RATES

As pointed out earlier, a rise in interest rates tends to affect bond values adversely, while a decline tends to enhance them. Stock prices are similarly affected.

The rate of interest is not an abstract or arbitrary figure. It is itself the result of the interaction of economic and political forces. Governments try to control the rate of interest to fit their fiscal policies. And it is directly affected by economic forces abroad, and at home, above all, by the profitability of industry. When their profits are mounting, business enterprises seek additional capital for expansion, and their competition pushes interest rates up.

---

[5] Arthur F. Burns and Wesley C. Mitchell, *Measuring Business Cycles* (New York: National Bureau of Economic Research, 1946), p. 467.

However, rising earnings have conflicting effects on interest rates and thereby on stock prices. Their direct effect is to push prices up. Indirectly, by raising interest rates, rising earnings tend to affect unfavorably the prices of stocks. While the effect of changes in earnings on stock prices is both immediate and telling, changes in stock prices that may be attributed to the effect of changes in interest rates are slow, working themselves out gradually throughout the general levels of bond and stock yields.

At first, the tendency toward declining stock prices brought about by the rise in interest rates is more than offset by the continued growth of earnings. In other words, the rise in interest rates then acts merely as a brake on the further rise of stock prices; it is not yet able to reverse their upward thrust. But interest rates continue to react upon the economic environment in which they were born. The interest rate is a derivative factor as far as the profits of yesterday are concerned; but it is itself a determinant of the profits of tomorrow. Higher interest rates ultimately bring lower earnings.

The conflicting influences of earnings and interest rates on stock prices are rooted in earnings. The rising profitability of industry, a phase of the rising tide of the cycle, is soon reflected in higher equity prices. But through a slow and subtle process it contains within itself its own counter-measure—its stimulating effect on the interest rate. Many other economic factors also carry within themselves opposing forces of propulsion and regression. Eventually, they reverse the effects they had originated. The fact that the rise in interest rates is due to a rise in earnings suggests that between them there may exist a certain characteristic lead or lag in cyclical timing.

Interest rates are listed among the lagging indicators in BCD and these students of business cycles have much evidence to support them. The monetary economists, as will be mentioned later, take the opposing view that interest rates lead far in advance of the cycle, rather than trailing a bit behind the previous business cycle. The evidence, of course, would support either interpretation.

STOCK PRICES, DIVIDENDS, AND EARNINGS

Since earnings are the source of dividends, there is a time lag between a decline or rise in earnings and in dividend payments. Occasionally this lag is so great as almost to obscure the causal relation. Corporations enjoying exceptionally strong financial positions and anxious to pay dividends regularly may draw on their surplus in bad years if earnings are inadequate. Conversely, if earnings are "plowed back" into the business, dividend payments may be small compared with net profits.

Because dividends do not always reflect a company's current financial affairs, "earnings have more influence than dividend payments in the determination of stock prices."[6] However, we should note that modern academic writers hold opposing views on that subject, as do financial analysts.

---

[6] Cowles, and associates, *Common Stock Indexes*, pp. 46 and 59.

If the stock exchange were strictly a value market, the relation between current earnings and stock prices would be considerably less pronounced, for current earnings would lose much of their direct and immediate influence on prices. They would determine stock prices to the extent that they contribute to the formation of stock values. Discounted in terms of future dividend payments over an infinite period, they would trace a much flatter curve. However, owing to the influence of speculation, stock prices are, for short periods, often only shadows cast by current earnings. And, like all shadows, they enlarge or dwarf the projected object, depending upon the position of the economic sun.

The very sensitivity of stock prices to earnings makes the latter unsuitable for forecasting. Stock prices often discount earnings before they are published. "Insiders" can take advantage of their advance information by buying or selling the stocks of companies with whose affairs they are familiar or that belong to the same industrial group. The stock market itself is likely to be the barometer of earnings, its movements preceding rather than following theirs. Both stock prices and corporate profits are classified in BCD as "leading" indicators. This does not prevent long lags from occurring between them. We saw in Chapter 5 the resulting misleading effect on price-earnings ratios in 1958.

STOCK PRICES, BUSINESS ACTIVITY, AND COMMODITY PRICES

Dividends, earnings, and interest rates—the prime determinants of stock values and prices—are not jut numbers passed around to statisticians after a turn of an economic lottery wheel. They are summaries of relations between forces generated by the actions of millions of men earning a living and are shaped by the physical, political, and social environment in which they happen to live.

The movements and trends of factors such as earnings must, therefore, have a counterpart in the economic developments that produce them, such as industrial production, commodity prices, wages, living costs, and money and credit conditions. Could indexes of general business activity and of some of their components be used for predicting cyclical movements of stock prices?

It is logical to expect that over long periods the curves of business activity, earnings, and stock prices will follow a fairly parallel course. Industry would not long be willing to expand production if it proved unprofitable or if prospects were bad. Nor would it be inclined to curtail output if the outlook for earnings was favorable. Undoubtedly there is a fundamental relation between business activity, earnings, and stock prices. But fluctuations in an index of business activity do not, therefore, necessarily forecast cyclical fluctuations of stock prices.

In fact, as is shown in the extensive research efforts of the National Bureau of Economic Research and others continually bringing the studies up to date in each month's BCD, stock prices tend to lead the economy—reaching their peak months before the peak in business activity and making their lows months before the economy reaches its nadir. For short stretches of time, and within relatively narrow limits, stock prices and business activity do move in opposite directions. But a divergence lasting for almost a full year—from November, 1961, to October, 1962—and of so drastic a nature, raised theoretical and practical questions about their typical time sequence. These questions acquired even greater significance because similar wide deviations had happened before. In 1946, a notable fall of stock prices took place in full view of a powerful rise of corporate profits. And the independence of stock prices from other segments of the economy was not always of a bearish nature. To repeat an expression used by Burns and Mitchell, stocks "skipped" the cyclical decline of business in 1926–1927. Still, in the light of long statistical records, such occurrences are exceptions, not the rule.

Studies have been made to determine the effect of changes in commodity prices on stock prices. On the whole, over long periods of time, rising commodity prices seem to coincide with a pattern of rising stock prices. Yet, the evidence is not striking on a shorter term or intermediate term basis. Stock market booms have sometimes been accompanied by a stable or even declining general price level. The two most brilliant periods in stock market history, 1897–1914 and 1953–1955, have been accompanied by stable commodity prices.

STOCK PRICES AND MONEY AND CREDIT CONDITIONS

To make demand for stocks effective, prospective buyers must have purchasing power at their disposal—capital or credit. In its broadest and most general terms, the question is: Can the quantity of money outstanding at any given time and subsequent changes in it indicate the level and trend of stock prices?

For a long time it was held that stock prices cannot be explained by the quantity theory of money.[7] The quantity of money in relation to the quantity of goods and the velocity of turnover could affect only the general level of the prices of all goods and services offered for sale. In any one sector of the economy the quantity of money had little influence, for the items that will be bought are those whose values at the moment are the most attractive in the entire field of production and consumption.

These observations were not intended to deny that changes in the supply of money did not influence stock prices. All phases of economic life are affected. But the effect on stock prices was felt to be indirect—through earnings and interest rates.

During the last 20 years, much effort has been expended in restoring the quantity theory of money to a position of greater eminence. Clark Warburton and Milton Friedman have done the main remoulding. In recent years, Professor Friedman has accomplished a prodigious amount of research in constructing both monetary statistical data and interpretive theory. He has become the fountain-

---

[7] See Albert Hahn, "Die Verfugbaren Mittel der Borse" Zeitschrift fur Nationaloekonomie, Bd. 6, Heft 5, Wien, 1935. See also Williams, *The Theory of Investment Value,* pp. 45–54.

head of new monetary theory based on changes in the stock of money. He sought to demonstrate that the stock of money reveals cyclical behavior and that shifts in the rate of change of the money stock have a relationship to corresponding changes in the rate of change of money income.

In their monumental work, Professor Friedman and Mrs. Schwartz trace in minute detail the relations of business cycles to the stock of money. In the latter, they include currency, demand and time deposits in commercial banks, deposits in mutual savings banks and postal savings deposits.

In The Summing Up (Chapter 13) Friedman and Schwartz write:

> Throughout the near-century examined in detail we have found that:
> 1. Changes in the behavior of the money stock have been closely associated with changes in economic activity, money income, and prices.
> 2. The interrelation between monetary and economic change has been highly stable.
> 3. Monetary changes have often had an independent origin; they have not been simply a reflection of changes in economic activity.[8]

To substantiate the conviction born from this extensive study that the stock of money is causal, the authors state that the relation between the latter and cyclical movements in economic activity has been highly stable.

> On the average, the stock of money rose at a higher rate than money income. . . . The rise was more rapid than usual during cyclical expansions and less rapid than usual during cyclical contractions. The rate of rise tended to slow down well before the peak in business and to speed up well before the trough. This pattern prevails throughout the period, in the very earliest cycle our data cover and also in the most recent.[9]

Beryl W. Sprinkel, vice president and economist of the Harris Trust and Savings Bank of Chicago, is the strongest current advocate of the causal and predictive power of changes in the rates of money supply with respect to both stock prices and business cycles.[10] He is a personal friend and former student of Professor Milton Friedman.

Like Wesley C. Mitchell, Sprinkel is a pragmatist. "The only acceptable test is one of predictive power," he says in his book.[11] The only acceptable demonstration that the Federal Reserve and the commercial banking system play a central role in the transmission mechanism that results in the cyclical fluctuations of the bond and stock markets must be statistical. Since Sprinkel's own monetary approach was first formulated in mid-1957, he had so far to be satisfied with testing his concept by statistical hindsight, taking his experiment back to 1918. On this basis, it showed a satisfactory record. It also worked well under real

---

[8] Milton Friedman and Anna J. Schwartz, *A Monetary History of the United States, 1867–1960* (Princeton, N.J.: Princeton University Press, 1963), p. 676.

[9] Ibid., p. 682.

[10] Beryl W. Sprinkel, *Money and Stock Prices* (Homewood, Ill.: Richard D. Irwin, Inc., 1964).

[11] Ibid., p. 133.

forecasting conditions in 1958, 1960, and 1969. It failed in 1962 and 1971. The 1962 collapse of stock prices was counter-cyclical, and stocks not only recovered but also made new highs.

Perhaps the weakest point for the practical application of Sprinkel's forecasting method is the difficulty of determining the actual liquidity peaks and troughs. In the hindsight tests this presented no problems. The highest highs and the lowest lows were used. In a recent private letter to the author, Dr. Sprinkel stated that when using this technique for forecasting under current conditions:

> It is necessary to make a judgment based on what is currently happening to monetary policy and the political environment as to whether a recent peak may remain a peak or whether it will be reversed by later monetary action. . . . Due to the long lead time prior to an adverse impact on stock prices and the economy of a declining monetary trend, one need not make a conclusion in the early phase of an apparent change. . . .

A NOTE ON LONGER CYCLES

Our age is attuned to the pragmatic experimentalism and quantitative measurements of the empirical school's methods of studying business cycles. The earlier literature on business cycles is immense and was largely theoretical and deductive. Many of its contributions are impressive works of outstanding and penetrating thinking. Its greatest monument is perhaps represented by the two volumes of Joseph H. Schumpeter's *Business Cycles,* published in 1939.[12] Investors and financial analysts who have little leisure for theoretical studies, would do well to read chapter 4 of volume 1, entitled "The Contours of Economic Evolution." Little else could give them a better feel of intellectually great deductive reasoning.

One of the difficulties of cyclical forecasting is the uncertain duration of the cycles themselves. Around the lines of the slowly rising secular trends, cyclical fluctuations trace their recurrent curves. In contrast to the quantitative researchers who usually limit their duration from two to five years, theoretical students of business cycles believed that they may last from less than one year to long waves of several decades.

Schumpeter classified the principal among them by the names of the economists who brought them, in a complete form, to the attention of the scientific community. In the descending order of their duration, he names the cycles *Kondratieff* (40 to 60 years), *Kuznets* and *Wardwell* (15 to 25 years), *Juglar* (10 years), and *Kitchin* (40 months).

Schumpeter remarks, however:

> Barring very few cases in which difficulties arise, it is possible to count off, historically as well as statistically, six Juglars to a Kondratieff and three Kitchins to a Juglar—not as an average but in every individual case. We shall make use of this

---

[12] Joseph H. Schumpeter, *Business Cycles: A Theoretical, Historical and Statistical Analysis of the Capitalist Process* (New York: McGraw-Hill, 1939).

fact in our exposition, but the writer is very anxious to make it quite clear, not only that no major result depends on this, but also that no part of his theoretical schema is tied up with it. There is nothing in it to warrant expectation of any such regularity. On the contrary, the logical expectation from the fundamental idea would be irregularity; for why innovations [this was the cause of business cycles in Schumpeter's own theory—*author's note*] which differ so much in period of gestation and in the time it takes to absorb them into the system should always produce cycles of respectively somewhat less than 60 years, somewhat less than 10 years, and somewhat less than 40 months, is indeed difficult to see.[13]

Modern economists have abandoned much of this classification. Kuznets, for example, describes them as "secondary secular trends," with each phase lasting from 6 to 14 years, and being a characteristic of the American economy since the last quarter of the nineteenth century. Both economists had in mind the same thing, but used different terms to describe it because their respective labels were more attuned to their thinking about economic trends.

To close this chapter, where much was said about the influence of credit and money on stock prices, we should raise the question about credit conditions more immediately related to the stock market—the amount of brokers' loans.

When brokers' loans are not banned, they tend to move in close relation with stock prices. It is the rise in stock prices that generates the increase in brokers' loans. But once started, the process forms a spiral; speculative purchases made on credit cause higher prices and a greater resort to loans, each action feeding the other. For practical purposes of forecasting, there are no appreciable time lags. Moreover, periods can be cited when big upswings of the market were not accompanied by increasing loans against securities or even occurred when loans were shrinking.

Inflated brokers' loans, especially in periods of overspeculation during the later stages of a bull market, are an indication that the technical position is vulnerable. But they tell nothing about the timing of selling. There is no way of picking the moment at which brokers' loans may be signaling that the breaking point in the stock market is near.

---

[13] Ibid., vol. 1, pp. 173–74.

10

Invitation to a Walk

ACCORDING to a well-known anecdote, when asked for an opinion concerning the outlook for the stock market, Thomas Lamont quipped that stocks will continue to fluctuate.

Lamont was a senior partner in J. P. Morgan & Co., and his pronouncement from the throne of financial power is oftentimes quoted as an irrefutable dictum condemning, with sarcastic brevity, ill-guided attempts by the ignorant or the presumptuous to predict the unpredictable. And this ironic verdict may also be construed to imply a general sweeping denial that stocks are subject to any laws governing their action.

Like the majority of financial analysts, this writer has a professional bias and therefore could not accept this view. Stocks will indeed fluctuate. But this writer has long believed that they moved around computable values. However, several years ago, doubts began creeping into my mind. As a result of a chance encounter with a leading scholar, I began to explore the academic literature for studies on the fluctuations of stock prices. At least a bird's eye view of the subject was acquired, but much effort could have been spared by waiting for Cootner's book of readings entitled *The Random Character of Stock Market Prices*.[1]

The major finding of most of these new explorations of stock market action by academic scholars was that there is no pattern to stock prices, the fluctuations are mostly random in character. They also found that stock prices do not respond to seasonal influences; there is no indication of any important cyclical frequency in their variations; no correlation exists between successive changes of stock prices; and the number of shares traded is not related to the behavior of stock prices. The preponderant number of writers in Cootner's collection asserted that fluctuations of stock prices were a chance phenomenon. Their papers were strong and convincing, drowning out, it seemed, the voices of the opponents.

---

[1] Paul H. Cootner, ed., *The Random Character of Stock Market Prices* (Cambridge, Mass.: M.I.T. Press, 1964).

The apparently erratic and aimless changes in stock prices were described, in statistical terms, as "random walks."

THE CURTAIN RISES

The fountainhead of the proponents of the random walk theory was a brief but pungent doctoral dissertation on the behavior of speculative prices written by Louis Bachelier in Paris in 1900.[2] Bachelier's thesis made little impact on economics until it was rediscovered by econometricians half a century later. Bachelier was approaching his 30s when he wrote his now famous work. He was hoping that it would open the doors of a distinguished academic career. Yet no appointments came until late in his life. He was then already an embittered man who had no premonition of his post-mortem fame.

While his contribution had left the economists cold and unreceptive, scientists were more impressed by Louis Bachelier. His mathematics fitted neatly into the theory of Brownian movement, first formulated in 1828 by the English botanist and physicist, Robert Brown. Nearly a century later, Albert Einstein gave it a definitive form and was awarded the Nobel prize for this work. It was an ironically backhanded way of honoring the greatest physicist since Newton. The theory of relativity was not eligible, since Nobel prizes at that time were rewarding applied science only.

PATTERNS OF STOCK PRICES

The cornerstone of the random walk hypothesis is that stock price changes are completely independent from one another in time. Since stocks move randomly, the record of past price changes provides no indication as to the changes which will take place in the future.

This hypothesis is sufficient for questioning the validity of the work of those "technical" analysts who rely on charts of past records of stock prices as a basis for predicting future moves of the prices of individual stocks and of the general market. Charts may have their limited use for a clear graphic picture of the present position of a stock or an average as compared to its historical performance. Yet, no valid conclusions may be drawn from so-called chart "patterns" concerning future probabilities of stock price movements.

The first economist to point out the frailty of chart "patterns" was Harry Roberts, professor of statistics at Chicago's Graduate School of Business. His demonstration originated in a discussion with a group of security analysts at the annual seminar sponsored by the Financial Analysts Federation. Out of Roberts' discussion an important study emerged, which serves as the lead article in Cootner's book of readings.[3] Roberts shows that there is a close resemblance between stock market action and that of simple chance devices. He demonstrates that

---

[2] Ibid., reprinted on pp. 17–78.

[3] Ibid., reprinted on pp. 7–16.

tables of random numbers produce patterns quite similar to those formed by stock prices to which "chartists" give meaningful predictive interpretation. He claims that stock price patterns are nothing but doodles scribbled by illusion and have no relation to reality.

Professor Roberts wrote his paper with modesty and restraint and makes no claims that his demonstration is the root of all wisdom about the stock market. While criticizing "patterns," Roberts recommends other methods of financial analysis, including the formal statistical techniques of industrial quality control. If a stock price falls outside the control limits, this gives a signal for the analyst to search for an explanation beyond the price series itself, such as company developments, economic changes, or governmental action.

SOME OTHER ASPECTS OF THE RANDOM WALK

Professor Cootner's well-organized compendium on the *Random Character of Stock Market Prices* is divided into four parts, each being preceded by the editor's helpful and excellent introductions. Part III is entitled "The Random Walk Hypothesis Reexamined." It contains an article by Eugene F. Fama, another professor from the University of Chicago.[4] This study is devoted to an examination of contributions to the random walk hypothesis by Benoit Mandelbrot.

From Bachelier on, the random nature of stock price movements was described by its theoreticians as a normal distribution. Mandelbrot claims that the bell-shaped normal curve (Gaussian) is not applicable to the study of stock prices. In presenting his case, he draws on the work of Wilfredo Pareto and his own famous teacher, Paul Levy. The latter's classic treatise, *Calcul des Probabilités*, published in 1925, is one of the foundations of the modern rigorous approach to the theory of probability. Mandelbrot calls the distributions which he considers as the appropriate tool for the study of stock prices as "stable Paretian." He related Levy's work to Pareto's study of the distribution of incomes which showed that incomes have an infinite variance. Thus, the finite Gaussian distribution appears only as a special case and is not a general rule governing all economic time series.

We could have omitted a discussion of Mandelbrot's work in this chapter. Whether or not successive price changes are random is quite a separate question from whether they are normally distributed or distributed in some other way. Mandelbrot's contribution is not symptomatic of inner conflict in the random walk camp. Whether a distribution is Gaussian, stable non-Gaussian, or something else, is a question that can be settled by the data. The key point of the random walk theory, at least of individual stocks, is that the changes (appropriately measured) behave very nearly like independent drawings from the same distribution, whatever it is. Nor is even the infinite variance feature really central to Mandelbrot's work. Harry Roberts notes in a letter to the author, dated

---

[4] Ibid., reprinted on pp. 297–306.

October 5, 1966, whose contents are also reflected in the immediately preceding lines, that a stable non-Gaussian distribution could be truncated very far out in either tail without producing noticeable differences in observed samples from the distribution. But the samples would behave very differently from Gaussian data.

If this author, who is not a mathematician, understands it correctly, the importance of Mandelbrot's contribution lies in its innovation which is relevant to the study of stock price movements by mathematical methods. After Mandelbrot's 1963 article, the Gaussian distribution looks like a very poor candidate for stock market analysis.[5] A new creative forward step has been taken, the first since the Bachelier thesis. Without attempting to destroy the Gaussian bell shape, Mandelbrot broadens the concept to include the normal distribution within a wider statistical framework.

Perhaps one could credit as being an intervening stepping stone a study published in 1934 by Holbrook Working, who was not familiar with Bachelier's work. His study begins with the following paragraph:

> It has several times been noted that time series commonly possess in many respects the characteristics of series of cumulated random numbers. The separate items in such series are by no means random in character, but the changes between successive items tend to be largely random. This characteristic has been noted conspicuously in sensitive commodity prices. On the basis of the differences between chain and fixed base index numbers King has concluded that stock prices resemble cumulations of purely random changes even more strongly than do commodity prices.[6]

It may be questioned whether an inner contradiction exists between random behavior of individual stocks and the tendency of stock groups and even of stocks in the overall market to move together. While this is far from being completely understood, it seems possible to reconcile individual anarchy with mass co-movements. An unforeseen change in the economic environment such as a sudden shift in the Federal Reserve Board's monetary policy could, for instance, cause most stocks to respond in the same way without creating a similar correlation in price changes.

A comprehensive study by Benjamin F. King discusses the phenomenon of covariance without sacrificing the basic random walk approach.[7]

Without King's contribution, much is inexplicable solely on the basis of the rest of the random walk theory. As a practicing financial analyst, the author believes that the samples used by King, and the classification of individual stocks into industrial groups, leave much room for improvement. Unsatisfactory as they are, their deficiencies do not undermine the conclusions of the study.

King demonstrates convincingly that the several methods of analysis which

---

[5] Ibid., reprinted on pp. 307–32.

[6] Holbrook Working, "A Random-Difference Series for Use in the Analysis of Time Series," *Journal of the American Statistical Association*, vol. 29, no. 185 (March 1934).

[7] Benjamin F. King, "Market and Industry Factors in Stock Price Behavior," *Journal of Business* (University of Chicago), *Security Prices: A Supplement*, vol. 39, no. 1, part III (January 1966).

he applied to his data give remarkable support to the hypothesis that the movement of a group of security price changes can be broken down into market and industry components. The implication of his results branch out into improving methods of construction of optimal portfolios and contributions to the theory of the cost of capital as well as for the design of indexes of change in security prices.

HOW PERFECT IS THE PERFECT MARKET?

Up to this point, our excursions in the academic literature on the random walk have been confined to those articles stressing shorter time spans and suggesting that it is futile to attempt to predict short term price movements in a stock market dominated by uncertainty. It is now time to consider the work of the proponents of the efficient markets hypothesis. We shall draw heavily on a nonmathematical review of the subject by Professor Fama.[8]

The real difference between an "efficient markets" theorist and a security analyst, thinks Fama, is rather in what each chooses to emphasize. Both would agree that at all times there are some stocks which are over- or under-priced in relation to their values. It is the analyst's job to find these stocks. The "efficient markets" theorist, on the other hand, being a scientist, is appropriately more interested in the process by which actual prices adjust to new information. He chooses to emphasize the close agreement between price and value, which, he thinks, is the normal situation. Though there are always stocks for which price and value are not equal, he feels such situations are difficult to identify. The financial analyst, on the basis of real life experience with numerous and extremely successful investors, who may or may not have followed the analyst's advice, is much more sanguine and optimistic in this respect. He does not necessarily have to be himself an unusually gifted money maker in the stock market to be aware that quite a few investors, with whom he has maintained a daily contact over a great many years, have succeeded in building large fortunes out of exceedingly modest initial ventures.

After this preamble, we shall summarize a section of Fama's nonmathematical paper.

Random walk theorists usually start from the premise that major security exchanges are "efficient" markets, i.e. markets where there are large numbers of rational profit-maximizers actively competing. The buying and selling of the participants is guided by their respective expectations of future prices of the stocks in which they deal. Important current information is almost freely available to them all.

This leads to a situation in which actual prices of individual securities already reflect the effects of both information and expectations. In other words, in an efficient market, at any point in time, the actual price of a security will be a good estimate of its value.

---

[8] Eugene F. Fama, "Random Walks in Stock Market Prices," *Financial Analysts Journal,* vol. 21, no. 5: 55–59 (September–October 1965).

Since in an uncertain world the value of a security can never be determined exactly, there is always room for disagreement among participants concerning just what the value of an individual security is, and such disagreement will give rise to discrepancies between prices and values. If the discrepancies between prices and values are systematic rather than random in nature, then knowledge of this should help intelligent market participants to better predict the path by which actual prices will move toward values. When the many intelligent traders attempt to take advantage of this knowledge, however, they will tend to neutralize any systematic behavior in prices. Uncertainty concerning values must remain, and actual prices of securities will wander randomly about their values.

Values themselves change over time as a result of new information. It may involve such things as the success of a current research and development project, a change in management, a tariff imposed on the industry's product by a foreign country, an increase in industrial production or any other *actual or expected* change in a factor which is likely to affect the company's prospects.

In an efficient market, *on the average,* competition will cause the full effects of new information on values to be reflected "instantaneously" in actual prices.

In fact, however, because there is vagueness or uncertainty surrounding new information, "instantaneous adjustment" really has two implications. First, actual prices will initially overadjust to changes in intrinsic values as often as they will underadjust. Second, the lag in the complete adjustment of actual prices to successive new values will itself be an independent random variable with the adjustment of actual prices sometimes preceding the occurrence of the event which is the basis of the change in values (i.e. when the event is anticipated by the market before it actually occurs) and sometimes following.

This means that the "instantaneous adjustment" property of an efficient market implies that successive price changes in individual securities will be independent. A market where successive price changes in individual securities are independent is, by definition, a random walk market. Most simply the theory of random walks implies that a series of stock price changes has no memory. Past price history cannot be used to predict the future in any meaningful way. The future path of the price level of a security is no more predictable than the path of a series of cumulated random numbers.

It is unlikely that the random walk hypothesis provides an exact description of the behavior of stock market prices. For practical purposes, however, the model may be acceptable even though it does not fit the facts exactly. Thus, although successive price changes may not be strictly independent, the actual amount of dependence may be so small as to be unimportant.

Most mathematicians, including those random walkers who write in mathematical terms, agree that there exist long-term trends in the stock market caused by underlying forces such as inflation. They also agree that money can be made in stock transactions as a result of informed knowledge of insiders. Such knowledge is not limited to a low voice discussion in the coffee lounge of the Downtown Association between the senior officers of two corporations contemplating merger. Less realistically and more romantically, it is not carried by a horseman galloping through the night to make an anxiously waiting financier the first possessor of the news of a great victory, or defeat, on a decisive field of battle. The most desirable advance information is repetitive and not accidental. It comprises an area as wide as the entire panorama encircled by our economic horizon. It offers countless opportunities for experienced probing leading to early judgment. It is surprising how long it often takes the "general market" to become aware of substantial differentials between prevailing prices and underlying values. Eventually they will be leveled out when the awareness is widespread. For investors or speculators it is unimportant whether the traveling of stock prices toward the valuation area follows a path of chance or a systematic pattern. They are interested in practical results. They know that new opportunities are constantly created by the ceaseless stream of economic change. It offers a never ending flow for exercising the professional skills of competent financial analysts.

We will close this section with a quotation from a respected financial analyst, Robert I. Cummin:

> Knowledge and insight are spread most unevenly over the whole wide mass of stockholders, and this includes institutional investors as well. Only a few have accurate knowledge about a stock's prospects at any given time. Those who have this knowledge hold it with varying degrees of conviction. A still smaller proportion has the insight or motive to take investment action, that is to make a trade. Among the small number of stockholders agreeing on a mutual price at a given time (and thus trading), one side is likely to be substantially better informed than the other.
>
> To have an effect on stock prices, investment knowledge must be accepted and understood by at least some stockholders. To endure, it should also be true. An important piece of knowledge is reinforced in its effect on price as more people hear of it. Their conviction increases as they understand it better and as later news confirms it. Doubters become believers, until at last the price fully reflects the knowledge, or more likely over-discounts it. Throughout this process there has been a large body of stockholders, some of them well informed, who do not trade, either being satisfied with the way things are going or restrained by taxes or other valid considerations. Thus, due to the delay in dissemination of knowledge and in comprehension of its import, price response to new information is gradual, not instantaneous; cumulative, not random.[9]

SUMMING UP

The main points to be kept in mind are elegantly stated in an unpublished letter to this writer by one of the pioneers in the random walk theory, M. F. M. Osborne:

> The gulf between financial analysts (including technical analysts) and the random walkers is really no gulf at all. If financial analysts wish to justify their existence,

---

[9] Robert I. Cummin, "Knowledge and Insight," *Financial Analysts Journal*, vol. 22, no. 4: 65–67 (July–August 1966).

it is necessary to assume that a better than random judgment is possible. It may be appallingly difficult, but still possible. Random walk theory allows for this possibility, but this possibility is not required. It simplifies random walk theory (and makes it easier to understand) to assume that superior judgments are impossible. Similarly, the biologist's understanding is greatly eased by assuming that there are no real qualitative differences between man and the rest of God's creatures. For a theologian, it is absolutely necessary to make a real distinction (the soul).[10]

Much of this book has been devoted to efforts to demonstrate that stock prices gravitate around computable values. However, it would be foolish for anyone to deny the existence of knowledge, both in its theoretical aspects and empirical demonstrations, that the traveling of stock prices around their value orbits shows no regularity. One should not disdainfully brush aside the accumulating evidence of random walks.

Stock prices oscillate back and forth across the orbit of value; but, contrary to intuition, their swings do not have to balance out. They are not symmetrical. A long bull market does not become vulnerable merely because of its duration. It is subject to many forces besides that of the passage of time.

Stock prices are the result of complex factors and therefore necessarily contain many elements of irregularity. During short segments of time, the irregularities predominate and produce random characteristics. But the longer the period, the more the irregularities are dissolved and smoothed out and lend themselves to a systematic analysis.

The financial community faces a difficult task to prove that it is possible to achieve consistently superior selection. Among those who are satisfied that they have accomplished this and have published their work are the technical analyst Robert Levy[11] and the Value Line Investment Survey[12] which is based upon fundamental methods of financial analysis. Additional studies along these lines will be needed before it can be stated convincingly that financial analysts are not mere parasites, but do have a justifiable role in attempting to seek a practical goal of above average security selections.

---

[10] M. F. M. Osborne, private letter to the author dated November 4, 1966.

[11] Robert A. Levy, "Random Walks: Reality or Myth?" *Financial Analysts Journal*, vol. 23, no. 6: 69–77 (November–December 1967).

[12] *Value Line Investment Survey*, (New York: Arnold Bernhard & Co., Inc.). Each quarter a review is made of their record, indicating that the results exceeded that of a random walk.

Part II

Abstracts of the Published Works of Nicholas Molodovsky

New Tools for Stock Market Analysis *

"This study is not journey's end, but rather its point of departure."

Part I of this monograph explores methods for valuing stocks. Part II describes some new tools for forecasting stock market moves. While value analysis is essential, its justification may take a long time. Meanwhile, the nerves of holders are subjected to many strains and stresses. Moreover, if investors are guided solely by values, they may remain out of the market during the most profitable period of a rise and reenter it long before the downtrend is reversed, suffering heavy losses.

Valuation analysis ranges from simple short cuts to complex methods. Yet dividends are the anchor, since the true investment value of a common stock is the present worth of all future dividends to be paid upon it. John Burr Williams and Samuel Eliot Guild are quoted among other pioneers of present worth theorists.

Value is easier to define than to compute. Yet some estimate of value must be attempted to decide whether the current price of a stock correctly expresses its value. Future dividends depend upon future earnings. To be complete, the study of a company's earnings cannot stop with the income account; the analyst must dissect the balance sheet with equal thoroughness. For profits do not drop as the gentle rain from heaven. They must be earned; their source is corporate assets.

The analyst's troubles will not be over even when he has completed his estimate of future earnings and dividends. An appropriate rate of interest must be selected to discount each estimated future payment.

Confronted with the vast array of imponderables that beset the analyst who tries to estimate future dividends, earnings, and interest rates, and not having the time and energy required for arriving at a reliable figure, investors frequently resort to short cuts. The most common is the price-earnings ratio. Students of security values are not satisfied with simplified measures or short cuts. After discussing an eight-point approach toward making a realistic evaluation of a stock, it is stressed that this valuation is still nothing more than an estimate.

Over reasonably long periods, average prices do not deviate from true investment values. However, in the course of their incessant movements, the prices

---

* Published by White, Weld & Co. Incorporated. First printing: December, 1946, pages 1–96. Second printing: June, 1947, includes Progress Report pages 97–114 in addition to the main monograph.

of stocks at times wander so far from values as to make the link between them more theoretical than real. Actual prices are essentially dynamic. They follow, even magnify, peaks and troughs of business cycles. However, business cycles are so highly individual that forecasting on the basis of comparisons with past cycles is impossible. Examination of the relations in the trends of stock prices and of the main economic factors such as interest rates, business activity, commodity prices, money and credit, shows their unreliability as forecasters.

The stock market indexes most commonly used for technical market analysis show surface conditions alone. They do not expose internal structural changes in the market which often betoken impending changes in trend. The author devised various indicators to measure internal market conditions from six angles. The 1946 market afforded a good testing ground for the new indicators. They acquitted themselves well, giving ample warning of the successive declines amounting to 23 percent from a peak of 212 on the Dow-Jones Industrial at the end of May to a trough of 166 three months later.

The greatest weight is given to the Index of Confidence, which is a ratio of the index of low-priced stocks to the index of high-priced stocks. The author found it necessary to construct his own stock market indexes for these groups. This was to ensure that both series were homogeneous and fully comparable. The chart below covers this Index of Confidence during the 1942–1946 bull market.

1942–1946 Bull Market

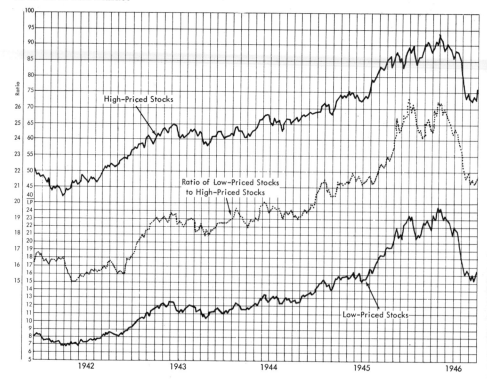

All stocks participated in the uptrend, but as long as low-priced stocks advanced at a faster rate than high-priced stocks, this was an indicator that investor confidence was continually strengthening. Eventually confidence reaches levels of speculative enthusiasm before a reaction and disillusionment sets in. This Index of Confidence provides a tool for objectively measuring the degree of speculative enthusiasm or disillusionment.

Various other indexes were devised to measure changes in different industry groups, demand and supply leverage, and historical relationships. These indexes proved to be less satisfactory as stock market forecasters, although they pointed out many interesting relationships.

The Progress Report section written in June of 1947 reported that the decline in the Index of Confidence continued during the six months following the original study. The refusal of the Confidence Index to participate in the late 1946–early 1947 rise served to confirm the basic assumption that 1946 had seen the cyclical top of the 1942–1946 bull market. It is a fact of outstanding importance that truly significant bull and bear markets are not unattached and haphazard fluctuations of stock prices, but are, on the contrary, deeply imbedded in the economic cycle itself. Stock prices themselves are one of the most sensitive cyclical factors, and their turning points usually precede by many months those of general business itself. A direct approach to the analysis of the fluctuations of stock prices attacks the problem where it is.

It should be strongly emphasized that the writer's approach implies no "reading of the charts." Charts are merely used as a convenience for the eye as a graphic illustration. No interpretation of chart patterns is ever attempted.

Other series are also reviewed and all seemed to confirm the conclusion of the Index of Confidence that the market was in an uncertain frame of mind, neither strongly bullish nor especially bearish. Market analysis has limitations of its own. It is useful in helping to solve the important problem of timing, but sound investment policy also requires decisions based on value analysis and economic analysis.

The Case for Scientific Stock Market Analysis *

Under present conditions of low bond yields and of the declining purchasing power of fixed incomes, few investors can afford to confine their holdings to securities whose price fluctuations can be disregarded with equanimity. They must hold common stocks—stocks which are doomed to fluctuate in price swings of lesser or larger magnitude. Capital appreciation is the fondest hope of invest-

---

* *Commercial and Financial Chronicle*, vol. 165, no. 4590: 1, 34–36 (May 1, 1947).

ment management, but preservation of capital worth is its starkest necessity and the acid test of investment policy.

In the author's monograph "New Tools For Stock Market Analysis," [see page 124 of this book] the conclusion was reached that the market had reached its cyclical peak at the 1946 highs, and then entered the downward phase of the stock market cycle. Once a working hypothesis is stated that at some point there will be another reversal of the cycle, the market analyst can concentrate his attention on locating the actual point of this reversal.

The balance of the article focused on the movements of the integrated index containing stocks of marginal investment quality and the failure of this index to rise when the quality stocks comprising the Dow-Jones Industrial Average began to recover in early 1947. This indicated that the recovery was not broadly based and hence would falter. Other tools were used to examine the situation and all seemed to indicate that a reversal in the market's downtrend was still to come.

When psychological influences dominate the market, the economist can provide little guidance to the investor. This situation will not persist forever. Value analysis, economic analysis, and market analysis, all are links in the chain of investment thinking and action. None is fully adequate by itself.

The Province of Market Analysis*

For a great many years, the writer approached the stock market exclusively as a student of economic conditions and security values. However, a market analyst deals exclusively with the realities of the present. Stated most simply, the purpose of market analysis is to determine, at any given time, the extent of the effective demand for stocks as well as the abundance and readiness of their supply. Studies of demand and supply are the essence of all economic analysis.

During the last decade, the curves of stock prices and of industrial production have moved in the same direction for 20 months. During 100 months they followed opposite courses. Thus, economic analysis is not the complete answer to an understanding of the stock market.

Effective demand and effective supply of stocks find a reflection in changes occurring in the internal relations of the time series describing the fluctuations of stock prices. The important statistical fact in this respect is that stock prices are not a chance series. They are not a number drawn from an economic lottery wheel. They are a time series with persistent trends and analyzable structures.

Current methods used by market analysts fall short of the possible attain-

---

* *Financial Analysts Journal*, vol. 5, no. 1: 12–14 (First Quarter, 1949).

ments. Scientific study of economic time series is a recent development of mathematical statistics. Its application to the analysis of stock price series is still newer. No more has been done so far than merely to scratch the surface of possibilities. Lack of understanding of the real nature of the problem and of the possibilities of its solution, as well as its costs in time and money, are our present enemies.

The two approaches of market analysis and value analysis are not enemies, but allies. Even the most orthodox value analyst need not fear market analysis. While his reasons were not developed, the writer indicated his conclusions that the stock market is still engaged in a long-term basic cyclical decline. Yet at the same time, he also believed that the market was at the inception of a significant intermediate rise.

Some Aspects of Price-Earnings Ratios*

This article was extensively revised and brought up to date to serve as Chapter 5 of this volume.

The price-earnings ratio is undoubtedly the most common yardstick for comparing the relative attractiveness of individual stocks, and for appraising whether the general market is relatively high or low. The most important characteristic of the price-earnings ratio is that it is a ratio. It is an expression of a relation between two factors. Price-earnings ratios have no independent existence as prices and earnings have. Yet somehow they have managed to acquire a personality of their own.

The existence of a high price-earnings ratio for a stock reflects the judgment of investors that the profits currently earned by the company in question are low compared to its future earning power. Similarly, when the price-earnings ratio of a stock is low, it expresses the opinion of buyers and sellers that the current earnings of that corporation are higher than its expected future representative earnings level. This includes not only expectations for future growth or stagnation, but also whether or not investors regard current earnings as being at a cyclical top or a cyclical trough, neither of which conditions will persist for long.

Two facts stand out as a result of this survey. First, no relation exists between price-earnings ratios and the levels or trends of stock prices. The second point is that the relationship allegedly existing between stock prices and price-earnings ratios in reality links changes in price-earnings ratios to cyclical fluctuations in earnings. The concept of average earning power is thoroughly examined in this article to indicate that it is the best basis for the valuation of common stocks.

---

* *Financial Analysts Journal*, vol. 9, no. 3: 65–78 (May 1953).

A Theory of Price-Earnings Ratios*

This article was extensively revised and brought up to date for inclusion as Chapter 6 of this volume.

A basic set of truths is laid out as background for the development of a theory of price-earnings ratios:

1. Stocks will fluctuate, but they move around a computable value. "They remain bound by gravitational force to that sun of the economic system."
2. Dividends form the hard core of stock values, supported by the expectation of future payments.
3. The "size of the future," is limited by present worth (sometimes called present value). It narrows down the problem of evaluating a never ending dividend stream because, beyond a certain point, further increments are no longer economically attractive. At the same time, though, present worth introduces the complication of selecting the proper interest rate to be used as the discounting factor.

Therefore, the author states, "the theoretical content of the true investment value of a common stock cannot change; it must always be determined by future dividends and interest rates." As dividends flow out of earnings, it is necessary, first, to estimate future earnings. Then, by capitalizing the future earnings, investors obtain a measure of value. The Molodovsky approach is based on hypothetical price-earnings ratios as capitalization multipliers, and the use of capitalized earning power as a measure of the value of common stocks.

Next, a hypothetical principle of the behavior of price-earnings ratios is developed and submitted to statistical testing with historical data. The essence of the concept is "the compensating principle" and the "rule of opposite movements." When current earnings fall below earning power, they must be compensated. Conversely, when current earnings rise above earning power, they must be discounted. This means that the price-earnings ratio increases (to compensate) when current earnings fall below expectations, and that the price-earnings ratio declines (to discount) when current earnings rise above expectations. Accordingly, current earnings and price-earnings ratios move in opposite directions (opposite movements), completing the theoretical concept.

To illustrate the concept diagramatically, a line called the "price orbit" is developed by capitalizing earning power. This line is "the central stem around which stocks will fluctuate . . . the operational value of investors." The deviations of current earnings from expected earnings, therefore, determines the extent of the required compensation or discount by the hypothetical price-earnings ratio.

To move from the theoretical realm into the practical world requires that the

---

* *Financial Analysts Journal*, vol. 9, no. 5: 65–80 (November 1953).

theory be capable of historical and statistical verification. To satisfy this requirement, Molodovsky explains two tests which were performed.

The first test, with Barron's indexes for the period 1934–1951 was made using ten-year moving averages of stock prices and the corresponding price-earnings ratios. Also, hypothetical price-earnings ratios and the "price orbit" (based on the theoretical approach already described) were used. The following results were shown:

1. For 1934, with current earnings well below the average, the price-earnings ratio was a high level.
2. For 1935, as earnings rose, the price-earnings ratio declined.
3. For 1936, as earnings rose above the moving average, the price-earnings ratio did not decline as expected. This, according to the author, ". . . showed that forces other than those of capitalization of earning power were exercising their sway. . . ."
4. Generally, the findings showed that the actual and hypothetical price-earnings ratios follow a similar course.

Molodovsky found the use of moving averages of past earnings to measure earning power as too crude, requiring constant adjustment, since investors are more interested in future earning power than in the historical averages. But, the proper adjustments can be made, and these averages can be used as the basis for the hypothetical price-earnings ratios which can be compared to actual price-earnings ratios. Any differential that exists between them, to the extent that no other influence is operating, reveals how the investors view earning power.

A second test, with data from the Cowles Commission dating from 1871 is performed, again using ten-year moving averages of earnings. The results serve as the basis for a detailed discussion of the other influences which may cause actual price-earnings ratios to diverge from the hypothetical, and how the analyst might handle them.

Three time periods were identified, 1880–1894, 1894–1914, and 1914–1937. For the "first panel of the historical triptych," the hypothetical and actual price-earnings ratios moved more or less in unison. Afterwards this relationship changed. For the decade following 1897, the actual price-earnings ratio moved sideways. This indicated a reappraisal by investors of the basic earning power of American corporations. For the period 1927–1929, the actual price-earnings ratios moved sharply above the hypotheticals, again revealing investor sentiment favoring a structural change in corporate earnings power (about which they were disappointed).

The article concludes with a discussion of factors unrelated to capitalization of earning power, such as investors' impressions about structural changes and psychological influences. The author suggests how these influences can be handled by the analyst, within the framework of the theoretical system, by using historical and projected price and earnings data to detect and measure these forces.

The Core and the Margin—Value Stocks and Vision Stocks*

Great selectivity has marked the movements of stock prices in recent years. The growing predominance of institutional investors has resulted in a wide diversity in the movements of different stock groups, whether classified by industries or by investment quality. Since there were no really satisfactory indexes classifying stocks by investment quality, the writer prepared two indexes covering prices, quarterly earnings and dividends, and the volumes of shares traded, beginning in 1937 and continuing through the time of this 1954 article.

An index consisting of 50 of the nation's strongest corporations, each among the leaders in its industry, was termed the index of Value Stocks. The other index included 50 stocks, each of which was closely matched to its counterpart in the Value Stocks index in terms of being widely held and being in the same industry. However, all of the stocks in this second index belonged to a secondary echelon of American industry and stood closer to the economic margin. This index of marginal quality stocks was termed a Vision Stocks index. Value Stocks are sought out predominantly on the basis of their estimated investment worth. Vision Stocks, on the other hand, are purchased primarily when the economic outlook, as "envisioned" by the buyers, looks promising for the prospects of marginal enterprises. Each index contained a broad cross section of the stock market, including railroads and utilities as well as industrial stocks. The indexes were probably arithmetic mean indexes.

Both the price action and the earnings records of the Vision Stocks proved to be much more volatile than the investment quality index:

	Value Stocks (percent)	Vision Stocks (percent)
Price Action		
1942–1944	+58	+167
1946 bear market	−23	−45
Earnings		
1949 decline	−30	−67
1950 advance	+71	+344
1951–1952 decline	−35	−61

Hypothetical price-earnings ratios were computed for each index in line with the procedures outlined in the preceding article and as elaborated in Chapter 6 of this volume. The hypothetical ratios for Value Stocks closely approximated the actual price-earnings ratios, but could not keep up with the wide swings in the Vision Stocks index.

---

* *Financial Analysts Journal,* vol. 10, no. 4: 17–31 (August 1954).

Applying Tinbergen's share-price equation method, the two indexes had the following equations:

$$\text{Value Stocks Price} = 1.0179 + .2051D \qquad + .4238Eq + .9281TM$$
$$\text{Vision Stocks Price} = .4593 + .2462D + 2541E + .0231Eq + .91TM$$

D = 12 months' dividends
E = 12 months' earnings
Eq = annualized quarterly earnings
TM = mean price in preceding quarter

The Value Stocks equation worked especially well with a standard error of only 3.6 percent of the mean price—in other words 95 percent of the time actual prices were within 7 percent of the calculated price. At the time of the article, Value Stocks were selling in line with their calculated value and Vision Stocks were significantly depressed. If the economy should continue its recovery, the more marginal stocks would appear to have the potential for a sharp rise. However, the superior potential of marginal stocks is based on the average experience of the past 17 years, and the factor of institutional demand for investment quality stocks may well upset this past relationship.

Stock Prices and Current Earnings *

Portions of this article were revised and included in Chapter 6 of this volume which represents the author's final thoughts on the subject. In this article he uses correlation analysis to show for the period 1871–1951 that (with one exception) current earnings and stock prices change at different rates. Their correlation ". . . is so low as to preclude the existence of any significant causal link. . . ." In examining the influence of dividends, trend momentum (cumulative influence of the price trend), and current earnings on stock prices, the author found that all three factors together accounted for slightly more than one-half of the total influence on stock prices, with current earnings showing the smallest influence. The exception occurred during a period (1894–1914) where a basic reappraisal of earning power was underway; investors identified current earnings with earning power, capitalizing stocks on that basis, because of the industrial changes taking place at that time and their projected impact on long-term earnings.

The author warns against the use of yardsticks based on current earnings: "When individual ratios of prices to current earnings are computed for quick ready reference, they carry a clear meaning. But, when they are used as capitalization multipliers and are confronted with one another, strange things begin to

* *Financial Analysts Journal*, vol. 11, no. 4: 83–94 (August 1955).

happen. . . ." Because the price-earnings ratios fluctuate so much, they are not true capitalizers. They must adjust for departures between volatile current earnings and the slow-to-change earning power.

Discussing the capitalizer for an index of share prices, the author states that only one multiplier can exist because the basic foundation behind appraisals of capital worth rarely changes and that, "Financially, it should not matter whether the return produced by capital is secured from the manufacture of steel or spaghetti." Only long-term earning power offers adequate foundation for values.

Price-earnings ratios, by reflecting the action of both prices and earnings, provide a tool for examining their interaction. Changes in prices, earnings, and price-earnings ratios fall into 13 combinations: five which cause price-earnings ratios to rise, five which cause them to decline, and three where no change occurs. A classification of all combinations based on data for the period 1871–1951 revealed that in the majority of historical cases, current earnings and price-earnings ratios moved in opposite directions. In other words, earnings moves are more volatile than price moves. In the author's words, "Stock prices tend to discount the rises of current earnings and to compensate for their declines."

Molodovsky lists capitalized earning power and economic momentum as two principal forces behind the stock market, and sets forth the phases of the market during a typical economic expansion (the scheme is reversed for a period of contraction):

1. Beginning with declines in price-earnings ratios, current earnings begin to rise faster than stock prices.
2. The advance of stock prices catches up to earnings. Price-earnings ratios continue to decline, but more slowly.
3. As both stock prices and current earnings increase, the price-earnings ratios move sideways.
4. Price-earnings ratios begin to move in the same direction as current earnings, amplifying the rate of price increase. This is the phase of over-speculation. The action of the price-earnings ratio indicates a change of trend.

Moving from a theoretical approach to the practical world, Molodovsky discusses the then current market situation. Current earnings can be relevant to the extent that they can bring about a reappraisal of estimated earning power. After a massive advance of prices fueled by "supercharged" investment demand, quality stocks became overvalued. Prices, earnings, and price-earnings ratios were rising. Usually, such circumstances would point to a change in the price trend.

Departing from value analysis, Molodovsky looks to the internal condition of the market for information about the possible trend of prices. The stocks of marginal companies were showing better earnings recovery than other, stronger firms. Additional room for price improvement in these stocks was seen, which suggests the possibility of a structural change in earning power (as viewed by investors) similar to that which took place at the turn of the century.

Among the factors mentioned as support for the possibility of a structural change in the earning power of American corporations are the technological revolution, the development of atomic energy, better international relations and the hope of more foreign trade, and the successful shift from a wartime to a peacetime economy. These factors could cause the acceptance of a higher level earning power to be used as a capitalizer. The Standard & Poor's Industrials had just reported 1954 earnings of $2.89, near their all-time high, and the index had moved up to an all-time high of 40. With the average price-earnings ratio of 13, the expectation of an increase to 15 is predicted. Molodovsky closes with the thought that the financial crisis which occurred following the structural change at the turn of the century is not likely to be repeated. Any interruption would be of short duration and should not develop into a protracted bear market.

An Appraisal of the Dow-Jones Industrial Average*

After showing why the price-earnings ratio is an inadequate measure, the writer discusses other methods of valuation based upon average earning power which indicate that even at the then current level of 540, the Dow-Jones Industrial Average was reasonably priced.

During most of 1958, stock prices and earnings had been moving in opposite directions. Divergencies in their relative action are not an unusual development. This time, however, they had been so striking that many experienced investors were shocked and bewildered. The most representative opinon was that stock prices had lost all contact with any reasonable measure of value.

Fluctuating current earnings cannot serve as a reliable capitalization base. They do not offer a strong enough foundation. A more stable form of earning power is needed by investors as a basis for market values. Charts were presented showing that the Dow-Jones Industrial Average during the last 20 years had generally fluctuated reasonably closely to valuation of 14.8 times normal earning power as defined by a moving average. Thus, investors have in actual fact based their valuations of the DJIA on average earning power—not on the results for any one year.

In considering an appropriate valuation for the DJIA, the pessimist will choose a 2 percent annual growth rate based upon recent earnings progress. The optimist will choose the 4 percent rate of earnings growth actually achieved by the DJIA since 1915. Using a 7 percent discount rate, the intrinsic values would be as follows:

	2% Growth Rate		4% Growth Rate	
	Normal Earnings	Intrinsic Value	Normal Earnings	Intrinsic Value
1958	$32.00	440	$24.00	530
1965	36.75	500	31.50	700
1970	40.60	550	38.50	850
1975	44.80	600	46.75	1050

* *Commercial and Financial Chronicle*, vol. 188, no. 5790: 3, 30–33 (October 30, 1958).

Valuation of common stocks is not a hopeless task. It is possible to compute a range of definite values for individual stocks as well as stock market indexes.

Valuation of Common Stocks*

Research in an important area such as the valuation of common stocks must be a collective effort. Many minds attack the problems from different angles. After reviewing other approaches, Molodovsky expresses his preference for defining value as the present worth of future dividends. The first application of present worth to valuing common stocks was published in two articles by Robert G. Wiese in *Barron's* in September, 1930. Samuel Eliot Guild, an associate of Wiese at Scudder, Stevens & Clark, published the first book on the subject a few months later. Guild had worked on his book for two years. John Burr Williams gave the most exhaustive and scholarly treatment of the valuation of common stocks by the present worth method in his 600-page volume *The Theory of Investment Values* published in 1938.

The two tremendous forces which shape the frontiers of investment value are growth and discount. Growth at even moderate rates compounds to almost unbelievable heights over extensive periods of years. At a 5 percent growth rate, one dollar would double in 15 years, triple in 23 years and grow to $131.50 in 100 years.

While growth is a powerful force, it is met in present worth valuation methods with the opposing force of the rate at which future dividends and investment values should be discounted. Today's value of one dollar payable 50 years hence would have a value of three cents if discounted at 7 percent, a value of two cents if discounted at 8 percent and a value of one cent if discounted at 9 percent. While growth projections can stretch out to infinity, 91 percent of the present worth of a stream of constant dividends is derived from the first 50 years if discounted at 7 percent. If dividends are growing, it will take longer to recover 91 percent of their present worth, but not a great deal longer at moderate rates of 2 percent or 3 percent, which is about the extent that most analysts would use when projecting earnings 50 or more years distant. Thus, the discount rate offsets the very large future values that will obtain in the long distant future. The analyst should not hesitate to use present worth techniques because of his doubts as to the ability of anyone to forecast the distant future. The bulk of the present worth applies to the next few decades which are, in any event, projections

* *Financial Analysts Journal*, vol. 15, no. 1: 23–27, 84–99 (February 1959).

required to be made under virtually any method of valuation. Value does not rest on an appraisal of one year.

Appraisal of General Motors
Common Stock*

This article estimates the theoretical intrinsic value of GM for 1959 at 52, a value closely in line with the then current market price of 50. The study was an updating of a privately circulated report of April, 1958, which estimated an intrinsic value of 45 and thereby urging purchase of GM common at the price of 35 which was then prevailing.

The valuation process begins with a projection of GM's earnings for the next 25 years. The past 25 year period of 1933–1958 is examined and interpreted as a 4 percent growth rate during the 1930s with a dramatic upward move during the immediate postwar years followed by a return to more moderate growth following the 1955 earnings peak of $4.26 per share. Earnings had receded to $2.22 per share for 1958, just announced at the time this article was written. Yet, it was assumed that the normal earning power of GM was $3.40 per share and would grow at a 3 percent annual rate during the next 25 years resulting in normal earning power of $5.00 in 1973 and $7.25 in 1985.

Despite the great length of this period, the projections were considered to be economically plausible. They were based, in part, on estimates by two analysts consulted by the author. Unit sales of GM had grown at a 4.4 percent annual rate during the preceding 20 years while deflated earnings per share (after adjusting for inflation) had risen at a 5.8 percent rate. After a fairly detailed examination of the reasons why GM had exceeded by far all past sales and earnings projections, the author considered his to be conservative: "It seems safe to say that none of these projections were inspired by a flight of pure imagination or poetic fancy. They are thoroughly earth-bound and practically iron-clad."

Using the valuation method outlined in his 1959 article and based upon normal earning power of $3.40 per share for 1959 growing at a 3 percent annual rate through 1983 followed by an indefinite 2 percent annual growth rate, the theoretical value for GM common was 52 for 1959 and 69 for 1970.

The essential elements governing GM's future outlook were reviewed, including the negative threats posed by the antitrust division of the Justice Department and the compact car which would probably carry lower profits for the auto makers than medium and large sized cars. However, economic necessities are stronger

* *Financial Analysts Journal,* vol. 15, no. 3: 67–72, 107–12 (May–June 1959).

than momentary whims. People not only want cars, they need them. The author also sincerely believed that this great organization will continue to produce the leaders it needs most in the particular economic environment in which it has to survive and prosper. It is undoubtedly no accident that so many of them came and went at precisely the right moment. Harlow Curtice, the latest, but undoubtedly not the last of the Mohicans, was ready to step down when his talents were no longer needed and leave the helm in the hands of a pilot attuned to the needs of a new day.

Stock Values and Stock Prices*

This article is a revision and extension of his 1959 article "Valuation of Common Stocks." The Standard & Poor's "500" index figures for earnings and dividends became available during the intervening year and this boosted the 1871–1955 earnings trend by 0.3 percent above Molodovsky's earlier conservative estimates. Adding four years to the period to extend the series through 1959 increased the growth trend another 0.2 percent. The effective yield from dividends and growth for the 89-year period now amounted to 7.6 percent, instead of 7.1 percent as indicated in the earlier study. Thus, a larger discount rate would seem to be appropriate.

The availability of additional data encouraged a deeper look at past earnings growth trends. Least squares trends for 21-year periods were calculated for all of the 65 sets of 21-year periods. When these trend lines were superimposed on each other, they clearly indicated that growth was not one smooth upsurge over the 89 years, but rather fell into the following general categories:

> 1871–1900 . . . . −2 percent annual growth in earnings
> 1900–1920 . . . . +4
> 1920–1940 . . . . −2
> 1940–1959 . . . . +7

The fastest growth trend ended in 1952, a 12.4 percent growth trend over the 21 years beginning in 1932. Elimination of the depression years from the base period resulted in a drop to the 7 percent growth rate by 1959. Examining the record of the last few years, Molodovsky believed that this flattening out of the growth trend would continue until growth came back to more sustainable rates.

Molodovsky then examined the earnings and dividend growth trends for the Dow-Jones Industrial Average and its individual components. He generally confirmed his 1958 article "Appraisal of the Dow-Jones Industrial Average." After examining many aspects of the past growth trends, he estimated that the DJIA

---

* *Financial Analysts Journal,* vol. 16, no. 3: 9–12, 79–92 (May 1960); vol. 16, no. 4: 53–64 (July–August 1960).

earnings would grow at a 5 percent rate during the decade of the 1960s, reaching $57 in 1970. With the average at 625, this implied a 6.5 percent growth rate for the 1960s and thus the market appeared overpriced. Estimates were developed for each of the 30 component stocks in the DJIA.

He concluded that ignorance of the future should be the great disciplinarian of investors. Value is a balance wheel spinning against the backdrop of a long perspective receding further and further into a thickening fog of uncertainty and doubt. Investors should not let their minds roam too far beyond the horizon. They have sufficient tools for organizing their forces under the banner of judgment drawn from knowledge and experience. Molodovsky's technique of valuation tries to trace firmly the boundaries between ascertainable knowledge, reasonable estimates, and honest ignorance in making an estimate of the investment value of a stock.

Dow-Jones Industrials—A Reappraisal*

The main purpose of this paper was to review changes in the estimates of earnings and the resulting appraisals of the 30 stocks in the Dow-Jones Industrial Average in the eight months elapsing since his last article. The earlier article had indicated that only 11 of the 30 DJIA stocks were undervalued and that the average itself at 625 was above its estimated investment value of 570. The DJIA subsequently declined to 564 and the relative ranking of the 30 components provided creditable results—all of the underpriced stocks subsequently rose and all of the overpriced stocks declined, as did the general market.

However, earnings and their projections into the future are subject to change with notable effects on the patient's health. Periodic checkups are necessary. The main reappraisal at this time concerned the steel stocks. In retrospect, as usual, it is much easier to enumerate the underlying troubles that were plaguing the industry and which came into focus as the year 1960 progressed. While U.S. Steel had risen moderately in price by the time of this article to 83, the changed economic environment and future outlook made a 20 percent reduction in its intrinsic value appropriate, making it and most steel stocks candidates for sale.

The revised investment values were 590 for the DJIA in 1961 and 765 in 1970. With the average at 649 and many of its component stocks also overpriced, it appeared to be a time for increasing caution. It seems difficult to discourage investors from participating in this powerful bull market whose main driving forces are psychological in nature. But let us try not to miss the signs when stock prices will be entering once more an area of cyclical reversal.

* *Financial Analysts Journal*, vol. 17, no. 2: 13–19 (March–April 1961).

The Summer of Our Discontent *

Following the election of President Kennedy in November of 1960, a honeymoon mood prevailed in Wall Street for five months. Despite the deepening economic recession, stock prices advanced with great vigor. Then a reaction set in with doubts and fears gripping the hearts of investors. Evidence soon developed that the business contraction had reached its trough in early 1961 and that industrial activity and earnings were starting to recover. Yet the market disregarded this good news as completely as it had previously disregarded the bad news of the recession.

Having just barely come out of a recession, we stand on a favorably situated observation platform. We should not be disappointed if the progress of the recovery is slow and uneven, since this has been the typical experience following mild recessions. But, we should not commit the error of setting too low the goals which the economy is likely to achieve.

Nearly every business expansion has carried total output, employment, and profits beyond the level reached at the preceding peak. We are undoubtedly justified in reaching the conclusion that the recent weakness in stock prices represents a normal correction of the first leg of a cyclical rise. This reaction should be followed by a resumption of the bull market which is likely to be especially dynamic and brilliant when earnings will be approaching their next cyclical peak.

Tables comparing stock market action for 76 stocks and for various stock market indexes were reviewed. These indicated that the reaction phase of the stock market seemed to be nearing an end, preparing the way for the next bull market rise.

The Many Aspects of Yields †

This article was brought up to date to serve as Chapter 7 of this volume. For some time now, stock yields have been declining while bond yields have been rising. This has given cause for alarm to those who have remembered past moves in the dividend yield cycle on the Dow-Jones Industrial Average:

1929	3.1 percent	1932	10.3 percent
1937	3.7	1942	7.9
1946	3.2	1949	6.9
1961	2.9		

* *Financial Analysts Journal*, vol. 17, no. 4: 81–88 (July–August 1961).

† *Financial Analysts Journal*, vol. 18, no. 2: 49–62, 77–86 (March–April 1962).

Since 1954, bonds have provided higher yields than common stocks, and yet the 1954 level of 350 on the DJIA did not spell disaster for the market—in fact the market doubled during the next seven years.

The article traced the history of stock yields from 1871 to the present. During the first 60 years of this study, bond yields and stock yields followed one another. During the depression era of the 1930's the relationship shifted with bond yields falling to a low level while stock yields remained fairly constant. Since 1949, bond yields have been in a generally rising trend and stocks have been in a declining trend and, as mentioned previously, bonds have provided larger yields than stocks since 1954. In view of this divergence in recent years do stock yields have any meaning at all? They do. They are a basic point of departure for measuring the total return from dividends. The effective yield including capital growth could be legitimately compared with bond yields.

*"It's Good to Own Growth Stocks"**

Demonstrations triumphantly drawn on vast stores of hindsight are often used to urge clients to buy growth stocks since they are depicted as ideal investments. The argument of the opponents of selling carefully selected growth stocks even to sidestep an approaching cyclical downswing—which, in any case, can never be forecast with certainty—is that cycles come and go while good growth stocks outlast them.

This reasoning is seductive. Unfortunately, it has a catch or two. When a crippling development becomes evident enough, the stock will be vulnerable to a sharp decline in its price-earnings ratio as its former premium multiple evaporates. Even if a growth company continues to prosper, it is still vulnerable to a general loss in confidence if investors should come to feel that the general economic and political environment will slow earnings growth for all companies.

During the 1962 collapse, growth stocks were among the worst battered. From a table of 25 superb growth stocks, *all* of which had shown strong earnings growth and a tenfold gain or better in stock price during the last ten years, almost all declined in price by 50 percent or more during 1962. This group included American Home Products, IBM, 3M, Polaroid, Xerox, and many other quality growth companies.

An Oxford scholar, Ian Little, had recently studied the records of 562 English companies operating in a variety of industries and found that there was no relation between past growth and future earnings growth. Dividend payouts and book values also proved useless in attempting to forecast earnings growth. The

---

* *Financial Analysts Journal*, vol. 19, no. 2: 75–86, 93–99 (March–April 1963).

study quantified our general impression of the difficulties involved in projecting earnings growth.

The analyst's problem is to find a way of determining the proper capitalization after taking into account the probable durations and changes in the respective rates of growth. The present worth method which can be applied to all stocks —average stocks as well as growth stocks—proved its mettle both during the long undervaluation prior to 1958 and the subsequent overpricing of stocks by the market. Use of these techniques, outlined in other articles, makes it possible to prepare comparative valuation schedules for an unlimited number of stocks. It should continue to be a good method.

*Economic Insight**

This article was revised to serve as Chapter 4 of this volume. The economic background for an industry is often of crucial importance in determining whether or not a company will prosper. To illustrate this, case sketches are presented of the postwar history of two major industries—motors and steels.

Projections of General Motors' post-World War II growth have been far exceeded by the actual results. The reasons were fundamental, but most analysts did not realize the intensity of the economic forces at work which were:

1. The automobile had become a necessity for the masses.
2. Wider distribution of income and the availability of installment credit made it possible for the masses to buy cars in large volumes.
3. The automobile had come to fulfill psychological needs as a symbol of economic victory and personal freedom.

The steel industry had experienced great growth in earnings during the postwar years, and steel stocks had been most successful investments. However, steel was not a true growth industry—tonnage shipped had shown only modest gains. The growth in earnings had been largely the result of higher selling prices which widened profit margins. Labor costs had been rising as fast as selling prices and if it should become difficult to continue to boost prices steadily, the steel industry's profits would soon come under pressure. Price restraints came in the form of competition from imported steel and the fundamental economic environment for the steel industry changed for the worse.

---

* *Financial Analysts Journal*, vol. 19, no. 4: 27–31, 74–82 (July–August 1963).

Stock Market—Lessons from the Recent Past*

The last two years saw a violent fall and a swift recovery of stock prices. These moves provided fresh experimental observations of the stock market's relation to other areas of economic activity.

We have known for a long time that stock prices are sensitive to cyclical timing. The National Bureau of Economic Research, after testing more than 800 series, selected 12 as being particularly worthy of attention as indicators generally leading the business cycle. One of these few chosen leaders was a common stock price index. Yet, the drastic decline in stock prices in 1962 had no effect on the strong business recovery. The same thing happened in 1946 and, going further back, the reverse situation occurred when stocks skipped the cyclical decline of 1926–1927.

Thus, lessons from the recent past confirm previous experience that while fluctuations of stocks are embedded in business cycles, at times they may have wide counter-cyclical swings as a result of outbreaks or terminations of war, flagrant and sustained departures of prices from values, and swings or shocks to sentiment.

The work of Bachelier, Godfrey, Granger, and Morgenstern in random walk theory is discussed. The main lesson is that the stock market, like life itself, is not deterministic. Stock prices oscillate back and forth across the axis of time; but contrary to intuition, their swings do not have to balance out. They are not symmetrical. A long bull market does not become vulnerable merely because of its duration. These random fluctuations in stock prices make the lot of the investor an uncertain one.

For the Record†

Ralph Bing's article (*Financial Analysts Journal,* vol. 20, no. 3: 118–24, May–June 1964) summarizing this writer's methods for valuing common stocks, along with those methods used by other analysts, shows that my communication with readers has broken down. I have never advocated the use of ten-year projections of earnings for every stock. Each issue is a different situation calling for different methods for making projections. Rather than using one growth rate for a lengthy period of years, quite often changing growth rates for the periods being projected are more appropriate.

---

* *Financial Analysts Journal,* vol. 20, no. 1: 50–54 (January–February 1964).

† *Financial Analysts Journal,* vol. 20, no. 3: 125–28 (May–June 1964).

Also, the discount rate of 7.5 percent mentioned in my studies is neither immutable nor sacred. Users should be free to select their own discount rate.

Bing was correct in rejecting irresponsible estimates of future earnings beyond the limits of reasonable projections. But his preference for "basic" price-earnings multipliers is unsatisfactory. Bing discusses recent years, but the bull market which went from 416 on the Dow-Jones Industrial Average in late 1957 to 688 a little over two years later proved the unreliability of averaging price-earnings ratios. Stock prices seemed to have lost all contact with any reasonable measure of value. Price-earnings ratios were high and kept rising, while earnings went from bad to worse.

Our own work is aimed at relative values, not absolute values. Valuation by present worth does not require projections of earnings any further into the future than other approaches to the valuation of a stock. The generation of financial analysts still in the classrooms will lean increasingly on mathematical statistics. Many of the rules of thumb we have been using in reaching investment decisions will wither away and be replaced with more effective probabilistic methods.

Tables of Stock Values *

This article served as a preface to a lengthy article by Samuel Eliot Guild adding to his pioneering 1931 book *Stock Growth and Discount Tables.* Guild's book appeared in the midst of the worst depression that has ever faced investors and thus did not gain much attention from the general investment public. In 1954 Clendenin and Van Cleave published an article on "Growth and Common Stock Values" which had a great impact on investment thinking in the bull market then under way.

Clendenin's view, as more fully developed in a subsequent report, was that variable discount rates should be used in different growth periods, reflecting that the uncertainty of future payments increases as the time periods become more distant. Bauman's book of investment analysis and tables also used variable discount rates since "the amount of investment income that an investor estimates he will receive from a stock in the more distant future is subject to greater error and hence the income is more uncertain than the amount of income he estimates he will receive in the near future." Other tables developed by Bell, Bates, and Soldovsky and Murphy were also reviewed.

All architects of stock value tables have rendered great service to investment analysis, but it still remains largely potential. None has so far succeeded in providing an adequate design for realistic investment practice. The difficulty with

* *Financial Analysts Journal,* vol. 20, no. 5: 78, 79 (September–October 1964).

all of these tables is that they require the investor to make a number of assumptions. The task for a more practical set of tables is to incorporate as many assumptions in the tables so as to leave the investor only the most vital judgments to make. This philosophy was carried out by Molodovsky in the tables presented in the Stock Valuator section of this volume.

A Brief Analysis of Capital Gains Tax Rates *

A great many analysts assume that long-term capital gains are taxed at the rate of 25 percent as is the case for most taxpayers. Actually, of course, the 25 percent tax rate is the maximum under present tax laws and many investors have an actual effective capital gains tax rate less than 25 percent—in some cases considerably less. After discussing some of the basic tax factors in computing the amount of taxable long-term capital gains, it is noted that the 25 percent maximum rate on capital gains is not reached until the single taxpayer has $20,000 of taxable income or the joint return taxpayer has $40,000 of taxable income, under 1964 rates. If the investor had no income apart from capital gains, he could have up to $80,000 in capital gains before reaching the 25 percent maximum capital gains rate for taxpayers filing joint returns. The article is basically an explanation of the Internal Revenue Code as it affects the average stockholder paying taxes on capital gains.

Common Stock Valuation †

WITH CATHERINE MAY AND SHERMAN CHOTTINER

This article presented stock valuation tables of a new type aimed at defining the valuation problem in a manner consistent with actual economic experience and in simplifying the mechanics so that the tables would be functional and simple to use. Catherine May assisted in the theoretical and practical evolution of this valuation method, while Chottiner assisted in preparing the computer-generated tables. Molodovsky and May subsequently revised the model, and the Stock Valuator section of this volume presents their definitive work in this area.

The basic concept behind the tables is that the value of a common stock is the present worth of its future stream of dividends. In order to provide a link

* *Financial Analysts Journal,* vol. 21, no. 1: 75, 76 (January–February 1965).

† *Financial Analysts Journal,* vol. 21, no. 2: 104–23 (March–April 1965).

between earnings and dividends, they use a hypothesis that companies with higher growth rates will tend to pay out a small proportion of earnings in the form of dividends, reinvesting the major portion of earnings in order to help finance their growth. As the company matures past its initial high growth period, growth will slow down gradually (or quickly in some instances), but the proportion of earnings paid out in dividends will increase now that capital growth requirements are less demanding. After some years of declining growth, a zero growth rate is reached which is extended indefinitely. An extensive multiple regression analysis provided the background both to indicate the general validity of the hypothesis and to indicate how dividend payout rates vary with differing growth rates.

The user of these tables selects the period and growth rate for the initial period of constant growth and then the number of years of declining growth which will take place before zero growth is reached. From these assumptions, the tables can be used to determine investment values. They can also be used to test the reasonableness of current market prices and what growth projections must be met in order to justify current market prices. In short, the tables were built to find stocks which are the most rewarding holdings for long-term investors.

Building a Stock Market Measure— A Case Story*

In 1926 *Barron's* requested William L. Crum, then an assistant professor of statistics at Harvard, to construct an index that would measure the fluctuations of the stock market more satisfactorily than the indicators which were already in existence at that time. Professor Crum spent a year in reviewing the possibilities and published six articles describing his research and the reasons he constructed the new index for *Barron's* using techniques somewhat different from those employed in constructing other stock market indicators.

This case history illustrates the types of statistical techniques and thinking relevant to the construction of measurements of trends and levels of the stock market. Analysts frequently encounter averages or indexes of stock prices; few, however, have real insight into their structure and special characteristics. Even simple averages raise intemporal problems; complex index numbers can reach high sophistication and still leave unanswered the question of what they succeed in measuring.

Molodovsky's discussion of the problems involved in constructing stock market indexes is contained in Chapters 2 and 3 of this volume. Professor Crum's index constructed for *Barron's* has only academic interest since it was carried by

---

* *Financial Analysts Journal*, vol. 23, no. 3: 43–46 (May–June 1967).

that magazine for little more than a decade before being abandoned. The Dow-Jones Averages as compiled by the publisher of *Barron's* provided a sufficient representation for investment quality stocks, in Crum's opinion. Therefore, he attempted to construct an index to reflect the speculative tone of the stock market. The index was composed of the 50 stocks which had had the greatest turnover during the past week—that is, the number of shares traded in relation to the number of shares outstanding. Thus, the stocks in the index would change from week to week and keep pace with the rotation of leadership in trading activity. The index was computed with link relatives, and it was weighted with each issue being given a weight equal to the total number of shares traded during the past week. This index never gained much attention; Crum's work was most valuable in spelling out clearly the strengths and weaknesses of the more popular indexes.

Recent Studies of Price-Earnings Ratios *

In the early days, "ten times earnings" looked to be a pretty good rule of thumb for common stock investment. Postwar inflation brought in its wake the adulation of growth stocks; in its extreme form, it abolished any limits on earnings multipliers. Some recent empirical investigations attempted to achieve a balance by stressing once more the virtues of low price-earnings ratios (P/E).

Nicholson's 1960 paper covering a sample of 100 industrial stocks of trust investment quality over the years 1939–1959 indicated that the 20 stocks selling at the lowest P/E ratios rose more than the 20 highest P/E ratio stocks both for the 20 year period and for 11 sub-periods. Cootner has pointed out the bias in this study resulting from the fact that the 100 stocks were chosen at the end of the 20 years. Many of the 20 lowest P/E stocks in 1939 were not universally regarded as being of investment quality; they achieved this rating over the subsequent years.

A Drexel & Co. study of the stocks in the Dow-Jones Industrial Average revealed similar results, as did another study by McWilliams. No doubt the basic reason for the difference in the performance of the low P/E stocks as compared with the high P/E stocks is the simple fact that investors' growth expectations are not always realized. Some of the high P/E companies will falter, and when they do so, their price performance will be poor. The low P/E stocks are held in low regard by investors, yet some will surely provide pleasant surprises in boosting earnings and achieving a better investment regard.

There are very real difficulties in using P/E ratios in a mechanical manner. The investor should be flexible, not buying every low P/E stock and not selling

---

* *Financial Analysts Journal,* vol. 23, no. 3: 101–8 (May–June 1967).

every high P/E stock. The studies found that the best performing stocks could be found in all groups—the high P/E issues as well as the low P/E stocks. The author gives a skeptical welcome to all such demonstrations as how to form an investment philosophy. He questions the validity of any mechanical approach to the subject of P/E ratios.

Portrait of an Analyst: Benjamin Graham *

This brief biographical sketch inaugurated a new series of Journal features. Subsequent issues will contain profiles of distinguished members of our calling. It seemed appropriate to open this gallery of analysts with the protrait of their illustrious leader—Benjamin Graham. [Profiles of Pierre R. Bretey and Abe Kulp were subsequently completed prior to Molodovsky's death.]

The wide range of Benjamin Graham's luminous mind was revealed early in his life. Upon his graduation from Columbia University in the spring of 1914, the Departments of Philosophy, Mathematics, and English—the latter headed by the great John Erskine—all invited the newly elected Phi Beta Kappa member to join their ranks. Each honor was hard to resist. If it had not been for the personal influence of Columbia's Dean Frederick Paul Keppel, and his predilection of orienting bright graduates towards practical business, Ben Graham would have become a distinguished resident of an Ivory Tower. Undoubtedly, the clarity of his thought would have resulted in notable academic contributions.

It was fortunate, however, that Graham descended into the canyons of Wall Street. The attainment of fame and financial reward in his chosen field were personal triumphs. Yet business history has known many successful financiers. It was Graham's great distinction that his achievements were also value-added to others. He became the acknowledged teacher of at least two generations of security analysts and investors.

Besides, in 1927, he returned to his alma mater as a part-time "lecturer" in finance. He is now not only professor emeritus at Columbia's School of Business, but also "resident professor" at UCLA. He says the latter is an ideal position since it carries no salary and no duties.

It is not our purpose to recount Ben's life in detail. Some day, no doubt, he will do so in his own personal way. We shall just touch on a few highlights illustrating how he applied analytical skills to practical investment decisions.

One hears a great deal these days about fabulous results achieved by so-called "hedge-funds"—with the implication that they constitute a new form of financial

* *Financial Analysts Journal*, vol. 24, no. 1: 15, 16 (January–February 1968).

operations, unknown to the dark ages of even the recent past. In fact, hedged or arbitrage positions were the hallmark of Graham's financial style throughout his entire career in Wall Street. Its beginning goes back to 1915—the dissolution of the Guggenheim Exploration Co. This concern held large interests in several important copper mines, all of which were actively dealt in on the New York Stock Exchange. When Guggenheim proposed to dissolve and to distribute its various holdings pro-rata to its shareholders, Graham calculated that the current market value of the various pieces to be received were appreciably higher than the price of Guggenheim shares. By buying the latter and simultaneously selling "short" the components, a substantial profit could be attained. Graham recommended the operation to the firm with which he was then associated. They arbitraged a fair number of shares. Several individual clients did likewise and Graham handled the operation for them. The dissolution went through without a hitch, and the profit was realized as computed. In this way, Graham entered upon the first operation in what was to prove one of his special fields of study and action.

In 1920, Benjamin Graham was made a junior partner of the firm and placed in charge of all the arbitrage and hedging operations for the firm's own account. A standard transaction consisted of buying convertible bonds around par and selling against them "calls" on the related common stock. A more elaborate variant was to sell the related common stock "short" and also selling "puts" against the short position. Profits were made regardless of whether the stock advanced, declined, or stood still.

After several years of successful experience, which included running hedge funds for a share of the profits, Graham took a big step. On January 1, 1926, he organized a fund under the name of "Benjamin Graham Joint Account." Most of the capital was contributed by old friends. This fund was the predecessor of the legendary Graham-Newman Corp., which operated for 20 years until Graham's retirement to California in 1956. The success of the fund was largely due to an unusual combination of Graham's talent for security analysis with the outstanding business and negotiating abilities of his long-term partner, Jerome A. Newman.

Graham-Newman's operations were restricted to a few well-defined categories, each of which promised a satisfactory rate of profit—say, 20 percent per annum, or better—against relatively minor risks. The latter were further minimized by wide diversification. The categories were entitled: arbitrages; cash payouts (liquidations); related hedges; unrelated hedges; current-asset stocks ("bargain issues"), and controlled companies—the special province of J. A. Newman. A careful check was kept on the result of each operation and class of operations.

One consequence of this continuous evaluation of results may seem surprising. The "unrelated hedges"—in which a "cheap issue" is bought and an entirely disconnected "dear issue" is sold against it—were found to be more trouble than their overall profit was worth, and they were accordingly dropped. The Graham-Newman "value approach" did not work well enough in the short-selling of highly popular and hence apparently over-valued issues, *unless* there was adequate protection through holding of a senior, convertible issue of the same company.

The "bargain issues" were practically all restricted to the purchase of common stocks at less than two-thirds of their net-current-asset value. Remarkably few final losses were shown in this category, comprising the purchase of many hundred such issues over a period of more than 30 years. However, it is both paradoxical and typical of financial experience generally that the most profitable Graham-Newman operation of all did not meet this exacting requirement. This was the purchase of a 50 percent ownership of Government Employees Insurance Company at a price only slightly below its asset value. This company was to show an extraordinary growth of sales, profits, and market value—and was to make millionaires of many of the Graham-Newman stockholders.

Among various ventures of the original "Benjamin Graham Joint Account," at least one deserves special mention. It shows how the penetrating mind of a great analyst, followed by courageous and persevering action, can achieve a well-deserved victory.

When the Standard Oil monopoly was broken up by the Supreme Court in 1911, eight out of the numerous new companies were small oil pipelines. Little was known about their finances, and still less was published. Graham discovered that these pipelines filed complete reports with the Interstate Commerce Commission. A trip to Washington laid before him, on a desk in the Commission's record room, detailed annual reports of all eight pipelines. To his amazement, he found that they all owned huge amounts of the finest railroad bonds. One of them, the Northern Pipe Line, which was then selling around 65 and paying a $6 dividend, was holding some $95 per share of what amounted to cash assets. They could be distributed to stockholders without the slightest drawback to the operations. Pipelines were then out of favor and no one bothered to investigate them. Most investors felt that the 9 percent dividend was a warning of trouble ahead. After careful but persistent buying, Graham acquired 2,000 shares out of the total 40,000 shares outstanding. This made him the largest private stockholder of record, second only to the Rockefeller Foundation which owned 23 percent.

To make a long story short, Ben Graham finally won a two-year battle with the reluctant management. He became the first "outside" director of a former Standard Oil subsidiary, and no less than $70 per share was distributed to the stockholders out of the relatively unproductive cash-funds.

Ben Graham is a sensitive and modest man, as is well known to all who have had the privilege of his personal friendship. During his rewarding years as an analyst, his sole regret was a too easy acceptance of financial success as the aim of life. He did not need to have such scruples. His writings and his lectures formed a new tradition and his approach to security analysis came to be a fountainhead for advances of knowledge in this complex field with its never ending quest.

In a charming recent letter from France, addressed to old analyst friends and former pupils, he writes how far he feels removed—not geographically but spiritually—from his old world of finance. Instead of commenting on the Dow, Detroit riots, or de Gaulle, he described four open-air theatrical and musical performances that he attended in Paris and Aix-en-Provence. His remarks are witty and perceptive. Those who must still struggle, and who derive much benefit from his teachings, may hope that their turn will come, after accomplishing their goals, to turn to fuller enjoyment of human culture.

Corporate Mergers and Antitrust Policy*

This article was designed to serve as the first of a series which would examine, in broad outline, the history and present status of American business corporations. This subject area is amply covered in the academic literature, but has received scant attention in financial analysis. Investment handbooks begin by discussing stocks and bonds as God-given entities. They rarely bother to consider their source and the role of business corporations in the overall economic structure.

Free enterprise, with unrestricted entry and unlimited competition, is the theoretical image of the American capitalist system. While this is the theoretical model, compromises are worked out by the ever-changing contingencies of life. The greater and the more complex the society in which they have to be achieved, the more intricate will be their network.

The original merger movement was concentrated in the form of horizontal mergers, i.e., combinations of direct competitors. Now these account for only 15 percent of all mergers because of the well-settled antitrust restrictions against such mergers when one of the parties already is of significant size. Vertical mergers, which combine a corporation either with its customer or supplier, have also declined in frequency and now account for 15 percent of all mergers. At present, conglomerate mergers are by far the most numerous, accounting for nearly 70 percent of the total number of mergers.

A detailed review of the history of antitrust legislation and judicial decisions concluded that the antitrust response was a deep-seated reaction to the merger wave of the closing years of the nineteenth century in which the main drive was to achieve monopolies or near-monopolies. The current wave of conglomerate mergers is bringing many changes to the American corporate panorama and after the nation's political forces begin to consolidate their positions about this newer phenomenon, corrective measures will no doubt be taken. Senate hearings and Antitrust Division statements are examined to note the direction which these corrective measures are likely to take.

* *Financial Analysts Journal*, vol. 24, no. 2: 23–33 (March–April 1968).

The Business Corporation*

This article was moderately condensed to serve as Chapter 1 of this volume. The author traces an informal outline of the history of business corporations. He points out the principal forces, such as the lever of limited liability and the industrial revolution, which have contributed to the rise of the modern corporate economy. The significance of the separation of ownership and control is discussed, both as it appeared to Berle and Means 36 years ago and in its present aspects. The consequences of the institutionalization of common stock investments, which has replaced the recent fragmentation of ownership by a new form of concentration, are also considered.

Selecting Growth Stocks†

This article illustrates the difficulties which frequently confront analysts and investors in identifying growth stocks. It reviews the subsequent fate of a stock recommended for purchase by two distinguished analysts and a widely respected investment review. The recommendations for purchase were made at the beginning of June, 1960. The stock rose 30 percent during that month to its all-time high of 80. It soon collapsed with a decline, almost without interruption, over a two-and-a-half-year period to 10. The two analysts did not issue additional reports commenting upon the stock, but the investment service recommended holding the stock all the way down to 16, at which point they recommended its sale.

The story has some lessons for the analyst wishing to avoid pitfalls in selecting growth stocks. The issue in question is UMC Industries, then known as Universal Match Corporation. The company's earnings had been rising sharply from $0.32 per share in 1954 to $1.17 in 1959. The analysts recommending the stock were looking for a further rise to $1.50 per share for 1960. The stock was obviously selling at a high price relative to current earnings, even for a growth stock. However, the company was about to introduce a unique paper currency accepting machine that promised to revolutionize the automatic vending business. There existed a need for the new product and, at least at the outset, there seemed to be no serious competition. The first machines would provide change for five dollar bills and one dollar bills and experimental models might take larger denominations. This would enable vending machines to offer higher priced merchandise as well as the traditional products offered for small coins.

---

* *Financial Analysts Journal*, vol. 24, no. 3: 29–31 (May–June 1968).

† *Financial Analysts Journal*, vol. 24, no. 5: 103–106 (September–October 1968).

This case illustrates the frequent helplessness of investors and their advisers in arriving at sensible decisions in buying or selling high P/E stocks. Great emphasis was placed on a still insufficiently tested innovation. We believe that it is possible to have an investment portfolio with growth as its main objective—yet, the stocks should be purchased at prices close to, and preferably below, their quantified values based upon current earnings and justified growth potential.

Stock Values and Stock Prices*

The 1953 article "Some Aspects of Price-Earnings Ratios" is revised in the light of 15 additional years of experience. Chapter 6 of this volume represents another revision and refinement of the concept of a theoretical price-earnings ratio.

The author's earlier studies of price-earnings ratios were largely based upon annual figures—the average market price for the year and the earnings reported for that year. This method has its limitations. Steep rises and deep declines in the stock market sometimes take place during the same year. Summarization in a single figure obliterates these moves. Use of annual earnings is also suspect since investors do not ignore financial results until the annual report is issued. Investors and speculators are keenly following and constantly appraising the direction and intensity of the flow of profits. They may be thinking in terms of an annual rate of earnings per share, but the current earnings level is not restricted to the confines of the calendar year; it is an everchanging flow.

Monthly average prices for the S&P 500 are easily available and this leaves monthly average earnings figures to be constructed in order to have monthly price-earnings ratios to analyze. First, annual earnings were centered at the midyear mark. Then quarterly figures were plotted and the monthly rates were obtained by interpolating between the quarterly figures. This method does not imply that the majority of analysts or investors can always accurately estimate earnings six months ahead. However, it implies that they attempt to do so and that this is a reasonable period for studying the situation.

The article then reviewed the history of the stock market since 1914 using monthly data and concluded that the best explanation for changes in price-earnings ratios was still the concept of changes in actual earnings as compared with normal earning power defined by a moving average. Experiments with quarterly earnings figures in calculating least squares trends proved to be virtually identical with trends calculated with annual earnings. In consequence, the monthly data proved to have limited value in attempting to refine an understanding of fundamental relationships in the stock market.

* *Financial Analysts Journal*, vol. 24, no. 6: 134–48 (November–December 1968).

ABSTRACTS OF OTHER PUBLISHED WORKS OF
NICHOLAS MOLODOVSKY

Germany's Foreign Trade Terms in 1899–1913*

This paper was a study aimed at understanding the interchange in Germany's foreign trade in real terms of physical volume. Obviously, price changes obscured the patterns presented by the traditional statistics expressed in terms of money. But price indexes were unavailable for the 1899–1913 period under study.

Physical quantities were studied for 30 important products exported and for 20 imports. This enabled the construction of indexes to measure for the first time Germany's trade balance in physical terms. Nonmerchandise trade patterns were also examined.

Germany imported about 25 percent more than it exported in most of the years under consideration when measured in terms of marks. (The year 1913 was an exception with an approximate balance.) Molodovsky's study showed that while there was a significant trade deficit in physical volume at the turn of the century, the situation steadily improved during the next dozen years and was in balance by 1913. The difference was not solely accounted for by results in 1913. The 1913 balance was a normal expectation; the deficits of the few years preceding 1913 reflected unfortunate price situations, the physical volume trade balance was sound. The conventional wisdom relative to Germany's foreign investments is also questioned since the fragmentary evidence available supported the contrary position.

Gold Clause in American Law †

The gold clause is the most typical device of all protective agreements by which creditors seek to safeguard the value of their claims against the risk of a depreciation of the money of payment stipulated in the contract. The validity of this clause is a much disputed question. In general practice it is pronounced inoperative and illegal by the courts of the great majority of countries as under-

---

* *Quarterly Journal of Economics*, vol. 41, no. 4: 664–83 (August 1927).
† *Foreign Trade* (published by the American Chamber of Commerce in France, July 1932).

mining the foundation of the national currency which should be accepted as the only and intangible measure of value. An exception is found in the case of the United States where the validity of the gold clause is accepted without question and enforced by the courts.

Molodovsky then reviewed the Civil War period, which was the only period in American history when the nation had a depreciated currency. In 1862, "greenbacks" were approved by Congress to serve as legal tender for all debts public and private. They rapidly depreciated in value and at one time were worth only 36 cents per dollar in gold. Seven years later, the Supreme Court rendered the opinion that Congress had exceeded its power and that the gold clause in pre-existing debts was still valid. Many other court cases reinforced the validity of the gold clause, and the U.S. Treasury included a gold clause in each of its debt issues floated during and after World War I.

In summary, the gold clause has received a proper enforcement at the hands of American courts and constitutes, at the present time, the most effective protection which an investor can receive in this respect on the international markets, at least so long as gold will remain the foundation of our systems of currency and credit.

Some Aspects of the European Automobile Industry*

NICHOLAS MOLODOVSKY AND NATHALIE MOLODOVSKY

France's automobile production had been growing to the 250,000 cars per year rate and in 1931 passed the United Kingdom's to become the largest auto-making country in Europe. Exports were weak since the U.S. auto makers had the economies of mass production which enabled them to sell cars at much lower prices than French companies. High tariffs were in rule in France and in the other major auto-making countries, U.K., Germany, and Italy. The Ford plant in England, designed to produce 200,000 autos per year, failed to achieve its goals since the economies of mass production were offset by tariffs.

The passenger car has been so far chiefly designed to appeal to the wealthier classes as an instrument of pleasure rather than as an economic tool. Yet, the passenger car may be used not only to aid in the observance of a new religious rite with abundant human sacrifice on the crossings of the highways, but also to meet more essential needs of the ordinary business of life.

---

* *Foreign Trade* (Paris, October 1932).

Shipping and Shipbuilding *

Conditions in shipping and shipbuilding all over the world were causing concern to the companies in these and allied industries. The world's freight traffic declined by 62 percent between 1929 and 1933 in terms of value. The decrease in volume was 26 percent. Volume was below the 1913 level even though the world's population had risen 15 percent and shipping capacity was 43 percent larger.

The energetic efforts of the United States during World War I to build more ships than German submarines could destory resulted in a commercial fleet of gigantic proportions. Japan, Italy, and Holland also built large fleets, with the result that capacity far exceeded demand. After reviewing the situation in France and in other leading maritime nations and the various proposals being advanced to attempt to solve the excess capacity problem, the author concluded that the outlook for both shipping and shipbuilding was dismal.

Principle of Comparative Advantage in International Trade †

The doctrine of comparative advantage as enunciated by David Ricardo in 1817 is reviewed in this article. Later economists developed the theory of international trade and established that the basic assumptions of comparative advantage are utility economics rather than the labor costs economics favored by Ricardo in the bulk of his work.

The doctrine states that a country tends to devote its labor and capital to those industries in which they work to greatest effect. There will be less emphasis on other industries which produce only small profits. The products of the high profit industries generally find a substantial export market while the low profit industries face hard competition from imports. In other words, under free trade and perfect mobility of labor and capital, each country and each region will specialize in whatever it can do most efficiently and use these receipts to buy other products from other nations which specialize in these lines. This works to the benefit of all nations. It is the dominant force in international trade, and when a foreign trade policy disregards this because of its simplicity, difficulties are bound to arise.

---

* *Foreign Trade* (Paris, March 1933).
† *Foreign Trade* (Paris, May 1933).

Review of Economic and Business Conditions *

On April 19, 1933, the United States went off the gold standard. The unusual and distinctive characteristic of this decision is that the reasons do not lie in the monetary field. Technically, the dollar continues to be strongly protected by ample gold reserves and by a favorable balance of payments. The reason most frequently advanced for the move was the government's desire to alleviate the dangers arising from the heavy debt structure of the country—$130 billion, including $35 billion owed by the federal, state, and local governments. Yet, France and Great Britain have far heavier debt loads.

The President has been granted wide powers by Congress in all monetary matters. Inflation is desired by the majority of public opinion and political leaders. It is questionable if inflationary measures can raise the level of commodity prices in any sound and constructive manner. There is great danger of embarking on any such policy, even with the best intentions of keeping it under control. The value of the President's inflationary powers must chiefly reside in what they can produce as a psychological stimulant of general business activity.

The events of the month have exercised an exhilarating effect on the stock market with the Dow-Jones Industrial Average rising to 82. We seem definitely moving toward higher markets. The present business improvement may be temporarily interrupted, the inflationary stimulus may lose much of its strength, and various international scares may help to depress the market from time to time, but it is nevertheless probably true that we are now riding on a major upward swing.

La Clause—Or aux États-Unis †

The question of the validity of the gold clause in the United States became a serious preoccupation in American financial circles during the preceding week. The U.S. Supreme Court had ruled that two New Deal laws were unconstitutional. This raises great doubts as to the nature of the decision that the Court will render in the pending case questioning the validity of the law of June 5, 1933, which abrogated the validity of the gold clause in all contracts, public and private, with retroactive force.

After a review of previous U.S. Supreme Court decisions on the gold clause from 1868–1889 which upheld the gold clause and a review of the voting charac-

---

* *Foreign Trade* (Paris, May 1933).

† *La Situation Économique et Financière* (Paris, January 18, 1935).

teristics of the justices (Brandeis and Cardozo have the most radical views), Molodovsky concluded that it was impossible to predict what the court would decide. If the gold clause were held to be valid, then the Administration and Congress would have to seek expedients to neutralize the consequences of the Supreme Court's decision.

Grandeur et Décadence du New Deal*

President Roosevelt and his advisers have elaborated a sort of new economic theory based on purchasing power. To increase purchasing power artificially, the NRA (National Recovery Administration) was designed to increase wages and prices of industrial commodities and services. The AAA's (Agricultural Adjustment Act) goal was to boost prices of farm commodities. Along with a vast public works program, these agencies were designed to assure victory over the depression. The progressive deterioration of the NRA, as it imposed increasingly rigid rules, exposed the weakness of the New Deal programs. The New Deal was attempting to direct with penury and restrictions an economy of abundance and fluidity. The restrictions prevented moves toward adapting to new circumstances.

La Mort de l'Aigle Bleu †

This is an eyewitness account of the oral arguments and final decision in the U.S. Supreme Court case which declared the NRA (National Recovery Act) unconstitutional. The Supreme Court's first challenge to the New Deal was to overturn President Roosevelt's dismissal of a member of the Interstate Commerce Commission before his term had expired. The Frazier-Lemke law with a five-year moratorium on farm mortgages had then been declared an unconstitutional deprivation of the rights of bankers. This was not a New Deal law, however, but rather one that resulted from the efforts of Huey Long, "l'enfant terrible of the Senate and a demagogue of great talent." The NRA had industry groups advise in the establishment of detailed codes of practice for each industry. The Court ruled that this was an unconstitutional delegation of Congress's lawmaking powers. Not only did the NRA (and its symbol the blue eagle) die, but other New Deal programs seemed to be equally likely to fall when tested by the Supreme Court.

---

* *L'Europe Nouvelle*, vol. 18, no. 910 (Paris, July 20, 1935).
† *L'Europe Nouvelle*, vol. 18, no. 911 (Paris, July 27, 1935).

*Y a-t-il eu une Révolution Roosevelt?**

Has there been a Roosevelt revolution? The first Democrat to become president was Jefferson, an advocate of "laisser faire," the least government possible. This doctrine was followed by most presidents, but FDR took office with totally different ideas. During the campaign he had advocated the establishment of an economic order. The official proclamation of a government department to direct the economy was created at the start of the Roosevelt administration. The NRA and the AAA were examples of mechanisms created for the reconstruction of economic life and at the same time serving to fight the economic crisis. The methods chosen were dominated by political considerations.

Roosevelt did not try to kill the individualistic economy all at once. There were many reprieves in the war against capitalism. He wished to conserve in the United States an economic system which would be able to produce the largest quantity of material. He did not wish to destroy the recuperative power of the American economy.

There had been another reprieve in the two months since the Supreme Court's overturning of the NRA. There have been no economic or political shocks in this period. Roosevelt will undoubtedly be given a second term in which he can introduce important reforms. These may not be revolutionary measures, but rather ones which will consecrate the New Deal's stamp in the evolution of the United States.

One more time America is engaged in a new avenue. It is doubtful if this will end in either communism or fascism. We should not be hypnotized by these forces. It is infinitely more probable that by a process of successive changes, the U.S. will develop a new economic structure of its own. Roosevelt is engaged in a fight between the ideals of social justice and a desire to preserve an economic system which has provided material success. He wishes to accomplish a synthesis of these opposing forces in building a new economic order in the United States.

La Mort de la Triple A †

The U.S. Supreme Court declared unconstitutional the Agricultural Adjustment Act. In the confusion and tumult of ideas and sentiments provoked by this judgment, it is well to keep in mind the capital importance of this case. The decision was written by Justice Owen J. Roberts, one of the candidates for the Republican nomination in this year's presidential campaign. Roberts appears as the savior of the Constitution and the best American traditions, defending them

* *L'Europe Nouvelle*, vol. 18, no. 914 (Paris, August 17, 1935).

† *L'Europe Nouvelle*, vol. 19, no. 936 (Paris, January 18, 1936).

against the violations and profanations of the head of the Democratic party. He is a leader in the battles between the conservatives and the liberals, the defenders of the Constitution and the revisionists, the inflationists and the friends of a money healthy and stable, the advocates of laisser faire and the apostles of an economy more or less completely directed by the government.

The Court's decision will decrease the purchasing power of farmers, since the AAA's price supports will be ended. The farm crisis has been present since the early 1920s and the AAA crowned the efforts of the preceding decade to find a remedy for the chronic farm depression. The success of the program is measured by the 55 percent increase in farm revenues from 1932 to 1935. The repercussions from the overturning of the AAA would be disastrous if nothing were done. For political reasons alone, President Roosevelt will be forced to try a new measure to help the farmers.

The Supreme Court's direct and rigorous interpretations of constitutional principles makes it difficult, if not impossible, to enact almost any kind of social legislation. The Court is a serious block in the way of progress. Amending the Constitution would be a dangerous election campaign platform, however, and the President will therefore be combatting the Court with one arm tied behind his back.

La Lutte contre la Crise Agraire aux États-Unis*

This book is the published version of Molodovsky's dissertation for the degree Doctor of Law awarded by the University of Paris in 1936. The title indicates the theme of the book—*The Battle against the Farm Crisis in the United States.*

Farmers comprised 21 percent of the American population according to the 1930 census, and fully 44 percent of the population lived in rural areas, including the farmers and those who supplied their requirements. Farm income had fallen from $12 billion in 1929 to $5 billion in 1932—mainly as a result of lower prices. The problem began when the World War took 50 million acres of farmland out of production in Europe and 40 million acres were planted in America to supply the food. The aftermath was a 40 percent decline in farm prices during 1920. The Europeans protected their farmers by doubling or tripling tariffs, so the export market fell drastically. The rise of the tractor also resulted in a decline in the horse population during the 1920s, further depressing the demand side of the market. The 1920s were years of low farm income at a time when urban America was prospering.

---

* *Libraire Technique et Économique* (Paris, 1936), pp. 1–173.

Many proposals were made to help the situation, and Congress passed the McNary-Haugen Act. A Federal Farm Board was established to reorganize the system of selling farm products. Farmers were encouraged to form cooperatives which would propose solutions and the Farm Board would assist them in carrying them out. Basically, it was hoped that the marketing of farm commodities would be done with one cooperative controlling the market for each commodity and supporting the price by refusing to sell in the U.S. market at low prices. The surplus would be sold in export markets at whatever price it would bring. The loss on export sales would be offset by a per-bushel tax charged each farmer on his sales through the cooperative.

The Federal Farm Board was established in 1929 with funding of several hundreds of millions of dollars to finance the initial stages of the marketing programs. The world grain markets were favorable as the harvest season of 1929 began, but the panic on Wall Street spread the next day to the commodities exchange. Prices fell and fell, and the efforts of the Farm Board to support domestic prices seemingly made no impact. Soon the Farm Board's funds were exhausted. This led to violent attacks against the Farm Board and against its president—by farmers and by the Congress. The liquidation of the Farm Board was urged, but it did not die until President Roosevelt took office in 1933. The Farm Board had been too fragile to withstand a major crisis in agriculture.

The Farm Board had urged farmers to reduce their plantings in 1930 so as to help end the oversupply problem that was depressing prices. Radio appeals and other means were used to encourage farmers to cooperate, but they did not do so. Governor Huey P. Long of Louisiana called a conference of legislators from the cotton growing states in 1930 with the object of having these states pass laws prohibiting the planting of cotton entirely during 1932 in the hopes of boosting cotton prices from 5 cents per pound to 20 cents. Louisiana voted the full vacation from cotton planting, while Texas, Arkansas, and Mississippi voted 30 percent reductions. While these efforts were not very successful, the idea grew that any successful program to raise farm prices would have to cut back on farm output so that the supply of farm products would become in better balance with demand.

Twelve days after his inauguration, FDR sent a preliminary text to Congress of the Agricultural Adjustment Act, and one month later the new law was signed. The grand innovation of the AAA consisted of its measures to control production. The farmer who reduced his acreage planted in accordance with the requests of the government was able to receive a subsidy for his crop while those farmers who did not reduce their acreage had to sell their crop at the free market price.

The AAA began its wheat program with a subsidy of 28 cents to 30 cents per bushel to participating farmers who agreed to cut back their acreage planted in wheat by 15 percent. Farmers holding 75 percent of the nation's wheat acreage signed contracts with the AAA in 1933. In the wheat belt states, nearly 90 percent of the land was included in the program. In 1934 the same acreage restrictions applied, but the drought enabled a removal of acreage restrictions in 1935. The program was financed by a tax of 30 cents per bushel on all wheat milled.

Similar programs were initiated in five other basic farm commodities which combined accounted for 50-55 percent of total farm revenues. The program was thus broadly based—and was quite successful in obtaining a large participation by farmers. From March of 1933, when the AAA was established, until March of 1935, the prices of all farm products nearly doubled. The prices of products purchased by farmers rose 26 percent during the two-year period, but the parity ratio of the index of the purchasing power of farmers rose from 55 percent to 85 percent. It must be noted that not all of this improvement was due to the efforts of the AAA. Three consecutive years of drought helped to reduce production as much as the AAA's efforts. The boll weevil also served to solve the problem of the oversupply of cotton.

Molodovsky concluded that the AAA was an attempt at solving the major problem of the chronic crisis in agriculture. It helped to reinforce one of the most vulnerable sectors of the national economy and to stop the disintegration of the social and economic tissue of the nation's farmers. Not only was a new program required by the farm crisis, it also met the political needs of the president and served as an important part of the general attack on the depression afflicting the entire economy.

The AAA must be considered as part of the New Deal approach toward the economy. The New Deal doctrine of economic and political thought was based on increasing purchasing power. It believed that this was the "open sesame" that would bring about economic prosperity. This is an erroneous conception of a complex economic organism. While economic gains in the New Deal's first two years had been substantial, it is infinitely more probable that these were the result of a normal cyclical recovery, not simply the result of New Deal programs. Among the lessons of the AAA is the realization of the immense administrative efforts needed to attempt to cope with the forces of a complex economy. Molodovsky was skeptical about the longer term prospects for administering the AAA and whether it would have a lasting effect for the good of American farmers.

La Vie Francaise

Molodovsky wrote seven monthly columns for *La Vie Francaise*, a financial newspaper published in Paris. The following are brief, freely translated excerpts.

April 22, 1960—The year 1960 is a year of transition. The current business expansion began 24 months ago and is reaching an advanced stage in its development. Business expansion in the ten cycles since World War I have lasted an average of 27 months. In much the same way as a grand leitmotif, the end of an era of expansion passes through numerous variations and modulations. Among other factors, we are living in an election year with the need to cajole voters, even though the present occupant of the White House is inclined to austerity in government spending.

* * *

May 20, 1960—The New York Stock Exchange has given the arrival of spring an almost glacial salute. In spite of the coming summit conference, the market is conserving its good disposition. (The Dow-Jones Industrials dipped below 600.)

* * *

June 24, 1960—After the derailment of the summit conference (by the U-2 affair), the first instinct of speculators in New York was to buy aircraft stocks. In other areas, Wall Street guarded its enthusiasm.

* * *

August 19, 1960—Deterioration continues in diverse branches of economic activity. The decline is perhaps prolonged by the actions taken to curb inflation. In the passage of time, the year might be seen as one of a short cyclical contraction.

* * *

September 23, 1960—As the Ides of March came for Caesar, the month of September is often full of menace for American stocks. Labor Day traditionally marks the start of a new financial season after the end of summer. Men of affairs, after returning from vacation, try to discern the contours of coming events. The results of their meditations often create decisive events for stock market history. It will be difficult to attribute the present weakness in the stock market to a simple crisis of nerves provoked by an occult superstition about Labor Day. The recent economic news has been unfavorable. Some statistics have been shocking.

* * *

December 6, 1960—The American economy continues to deteriorate. It is not an isolated case or two, but a general situation. GNP has even declined slightly. Independent of general stock market trends are the individual issues distinguished by the grand romantics of Wall Street as "growth stocks." Among the premières danseuses are IBM, AMF, Polaroid, Litton, and Mead Johnson, which introduced this year the celebrated product, Metrecal.

* * *

February 17, 1961—The flagrant contradiction between the downward movement of business and the rise in the stock market continues. President Kennedy has announced a program to fight the recession. We have a word of consolation. In spite of the distance already covered, the new stock market rise is young for a normal cycle. The prime forces are less economic than psychological, however.

Part III

"Value and Return in the Stock Market"

WHAT ARE YOUR STOCKS
REALLY WORTH?
VALUE AND RETURN
VIA
THE STOCK VALUATOR

By
Nicholas Molodovsky
and
Catherine May

To
the memory of
Nicholas Molodovsky
(1898–1969)
first recipient
of the Nicholas Molodovsky Award
which he inspired
presented by The Financial Analysts Federation
only to those persons
who have made contributions
so powerful and effective as to change
the direction of the profession
or
lift it to higher standards of accomplishment

Preface

His ENERGY completely depleted by overwork—because of his love for it—the distinguished senior author, Nicholas Molodovsky passed away peacefully in his sleep, in Mexico City, on March 7, 1969. I can still hear what were almost his last words to me: "If I weren't getting so old and so tired, I wouldn't have to waste these ten days on vacation."

Having worked closely with him since 1950, I have felt the full impact of the loss of a wonderful and warm friend as well as a guiding light in research.

In addition to the immeasurable loss to his family and personal friends, it is most unfortunate for the financial community that he had to pass from our midst before bringing to fruition all the dreams which he had conceived.

Besides his relationship of 36 years with White, Weld & Co. Incorporated and his editorship of the *Financial Analysts Journal* for over five years, he had begun or planned three most important books. At the time of his death he was working on a huge, scholarly work which kept growing in his mind until it would have included just about every phase of finance and economics. The work he completed comprises Part I of this volume.

The next book planned was a relatively short book on the subject of valuation of common stocks. This would have covered the discovery and refinement of our valuation system, based on the theory of present worth, as well as a description of its application in the uniquely developed tables. The third book would have consisted mainly of these tables, the only text being an explanation of how to use them.

Since the book which would have expounded the logical development of the principles of our method of valuation was never written, it was necessary to include in this book of tables a few extra chapters which cover the barest minimum of necessary background for an intelligent understanding of these tables—to which have been given the distinctive title, *The Stock Valuator.*

The first chapter shows the great need for determining the value of stocks by a relatively simple method which any intelligent investor will find practical for everyday use. The second chapter gives an outline of previous efforts toward this end. A simplified presentation of the meaning of the theory of present worth and of the additional relationships which have been built into these tables makes up the third chapter. The built-in relationships between growth of earnings and payout, in conjunction with the "open end" assumption about the stock universe, not only reduce the necessary input to a minimum—projected earnings—but also confine the subjective elements to the hypotheses concerning earnings and so protect, as far as possible, the comparability of stocks evaluated. Thus, there are greatly expanded possibilities for mass selection and ranking of stocks, portfolio selection, and such matters. After clarifying a few important and helpful concepts, the fourth chapter demonstrates the method of using the Valuator. It includes various examples which show how the tables can be helpful in the solution of different types of common stock investment problems. Our readers will find many more approaches and uses for *The Stock Valuator.*

The real bonus is the ease with which value can be determined. This not only brings convenience to the few but also infinitely broadens the field of potential users, and in this way hastens our advance toward that far more important goal—the ultimate stabilizing effect which widespread acceptance of an authoritative method of valuation can be expected to have on erratically fluctuating price swings.

Insofar as possible, actual writings of Mr. Molodovsky have been woven into the text in this book. Much of the second chapter was based on a more comprehensive draft he had written for a book which was never published. Many excerpts from various articles by him, published from time to time in the *Financial Analysts Journal,* have been included in all chapters, especially Chapter 1.

My aim throughout this book has been to make it as readable and as easy to understand as possible. For reasons suggested above, I have tried to present it, not only for the professional analyst and the exceptional investor, but also for every intelligent investor and investor-to-be who has enough interest in his portfolio to investigate the prospects of the companies in which he invests his money.

Those of our readers who are familiar with the present worth theory—as well as those who are pressed for time—will find that Chapter 4 covers all the necessary concepts and explanations for the practical application of *The Stock Valuator.* Those even more pressed for time may refer at once to the worked out examples that begin on page 221.

ACKNOWLEDGMENTS

I am most grateful for the invaluable assistance of Mr. Oliver G. Selfridge of the Massachusetts Institute of Technology who did the FORTRAN programming. The programs were run on an IBM Model 360/65, and their output printed on an IBM line printer exactly as they appear in this book.

I also wish to thank Mrs. Katharine Molodovsky for her kind cooperation and encouragement. Special acknowledgment is due to Mr. James R. Morse, senior vice president of White, Weld & Co. Incorporated and to Mr. John Fountain, also at White, Weld & Co. Incorporated, who encouraged me to complete the work on this method of valuation and critically reviewed the manuscript. I wish to express my appreciation to Mr. Irving Kahn, partner of Abraham & Co., for his valuable suggestions. Recognition is due to Mr. Joseph Valentine who expertly drew the charts and to Mrs. Mary Elizabeth Farrell who typed the manuscript and offered helpful suggestions. Finally, I wish to express my gratitude to all who have generously given permission to refer to their works and to all who have stimulated me in the preparation of this manuscript.

C. R. M.

CONTENTS

174   *Investment Values in a Dynamic World*

Chart of Value and the Rate of Return
More About the Rate of Return
A Word of Warning

4. A METHOD FOR STOCK VALUATION 211

The Computer Program
The Magic of Growth
Growth Rate of Earnings
Value and the Rate of Return (Discount Rate)
High Growth Stocks and Value
Cycles in the Stock Market
Normal Earnings Clarified by Diagram
The Stock Valuator—Tables for the Valuation
    of Common Stocks
Some Practical Illustrations
No Conflict—And It's So Easy!
Summary and Conclusions

APPENDIXES 231
  A. Amount of $1 at Compound Annual Growth, 233
  B. Present Value of $1 Discounted Annually, 234
  C. Graphs of Earnings and Earnings Trends, 236
  D. The Stock Valuator—Industrials, 253

Chapter 1

WHY DO WE NEED A VALUATOR?

"THE MARKET will tend to fluctuate." This phrase is often uttered with the same smugness as "boys will be boys." The famous saying is attributed to Morgan the Elder. This pronouncement from the throne of financial success and power is used as an irrefutable dictum condemning, with sarcastic brevity, ill-guided attempts by the ignorant or the presumptuous to predict the unpredictable.

If Mr. Morgan did have this notion, he was, without knowing it, an early apostle of the hypothesis of the random walk. His ironic verdict may also be construed as a general sweeping denial that stocks obey any law.

We cannot subscribe to the latter view. Stocks will fluctuate. But whether their movements follow a path of chance or a systematic pattern, they lead to a computable value. Stocks remain bound by gravitational force to that sun of the economic system.

Paraphrasing Voltaire's famous saying, if value did not exist, it would have to be invented. It is our only anchor. If stock prices are engaged from here to eternity in a random dance and do not feel the pull of value—if they move in a value vacuum—it would be appropriate to erect a new stock exchange building in Las Vegas instead of Manhattan.

NOTE ON A PITFALL

It seemed almost as if Las Vegas had established a branch in New York when the stock of a well-known company rose from 3⅞ in October, 1957, to 80¾ in June, 1960, as investors scrambled wildly, intoxicated with blind hope which begot dreams of castles in the air. Do not misunderstand. There was real basis for optimism and promise from that fabled attribute called "growth." However, there were also the ever-present hazards characteristic of such ventures. Thus, there was also real need for cool calculation of how high one could reasonably bid. This was proved only too painfully for those who held on too long under

175

the hypnotic spell. The earnings balloon was battered by both increased expenses and reduced industrial activity and, punctured badly, it fell back to earth bringing with it the high-flying price—down from 80¾ to 10⅝ by October, 1962. And the sad epilogue is this: Even though earnings recovered and surpassed their 1960 level, the price of UMC Industries not only has not yet reached even 30 again, at the time of this writing, but, in the face of a lean year, dropped back to 9½—an 11-year low—in the dark days of May, 1970.

It is a cold, hard fact of financial life that as soon as investors lose faith that a high-flying stock will continue to make money at a rapidly growing rate, the same thing happens as when an aircraft loses speed—it starts falling. The trouble is double-barrelled. When prospects are bright, we bid too high. But the appearance of clouds on the horizon so shatters us that we panic and offer too low. Why are we of so little faith? Simply because we do not know how much the stock is really worth.

"It's Good to Own Growth Stocks!" was the alluring headline of an advertisement frequently appearing on financial pages before the 1962 market break. The advertisement supported its claim by a tabulation showing the much steeper percentage increases in the prices of stocks of fast-growing companies than in the averages of the general market. For a consideration, it offered guidance in this exciting investment field.

Many other statistical organizations and investment counselors have also often urged their clients to buy growth stocks, since they represent such an ideal investment. Demonstrations triumphantly draw on vast stores of hindsight, bringing up heavy statistical artillery for assaulting a fort without defenders. By laboriously comparing stock price histories of successful companies with those whose record is mediocre, the conclusion is reached that growth is financially preferable to stagnation.

THE CASE OF IBM

Typically, IBM is used for illustration. The presentation usually begins with the assertion that a thoroughbred growth stock "discounts" its prospects far ahead. And since IBM's past progress promises to continue, investors can purchase the stock practically blindfolded, especially if it can be caught off guard in a reaction.

This advice was not merely offered but faithfully followed. At the 1961 year-end, IBM was the largest dollar value holding of American investment funds. Fifty-seven leading funds were holding a total of 1,210,536 shares of this stock, representing a market value in excess of $700,000,000. These funds' holdings of American Tel. & Tel. and of General Motors amounted at that time respectively to $261 million and $222 million.

To show how faithfully this advice is still being followed we cite the comparable figures for mid-1970. Seventy-five funds held a total of 5,073,350 shares of IBM with a total market value in excess of $1.25 billion, as compared with holdings of American Tel. & Tel. and of General Motors worth approximately $457 million and $306 million, respectively.

In its weekly summary of outstanding reports by financial analysts, a daily newspaper with a national circulation, called attention some years ago to a study by a research expert of an investment banking firm. This analyst pointed out that $3,000 worth of IBM stock purchased in 1914 would have grown into $2,164,000 in cash and stock by May, 1956. We might add that by the year-end 1961, this $3,000 investment would have represented a market value in excess of $12,-000,000, and over $29,000,000 in January, 1970, when IBM reached its all-time high up to the time of this writing.

Proper homage was paid IBM by an analyst who said it was not a stock but a religion. To spell out its name in full would have been sacriligious and an uncivil doubt of the readers' *savoir vivre*. This reverence, however, was a bit shaken in 1962 when IBM's price declined slightly over 50 percent—from 607 in October, 1961, to 300 in June, 1962 (i.e., from 120 to 62, after adjustment for stock dividends and splits through 1973). This collapse, furthermore, took place against the background of an uninterrupted rise of earnings at the sizable pace of over 20 percent per year.

In this case great "value" was still there. The question was "How much?" Faith had been shaken by an announcement that a change was taking place in IBM's data processing mix. Customers were to be permitted either to buy or to rent IBM systems machines, which were formerly available on a rental basis only. Some feared that IBM might lose its former stability of earnings. But there was also another great fear which troubled investors—the nagging suspicion that very probably they had bid up the price too high. How much too high? If only they could know! In their dismal disillusionment they proceeded to cut down their idol to half its stature!

In the case of the venerable IBM, however, faith was gradually restored as earnings continued to grow without interruption at close to 20 percent per annum. Nevertheless, it was May of 1964 before its price again reached the high of October, 1961. Since then, there have been periodic setbacks, but up to this writing there has been none quite so great percentagewise. The market reversal of 1966 saw IBM fall 23 percent, and the 1968–69 decline was 22 percent. However, the 1969 "low" of 224 (adjusted to 1973) was nearly double the 1961 "high." Improved prospects seasoned with renewed hope and faith then sent IBM charging ahead again, counter to the general trend, to another new high of 310 in January, 1970. But no sooner had the top been reached than doubts and fears begotten by the adversities of the 1970 recession pounded it down 44 percent. IBM once again was one of the better performing stocks in the subsequent recovery reaching another new peak at 365 in 1973, before dropping somewhat more than 50 percent the following year. The point of this recitation of market history is to illustrate that even a high quality, well known growth stock is subject to rather extreme price swings even though earnings are continually showing excellent growth all the time.

PRICE AND VALUE

True blue value, such as IBM's, must eventually pull price upward as earnings continue to climb ever onward and upward. How long it takes, however, depends not only on the performance of earnings but, fully as much, on how long it takes to restore that phantom confidence. In our first example, UMC Industries, it certainly has not yet been restored, for various reasons which need not be gone into here.

A loss of confidence may have many facets. It may pertain to the earnings outlook of a single stock. But it can also be of a general nature if investors should come to feel that the economic and political environment has become less propitious for companies to make profits. A company with a greater than average earnings growth is bound to suffer more than the average stock from unrealized growth expectations. While all goes well, its rate of earnings increase produces a cumulative effect and strengthens the anticipation of a continued favorable trend. This widens the differential spread of the earnings capitalizer compared to stocks of companies with profits growing at slower rates. But when confidence begins to wane, the decline of the stock's price will be the steeper and in direct relation to its speed of growth.

A similar situation arises, and for the same reason, when an unfavorable overall rate change is made by a public utility regulatory commission. An expanding utility would suffer more from such a change. Both its growth rate and market capitalizer would, in all likelihood, decline more than those of a company with more stable earnings.

Changes of psychological climate can overtake any stock, or an industrial group, or even the entire market. They may develop slowly, leaving ample time for reflection and action; but they can also strike with the flash of lightning, leaving even a rabbit no time to run. For the most part the changes are cyclical. These are difficult to gauge since stock prices are among the most sensitive of the leading cyclical series and their holders cannot detect advance tracks of the approaching tread of the bear or bull. Yet sometimes even the cyclical elements are missing, and the mystery of the sudden turn may not be solved until long after the event.

How often, in moments of reflection, have we wondered why, as we watched prices gyrate? If a share of stock represents a fraction of the net worth of a corporation, how can it vary so much in a few months, even a week, a day, alas even an hour? It's a logical question.

Soon after the thunderous collapse of stocks on Blue Monday, May 28, 1962, an advertisement was published by a major investment firm. It pointed out that on February 6, when General Motors sold at its 1962 high of 57¼, the corporation might have been considered to be worth in excess of $16 billion. On May 29, when GM opened at 46, that valuation had dropped to just over $13 billion, based on its outstanding shares of common stock.

What serious reverses had GM suffered to account for a three billion dollar loss? The answer was: None!

After turning its spotlight on GM's excellent short-term and long-term outlooks, the advertisement asked investors two additional questions: Was GM overvalued on February 6, 1962, when it was selling at roughly 18 times 1961 earnings? Or was it undervalued on May 29, when it was selling on a basis of 11 or 12 times indicated 1962 earnings?

The advertisement did not answer the questions, but it said they were worth some serious thought. It recommended, in conclusion, that investors ask themselves such questions about other securities too.

As a sequel to this advertisement, we might note that by October, 1965, the price of General Motors had risen to 113¾, only to shrink to 59½ in May, 1970. Does this mean that there had been a variation of about $15.5 billion in the net worth of General Motors Corporation—from roughly $32.5 billion to $17 billion? Hardly! How then can real value be determined?

"THE GOOD OLD P/E"

We agree that a stock's value is the standard for measuring its price. The problem is how to determine this elusive thing called value. It has long been a habit in Wall Street to use price-earnings ratios as a guide. As mentioned in an article in the December, 1944, issue of *The Exchange*, in "the buoyant 1920's, when an industrial company's shares were selling at around 10 times earnings, actual or closely estimated, the price was considered by the trading fraternity as reasonable, meaning reasonably low."

When earnings remain stable, a constant capitalizer makes sense. However, the multipliers must reflect changes in earning power. This fact is generally recognized today. In a more recent article in *The Exchange*, Sam Shulsky, who writes a nationally syndicated newspaper column of advice for investors, points out that the P/E ratio of a stock "can, and does, change from hour to hour, day to day, and season to season. . . . One stock selling at 40 times its earnings may be a bargain—as only future events can prove—while another selling at 12 times earnings may prove to be overpriced."[1]

GM as a kind of "model stock" can serve very well to demonstrate how confusing and untypical the price-earnings ratio can be. Between 1946 and 1949, GM's per share earnings soared from $0.29 to $2.44, rising almost ten times. Simultaneously, the price-earnings ratio, based on the average price of each year, tumbled from 37.7 to 4.2. Even if 1946 and 1947 only are considered, i.e., two immediately adjacent years, earnings advanced from $0.29 to $1.04 per share, while the price-earnings ratio fell from 37.7 to 4.4. If we compare the same factors

---

[1] Sam Shulsky, "P/E Ratio—How Good a Yardstick?" *The Exchange*, p. 9 (February 1970). *The Exchange* is published by the New York Stock Exchange, but any opinions expressed are those of the writers and do not represent any official point of view.

for 1955 and 1956, we observe a decline of per-share earnings from $4.26 to $3.02 and a lift of the price-earnings ratio from 9.1 to 15.0. Again, in 1970, as a result of a long strike, earnings collapsed from $5.95 in 1969 to $2.09, thus raising the average annual price-earnings ratio for 1970 to 33.7 from 12.9 in 1969. In 1971 earnings rebounded to a more normal level of $6.72 and the average annual price-earnings ratio returned to 12.2.

These examples suggest that valuation by means of a price-earnings ratio can be erratic. This ratio is an ever-changing factor which swells when current earnings contract and shrinks when they expand. Nor are its inverse movements even proportionate to the rates of changes in earnings.

A ratio is a quotient. How can it become a capitalizer of one of its own two terms?

Value is the yardstick we seek for measuring whether price is high, low, or in line with the standard. When we use price-earnings ratios we are prisoners of price. Even when such "multipliers" have been refined by filtering them through comparative experience, they still are derived from price, which they are supposed to measure. We are spinning inside a looping Hula-Hoop. And when we attach the ratios to fluctuating current earnings, we perform the circling act on quicksand.

More confounding by far is the confusion when applied to the glamorous "growth stocks." If two stocks will each earn this year one dollar per share, with the earnings of stock "A" growing at a compound annual rate of 3 percent, while those of stock "B" increase at the rate of 30 percent, and if this differential is expected to prevail for a while, it is self-evident that the earnings of these two stocks will not be valued by applying to them an identical multiplier. The analyst's problem is to find a way of determining the proper capitalizers after taking into account the probable durations and changes in the respective rates of growth. The magnitudes differ, yet the nature of the problem is identical in both cases.

Could it be that the classification of certain equities as "growth stocks" is essentially an attempt to escape from the unpleasant analytical necessity of developing a single method of appraisal that is valid for all stocks? Do "growth stocks" exist as an independent logical category? When they are set up as such, is it not done for the sake of claiming that their valuation needs special treatment? The rest of the stocks can then be left to be handled by other and, perhaps again, varying rules of thumb.

THE STOCK VALUATOR

We have encountered the most crucial question in the entire field of invest-ment. To solve it, financial analysts require a full measure of economic insight. But solution is imperative. It is a challenge that had to be met. There had to be a better way than that blind skyrocketing which too often lured the "little man" only to ruin him in a tailspin.

Our answer is the Stock Valuator—a set of tables for determining "value," if hypothesized assumptions are realized. The basic principle is the "theory of present worth" which was already well known in intellectual circles in the 1930s. The earliest substantial pioneering work on the subject came out in 1931 when Samuel Eliot Guild published his *Stock Growth and Discount Tables.* More will be said of this in the next chapter.

John Burr Williams gave the most exhaustive and scholarly treatment of valuation of common stocks by the method of present worth in a doctoral dissertation, *The Theory of Investment Value,* numbering over 600 pages and published in 1938 by the Harvard University Press. We shall have occasion to refer again to this distinguished work.

Research in an important area must be a collective effort. Many minds attack the problem from different angles. It is a never-ending process. Our part in it was long and tedious and encompassed years of research and development, of questioning, experimentation, and double-checking. But it produced what we believe to be the most refined and the only existing method of valuation which requires only one assumption—that of expected growth of earnings—which the user obtains from any of various sources, probably most often from the research analysts at his investment house. It is also a happy development that company officials are tending more and more to give out just the information needed: estimates of the expected growth rate of earnings and the number of years they foresee at that rate.

A PRACTICAL MEASURE OF VALUE

We are not so presumptuous as to guarantee that use of the Valuator will bring riches in abundance within a short period of time. It will give the "value" corresponding to the expected growth which, incidentally, can be varied at will. The Valuator can also be used to determine the range from optimistic to pessimistic expectations. Even this, however, unless widely known and followed—as we trust this book will make it—cannot assure success. To clarify this point, let us transport ourselves in spirit say a quarter of a century into the past and assume that one of us, perhaps at high personal cost, had procured straight from the devil, reliable data concerning precise annual true values of a certain number of stocks for each of the next 25 years. Such full disclosure would undoubtedly have seemed to promise a lot of coin. But even if he had been as smart as his friend the devil in picking the growingest of all the growth stocks, he would most likely have come to a sad end from exhaustion and frustration, because all the other investors and speculators trading in that particular stock, unable to lift even one of the seven veils concealing the future, would have operated in the dim light of their exceedingly limited vision.

The point of this parable is that to make real money it is not only knowledge of real value that counts. Considerably more practical and infinitely more precious would be some reliable standard for comparing the investment values of all existing stocks without attempting to transgress the boundaries of such readily accessible information and modest imagination as constitute the frontiers of our so-called minds. If a standard does not exist, why should we not try to make one?

Such a standard of comparison is supplied by the Valuator. For example, an investor requires 12 percent return on his money. He therefore confines himself to the 12 percent return group of tables. After determining what price he can afford to pay for each selected stock and still have a probable chance of realizing 12 percent return, the next step is to compare current prices with these guide-posts. This is the clincher which sifts and sorts the candidates.

In order to be as practical as possible, a standard of investment value should conform to several requirements. The method of its construction must be consistent with scientific procedure. Its capitalization base must have unquestioned validity. The valuation formulas should be suitable for programming for electronic computers, then data processing will make it possible to classify appraisals rapidly and in accordance with any desired specifications, thereby meeting any and all investment objectives.

Coming from such an eminent authority it was most gratifying when the senior author received a personal letter from Samuel Eliot Guild in which he said:

> I really believe that any general acceptance of such tables might tend to at least modify such extreme fluctuations as occur under present conditions. If this should ever prove to be the case I further believe it might have a steadying effect on our whole financial picture, but this may be only an unduly optimistic daydream.

We dare to believe that the wider the use of these tables, the closer to reality will this dream become. The Las Vegas game may be fun for those who can afford it. Today, however, investment is no longer for only the wealthy, and the unjust exploitation of the many for the benefit of the few must be phased out—but naturally, by evolution.

There comes to mind at this time the inscription on a Hallmark Contemporary Card:[2]

> They laughed at Edison!
> They laughed at Columbus!
> They laughed at Bell!
> They laughed at Marconi!
> And they're beginning to smile at you!

---

[2] © Hallmark Cards, Incorporated. Reprinted by permission.

Chapter 2

THE EVOLUTION OF
STOCK VALUE TABLES

IN ANCIENT GREECE the science of mathematics was already greatly advanced. But, as life and times change and become more complicated and involved, new needs arise. Gradually, new practical applications of mathematics develop to serve these needs. Oftentimes—especially where many varying influences are at work—it is a slow and tedious struggle to develop a workable system. High on the list of these problems is the development of a satisfactory method of determining the value of common stocks.

HISTORY OF BOND TABLES AND STOCK VALUATION MODELS

All investors are familiar with the use of bond yield tables, but few could pass the test of a detailed description of the technique of their construction; fewer still could answer the question of their origin. An interesting "Note" under the title of the above headline was published in the March, 1966, issue of *The Journal of Finance* by Professor Robert M. Soldofsky of the University of Iowa, an associate editor of that journal.[1]

Professor Soldofsky relates that through his research, a part of which was done at the New York Public Library and the Library of Congress, he discovered that the first bond yield tables were prepared by a New York banker, Joseph M. Price, and were published in 1843 in New York. The introduction to Price's tables stated that the tables were calculated with the aid of Callet's Tables of Logarithms. The yields and prices are the same as those given in bond tables now in use. They were relatively narrow in the scope of yields and maturities, but expanded tables were given in an edition published in 1862. The original tables were so well done that Mr. Soldofsky wondered whether they had had forerunners, but none could be found.

According to the author of the same "Note," the earliest English bond tables did not appear for almost twenty years after Price's work.

Of more direct interest are Professor Soldofsky's remarks in the same "Note"

---

[1] Robert M. Soldofsky, "A Note on the History of Bond Tables and Stock Valuation Models," *The Journal of Finance*, pp. 103–11 (March 1966).

concerning the history of equations suitable for stock valuation models. He states that the "expression of one of these equations dates back to at least 1869." According to Soldofsky, a textbook of the Institute of Actuaries, published in England in 1882, contained a section on varying annuities. The author of the textbook stated that "annuities may be increasing or decreasing, that their progressions may be arbitrary, arithmetic, geometric, or follow some other law of progression." The textbook referred to a leading paper on the subject published in 1869 by the *Journal of Institute of Actuaries, and Assurance Magazine.* ". . . actuaries were hired as consultants to estimate the value of real property. The procedure in the case of a mining property was to estimate the prospective receipts, the prospective expenditures, and to discount each back to the date designated." The editor of the above-mentioned journal, Mr. T. B. Sprague, a very distinguished person in his own field, gave at the end of the paper a formula for computing annuities increasing geometrically.[2] This was the seed from which tables for stock valuation very gradually developed.

THE PIONEER

We cannot approach this subject without rendering due homage to Samuel Eliot Guild, the unquestioned pioneer of stock value tables.

It was on January 1, 1939, in Boston that Mr. Guild (rhymes with mild) wrote the acknowledgments to those who helped him prepare his stock growth and discount tables. The first man to whom Guild expressed his thanks was "Dr. T. H. Brown of the Statistical Department of the Harvard School of Business Administration, not only for his invaluable assistance in developing the philosophy upon which these Tables are based, but particularly for his patience and genius in calculating the formulae used in their computation."

In April, 1931, the Financial Publishing Company of Boston brought out the book entitled *Stock Growth and Discount Tables* by Samuel Eliot Guild.[3] As with so many other efforts to blaze new trails, it would be an exaggeration to say that it met with instant recognition. Few copies were sold when it came out. Guild worked on his book for two years and published it at his own expense, which was quite high as all the calculations had to be done longhand. Many Harvard students were enrolled for the job. As mentioned above, for expert guidance and the mathematical construction of his formulas, Guild leaned on Professor Theodore H. Brown of the Harvard Business School, who had also taught mathematics, economics, and business subjects at Yale, Brown, and Columbia. He is now Professor Emeritus of Business Statistics of the Harvard Business School. This author felt that it was very fortunate that he was able to prevail upon him to write a companion piece in the same issue of the *Journal*

---

[2] Ibid., p. 107.

[3] Samuel Eliot Guild, *Stock Growth and Discount Tables* (Boston: Financial Publishing Co., 1931).

in which Guild's article was published.[4] Guild's other expert collaborator was the late Stephen Heard, partner in charge of research of the State Street Research and Management Corporation. Outside of general advice and help, Heard also contributed an appendix to the book on the valuation of warrants.

In his article published in the September–October, 1964, issue of the *Financial Analysts Journal*,[5] Guild wrote of his theory as follows:

> There is one fact which no investor can ignore—"The Bloodless Verdict of the Market Place." As related to the current price of an individual stock, this "verdict" often turns out to have been unrealistic when reviewed by hindsight. The analyst's work is to decide whether the current price is too high or too low as related to his own estimates of the stock's future prospects.
>
> Admittedly, we can never make anything approaching such exact estimates of the returns we will receive from our stocks as bondholders can from their bonds.
>
> However, for any given *rate of return*, we can at least eliminate guesswork as to whether the current price of a stock is too high or too low, insofar as it reflects our estimates of the future *trend of growth* of its earnings; the probable percentage *dividend payout* from such earnings; the *number of times its earnings* it can reasonably be expected to sell for at the end of any given *period;* and know the *current price* at which a stock should be bought to produce the desired return upon the basis of our estimates.
>
> There are thus six variables for a stock against only four for a bond, all of which are known and not estimated. For any *yield to maturity* a Bond Yield Table will combine the *rate of a bond's coupon* with its *years to maturity* and give us the *current price* at which a bond should be bought to produce any given return.
>
> If a bondholder buys a 5% bond payable at par, he can capitalize his $50 income from his coupons upon a 5% basis and count upon receiving $1,000 when his bond is redeemed at maturity. This is not true in the case of a stockholder

Guild's method of computing the present worth of common stocks consists in a clear-cut separation of the discounted income stream, received before the sale of the stock, from the discounted value of the sale's proceeds. The sale may be purely conceptual. In appraising the stock's value, an investor may project, as far into the future as he deems reasonably visible, the income to be received from the stock, discounting each annual payment to find the sum of their present worths. He is then faced with the additional problem of estimating the probable price at which the stock could be sold and discounting the price of the sale at the same rate of return as was applied to dividend payments. The sum of the present worths of income payments plus the present worth of the conceptual resale represents the present value of the stock. Guild emphasizes this point on page 42 of his book. He states that, in actual practice: "Stocks are bought for appreciation of principal as well as for an anticipated increase in their rate of

---

[4] Theodore H. Brown, "Price-Earnings Discount Chart for Growth Stocks," *Financial Analysts Journal*, Vol. 20, no. 5: 98–103 (September–October 1964).

[5] Samuel Eliot Guild, "The Case for Stock Value Tables," *Financial Analysts Journal*, vol. 20, no. 5: 80 (September–October 1964).

dividend, so that these two factors together represent the rewards upon which the value of a common stock is based. The sum of these two rewards may be termed the 'investment return' or 'total investment return' as contrasted with the 'dividend return'."

AT LONG LAST INTEREST IS REVIVED

The fact that Guild's book came out in the depth of the depression, when interest in common stock values was at its low, was another factor contributing to the silence which engulfed its appearance. But general indifference and ignorance of the subject by analysts and investors was probably even more to blame. The interest in the theory of present worth and the possibilities of its applications to the solution of investment problems failed to be revived even by the monumental work of John Burr Williams, already mentioned. Two decades had to elapse before Professor John C. Clendenin of the University of California in Los Angeles (now Professor Emeritus) created a stir in academia and among financial analysts by publishing in the February, 1957, issue of *Trusts and Estates* an article on "Common Stock Values."[6] It called attention to dividend growth as a determinant of common stock values and to the use of the present worth method. It stated that "the value of a share at any given time is simply the present value of the probable future dividends as foreseen at that time."

The groundwork for a favorable reception of this thesis had been already laid by a previous article by Clendenin in co-authorship with Maurice Van Cleave, a retired navy officer who was at the time teaching at San Diego State College. This study, "Growth and Common Stock Values," was published in the December 1954 issue of *The Journal of Finance*.[7] These two papers contained examples of calculations and brief stock value tables. Neither mentioned Guild's name but both referred to the "Theory of Investment Value" by John Burr Williams.

In the middle 1950's investors were watching the unfolding of a powerful bull market and their interest in stocks was high. Clendenin's 1957 brochure met with keen response. To meet the demand Professor Clendenin enlarged his pamphlet and later in the year the UCLA Bureau of Business and Economic Research brought out his *Theory and Technique of Growth Stock Valuation*.

Not many papers had so strong an impact on analysts' thinking as the Clendenin-Van Cleave article. Guild's book appeared in the midst of the worst depression to face disillusioned investors. Clendenin's and Van Cleave's study showed up when a great bull market was once more in full swing. Investors were again avidly seeking concepts of growth stocks and methods of appropriate

---

[6] John C. Clendenin, "Common Stock Values," *Trusts and Estates*, pp. 104–7 (February 1957). Note: This is an abridgment of a longer study published under the title *Theory and Technique of Growth Stock Valuation* by the Bureau of Business and Economic Research, University of California, Los Angeles (1957).

[7] John C. Clendenin and Maurice Van Cleave, "Growth and Common Stock Values," *The Journal of Finance*, pp. 365–76 (incl.) (December 1954).

valuation. Tabulations of appraisals presented by the coauthors were, like Guild's, based on the principle of present worth. But their statistical material consisted of illustrations rather than elaborate and fully developed tables as contained in Guild's book. Depending on a writer's investment philosophy, the unknowns in a present value formula can be interchanged and solved in different terms. In his 1957 pamphlet, Clendenin assigns variable discount rates to different growth periods for measuring the uncertainty of future payments in relation to their position in time. A more recent book by Professor W. Scott Bauman used a similar method.

In the February, 1959, issue of *The Analysts Journal* we published an extensive article on the "Valuation of Common Stocks."[8] It was not addressed to academic scholars, but to financial analysts and investors. It reminded the readers that Benjamin Graham and David L. Dodd had mentioned in their famous work on "Security Analysis" that the doctrine of present worth had become an "accepted tenet of financial theory" (3d edition, p. 433). It discussed Guild's work at great length and with much praise. The paper was well received. In early June of the same year, the senior author was invited by the Boston Security Analysts Society to give a talk on the subject. Bill Hammond, then the partner in charge of the Boston office of White, Weld & Co. Incorporated, must have done a good public relations job, for the large auditorium was jam-packed; even the standing room was tightly crowded. At the luncheon preceeding the talk numerous members of the Boston Security Analysts Society were present. The author felt very proud, but the audience must have felt disillusioned when he had to explain that estimating a stock's investment value was not equivalent to forecasting its price.

After the talk, John Burr Williams, Eliot Guild, and this speaker walked over to Eliot's lovely apartment on the bank of the Charles River basin. It was good to meet Williams, having corresponded with him for many years. Dinner at the Harvard Club closed this memorable day.

This author had often wondered how much his appearance before the Boston Security Analysts Society and his numerous other talks over the years to other analysts societies throughout the country have contributed to the advancement of financial analysis. Yet his 1959 article—and his Boston address—gave a great boost to Eliot Guild's book of tables and indirectly may have stimulated other financial experts to compose other stock value tables, even though they did not follow each other as a forest fire, but took years to appear.

In any case, Guild's book sold more copies in 1960 than in its previous 28 years of existence. At some point in the long years since 1931, Guild had stored a few hundred copies in an old barn on his estate near Boston. When he reentered the barn to retrieve the books, he found that the bindings had been attacked by bookworms of the wrong kind. The books had to be fumigated before being reoffered for sale.

---

[8] Nicholas Molodovsky, "Valuation of Common Stocks," *The Analysts Journal*, vol. 15, no. 1: 23–27 (incl.) and 84–99 (incl.) (February 1959).

TABLES: RAISON D'ETRE

There exists an obvious need for stock value tables. Bond yield tables are now taken for granted. No professional or investor could operate without them. Yet they deal with the combinations of four factors only; if one excludes the risk of bankruptcy, all the four factors are finite and are expressions of certainty—they need no estimates. On the other hand, factors determining stock values are predominantly subject to uncertainty; they are so numerous and so complex that they cannot be effectively synthesized. Besides, many of these factors themselves which appear self-explanatory to the layman are often the subject of great debates on the scientific level of academic study as to their true nature and investment criterion merits. The frequent self-defense attitude of the practical man is that he does not care about the lucubrations of the eggheads; just give him the facts and let his common sense decide. Yet the so-called facts are often treacherous, hiding many unknowns; and the so-called common sense often leads to no sense at all when it wields its heavy axe on delicate structures which can be dissected only by the scalpel of the most sophisticated logic.

The time needed for the solution of a problem is also an important consideration. The examples in our 1959 article were all handmade valuations, laboriously worked out with the aid of a trusty table of logarithms. It is a standing joke with us that this faithful friend qualifies as a museum piece. Over the years of development and testing of our method, the pages have become so fragile that they must be handled with the utmost care and, in some places, the ink is worn off to such an extent that they are completely illegible and a substitute table has to be used as a supplement, albeit reluctantly. Furthermore, if, after working up the value based on what we thought was the outlook for a company, unexpected developments or newly acquired information changed the prospects, all new calculations had to be made. With reliable tables, the different values under changed conditions could be read off the table with no more work to be done beyond possibly a simple multiplication.

THE NEWCOMERS

Among the newcomers to the field of stock value tables, the one whose tables are closest in theory to Guild's is probably George E. Bates, James R. Williston Professor of Investment Management, Emeritus, of Harvard University Graduate School of Business Administration, George F. Baker Foundation. He is the author of "Comprehensive Stock Value Tables," which appeared in the January–February, 1962, issue of *Harvard Business Review.* His "Letter of Comment" followed in the May–June *HBR* of the same year.[9]

---

[9] George E. Bates, "Comprehensive Stock Value Tables," *Harvard Business Review,* pp. 53–67. (January–February 1962). Also "Letter of Comment," *HBR* (May–June 1962). Note: The original article, corrected, the material in the "Letter of Comment," and some subsequent minor additions are available in a single reprint issued by the *Harvard Business Review.*

Although his tables were developed only in 1961, Professor Bates explained to the senior author of this book in a letter dated September 27, 1966, that, as far back as the academic year 1928–1929, when giving a course in investment banking at Harvard, ". . . the discounting of future earnings implicit in the prices of many stocks led [him] to develop a formula for testing the assumptions presumably underlying the increased multiples being applied to earnings." At that time, however, he had no thought of using it to develop tables for general use. When Mr. Guild's tables appeared, however, he always had them on the library reference shelves and brought them to the attention of his students. Professor Bates explained further in his letter that the high multiples at which many stocks were selling in 1960 and 1961 caused him to "emphasize to students . . . the desirability of using the Guild tables." The problem was, however, that the library had only one or two copies while their cost was prohibitive for students. It was this need which inspired Bates to "concoct tables which would fit into the compass of a *Harvard Business Review* article."

Professor Bates did accomplish the difficult feat of presenting full-fledged tables within the concentrated space of two pages of *HBR*—two pages which actually include considerably more than is covered in the 128 pages of Guild's basic Table IV. In addition, he added some refinements to Guild's work, such as a subdivision of the tables for pre-tax and after-tax yields. The reduced size of his tables has its advantages, though some investors might not find it an unmitigated blessing. As Professor Bates put it in his letter, the disadvantage is that "the user has to do a little pencil-pushing." We might add that, although this pencil-pushing does not require complete understanding of the theory and formulas behind the actual tables—since instructions and examples are given— nevertheless a quite comprehensive understanding of the investment principles involved is necessary to make intelligent estimates for the various necessary assumptions. This the students had. But do all investors?

With some variations, both Guild and Bates enter their tables with similar investment requirements and estimates. Essentially they try to solve the present worth problem in terms of a future price-earnings ratio in order to find a desired yield.

In 1963 the Bureau of Business Research of the University of Michigan offered a "study of the present value theory and a practical solution to the problems of common stock valuation." This was the subtitle of a book of investment analysis and tables, written and computed by Professor W. Scott Bauman, then of the University of Toledo and now Executive Director of The Institute of Chartered Financial Analysts, and carrying at its masthead the words "Estimating the Present Value of Common Stocks by the Variable Rate Method." In this book Dr. Bauman held to the idea that the size of the discount rate should be related to the passage of time, and this concept underlies the computations of the tables included therein. He emphasized that the "amount of income that an investor estimates he will receive from a stock in the distant future is subject to greater error and hence to more uncertainty than his estimates for the near future."[10]

Recently, however, Dr. Bauman wrote to this author that he has given additional thought to the idea of increasing the size of the discount rate over future time. He now feels that, "although this concept is theoretically sound, it has several undesirable limitations from a practical standpoint." The first is that investors are much more accustomed to using a single (or constant) discount rate—which can be compared with other commonly used rates such as bond yields to maturity and portfolio rates of return. Not the least of these limitations is the difficulty of determining by what amount future discount rates should be raised.

Dr. Bauman's latest model and present value tables—which give "Dividend Multipliers and Dividend Yield Percentages"—are described in his article entitled "Investment Returns and Present Values" in the November–December, 1969, issue of the *Financial Analysts Journal.* This article has been reprinted along with an Appendix of forty-five Tables by the College of Business Administration of the University of Oregon.[11]

COMPOUND INTEREST TABLES

In order to determine what the earnings of a stock will be after a given period of expected growth, compound interest tables are most helpful and easy to use.

One of the best of such tables was first published in 1956 by Borden Helmer, economist of Union Carbide Corporation. It includes growth rates up to 100 percent and can be applied to many uses. It was frequently revised by its author who also often expanded its introduction. Mr. Helmer has now retired, but Union Carbide still gives the tables for the asking as a gesture of good will.[12]

A splendid brief manual on the use of compound interest and annuity tables in equity valuation and portfolio management was composed by W. Edward Bell, C.F.A., then vice president of Crocker-Citizens National Bank and past president of the Security Analysts of San Francisco. His study was published in the

---

[10] W. Scott Bauman, *Estimating the Present Value of Common Stocks by the Variable Rate Method* (Ann Arbor: Bureau of Business Research, Graduate School of Business Administration, the University of Michigan, 1963) Michigan Business Reports Number 42, p. 11.

[11] W. Scott Bauman, *Investment Returns and Present Values and an Appendix of 45 Tables,* (Eugene, Ore.: College of Business Administration, University of Oregon, 1969), Faculty Studies in Business Administration, Reprint Series No. 97.

[12] *Compound Interest Tables,* distributed by the Public Relations Department of Union Carbide Corporation, 270 Park Avenue, New York, New York 10017.

Other Compound Interest Tables:

"Compound Interest Tables for Long-Term Planning in Forestry" Agriculture Handbook No. 311, U.S. Department of Agriculture, Forest Service. (For sale by the Superintendent of Documents, U.S. Government Printing Office, Washington, D.C., 20402.)

"Financial Compound Interest and Annuity Tables," 5th edition, Financial Publishing Co., 82 Brookline Avenue, Boston, Massachusetts 02215. (This is probably the most complete book of such tables available, containing 1640 pages.)

May-June, 1964, issue of the *Financial Analysts Journal.*[13] At present Professor Bell teaches finance and management at San José State College, California.

OTHER STOCK VALUE TABLES

Another relatively recent book, *Growth Yields on Common Stock: Theory and Tables,* was published by the State University of Iowa in 1963. Its authors are Professors Robert M. Soldofsky of the University of Iowa and James T. Murphy of Tulane University.[14] Like most of the other analysts using the present worth approach to equity valuation, Soldofsky and Murphy dismember each stock into two distinct components: the dividend stream and the price of resale. However, in drawing a dividing line at the point of the expected selling price, they compute present value as the sum of two separate, discounted, income streams, before and after the conceptual sale.

Beginning with S. E. Guild, all architects of stock value tables have rendered great service to investment analysis; but it still remains largely potential. The number of assumptions to be made by the investor must be reduced. Such assumptions will still be estimates as against the known variables for the valuation of bonds. Their number, therefore, must be a minimum.

The task is to dissolve as many unknowns as possible in computer-generated relationships, thus leaving the investor to make only a few vital judgments. The resulting valuations offered by such simplified tables could be used for appraising individual stocks. By means of some additional data processing, they could also serve for portfolio construction by private and institutional investors.

In 1965, in the March-April edition of the *Financial Analysts Journal,*[15] we presented tables which were basically a mechanization of the handmade valuations made in our above-mentioned 1959 article on "Valuation of Common Stocks." Here, the only necessary assumptions were the projected growth rate of earnings and the years of constant and declining growth expected. These were in the nature of a test of the practicability of constructing tables with the aid of the computer. We believe that this test was successful.

THE ROAD AHEAD

As we have indicated, the result we sought was to set up computer-generated tables which would not only greatly simplify the appraisal of stocks but also reduce the margin of error and make comparisons of stocks more valid by putting

---

[13] W. Edward Bell, "Compound Interest and Annuity Tables and Their Use in Equity Valuation and Portfolio Management," *Financial Analysts Journal.,* vol. 20, no. 3: 111–117 (incl.) (May–June 1964).

[14] Robert M. Soldofsky and James T. Murphy, *Growth Yields on Common Stock: Theory and Tables* (Ames, Iowa: State University of Iowa, 1963).

[15] Nicholas Molodovsky, Catherine May, and Sherman Chottiner, "Common Stock Valuation— Principles, Tables and Application," *Financial Analysts Journal,* vol. 21, no. 2: 104–123 (incl.) (March–April 1965).

them on a common denominator. The Valuator included in this book is the product of our efforts. In these tables, as a result of considerable experimentation and discussion, we have followed more faithfully the 1959 method of determining the relationship between growth of earnings and payout. Furthermore, completely independent relationships have been developed for industrials and for utilities. Thus there are completely separate sets of tables for use in evaluating these different types of stocks. The residual growth rate has also been revised in the light of present conditions.

The development of our theory and its advance to full fruition in the tables in this book are covered in Chapters 3 and 4.

Before closing this historical chapter, we must not neglect to mention a very significant newcomer to the field of stock valuation—the time-sharing computer. Professor J. Peter Williamson, of the Amos Tuck School of Business Adminstration of Dartmouth College, in 1966 sent us a copy of the running of a computer program written by one of his students to handle our method of calculating theoretical value. At the time, Williamson pointed out that it offers a little more flexibility than the tables do and, on the whole, is a "very useful substitute for the tables . . . at least for anyone who has access to a time-sharing computer." (If only everyone did!)

In the summer of 1970, Professor Williamson combined some earlier programs into an improved one which applies the intrinsic value theory and which is available to anyone using the Dartmouth computer. In acknowledgement of the source of the theory, the program has been officially named NICKMOL. The latest revision and write-up of the program is contained in the manual in a book of computer manuals published in September 1970 by the Amos Tuck School, Dartmouth College.[16]

This is just the beginning of what can and surely will develop in this era of technology. But for the time being, until all investors have ready access to a time-sharing computer, tables are the "next best."

---

[16] J. Peter Williamson and David H. Downes, *Manuals for Computer Programs in Finance and Investments* (Hanover, New Hampshire: The Amos Tuck School, Dartmouth College, 1970) Manual No. 5.

Chapter 3

A THEORY FOR
STOCK VALUATION

"To bring the hopeful out of the wilderness," says a master and teacher extraordinary, "I have endeavored to show that building one's best skill is basically a matter of laying one little essential brick of fact on top of another. The confusion comes from the readiness of the uninformed to believe that this skill is an abstruse affair with secrets deeply concealed instead of a fundamentally simple thing for human enjoyment."[1]

These sage remarks about golf can be applied to investment. It too is really a simple activity devoid of magical secrets, conducive to human satisfaction and welfare, and in which proficiency is attained by clearing away the incidentals and, brick by brick, building a structure of fundamental facts.

Another great teacher and master, whose career has also been unfolding in demanding areas, but in somewhat different fields of endeavor, tells about a scientist and his efforts "to clear a space in the tangled underbrush of fact and fancy so closely interwoven and cemented by strange words."[2]

President Conant enriches the advice of Tommy Armour. We shall be guided by both the educator-diplomat and the philosopher-pro. After clearing some ground we shall start laying brick on brick.

COWLES COMMISSION FOR RESEARCH IN ECONOMICS

The foundation on which we built had to be sound. In 1939 the Cowles Commission for Research in Economics published monthly indexes of common stock prices for the years 1871–1938. They also provided, on an annual basis, earnings-price ratios and yields and the corresponding indexes of earnings and dividends as well as a price index of stocks for which earnings data were available. The Commission had originally planned to take its indexes back to a still earlier period. An extensive survey, however, revealed the scarcity of data. Information on capital structure, earnings, and dividends of industrial and utility stocks was

---

[1] Tommy Armour, *How to Play Your Best Golf All the Time* (New York: Simon & Schuster, 1953), p. 148.

[2] James B. Conant, *On Understanding Science* (New Haven: Yale University Press, 1947), p. 80.

193

practically nonexistent for the years before 1871. Consequently, the period covered by the indexes could not have been longer nor their scope wider.

As stated in the introduction to its Monograph 3:

> The purpose of the Cowles Commission common-stock indexes is to portray the average experience of those investing in this class of security in the United States from 1871 to 1938. The indexes of stock prices are intended to represent, ignoring the elements of brokerage charges and taxes, what would have happened to an investor's funds if he had bought at the beginning of 1871 all stocks quoted on the New York Stock Exchange, allocating his purchases among the individual issues in proportion to their total monetary value, and each month up to 1938 had by the same criterion redistributed his holdings among all quoted stocks.[3]

In brief, the Commission set itself the task of putting together the longest and broadest historical record of average common stock experience. In order to make it possible to extend its indexes into the future, it spliced them to the indexes of Standard Statistics Company, which, by merger, has since become Standard & Poor's Corporation.

THE "500" INDEX

This great statisical organization has fully lived up to the trust placed in it by the Commission. On March 1, 1957, it initiated a price index of 500 stocks, representing more than 90 percent of the market value of all common stocks listed on the New York Stock Exchange. These 500 stocks are the composite of 425 industrials, 55 public utilities, and 20 railroad stocks. "These Standard & Poor's Stock Price Indexes, which are based on the aggregate market value of the common stocks of all the companies in the sample, express the observed market value as a percentage of the average market value during the base period. . . . On March 1, 1957, the current base, 1941–43 equal to 10, was adopted."[4]

In order to provide as long and as comparable an index as possible, Standard & Poor's, in turn, has converted, to the 1941–1943 base, the Cowles Commission Price Indexes for the years 1871–1917. For 1918–1925, they used the S&P Weekly Indexes based on 200–416 stocks, adjusted to the new base. After being likewise converted to the new base, the S&P Daily Index of 90 stocks was used for the period from 1926 through February 28, 1957.

Regarding earnings and dividends, Standard & Poor's has used those series of their 90-stock index, for 1926–1957, and converted them to the 1941–1943

---

[3] Alfred Cowles 3rd and Associates, *Common Stock Indexes—Monograph No. 3 of Cowles Commission for Research in Economics* (Principia Press, 1939, out-of-print), p. 2.

[4] *Standard & Poor's Trade and Securities Statistics,* Standard & Poor's Stock Price Indexes—Description of Method Used in Computation (New York: Standard & Poor's, 1970), p. 2.

base. Beginning in 1957, the earnings and dividend series are based on the 500 stocks.

NECESSARY ADJUSTMENTS IN THE INDEXES

For our research involving relationships among prices, earnings, and dividends, however, it was imperative that only strictly comparable data be used. In order to achieve this to the greatest possible degree, certain adjustments had to be made in the data of the early years.

The price indexes, as published by S&P for the years 1871–1917, could not be used because, although they were computed from the prices of all stocks quoted on the New York Stock Exchange, earnings and dividends were not available for all of them. Thus relationships between these series would be invalid. Fortunately, the Cowles Commission had foreseen such a need and had prepared, on an annual basis, a price index of "stocks for which earnings data are available," as well as yields based on those same stocks. By adjusting this price index to the 1941–1943 base for the years 1871–1917 and splicing it to the S&P "500" from 1918 to date, there emerged a price index for the entire period from 1871 which could logically be related to available earnings data.

At the time of this writing, S&P had given us series of earnings and dividends adjusted to the price indexes, only from 1926 to date. Again it was necessary to go back to Cowles and apply to the adjusted price index, described in the preceding paragraph, the appropriate earnings-price ratios and yields (of stocks for which earnings data were available). Thus we produced probably the best possible earnings and dividend series adjusted to the longest and best available comparable price index.

From 1926 to date S&P's earnings and dividend series were used as published with only one exception: 1932 earnings. In this case, in order to give recognition to the many deficits in earnings that year, the earnings were calculated from the Cowles Commission Earnings-Price ratio. The S&P earnings were calculated by using zero for all deficits. This produced, in the case of the "500" Composite Index, an earnings figure of 0.41 and a P/E ratio of 16.9, in 1932, as compared with earnings of 0.05 and P/E of 138.9 when the Cowles E/P is used. The latter is more representative of the bottom of the most severe of all bear markets.

CHART OF BASIC RELATIONS

This period from 1871–1970—a full century—is so long and the indexes used are so broad that the relations they depict are the quintessence of the general. Some shorter segments of this period, or less comprehensive indexes, would be likely to produce different numerical results, colored by the characteristics of the segment and the nature of the indexes chosen. However, our chart, entitled Basic Relations in the Stock Market, records the basic traits shared in common by the entire species and which are, therefore, typical of all its members.

FIGURE 3.1
Basic Relations in the Stock Market

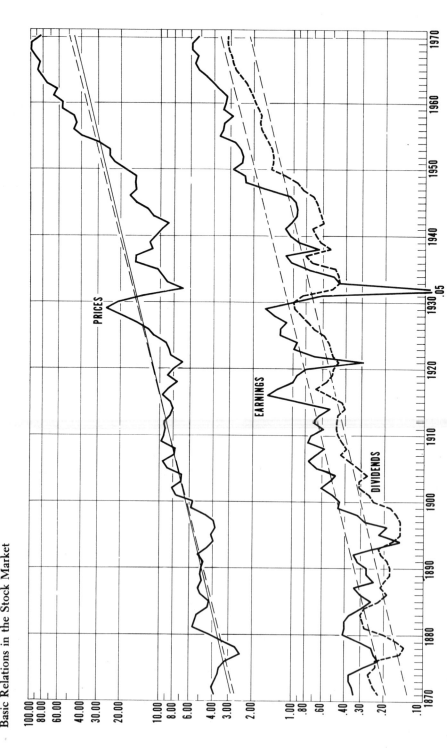

Through the curves of prices, earnings, and dividends long-term trend lines can be drawn. These 100-year trend lines were fitted to the logarithms of the data by the method of least squares. Thus, on our chart—with semi-logarithmic ruling—trends are straight lines representing constant compound annual growth rates. The significant thing about these trends is that all three are virtually parallel. Prices grew at an average rate of 3.04 percent, earnings at 3.00 percent, and dividends at 2.84 percent. Differences are so small as not to be significant, being due chiefly to rounding out decimals—and this in spite of the fact that it was impossible to use precisely whole numbers of cycles in each case. It is interesting at this point to look back at the corresponding trend lines found in our 1959 study.[5] During the period from 1871–1958 prices grew 1.99 percent per year, earnings 2.13 percent, and dividends 2.12 percent. Since that study was made before the powerful surge of the 1960's, the growth rates were considerably lower. But the important thing is that the fundamental, underlying bond of relationship among these three principal factors of the stock market was just as conspicuously there.

Logic also confirms that these variables should move similarly. Dividends obviously flow out of earnings, and thus earnings are the main source of the "value" which the prices purchase. They may pull apart temporarily for one reason or another, but in the long run, variations even out, and the long-term trends continue to follow parallel paths.

Various other useful observations can be made from our chart by exploring the mutual relations of the trend lines. Based on their midpoints, the average current yield (i.e. the percentage which the dividends are of price) was shown to be 4.67 percent for the entire 100 years from 1871–1970. This is somewhat lower than the 4.96 percent which had been found for the period ending with 1958. This difference also is in accord with the laws of financial life, because current yield tends to vary inversely as the growth rate of earnings. A similar observation can be made in regard to the average payout—i.e., the percentage of earnings which is paid out in dividends. For the entire period shown on the chart, the mean payout was 63.60 percent, whereas for the shorter period of slower growth it was 67 percent. We shall have more to say about payout later in this chapter.

Our chart passes through most of modern American economic history. During its 100 years, stock prices and their earnings and dividends have been subject to an infinite variety of events and changes, to virtually all conceivable economic and political developments and contingencies short of the destruction of the free enterprise system. And, as already stressed, the data used to reflect their vicissitudes are as all-inclusive as the period itself.

The year 1970, the most recent to appear on the chart, was the last port of call on a long historical voyage. Thus the points which the trend lines touch in 1970 reflect not only current conditions and those governing the recent past,

---

[5] Nicholas Molodovsky, "Valuation of Common Stocks," *The Analysts Journal,* vol. 15, no. 1: 25 (February 1959).

but also the relations prevailing in every single year since 1871. They are just as representative of the interrelations between stock prices, dividends, and earnings that are typical for the great bull market since World War II as for the times of World War I, or even of the years after the Civil War. In fact, what our chart offers is not a measure for any particular year of the period it covers, but an expression of historical norms of interrelations between prices, earnings, and dividends of common stocks.

The existence of various historical relations which can be read from the basic chart suggests the intriguing thought that they could be used for evaluating and comparing stocks. They are the ultimate common denominators to which all stocks can be reduced, revealing conditions underlying the economics of the stock market. If we could distill from all stocks the measurements they have in common, we could appraise each in terms of all the others.

Such a generalization or normalization of value would not destroy or drown out any individual characteristics of the particular stock we may wish to appraise. On the contrary, against the background of the merged features typical for the entire species, its own special traits will stand out in bolder relief. The most desirable of all conceivable standards of value, it would measure all stocks in terms of one another by what they have in common beneath their separate superstructures.

THEORY OF PRESENT WORTH

Basic relations is a challenge. It points unquestionably to the theory of "present worth." This doctrine in its simplest form is found in compound interest tables. Furthermore, it is the underlying principle on which bond tables are constructed.

More complicated is its application to common stocks, although it has not lacked able defenders. The earliest published work in this connection that we have been able to find was made by Robert G. Wiese. Two articles by Wiese appeared in *Barron's* in September, 1930.[6] The earliest substantial pioneering work on the subject was the tables of Samuel Eliot Guild which appeared a few months later. (See Chapter 2 for comments on his tables as well as a brief history of other stock value tables.)

Now it is our aim to carry the ball a few yards farther down the line.

RATE OF RETURN

Essential to the idea of present worth is the discount rate, or rate of return, which may also be thought of, in connection with stocks, as "total or effective yield."

Obviously, the current dividend yield falls far short of measuring the effective

---

[6] Robert G. Wiese, "Investing for True Values," *Barron's* (September 8 and 15, 1930).

yield when dividends continue to grow from year to year. The total return must also take into account the full effects of this growth. As a simple example, suppose you invested $10,000 in stocks which, in the first year, paid dividends totaling $500, you would receive a current yield of 5 percent the first year. If, however, the dividends continue to grow at the average rate of 4 percent per year, each subsequent year's dividends will represent a larger percentage of the $10,000 investment. This is the reason for the concurrent increase in the "value" of the stocks. Assuming that the average current yield continues at 5 percent, capitalizing the increased dividends at 5 percent would make each increment in the value of the stocks 20 times as much as the corresponding increment in the dividends. Actually, the total effective yield, in this example, would be at the rate of 9.2 percent per year.

In the case of our chart of Basic Relations in the Stock Market (Figure 3.1), the average rate of return over the 100 years has been 7.81 percent. If this is used as the discount rate of future dividends growing continuously, ad infinitum, at the rate of 3 percent per annum, then the sum of the present values of all such future dividends, i.e., value, at any point in time, would equal 21.4 times the corresponding point on the dividend trend line. This result is the same as if the dividends are capitalized at 4.67 percent—which is the average current yield for the 100 years.

This line of present worth has been drawn on our chart; indeed it is almost superimposed upon the trend line of prices. Most of the time the two lines are so close that they can scarcely be separated. They cross approximately in the center of the period and only at its two extremes is the distance between them measurable.

Since the line of present worth is the same as the capitalized dividend trend line, it also exactly parallels the latter. Those of our readers who remember the formulas for compound interest and geometric progressions can double-check us.

Let d = any particular point on the dividend trend line

ΣPV = sum of the present values of all future dividends from the chosen point in time ad infinitum

CCD = capitalized current dividend

In our simple example above:

$$\Sigma PV = \frac{1 + .04}{.092 - .04} \times d = 20 \times d$$

$$CCD = \frac{1}{.05} \times d = 20 \times d$$

In our chart of Basic Relations:

$$\Sigma PV = \frac{1 + .03}{.0781 - .03} \times d = 21.4 \times d$$

$$CCD = \frac{1}{.0467} \times d = 21.4 \times d$$

On the other hand, the trend line of prices was independently fitted to the entire price series. The virtual identity of these three lines not only confirms the logic of the theory of present worth as applied to stocks but also the concurrence of average price with value. This is the foundation on which our theory of valuation is built.

NATURE OF THE COMMON STOCK UNIVERSE

In describing above the reasons why the total rate of return on stocks is greater than the annual current yield whenever growth is present, reference was made not only to the increasing dividends but also to the important increases in value resulting therefrom as time passes on. We then proceeded to demonstrate that "value" is expressed in full by the sum of all discounted future dividends ad infinitum. A moment's thought makes the logic of this apparent. Since the initial and near-term dividends are increasing from year to year, the total of all their present values must increase.

It is possible, even natural, to think of the value of common stocks as the sum of dividend income received plus resale price. The prevalence of short-term trading keeps this image before us. This does not, however, represent the true nature of stocks. Regardless of the number of times that ownership of a stock may change, its basic value remains unaffected. This must be so because value is essentially a relatively stable thing which reflects the corporate health of a company.

Stocks have no maturity. They keep moving through time. As long as the company whose stock we are appraising remains afloat on the industrial stream, no terminal point will be in sight for its actual or potential dividend payments. In contrast to bonds, whose future is precisely delineated and finite, stocks dwell in an "open end" world. The "open end" nature of the common stock universe is clearly apparent from the chart of Basic Relations in the Stock Market (Figure 3.1). Time constitutes its most important dimension.

Furthermore, an investor who has mentally cut up the essential unity of a stock into conceptual income and principal segments in order to simplify his thinking must be exceedingly careful how he appraises the resale price.

Even a purely conceptual seller cannot set the price at which his stock should be sold without estimating the probable future prospects at the time of his theoretical resale. He must determine the prospective capitalizer of estimated future earnings. This multiplier must have a direct numerical functional relation to the future rate, or rates, of the estimated growth of dividends and earnings.

It is considerably more hazardous to make projections into the future from the point of potential resale, in order to estimate its present value, than to begin projections into the future from the present only. It was because of all the uncertainties surrounding each of the future unknown variables that we worked to develop a method of valuation which required an absolute minimum of assumptions.

THE HYPOTHETICAL OR NORMAL DIVIDEND

As we mentioned above, the present worth theory has long been recognized. One of the most important works in which it was applied to the valuation of common stocks is John Burr Williams's *Theory of Investment Value.* He states very clearly and concisely that "a stock is worth the present value of its future dividends, with future dividends dependent on future earnings. . . . True value thus depends on the distribution rate for earnings, which rate is itself determined by the reinvestment needs of the business."[7]

As shown above, the chart of Basic Relations in the Stock Market confirmed that value was equal to the present worth of all future dividends. It demonstrated, likewise, that dividends followed on the heels of earnings, being, in individual years, varying percentages of earnings, but, in the long run, following a parallel trend. It was also pointed out that in the shorter period (ending in 1958), when the average growth rate was lower, the payout rate was somewhat higher than in the 100-year period. This too is logical because the faster a company is growing the larger is the percentage of its income which must be plowed back—retained earnings—for use in the development and expansion of the business, and therefore, the lower is the percentage which can prudently be paid out in dividends.

These relationships suggested that if present worth could be computed directly from earnings, thereby completely sidestepping any need of estimating actual future dividends, much work would be avoided and the margin of error reduced.

As mentioned above, though the trend lines of earnings and dividends run parallel and are interchangeable as a capitalization base on our chart, this long-

---

[7] John Burr Williams, *The Theory of Investment Value* (Cambridge, Mass.: Harvard University Press, 1938), p. 397.

For Further Reading about Present Worth:

Frederick R. Macaulay, *Some Theoretical Problems Suggested by the Movements of Interest Rates, Bond Yields and Stock Prices in the United States since 1856* (New York: National Bureau of Economic Research, 1938), pp. 129–35.

Gabriel A. D. Preinreich, *The Nature of Dividends* (Lancaster Press, 1935).

Edward Sherwood Mead and Julius Grodinsky, *The Ebb and Flow of Investment Values* (New York: Appleton-Century, 1939), pp. 65 and 84.

Chelcie C. Bosland, *The Common Stock Theory of Investment: Its Development and Significance* (New York: Ronald Press, 1937), p. 67.

Willford I. King, "Price-Earnings, Price-Dividends and Price-Surplus Ratios in Depressions," *The Analyst* (January 2, 1931).

Michael W. Keran, "Expectations, Money, and the Stock Market," *Review,* vol. 53, no. 1: 16–31 (incl.) (January 1971). (Published by the Federal Reserve Bank of St. Louis.)

NOTE: In his "Conclusion" (p. 31) Keran states in part: "It is shown that the standard theory of stock price determination, that is, discounting to present value expected future earnings, provides a solid theoretical base for a reasonably good empirical explanation of stock price movements in the past fifteen years. The major factors determining stock prices are shown to be expected corporate earnings and current interest rates. The interest rate in turn is determined by expectations of inflation, the real growth rate, and the change in real money."

Daniel Seligman, "A Bad New Era for Common Stocks," *Fortune,* vol. 84, no. 4: 72–75, 168–79 (incl.) (October 1971).

term historical relation will not necessarily prevail during shorter periods even for indexes of the general market and still less so for individual stocks. It was necessary, therefore, to find norms of relations between earnings and dividends under varying rates of their respective growths.

In order to discover these special norms of relationships, exhaustive series of overlapping trend lines of earnings and dividends for the Standard & Poor's index of 425 industrial stocks had to be worked up. Overlapping periods were used in order to get as large a sample as possible. Based on these periods—58 in each group, industrials and utilities—earnings growth rates and their corresponding payout ratios were determined and correlated to get the regression equations which express algebraically the mean relationship between earnings growth and payout for each group. These lines also were fitted by the least-squares method in order to eliminate any possibility of subjective influence and also to assure that the resulting equations would be completely manipulable algebraically. This is essential for inclusion in the computer program as part of the valuation formula— which is basically a combination of the formulas of compound interest and of geometric progressions.

These regression equations, by expressing the average relationship between payout and the growth of earnings, actually express dividends in terms of earnings and the growth rates of earnings. In other words, a corresponding hypothetical or normal dividend can be computed for any rate of growth or decline in a short-term trend line of earnings. Even though these relations are not immutable natural laws, and are subject to change, they are a reflection of average past experience and are by far more consistent than actual dividends may be in many particular cases—subject, as they are, to widely varying policies of management and quite often completely absent in rapidly growing companies.

THE GREAT TEST

We can hear the skeptics protesting that what is true of these century-long basic trends and relations may not even remotely resemble the results derived from a sequence of short-term trends such as must be used when estimating value today from projected future trends of earnings. As a matter of fact, this writer is the greatest skeptic of all, the personification of the double-check.

Instead of the long-term overall trend lines, short periods of fluctuating actual earnings were taken. Into these were fitted numerous short-term trend lines, each with its own particular and widely varying rate of growth or decline. From these short periods theoretical normal dividends were computed and present worths were based on them. It was consoling to see the normal dividends weave around the actual dividends. The indescribable thrill, however, lay in the final result. After six large pages full of algebraic manipulations of minute figures, a theoretical value estimate was arrived at for the year 1881. Fearfully, with bated breath, we checked the two figures which that result should resemble: the corresponding point on the trend line of prices was 4.17; the capitalized dividend trend point was 3.99. Based on the fifteen short periods, followed by an assumed continuation ad infinitum at the average secular growth rate, the calculations produced a present worth in 1881 of 4.03. Several other points along the way came out equally satisfactorily. The fundamental soundness of the hypothetical dividend, as well as of the calculation of present worth from a series of varying short-term trends, were substantiated.

THE "IGNORANCE RATE"

The purpose and great advantage of building the payout-to-growth relationship into the formula is the reduction in the number of assumptions necessary for determining value. Now, only earnings projections are needed because their growth rate indicates the payout and, therefore, the normal dividends whose present worth represents the theoretical value of a stock.

Future trends may be more clearly discerned in some cases than in others, but there will always be a certain point in time, varying for each stock, beyond which even the highest professional skill cannot make reasonably accurate projections. From this point onward we assume, as an expression of our ignorance of the future, a floating along in the mainstream of the economy at its average long-term rate.

The 3 percent growth rates shown on the chart of Basic Relations in the Stock Market (Figure 3.1) are the mean rates for the past century. However, although the interrelationships will remain, the growth rates will not necessarily remain the same. This is evident in the lower mean growth rates for the period ending in 1958, as mentioned above. It appears that various factors are working together to increase the long-term growth rate of the economy to such an extent that the average 3 percent secular trend of the past 100 years has become an understatement for the future.

A few calculations helped suggest an appropriate rate to use as the final "ignorance rate." The growth rate of the population of the United States during the last half century has been about 1.3 percent per annum. As a rough indication of the inflation rate, the Wholesale Price Index of the Bureau of Labor Statistics of the U.S. Department of Labor can be used. The average annual increase in this index since 1913 has been about 1.7 percent. The fact that the product of 101.3 percent × 101.7 percent is 103.0 percent and indicates precisely the 3 percent secular trend of our chart of Basic Relations in the Stock Market is definitely a coincidence. However, a similarity between the increases is not unreasonable but is to be expected because the growth of population requires at least that the basic economy keep pace to minister to its needs. Furthermore, this must be a "real growth," undiluted by inflation. Therefore, to compensate for the changes in the purchasing power of the dollar, the growth rate of these series of variables must include that also.[8]

---

[8] It would not be practical to use data adjusted for inflation, i.e., expressed in constant or "real" dollars, because the basic reality available for use by investors, when estimating value, is "reported per share earnings after tax" expressed in current paper dollars.

At the risk of being accused of oversimplification, which admittedly it is, a similar trend of thought was followed in connection with the future. A check with the Census Bureau revealed that the population of the United States reached 204,765,770 in 1970 and that the projection for 1975 is 219,101,000. If attained, this will represent a growth rate of close to 1.4 percent per year for these five years. Furthermore, as we are all aware, inflation has increased to extreme proportions. To use the excessive current rate, which has precipitated controlling pressures by the national government, would be unreasonable.[9] The average growth of the Wholesale Price Index from 1964 to 1970 was 2.5 percent per annum. Inflation in the 1970's has been much faster and expectations are widespread that inflation will continue at much higher rates than prevailed in the past. Even using a low estimate of 2.5 percent for the inflation rate and 1.4 percent for the population growth rate, a 4 percent basic growth rate seems to be indicated by these two factors alone.

It can also be argued that the new technology, which is bringing ever-rising standards of living, indicates a still higher growth rate in the future.

This may be so but, as the old saw goes, "discretion is the better part of valor." For a basic minimum rate to be built into the tables as the final rate of growth ad infinitum, it is far better to be conservative than to give too high values and so create "disappointment ad infinitum." Whenever a user feels that this is too conservative, his optimism can very easily be handled by the tables. He can assume a higher growth rate, for a longer period of time, and/or assume a longer period of reduction to the 4 percent ad infinitum rate. Furthermore, the further removed this "ignorance rate" is from the present, the less is its significance in terms of present value. On the other hand, if too high a terminal rate were built into the tables, there would be no easy way of adjusting for it.

WHAT RATE OF RETURN SHOULD BE USED?

As mentioned above, under "Theory of Present Worth," a decision about the discount rate, or rate of return, is an absolute essential if present value is to be calculated. Not only is it essential, but its magnitude is most important. This is obvious even to the layman, who may be allergic to mathematics, when he realizes that for each different rate of return there is a different present worth. You have but to stop and think it out logically to understand this. Suppose that you give a discounted loan to someone who promises to repay you $100 in a year.

---

[9] An indication of the importance of expected price increases is demonstrated by the spread between the "real" and "nominal" interest rates of Aaa corporate bonds on the chart prepared by the research department of the Federal Reserve Bank of St. Louis. Recently revised data indicate that, although the average nominal rate declined from a high of 8.48 percent in June, 1970, to 7.64 percent in December, the spread between the "nominal" and the "real" rates has continued to increase to a high of 4.93 percent in December, 1970. This compares with a spread of 2.03 percent in January, 1967, and 1.08 percent in January, 1962. Probably more surprising is the indication that the "real" rate has dropped from a high of 3.80 percent in June, 1970, to 2.71 percent in December, 1970—the lowest in the past ten years.

If you are satisfied with a 5 percent return, you can give him now $95.24. However, if you require a return of 10 percent, you must give him no more than $90.91, since that is the present value of $100 discounted at 10 percent for one year.

To demonstrate the significance of a change in the rate of return required from stocks, let us go back to our simple example used earlier in this chapter. It was found that the rate of return, or effective yield, was 9.2 percent per annum if $10,000 was paid for the stocks, while $500 was the total annual dividend at the time of purchase, and this dividend was to grow ad infinitum at the rate of 4 percent per year. If, instead, 10 percent return were desired, while the dividends and their growth rate remain the same, one should not pay more than $8,667 instead of $10,000 for the stocks. In other words, the present value of these dividends when discounted at 10 percent is only $8,667. There might have to be a search for new stocks.

In Thor Hultgren's[10] opinion, the yield (i.e., rate of return) an investor should look for as a minimum will depend on many circumstances, including his alternative opportunities. These circumstances are not the same for all investors at any one time, or even for the same investor at different times.

Likewise, the average return of the market in general varies considerably during different shorter periods. Changes in the economic climate are accompanied by compensating changes in the basic interest rates. These changes in turn affect the average return on stocks. For individual stocks, returns vary still more widely.

CHART OF VALUE AND THE RATE OF RETURN

The purpose of Figure 3.2 is to clarify further these concepts of value and the rate of return and portray their relationship to the basic data. Shown are the price ranges, earnings, and dividends of a very well-known stock which needs no introduction—American Telephone and Telegraph. The period covered is 1949–1970. During this period the growth of earnings was quite steady and averaged 4.3 percent per annum for the 21 years.

Dividends, on the other hand, were quite unusual before 1958. As everyone knows, Mother Bell had faithfully paid a $9 annual dividend, through good times and bad, from 1922 to 1958, thus becoming the most-wanted stock for widows, orphans, and just about everyone else. (This $9 dividend appears on Figure 3.2 as $1.50 because all figures have been adjusted for the subsequent splits—3-for-1 in April, 1959, and 2-for-1 in May, 1964.) Such a constant dividend policy, however, is not in accordance with the natural laws of finance. Dividends are the portion of earnings distributed to the stockholders, and normally vary more or less as earnings do.

---

[10] Thor Hultgren, formerly with the National Bureau of Economic Research, has been a visiting associate professor of economics and is at present a lecturer at the University of Wisconsin at Milwaukee.

FIGURE 3.2
Value and the Rate of Return

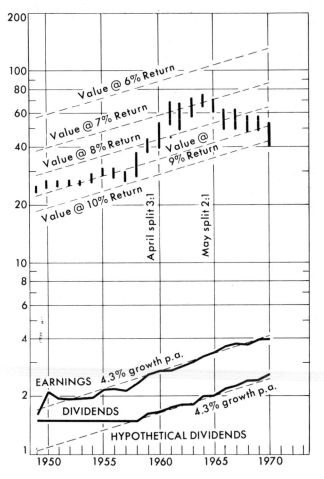

On the chart, along with the actual dividends, are shown the "hypothetical dividends" calculated from the general regression line of relationship between payout and growth of earnings, as described earlier in this chapter. These point out just how much the actual dividends exceeded the "normal dividends" in the years before 1958. But, in spite of the fact that the actual dividends were above normal, the price action of the stock was sluggish, increasing less than 3 percent per year on the average during 1949 to 1956—a period when the general market went wild, with the DJIA prices increasing over 15 percent per year, and the "500" over 17 percent per annum. At least part of the reason was the fear that Mother Bell might persist in paying the same constant dividend even though earnings continued to grow. Like typical investors, most faithful when they were getting more than their share, AT&T holders soon became disgruntled when they feared they might be left with less than their "fair share."

In 1958 the normal dividend was exactly the $1.50 paid that year, and so was perfectly fair and just. Then came the bombshell! The dividend was increased to $1.575 in 1959 and continued to grow with earnings in subsequent years. Although there were also other favorable conditions which certainly helped AT&T, it cannot be denied that the big boost which lifted the tarnished blue chip out of the doldrums was the reality of the "growing dividends." These created "growing value" and prices bounded up. But, alas, with investors not knowing how much the stock was really worth, they bounded too high—only to make again many unhappy stockholders, this time the eager newcomers who had flocked to the resuscitated fairy godmother.

The chart shows very clearly how faithfully the actual growing dividends followed the general norm for payout from 1959 to 1970, when this is being written. The line of hypothetical dividends is practically identical with the trend line fitted to the actual dividends. Thus the theory and the sample stock double-check each other, and we have a very good as well as a very interesting subject to demonstrate the application of the theory of present worth.

Value is determined by these dividends growing at the average rate of 4.3 percent per year until 1970 and then projected at the assumed basic rate of 4 percent ad infinitum. The sums of all these discounted dividends (their present worth) are calculated for various rates of return—6 percent to 10 percent. Lines showing the levels of "value" at these different rates of return are drawn in on the chart through the price range bars and so serve also to indicate the significance of the actual prices. For example, during the first half of the 1950's, AT&T was selling at about a 9 percent return level. A purchase made at this level, say at 28 (adjusted) in 1954, and sold at 53 in the spring of 1970 would have rewarded its holder with a return, or total effective yield, of just about 9 percent on his investment. Obviously, if a stock is bought below the level of value at the desired return or sold above value, the happy stockholder is rewarded with a proportionate bonus.

During cyclical highs, prices are at a level which represents, for the buyer, a lower than average rate of return. This is clearly pictured on the chart, which also shows the extent to which lower costs offer promise of higher return. I am not saying that one who buys at a high cost must lose or realize only very low return. My point is that his odds are poor. To win, he must be lucky and sell before the prices start to decline again. For instance, the buyer of AT&T at about 61 in 1961 would have had to "dump it" quickly in 1964, before it dropped below 69, in order to make only a 7 percent return on his investment. By 1971 he would have to sell at 90 to realize even that modest 7 percent total effective yield. These facts make it clear why the discreet investor should pay no more, and preferably less, than the "value" of a stock at the rate of return desired. Thus the importance of knowing what is the "value" of stocks in which one is interested—as well as the effect on value of changes in the rate of return. Many may be surprised at the magnitude of the change in value resulting from a change of only 1 percent in the rate of return, especially between the lower rates of return where the percentage difference is considerably greater, other things being equal.

MORE ABOUT THE RATE OF RETURN

Apropos of the rate of return, in his *Theory of Investment Value* (page 260), John Burr Williams states that:

> It is in the bond market, not in the stock market, that the long-term rate of interest is determined. The bond market, not the stock market, is where savings compete for an outlet, and where enterprises compete—really compete—for financial support. . . . The rate of interest that thus emerges . . . , whatever it may be, is merely carried over without further change into the stock market, and applied to the appraisal of common stocks there.

This statement finds a considerable degree of verification in conditions as they existed during this past year. In early 1970, short-term Treasury bills returned a yield as high as 8.02 percent, while the prime lending rate of the nation's banks—the very lowest rate charged to their best customers—was 8.5 percent. Yields of highest grade, seasoned corporate bonds, reached, on the average, a peak of 8.60 percent in mid-1970, and high-grade utility bonds with coupons of 9 percent and over were being issued. The coupons of some corporate debentures of lesser quality ranged to over 11 percent. Even long-term U.S. government bonds were yielding over 7 percent.

At about this same time the stock market was groveling in the dust of the bear market. While AT&T's newly-issued Aaa 8.75 percent debentures slipped below par to yield a bit more than the coupon indicated, the price of its common stock sank down below even the 10 percent total return level.

The general stock market indexes were at levels indicating similar returns for buyers. Assuming a conservative long-term 4 percent growth of earnings ad infinitum, from 1970 on, the approximate "values" for the S&P "500" composite index are as follows:

Total Return (percent)	Approximate 1970 Value of "500"
10	65
9	78
8	98
7.5	112

These are approximations because the "500" is a composite of industrials, utilities, and transportation stocks. Since each group has different relationships between payout and growth of earnings, the values were calculated by using an "intermediate" relationship. In spite of this difficulty, the results tend to bear out the thesis under discussion. While corporate bonds were returning over 9 percent, the "500" price dropped on May 26, 1970, to a low of 69.29. Interpolation indicates that this represented "value" at about 9.625 percent total return. Toward the end of 1970 interest rates declined considerably and yields on high-grade corporates were varying mostly between 8 percent and 8.5 percent. In mid-December the "500" reached 90, which would correspond to an average return of about 8.375 percent for buyers.

As a double-check we might investigate the Dow-Jones Industrial Average (DJIA) in a similar manner. Since these are all industrials, the appropriate relationships between growth and payout are those of industrials and the Valuator for Industrials in this book can be used. The trend line was fitted to earnings for the period 1948 to 1970—just as was done for the "500." The average growth rate for this period was found to be about 4.25 percent, and the 1970 level of this trend line was just about 57. Assuming again the basic 4 percent growth rate of earnings ad infinitum, the approximate "values" for the Dow-Jones Industrial Average are as follows:

Total Return (percent)	Approximate 1970 Value of DJIA
10	605
9	725
8	905
7.5	1030

All except the value at 7.5 percent return can be calculated by the reader directly from the 4 percent growth tables in the proper rate of return sections. You need only to multiply the figure in the tables by the normal earnings figure of 57. Looking at these values it can be seen immediately that they confirm the conclusions arrived at above from the table of "500" values. The May 26 low of 631.16 represented "value" at about 9.75 percent total return, while the 830 area reached in mid-December corresponded to a return of about 8.375 percent—the same as that indicated by the "500."

As mentioned in Chapter 2, some of the disciples of the present worth theory have proposed using a higher discount rate to compensate for a lower degree of certainty regarding projected earnings. This approach tends to give an entirely different significance to the idea of the discount rate. Our method of attacking the problem of very uncertain future earnings is rather to be more conservative in the projection while keeping the discount rate constant. By putting all the stocks under consideration for a certain purpose on the same common denominator, we preserve their comparability. Furthermore, the possibility of selection by computer is protected. Unless all stocks are expressed in terms of a standard return, it is impossible to rank them according to the relation of their current price to value and thus determine their relative attractiveness.

To provide as wide a range of returns as would be reasonably expected to satisfy most requirements, the tables in this book include returns from 7 percent to 10 percent, as well as 12 percent.

A WORD OF WARNING

The tables give the theoretical values, i.e., the trend values, corresponding to the hypotheses which are used. If a stock is purchased today at its present theoretical value and sold at some future time at the corresponding theoretical value of that moment, the return realized will be equal to that of the table used in the determination of these values. Obviously, by the same reasoning, if the stock is purchased below its present value or sold above value, the return for this happy trader would be greater.

If earnings projections are reasonably accurate—and the rate of return used approximates the facts of financial life at that time—we may assume that the market price will move in the direction of value until they are joined. Yet the market's traveling speed toward that goal will be conditioned by the degree and timing of investors' sanction of the projections as well as by the cyclical convolutions of the road.

No appraisals of investment values should be considered Judgment Day verdicts. They are merely expressions of present conditions and reasonable estimates of the future. If either or both change, the theoretical value must be adjusted accordingly. Indeed, values must change inevitably. The future becomes clearer as time passes. Thus today's appraisals of future value must be considered subject to change.

Besides cyclical influences, stocks are responsive to many other pricing impulses. The market, i.e., the consensus of countless investors and traders who compose it, gives varying treatment, in terms of earnings capitalizers, to stocks belonging to different groups. Some of such special attitudes of the market are long established habits; others are quickly changing "fashions," lasting a season or two. Some, especially in regard to stocks in the high growth category, result from confusion about how high a capitalizer is reasonable. Emotion, instead of cool calculation, too often rules the bidding.

As mentioned in Chapter 1, it is our dream that these tables may gradually pare down the extent to which prices stray away from value and so eventually change the image of the "market" from that of something akin to a "game of chance" to what it was intended to be: a medium for investment of money—a very special medium which would offer, with a reasonable degree of reliability, a choice of different types of investments with different rates of expected or probable return (reflecting varying degrees of risk), but with a very gradually increasing degree of predictability.

The tables in this book combine all the facets of this theory and bring them down from the ethereal realm of the abstract to terra firma. They provide a practical method for everyday use, which is simple enough for any investor to use. This method is described and demonstrated in the next chapter.

Chapter 4

A METHOD FOR
STOCK VALUATION

EVER SINCE the first stock issue, investors have been searching for a way to determine the value of a share. Many approaches have been tried, but none can stand up against every question that can be raised. None ever will be found by mortal man which will give the absolute and incontestable solution to this great mystery. This fact, however, could not be allowed to deter us from trying to improve on our methods and develop them to the point at which they can be as helpful as possible to all investors.

The last chapter described in considerable detail a further development of the theory of present worth for application to the valuation of common stocks. This alone, however, is of little help to the man in the street. Even for the professional, who has the mathematical facility to calculate values from the formula, it is too time-consuming to work out by hand any number of valuations. Therefore, since we are no longer in the age B.C.—Before Computers—we have done something about it. We have put to work one of these great machines. Into it was fed the formula with all its ramifications. In return, the iron brain gave us the tables in this book. Now the necessary calculations are reduced to a simple multiplication.

THE COMPUTER PROGRAM

A computer requires that directions be given precisely and completely down to the minutest detail. Mathematical formulas must be expressed in a special manner and the range of desired values of variables specifically noted. The manner in which the results of the computations are to be displayed on the final page must likewise be carefully delineated. The composite of all these instructions makes up the "Computer Program."

Besides all these demanding specifications, there is the problem of handling the endless variety of possible growth patterns. Theoretically, one can work out "value" by hand for any sequence of growth rates. I say "theoretically" because in actual practice it will often be quite impossible because of the overwhelming amount of computation involved. There is a real limit, however, to the amount of variation that it is practical to include in tables.

211

Since the tables will most often be used to estimate "value today" based on projections into the future, the assumed growth pattern obviously cannot have a high degree of precision. Nevertheless, it is necessary to provide for a wide range of initial growth rates as well as for quite a comprehensive coverage of subsequent variations. There are separate tables for each initial growth rate. Each table allows this growth rate to remain constant for selected numbers of years from 1 to 25 years, and then to gravitate toward the basic 4 percent rate during selected periods ranging from 2 to 20 years.

A bit of a problem is created, however, by one of the economic facts of life, namely, that changes in dividends usually lag behind when earnings growth rates change. Considerable experimentation was done in order to arrive at a practical solution which could be handled by the tables. The results of the testing indicated that, only when the growth rate of the recent past is greatly different from that assumed for the near-term future, does the resulting valuation show a significant difference from what it would have been if the same rate of growth had continued from the immediate past to the immediate future and then, after that, increased (or decreased) to establish the average growth rate assumed for the period beginning with the present—that is, the initial "Years Constant Growth" shown in the tables. This is not so complicated or compromising as it may seem at first. It is obvious to all that any growth rate achieved in the past, or assumed for the future, is an average rate for the period to which it applies. Therefore, it is not unrealistic to assume that, for example, in the transition from an average growth rate of 3 percent per annum (p.a.) for the past five years to an expected 5 percent p.a. for the next five years, the current rates for the year immediately past and the year immediately ahead may be quite similar. This being so, it was concluded that we can reasonably assume in the tables that the rate of growth of the immediate past is practically the same as that projected for the immediate future. The rare case in which exceptional circumstances make probable a drastic and sudden change in the growth rate can be taken care of by means of special longhand calculations.

The next problem is the number of years during which the initial growth rate can be expected to settle down to 4 percent—the "ignorance rate" described in Chapter 3. These are called the "Years Settling Growth" and will actually be years of rising growth when the initial growth rate is less than 4 percent, and years of diminishing growth when it is initially more than 4 percent. The stability and characteristics of the particular company in question will usually suggest whether this will be a short or a longer period of years.

Another complication in connection with the years of settling growth is the pattern which is followed as the growth rates decline or rise. Linear functions are used to describe this changing rate. If the settling period is less than five years, the annual change in the growth rate is equal to the difference between the initial rate and 4 percent, divided by $(n + 1)$, where n is the number of settling years. For example, if an initial growth rate of 9 percent declines to 4 percent in four years, the growth rates during these four settling years are 8 percent, 7 percent,

6 percent, and 5 percent. Then, from the fifth year ad infinitum earnings are assumed to grow 4 percent per annum. When the settling period is greater than five years, a little refinement is added to compensate for the lag of the dividends as earnings growth rates change. To accomplish this, the rate of decline or rise during the first three years is one-half that of the balance of the settling period.

Finally, the computer programs provide for complete sets of tables for each integral rate of return from 6 percent to 15 percent (although tables for only the 7 percent to 10 percent and 12 percent are given in Appendix D), with the only difference from set to set being the rate of discount. Many readers may be startled by the magnitude of the difference which a variation of only 1 percent of total return can make in the resulting investment value.

THE MAGIC OF GROWTH

Before describing the use of these tables, a few pertinent concepts should be made very clear.

An understanding of the power of compound annual growth is a most important precaution against the temptation to make over-optimistic projections. Few are fully aware of the great extent of this power. When the growth rate is high, it bombards the walls of our limited economic world with almost terrifying violence. Were it not for the countervailing pressure of discount, they would be destroyed as if in an atomic explosion. The discount rate determines the extent to which the present value of growing payments diminishes with the passage of time.

According to an ancient legend, failure to understand the hidden power of geometric progression cost a sovereign his kingdom. Once upon a time there lived in India a rich and powerful ruler who was so fascinated by the game of chess invented by one of his subjects, a Brahmin by the name of Sissa, that he offered any reward, however precious. Sissa requested that a single grain of barley be placed on the first square of the chessboard, two on the second, and so on, doubling each time up to the sixty-fourth square—the total number of squares on the board.

"You are not only a great inventor, Sissa," exclaimed the king, "but a modest man as well. You could have asked for half my kingdom; yet you are content with a few grains."

Sissa's shrewdness soon became apparent: the gift exceeded all the king's treasures.

A chess historian has figured that at the rate of production prevailing when he made the computations, two billion square miles would have been required to grow enough barley in one year to pay off Sissa. This is equivalent to the land surface of 38 terrestrial globes. Expressing the value in pounds sterling, a nineteenth-century chess writer arrived at £3,385,966,239,667 and 12 shillings, a tidy sum even at the present rate of exchange. As we do not have to pay the forfeit, we shall not check the calculations.

The income from an investment does not normally double the latter from year to year. In practical investment problems geometric progression often appears in the form of compound interest. Still, even at 5 percent, one dollar would double in 15 years, triple in 23 years, and grow to $131.50 in 100 years.

GROWTH RATE OF EARNINGS

Another application of this same principle is in connection with the growth of earnings. Earnings which are growing at the compound rate of 5 percent per year will, likewise, double in 15 years. Therefore, the same tables can be used to check the reasonableness of an assumed growth rate over a period of years.

In Appendix A, for the convenience of our readers, there is a table showing the amount of one dollar growing at various rates for one to 60 years. By clearly pointing out the full impact of a certain growth rate for an indicated number of years, this table not only can be helpful in deciding on the rate to use, but also can conceivably serve as a deterrent from using too high a growth rate, or assuming that it will continue for too long a period of years.

The need for caution in deciding on the growth rate assumed for future earnings is expressed very well by Professor W. Edward Bell of San José State College:

> It will generally be desirable to have a conservative bias in the growth rate projections, particularly where high rates are involved. The compounded error which would result from too liberal a projection can easily lead to purchases at speculatively high prices. A conservative approach will also reduce the risk of buying stocks at inflated prices which, while appearing reasonable in relation to past performance, are not justified in the light of a company's possibly less dynamic future prospects. Much attention has been given to the frequently transitory nature of growth, and not infrequently today's growth stock may become tomorrow's income stock.[1]

VALUE AND THE RATE OF RETURN (DISCOUNT RATE)

These concepts were explained and demonstrated in considerable detail in Chapter 3, and so will be just briefly summarized here.

According to the present-worth theory, the value of a share of stock is equal to the sum of the present values of all future dividends.

If a share of stock purchased at $20 pays a constant dividend of $1 per year, a current yield of 5 percent per year is realized by the stockholder on his investment. If no growth is foreseeable, this 5 percent current return is equal to the total return on this investment. Annuity tables indicate that the present value of $1 per year ad infinitum, discounted at 5 percent, is equal to $20. This confirms that the price paid was equal to "value for a 5 percent rate of return." Very few investors would be satisfied with this stock.

---

[1] W. Edward Bell, "The Price-Future Earnings Ratio, A Practical Aid to Stock Valuation," *The Analysts Journal*, vol. 14, no. 4: 25 (August 1958).

Since 4 percent has been indicated as a conservative estimate of the average basic rate of growth of the economy, this is the minimum growth rate which investors should expect under normal circumstances. It is quite possible at this time, when relatively high returns are prevalent, to find stocks which pay a 5 percent current yield and offer about 4 percent growth besides. Our investor may possibly find a stock with growing dividends selling at $20 per share and also paying a $1 dividend this year. If this dividend continues to grow at the average rate of 4 percent per year, his total return on this investment will be 9.2 percent, as compared with 5 percent in the first example. Each year's larger dividend will represent a proportionately larger percentage of his original investment. Furthermore, the current value of the shares increases along with the dividends, so that, theoretically, if the investor should sell his stock, he will be compensated for the future uncollected dividends by the higher price which the buyer will have to pay him.

The reader is referred to Figure 3.2 in Chapter 3, page 206, for a graphic demonstration of the meaning of value and the effect on value of changes in the rate of return.

HIGH GROWTH STOCKS AND VALUE

As for the investor who, at this point, may wonder about his return from a high growth stock which is paying a very small dividend—or none at all at the moment—we hasten to reassure him that the proportionately low dividend is taken into account in the tables by the built-in relationship between payout and growth of earnings described in Chapter 3. Furthermore, he should remember that, although the dividend may represent a relatively low percentage yield, these dividends, following in the path of the earnings, are growing so rapidly that the sum of their present values, which is the value of the stock, increases much more from year to year than in the case of the average stock. This is logical. Theoretically, the smaller the percentage of the earnings paid out in dividends, the greater are the retained earnings and, therefore, the greater the growth which is expected in the future—and the greater the increases in the value per share of stock. The tables serve to indicate precisely what this value is if—and it is a big *if*—the expected future growth actually materializes. Obviously, we are working with probabilities, and the "value" which we determine is only as accurate as the assumptions on which it is based. From a practical point of view, therefore, it is advisable to use conservative assumptions. Isn't it better to be pleasantly surprised by a larger gain than expected, than to be disappointed by a lesser gain, or even a loss?

In Appendix B is a table showing the Present Value of $1, discounted at various rates of return relevant to investments—7 percent to 12 percent—for one to 25 years. This is included as a convenience to help the reader to visualize the significance of present value and the power of the discount rate.

For more extensive tables of both growth and present value, the reader is referred to the Compound Interest Tables, published by Union Carbide Corporation, and other tables mentioned in Chapter 2.

CYCLES IN THE STOCK MARKET

Another point to bear in mind is the fact that changes in the economic climate are often accompanied by changes in the interest rates on bonds and, in turn, in the rates of return available from common stocks. Thus in times of cyclical lows as in 1970, it is generally possible to purchase stocks at a relatively lower price—that is, at a level corresponding to value at a higher rate of return. At cyclical highs, the opposite is usually the case. Figure 3.2 in Chapter 3 helps to clarify these characteristics of value and the rate of return.

The sale of stocks in the future at the same value level at which they were purchased—say, at a 9 percent return level—would indicate a total rate of return of 9 percent for the investor. However, sale at a price higher than value at 9 percent return, on the date of sale, would reward the stockholder with a higher total rate of return. This is why it is usually more profitable to buy at cyclical lows. By the same token, it is ordinarily risky to buy at cyclical highs because most stocks are selling at prices which represent value at lower than average total returns.

By this we certainly do not mean that no one should ever buy stocks at a cyclical high. As we have learned from past experience, only God knows when the top of the cycle has actually been reached. Furthermore, although all stocks are affected by powerful tides of the economy, many can "buck the tide" quite forcefully, especially those which at the time may be enjoying exceptional growth with very real prospects of continued increasing demand for their products. What we do mean is that, before making purchases at such a time, the most probable value of the stock in question should be carefully considered.

By the same reasoning it is evident that, at times when stock prices are relatively high, it is imperative to recheck the future prospects and values of all stocks already in one's portfolio in order to segregate those that have reached prices which definitely exceed their most probable estimates of value—always taking into consideration the level at which they were purchased, the rate of return desired, and the level and most probable direction of the market in general. These are the candidates for sales.

NORMAL EARNINGS CLARIFIED BY DIAGRAM

Present worth is calculated from a formula which describes a smooth curve—not too unlike the path to the moon followed by our astronauts. The slopes and levels of this curve of value are determined by the company's earnings and the sequence of growth rates of these earnings, as well as by the discount rate—as shown in Figure 3.2, Chapter 3.

It must be obvious even to the layman that it would not be logical to project from either the top or the bottom of a cyclical swing. Consequently, the only reasonable earnings magnitude to use in determining value is that which lies along a trend line drawn through the fluctuating annual figures—the "normal earnings" for the focal year. The slope of this trend line of earnings measures their average growth rate during the period of years which it covers.

If a company's earnings follow a relatively steady path, it may be possible to draw, by eye, a trend line which is quite accurate. On the other hand, in the case of companies whose earnings are very unstable or trace a widely cyclical path, it is generally necessary to fit mathematically a long-term trend line to determine a correct average growth rate and a representative normal earnings figure. In these cases the method of least squares is the best to use in fitting the trend line. Furthermore, care should be taken to work with only whole cycles, and preferably more than one cycle unless there is a definite change of trend, as fractional cycles distort the results. The compound growth table in Appendix A, or other compound interest tables, can be very helpful in checking growth rates.

In Appendix C are earnings charts for 50 companies. These were selected from among those whose stock is most widely held, but also with consideration given to the various industries as well as to some individual companies in which there has been special interest. If demand requires it, the number of companies covered will be expanded in future editions. The diagrams include earnings from 1949 (when available) to 1971 (estimated). Since these charts were prepared at the end of 1970, of necessity both the 1970 and 1971 figures are estimates. Trend lines are drawn through the earnings and their growth rates are shown. Also indicated in each case is the estimated normal earnings figure for 1971—the point of departure which can be used for projecting future earnings.

Analysis of a company's past earnings is helpful, not only in determining the present level of normal earnings, but also in getting an idea of the growth pattern and stability. These characteristics of a company suggest how confident, or how cautious, one should be in estimating future growth rates.

Value, however, depends on the path that earnings will follow from the present into the future. Certainly, actual earnings of a company cannot be estimated for each year far into the future in order that trend lines may be fitted. However, the trend of earnings of the recent past can be estimated either to remain the same, increase, or decrease in the near-term future. The magnitude of the average expected growth in the more-or-less near-future can be estimated by analysts from information obtained during interviews of company officials, studies of the industries, analysis of economic conditions in general, etc. A very practical tendency is developing among company officials whereby they sometimes give out for publication predictions of expected growth of earnings and the number of years they foresee at that rate. These are helpful but must still be used with discretion.

Apropos of estimates of future earnings, Professor W. Edward Bell had stated very clearly in 1958, an important consideration which we have always emphasized, namely, that:

All of the known characteristics of a stock can be reflected in the assumed growth rate. For instance, cyclical exposure, dependence on defense orders, and other factors which may be considered qualitative weaknesses can be reflected through an appropriately conservative assumed growth rate. The modification of the growth rate to reflect differences in quality is a subjective problem relying primarily on the analyst's experience and judgment.[2]

Even the quality of management can be expressed by raising or lowering the rate of projected earnings growth and extending or shortening the number of years of its projection into the future.

THE STOCK VALUATOR—TABLES FOR THE VALUATION OF COMMON STOCKS

Present worth has many applications, and it would be gratifying if these tables were found to be adaptable for various types of valuations. In this book, however, the only consideration has been the valuation of common stocks.

Appendix D contains the tables especially constructed for industrials. The investment value of a share of common stock is readily determined from the appropriate table after the following hypotheses have been decided upon.

1.   Normal Earnings

Normal earnings are just what their name implies—normal, not extreme, possibly average. Their's is a smooth path through the fluctuating year-to-year actual earnings.

Probably the most satisfactory means of determining normal earnings is to fit trend lines to the actual earnings. As explained above, and demonstrated by the charts in Appendix C, trends can often be fitted by eye if the earnings are relatively stable and hold to a more or less constant growth rate. The percentage growth rate can then be determined from the table in Appendix A. If the earnings are very erratic, or follow a wide cyclical pattern, it is advisable to fit a trend line by the least squares method.

Because, as explained above, the normal earnings level is the important figure for valuation, this is what is shown on the earnings charts in Appendix C.

The figures in the tables represent "investment value" for normal earnings of $1.00 per share.

Value for a particular stock is, therefore, equal to the appropriate table entry multiplied by the normal earnings for the year in question.

2.   Projected Growth Rate of Earnings

This growth rate, projected from the present, may be the same as the rate in the immediate past, or it may be higher or lower, depending on circumstances

---

[2] Ibid., p. 25.

which may or may not be powerful enough to alter significantly the earnings trend.

As pointed out above, a scientific projection is a task for a good analyst. A rough estimate, however, may be made in some cases with the aid of the growth table in Appendix A along with an earnings sketch similar to those in Appendix C.

The valuation tables include a range of growth rates for industrials projected from the present as follows: 1 percent to 20 percent consecutively and 25 percent.

Note. The tables do not include negative growth rates. In a case where a relatively quick recovery is not expected, there would ordinarily not be sufficient interest in the stock to warrant making negative rate tables. [As regards short-term declines, see note at the end of Item 4: *Years of Settling Growth.*]

3. Constant Growth Period—Years Constant Growth

This is the number of years during which the growth rate of earnings, projected from the present, is expected to be maintained.

An estimate of its duration would be suggested by the same analytical considerations as were used to estimate the projected growth rate.

All the tables include the following numbers of years of constant growth:

1 to 10 years, consecutively

12 to 20 years, by 2's, and 25 years

4. Years of Settling Growth

This is the number of years—after the period of constant growth—during which the earnings growth rate moves toward the "ignorance rate" of 4 percent per annum, which is then assumed to continue ad infinitum. These "settling" years will be years of *diminishing* growth when the initial rate is greater than 4 percent, and years of *rising* growth when the initial period of constant growth is at a rate of less than 4 percent per annum.

The length of the period depends to a great extent on the special characteristics of the company under consideration. For example, a company with brilliant promise of growth far into the future might be allowed quite a long period of diminishing (settling) growth. Alternatively, a firm may have enjoyed a period of high growth as a result of some special product, or other exceptional situation, and now has little chance of continuing this extraordinary growth. In this case the settling period would be correspondingly short.

A company with average prospects might be assumed to be growing at the rate of 4 percent per annum from the present, in which case there would be no years of settling growth since 4 percent is the assumed rate ad infinitum. A glance at any one of the 4 percent growth tables confirms this by the fact that every figure in the table is the same.

The tables include the following choice of years of settling growth: 2 to 20 years, by 2's and 25 years.

Note. In the case of relatively *short-term declines,* a 0 percent rate of growth can be assumed to continue throughout the period of decline and beyond until sufficient recovery can be expected to make the average rate for the "constant growth period" equal to 0 percent. The "settling years" would then be years of rising growth, and their duration would be decided upon after consideration of the reasons for the poor period and a realistic appraisal of the company's future prospects. [As an example, see the sketch of U.S. Steel earnings in Appendix C.]

5. Rate of Return

For the investor who is considering purchases, this is his desired rate of total return from long-term common stock investments. It should bear some relation to the returns available from alternative investments, such as bonds, real estate, proprietary business, savings accounts, etc.

Also helpful as a guide in deciding on a realistic rate of return is the range of typical returns suggested by the indexes for cyclical highs and lows, as well as the long-term average return of slightly under 8 percent. At major peaks average total return for the buyer may drop to about a 7 percent basis, at lesser tops to about 7.25–7.50 percent. At troughs average return rises, often to about a 9 percent basis. The 1970 major bottom saw the average return, as measured by the indexes, rise to about 9.75 percent, and to over 11 percent for public utilities. Individual stocks, of course, may vary more widely, or less widely, than the indexes. Some stocks may be "cheaper," i.e., selling at a higher return basis than others, all things considered. This is why the skillful investor will compare the values of all probable candidates with their current cost prices and in this way choose the "best buys."

In order to pass a fair judgment on the "significance of the current market price" of a stock one should use the approximate prevailing level of return. In this way he can determine what earnings growth prospects are "implied" by the current price. Then he can decide whether, in his opinion, it is "over-valued" or "under-valued." The tables can also translate his projections into a definite value figure at whatever return basis he may wish.

The seller, likewise, should be concerned about the return basis at which his holdings are selling. The candidates for sale should be those stocks which are definitely over-valued, high-priced that is, selling at a considerably lower return basis than the general market at the time.

The Stock Valuator includes complete sets of tables for each integral rate of return from 7 percent to 10 percent and 12 percent.

SOME PRACTICAL ILLUSTRATIONS

The mechanics of using the Stock Valuator can be best demonstrated by a few examples. In these examples the hypotheses are more or less arbitrary assumptions whose sole purpose is to illustrate some of the uses of the tables and the procedure for solving these various problems.

Example 1

The common stock of Company A, an industrial, is currently selling at 53.

An investor is considering purchase of Stock A. He would, however, like to realize a 9 percent total return on a long-term investment. In order to decide if his goal is probable at this time, determine the investment value of this stock on the basis of the following hypotheses:

Rate of return.	9 percent
Projected earnings growth rate.	4 percent
Constant growth period.	ad infinitum
Normal earnings.	$4.30

In the 9 percent return group of tables for industrials find the tables for 4 percent projected earnings growth.

As explained above, all figures in this table are identical because the assumed residual "ignorance rate" is 4 percent. Therefore, in the case of 4 percent growth projections there is no subsequent rising or diminishing rate of growth—no settling period.

On a 9 percent return basis this capitalizer (corresponding to "times earnings") is 12.7, which would be the investment value corresponding to normal earnings of $1.00.

Since, in this example, normal earnings are $4.30, investment value is equal to (12.7) X (4.30) or about 54.5—say 54 to be conservative.

As the market price is not significantly different from this hypothesized value, the stock is fairly priced for a 9 percent return to the buyer in the long-term investment perspective, as it seems today.

Example 2

Industrial Companies C & D have both enjoyed average earnings growth of 5 percent per year for about 20 years.

On the basis of the following assumptions determine which is the "better buy."

	Stock C	*Stock D*
Projected earnings growth rate.	5%	5%
Constant growth period.	6 years	5 years
Years of settling growth	6 years	4 years
Normal earnings.	4.10	2.20
Market price.	46	37

Determine the capitalizer for each stock:

$$\text{Stock C: } (46) \div (4.10) = 11.2$$
$$\text{Stock D: } (37) \div (2.20) = 16.8$$

The 10 percent return table for 5 percent projected growth, for six years of constant growth plus six years settling, indicates a value of 11.2 per $1.00 of normal earnings. Thus Stock C is selling at a 10 percent return basis.

The fact that Stock D's capitalizer is higher for the same growth rate immediately suggests looking in a lower return table, say 8 percent. At 8 percent return, 5 percent projected growth, for five years of constant growth plus four years settling, would indicate a capitalizer of 16.7. Thus Stock D is selling at about an 8 percent return basis.

Conclusion: If the hypothesized assumptions are realized, Stock C should eventually prove to be a considerably more rewarding purchase than stock D.

Example 3

Company E is an industrial which has been enjoying a very high growth rate for quite a few years.

An investor who is seeking a 10 percent return wishes to make a judgment as to whether or not this high-growth stock will satisfy his requirement.

If the current market price is 90 and the normal earnings 2.20, what rates and durations of growth would justify this price on a 10 percent return basis?

To determine the value per $1.00 of normal earnings, divide 90 by 2.20. This indicates a capitalizer of 40.9 which must be located in the 10 percent return tables.

The following tabulation lists several growth patterns which would make Stock E satisfy this investor's requirements:

Projected Growth Rate (percent)	Constant Growth Period (years)	Settling Growth Period (years)
12	25	16
16	16	4
20	8	8
25	4	9

The problem for the investor now is to appraise the realism of these projections and, on this basis, decide on his market action.

Example 4

Stock E, being a "highflier," can serve very well to demonstrate the technique of determining a range of values—from optimistic to pessimistic. This is suggested when it is difficult to make a definitive projection.

Assumptions	Optimistic	Pessimistic
Projected earnings growth rate	20%	10%
Constant growth period	7 years	10 years
Years of settling growth	10 years	6 years
Normal earnings	2.20	2.20
Rate of return desired	10%	10%
Investment value of $1 normal earnings	40.5	17.4
Investment value of Stock E	89	38

Comment. The wide spread between these investment values emphasizes the caution which must be exercised when buying high-growth stocks. These are the stocks we look to for higher than average return. Unfortunately, however, all too often their prices have been bid up so high that the chances of losing are greater than those for high gain. A slight rocking of the economic boat is enough to cause a considerable drop in price—even an unfounded rumor can shake the idol. Although these jolts may have only temporary effects, they can cause a good deal of anxiety.

We must, therefore, be very wary about the price which we pay for these high-growth stocks. Projections should always be on the conservative side. After deciding on what we feel to be the most probable future prospects, all things considered, including general economic conditions and the current position in the business cycle, it is very important to determine the value which these assumptions would represent not only at the desired rate of return but also at the current return of the market in general.

We might also check the range of values at a lower rate of return, which might be acceptable. As we all know, favorable developments, in this stock and in the business cycle in general, coupled with wise decisions about when to hold and when to sell, could bring about the eventual realization of a considerably higher return than the estimated basis at which the stock may have been purchased. Never forget, however, that these pleasant surprises develop from carefully planned, conservative beginnings.

See Example 5 for a comparison of the values of Stock E at different rates of return.

Example 5

Using the same range of assumed projections as above for Stock E, compare the corresponding values at each return basis from 7 percent to 12 percent.

Comment. In appraising these values it is important to remember that the level at a 7 percent return basis is probably about the highest that the price will normally reach. This is indicated as a probable upper limit by the fact that the major indexes did not even reach that level at the peak of the last great bull market. The S&P "500" at its 1968 top of 108.37 was at about a 7.3 percent return basis, while the DJIA's 1966 high of 995.15 represented about a 7.1

Total Return Basis (*percent*)	Range of Values			
	Optimistic		Pessimistic	
	Capitalizer*	Value	Capitalizer*	Value
7	102.4	225	39.4	86
8	70.8	155	28.3	62
9	52.4	115	21.7	47
10	40.5	89	17.4	38
11	32.3	71	14.4	31
12	26.4	58	12.2	27

* Capitalizer represents investment value of normal earnings of $1.00.

percent return. To plan to sell above this level is like planning to win the lottery. To buy at this level is to be a fool.

In making a judgment about how low a price may be probable, it is helpful to realize that at the major 1970 low the average return basis of the stocks in the above-mentioned indexes was about 9.75 percent.

These levels are just guidelines. They are average figures for what have been chosen as groups of representative stocks. Individual stocks may vary quite widely from the average.

It is interesting here to check Stock E's performance. Analysis of its 1970 low revealed that that price represented a 10 percent return for projected growth of 15 percent per year for 10 years plus 12 years of settling growth. Since this growth pattern is roughly midway between our optimistic and pessimistic assumptions for Stock E, it represented a typical value for a major cyclical low—a 10 percent return basis for a relatively conservative projection of the earnings of a high-growth stock.

Thus we have confirmation for our strong recommendation that investors should not plan on miracles—the "most probable" is usually the wisest basis for action.

Example 6

An investor holds Stock F which he feels may be over-valued and, therefore, a good stock to sell.

Although there were periods of higher growth, the average growth rate of the earnings of Stock F over the past 20 years has been about 4 percent per year.

On the basis of the following hypotheses, determine the investment value of Stock F at the current return basis of the general market. Also, determine the return basis at which the stock is now selling.

Current return basis of market	approximately 8 percent
Projected earnings growth rate	4 percent
Constant growth period	ad infinitum
Normal earnings	$2.10
Market price	53

At 8 percent return Stock F would have an investment value equal to (15.9) × (2.10), or about 33. On this basis the stock is greatly over-priced at 53 and is a good sale.

To determine at what return basis Stock F is selling, find the earnings capitalizer by dividing price by normal earnings: (53) ÷ (2.10) = 25.2. Check the tables for the investment values of $1 normal earnings projected at 4 percent growth ad infinitum. Interpolate to estimate the return:

$$\left.\begin{array}{ll} 6\text{ percent return} & 31.7 \\ ? & 25.2 \\ 7\text{ percent return} & 21.1 \end{array}\right\} \begin{array}{l} 6.5 \\ \\ \end{array} \right\} 10.6$$

Thus, the current price of Stock F is at about a 6.625 percent return level—based on a continuation of the 4 percent growth rate of earnings ad infinitum.

Comment. As we have emphasized time and again, the investment value determined for a stock is only as good as the earnings projection on which it is based, and 100 percent correct projections are beyond the reach of our finite minds. This being so, we must be satisfied with the best available—that arrived at by a skilled analyst after exhaustive study and analysis.

In the case of Stock F, for demonstrative purposes only, we projected the growth rate of the past 20 years. On this hypothesis, the stock is so over-priced that we are led to the conclusion that the majority of investors must be assuming a much higher growth rate in the future. At an 8 percent return basis, an investment value of 25.2 per $1 normal earnings implies, for example, a future growth of earnings at the rate of 10 percent per year for five years, followed by ten years of diminishing growth before the basic 4 percent is again assumed. As shown in Example 3, various growth patterns could justify this price, but they would all be at a high rate of growth.

The conclusion is that a thorough analysis must be made in order to determine the best possible projection of Stock F's earnings. Only this can give us a reliable estimate of its investment value. However, unless there is something very dynamic and extraordinary in Company F's future, the stock still seems over-priced and its sale should be seriously considered.

Example 7

An investor holds Stocks G and H and must sell one in order to raise needed cash. Determine which would be the better sale, which is selling higher as compared with its value at the current return level of the market.

Assumptions	Stock G	Stock H
Projected earnings growth rate	12%	9%
Constant growth period	6 years	6 years
Years of settling growth	10 years	10 years
Normal earnings	2.80	3.75
Market price	87	103

Current return basis of market = approximately 8 percent

Determine the capitalizer for each stock:

$$\text{Stock G: } (87) \div (2.80) = 31.1$$
$$\text{Stock H: } (103) \div (3.75) = 27.5$$

The 8 percent return tables indicate the following values if these hypotheses are realized:

Return Basis	Stock G		Stock H	
	Capitalizer	*Value*	*Capitalizer*	*Value*
8%	31.2	87	24.1	90
Market Price		87		103

Based on comparisons of price with value, the conclusion would be that Stock H is the better sale because it is selling at a considerably higher price than value at the current return basis of 8 percent, while Stock G is selling at just about its 8 percent return level.

Cost prices should also be taken into consideration before making the final decision about which stock to sell. It is possible that the stockholder may have a large capital gain in Stock G and a large loss in Stock H, and tax considerations may have an important influence on his final decision.

Comment. At this point it is advisable to emphasize again that a buyer must consider value at the rate of return which he desires, and his cost price should not exceed a stock's value on that basis. On the other hand, a seller aims to sell as high as possible. He must consider the current return basis of the market in general and should not sell at a price lower than the stock's value on that basis, unless, of course, he has some other compelling reason for selling.

NO CONFLICT—AND IT'S SO EASY!

This final presentation is included here, in all its minute detail, to demonstrate not only the validity of our theory but also the fact that the Valuator, having been developed from the same fundamental principles, has no conflict whatsoever with other tables which have been based on the theory of present worth. (See Chapter 2 for a sketch of other stock value tables.)

The difference is that our theory has reached a greater degree of refinement. The open-end nature of the common stock universe is not new. It has always existed, just as energy always existed in the atom. The relationships between growth of earnings and payout are a development which created hypothetical dividends and made it possible to estimate the investment value of a stock from a minimum number of assumptions.

To prove our theses, a test will be made with the aid of hindsight. All but the projection from 1970 into the future is history. Admittedly, this last projection is not based on exhaustive study, but it is reasonable and conservative and will serve our purpose here.

Procter & Gamble has been chosen as the guinea pig. Its graph—in Appendix C—shows a steady growth of earnings at the rate of 9 percent per year since 1952. This stability suggests that we might reasonably project continuing growth at 9 percent to 1975, and then assume a diminishing rate over the following six years to the basic 4 percent "ignorance rate."

In this example we hypothesize a purchase of Procter & Gamble in the latter part of 1960 at about an 8 percent return level. Sale of this stock is assumed to have been made ten years later in the latter part of 1970, also at an 8 percent return basis.

Following are the hypotheses:

Hypotheses	1960 Purchase	1970 Sale
Projected earnings growth rate	9%	9%
Constant growth period	15 years	5 years
Years of settling growth	6 years	6 years
Normal earnings	1.08	2.56
Price range of year	20⅞–35	40⅛–60¾
Return basis of transaction	8%	8%
Determined by Means of Valuator		
Investment value of $1 normal earnings	29.5	21.9
Investment value of Procter & Gamble	32	56
Hypothesized transaction price	32	56

We shall demonstrate, by an entirely different method, that the investor would actually have realized a total return of just about 8 percent—as indicated by the Valuator.

To prove our theses, not only should we use a different procedure, but it should be simple and clear-cut. This is possible because we have already determined the purchase and sale prices; and the dividends which would have been received during the ten-year period are history. All that is needed is to prove by compound interest that these hypotheses would actually have rewarded a stockholder with an 8 percent total return on his money invested.

Invested in the latter part of 1960: $32 per share.

Note. Each payment subsequently received as a result of that investment must be discounted at 8 percent per year for the number of years from 1960 to the year when it was received. This determines its present value in 1960 on the basis of an 8 percent return on the 1960 investment. (The reciprocals of the figures for compound growth given in Appendix A are the discount factors.)

Dividends Received	Actual	Discount Factor	Present Value in 1960
1961	.67	.926	.620
1962	.73	.857	.626
1963	.78	.794	.619
1964	.84	.735	.617
1965	.90	.681	.613
1966	.97	.630	.611
1967	1.05	.583	.612
1968	1.15	.540	.621
1969	1.25	.500	.625
1970	1.33	.463	.616
Total 1960 value of dividends			6.180
1970 sale price	56	.463	25.928
Total 1960 value of all receipts			32.108

The calculations above demonstrate that if the $32 per share 1960 cost price were broken down into 11 component parts (representing the 10 annual dividends and the 1970 sale price) and if each of these were to increase 8 percent per year for the appropriate number of years, each would grow to the amount of the respective actual dividend received, and the balance to the 1970 sale price. This proves that every dollar of original investment would have increased 8 percent per year for every year that it was invested, that is until it was recovered by the investor. It would be a good exercise for remaining skeptics to take these 1960 components and, with the aid of the table in Appendix A, determine to what each would increase at 8 percent compound interest.

Comment. The very small discrepancy between the results shown above (32.11 versus 32, or one-third of 1 percent error) becomes all the more amazing as we think of all the different possible sources of minor discrepancies:

1. To begin with, in the Valuator, the investment value is based on the hypothetical dividends determined by the relationship between growth of earnings and payout. This is an average relationship developed by correlation from the S&P indexes. The regression line describes the most typical relationship and, therefore, it cannot be expected that the hypothetical dividends derived from it will always precisely equal the actual dividends—determined, as they are, by the particular management policies of the individual companies.

2. All along the way—in both procedures—there was a good deal of rounding off. The tables carry only two decimal places; the investment values were rounded off to the nearest dollar; the normal earnings were rounded off to the nearest penny; the dividends were all rounded off to a certain extent.

This is more than enough to prove our point.

Observations. One of the fundamental concepts of the present worth theory can also be clarified by the above experiment:

If the investment value in 1960 is equal to the sum of the present values of all future dividends from 1961 ad infinitum, and

If the investment value in 1970 is equal to the sum of the present values of all future dividends, from 1971 ad infinitum,
Then, the difference between the 1960 and 1970 values must equal the sum of the dividends received during the intervening ten years.

To measure this difference in comparable dollars and cents, each item must be expressed in terms of its 1960 value. To accomplish this, each item must be discounted back to 1960 at the 8 percent rate of return realized by our hypothetical investor.
As shown in the calcuations above:

1960 cost price:	32.00
1960 value of sale price:	25.93
Difference	6.07
1960 value of dividends received	6.18

(The slight discrepancy is the accumulated error of 11¢ explained above.)

This demonstrates that, *after making adjustment for the 8 percent return during the ten years of holding,* the 1960 value actually exceeded the 1970 value by precisely the sum of the dividends paid during those ten years. This confirms the theorem that the value of a share of stock is equal to the present worth of all future dividends.

Thus besides giving evidence of the practicality of the tables, this illustration also bears testimony to the validity of our theory regarding the open end nature of the common stock universe. Furthermore, the results arrived at by means of the Valuator are shown to be accurate when double-checked by compound interest.

SUMMARY AND CONCLUSIONS

The Stock Valuator cannot and is not intended to substitute for the vital and indispensable work of financial analysis. To arrive at a meaningful estimate of value, the use of the tables must be preceded by competent security analysis. Furthermore, corporate developments have to be constantly scrutinized. Various events and new facts can affect the projections of future earnings as well as of normal earning power.

Not current dividends but the entire stream of future dividends determines value and return from common stocks. The tables were developed from this premise. Through statistical techniques, dividends were replaced by earnings growth rates as the operational input. This allows for efficient practical use while maintaining a sound theoretical structure.

The Stock Valuator can be used to determine, from estimates of the future growth of earnings, value at a desired investment return. It can also be used to test the significance and reasonableness of current market prices. By appropriate processing to meet specific requirements, the Valuator can serve for portfolio planning for private and institutional investors.

An inestimable advantage of these tables lies in the speed and ease with which the investment value of a stock can be found. Any change of opinion regarding a projection can be reflected at once in a different valuation figure. A range of projections can be translated immediately into a range of values.

These tables are not racing forms designed for picking the winners of the next stock market run. They were built to find stocks which will be the most rewarding holdings for long-term investors.

We earnestly feel that our Stock Valuator will be an increasingly useful tool not only for financial analysts but for practically all investors. Its usefulness could approach that of bond yield tables. In fact, this is a basis book for common stocks.

Appendixes

Appendix A

AMOUNT OF $1 AT
COMPOUND ANNUAL GROWTH

$$F_n = P(1 + r)^n$$

Pe-riods	2%	2½%	3%	4%	5%	6%	8%	10%
1...	1.0200	1.0250	1.0300	1.0400	1.0500	1.0600	1.0800	1.1000
2...	1.0404	1.0506	1.0609	1.0816	1.1025	1.1236	1.1664	1.2100
3...	1.0612	1.0769	1.0927	1.1249	1.1576	1.1910	1.2597	1.3310
4...	1.0824	1.1038	1.1255	1.1699	1.2155	1.2625	1.3605	1.4641
5...	1.1041	1.1314	1.1593	1.2167	1.2763	1.3382	1.4693	1.6105
6...	1.1262	1.1597	1.1941	1.2653	1.3401	1.4185	1.5869	1.7716
7...	1.1487	1.1887	1.2299	1.3159	1.4071	1.5036	1.7138	1.9488
8...	1.1717	1.2184	1.2668	1.3686	1.4775	1.5938	1.8509	2.1436
9...	1.1951	1.2489	1.3048	1.4233	1.5513	1.6895	1.9990	2.3589
10...	1.2190	1.2801	1.3439	1.4802	1.6289	1.7908	2.1589	2.5938
11...	1.2434	1.3121	1.3842	1.5395	1.7103	1.8983	2.3316	2.8532
12...	1.2682	1.3449	1.4258	1.6010	1.7959	2.0122	2.5182	3.1385
13...	1.2936	1.3785	1.4685	1.6651	1.8856	2.1329	2.7196	3.4524
14...	1.3195	1.4130	1.5126	1.7317	1.9799	2.2609	2.9372	3.7976
15...	1.3459	1.4483	1.5580	1.8009	2.0709	2.3966	3.1722	4.1774
16...	1.3728	1.4845	1.6047	1.8730	2.1829	2.5404	3.4259	4.5951
17...	1.4002	1.5216	1.6528	1.9479	2.2920	2.6928	3.7000	5.0545
18...	1.4282	1.5597	1.7024	2.0258	2.4066	2.8543	3.9960	5.5600
19...	1.4568	1.5987	1.7535	2.1068	2.5270	3.0256	4.3157	6.1160
20...	1.4859	1.6386	1.8061	2.1911	2.6533	3.2071	4.6610	6.7276
22...	1.5460	1.7216	1.9161	2.3699	2.9253	3.6035	5.4365	8.1404
24...	1.6084	1.8087	2.0328	2.5633	3.2251	4.0489	6.3412	9.8498
26...	1.6734	1.9003	2.1566	2.7725	3.5557	4.5494	7.3964	11.9183
28...	1.7410	1.9965	2.2879	2.9987	3.9201	5.1117	8.6271	14.4211
30...	1.8114	2.0976	2.4273	3.2434	4.3219	5.7435	10.0627	17.4495
32...	1.8845	2.2038	2.5751	3.5081	4.7649	6.4534	11.7371	21.1140
34...	1.9607	2.3153	2.7319	3.7943	5.2533	7.2510	13.6901	25.5479
36...	2.0399	2.4325	2.8983	4.1039	5.7918	8.1473	15.9682	30.9130
38...	2.1223	2.5557	3.0748	4.4388	6.3855	9.1543	18.6253	37.4047
40...	2.2080	2.6851	3.2620	4.8010	7.0400	10.2857	21.7245	45.2597
42...	2.2972	2.8210	3.4607	5.1928	7.7616	11.5570	25.3395	54.7643
44...	2.3901	2.9638	3.6715	5.6165	8.5572	12.9855	29.5560	66.2648
46...	2.4866	3.1139	3.8950	6.0748	9.4343	14.5905	34.4741	80.1804
48...	2.5871	3.2715	4.1323	6.5705	10.4013	16.3939	40.2106	97.0182
50...	2.6916	3.4371	4.3839	7.1067	11.4674	18.4202	46.9016	117.3920
60...	3.2810	4.3998	5.8916	10.5196	18.6792	32.9877	101.2571	304.4846

Source: Myron J. Gordon and Gordon Shillinglaw, *Accounting: A Management Approach*, 4th ed. (Homewood, Ill.: Richard D. Irwin, Inc., 1969), p. 784.

Appendix B

PRESENT VALUE OF
$1 DISCOUNTED ANNUALLY

$$P_A = A \left[\frac{1 - (1 + r)^{-n}}{r} \right]$$

Periods (n)	1%	1½%	2%	2½%	3%	3½%	4%	4½%	5%	6%	7%
1....	0.9901	0.9852	0.9804	0.9756	0.9709	0.9662	0.9615	0.9569	0.9524	0.9434	0.9346
2....	1.9704	1.9559	1.9416	1.9274	1.9135	1.8997	1.8861	1.8727	1.8594	1.8334	1.8080
3....	2.9410	2.9122	2.8839	2.8560	2.8286	2.8016	2.7751	2.7490	2.7232	2.6730	2.6243
4....	3.9020	3.8544	3.8077	3.7620	3.7171	3.6731	3.6299	3.5875	3.5460	3.4651	3.3872
5....	4.8534	4.7826	4.7135	4.6458	4.5797	4.5151	4.4518	4.3900	4.3295	4.2124	4.1002
6....	5.7955	5.6972	5.6014	5.5081	5.4172	5.3286	5.2421	5.1579	5.0757	4.9173	4.7665
7....	6.7282	6.5982	6.4720	6.3494	6.2303	6.1145	6.0021	5.8927	5.7864	5.5824	5.3893
8....	7.6517	7.4859	7.3255	7.1701	7.0197	6.8740	6.7327	6.5959	6.4632	6.2098	5.9713
9....	8.5660	8.3605	8.1622	7.9709	7.7861	7.6077	7.4353	7.2688	7.1078	6.8017	6.5152
10....	9.4713	9.2222	8.9826	8.7521	8.5302	8.3166	8.1109	7.9127	7.7217	7.3601	7.0236
11....	10.3676	10.0711	9.7868	9.5142	9.2526	9.0016	8.7605	8.5289	8.3064	7.8869	7.4987
12....	11.2551	10.9075	10.5753	10.2578	9.9540	9.6633	9.3851	9.1186	8.8633	8.3838	7.9427
13....	12.1337	11.7315	11.3484	10.9832	10.6350	10.3027	9.9856	9.6829	9.3936	8.8527	8.3577
14....	13.0037	12.5434	12.1062	11.6909	11.2961	10.9205	10.5631	10.2228	9.8986	9.2950	8.7455
15....	13.8651	13.3432	12.8493	12.3814	11.9379	11.5174	11.1184	10.7395	10.3797	9.7122	9.1079
16....	14.7179	14.1313	13.5777	13.0550	12.5611	12.0941	11.6523	11.2340	10.8378	10.1059	9.4466
17....	15.5623	14.9076	14.2919	13.7122	13.1661	12.6513	12.1657	11.7072	11.2741	10.4773	9.7632
18....	16.3983	15.6726	14.9920	14.3534	13.7535	13.1897	12.6593	12.1600	11.6896	10.8276	10.0591
19....	17.2260	16.4262	15.6785	14.9789	14.3238	13.7098	13.1339	12.5933	12.0853	11.1581	10.3356
20....	18.0456	17.1686	16.3514	15.5892	14.8775	14.2124	13.5903	13.0079	12.4622	11.4699	10.5940
21....	18.8570	17.9001	17.0112	16.1845	15.4150	14.6980	14.0292	13.4047	12.8212	11.7640	10.8355
22....	19.6604	18.6208	17.6580	16.7654	15.9369	15.1671	14.4511	13.7844	13.1630	12.0416	11.0612
23....	20.4558	19.3309	18.2922	17.3321	16.4436	15.6204	14.8568	14.1478	13.4886	12.3034	11.2722
24....	21.2434	20.0304	18.9139	17.8850	16.9355	16.0584	15.2470	14.4955	13.7986	12.5504	11.4693
25....	22.0232	20.7196	19.5235	18.4244	17.4131	16.4815	15.6221	14.8282	14.0939	12.7834	11.6536
26....	22.7952	21.3986	20.1210	18.9506	17.8768	16.8904	15.9828	15.1466	14.3752	13.0032	11.8258
27....	23.5596	22.0676	20.7069	19.4640	18.3270	17.2854	16.3296	15.4513	14.6430	13.2105	11.9867
28....	24.3164	22.7267	21.2813	19.9649	18.7641	17.6670	15.6631	15.7429	14.8981	13.4062	12.1371
29....	25.0658	23.3761	21.8444	20.4535	19.1885	18.0358	1o.9837	16.0219	15.1411	13.5907	12.2777
30....	25.8077	24.0158	22.3965	20.9303	19.6004	18.3920	17.2920	16.2889	15.3725	13.7648	12.4090
40....	32.8347	29.9158	27.3555	25.1028	23.1148	21.3551	19.7928	18.4016	17.1591	15.0463	13.3317
50....	39.1961	34.9997	31.4236	28.3623	25.7298	23.4556	21.4822	19.7620	18.2559	15.7619	13.8007

Source: Myron J. Gordon and Gordon Shillinglaw, *Accounting: A Management Approach*, 4th ed. (Homewood, Ill.: Richard D. Irwin, Inc., 1969), pp. 788–89.

8%	10%	12%	14%	15%	16%	18%	20%	22%	24%	25%	26%	28%	30%	40%	50%
0.9259	0.9091	0.893	0.877	0.870	0.862	0.847	0.833	0.820	0.806	0.800	0.794	0.781	0.769	0.714	0.667
1.7833	1.7355	1.690	1.647	1.626	1.605	1.566	1.528	1.492	1.457	1.440	1.424	1.392	1.361	1.224	1.111
2.5771	2.4869	2.402	2.322	2.283	2.246	2.174	2.106	2.042	1.981	1.952	1.923	1.868	1.816	1.589	1.407
3.3121	3.1699	3.037	2.914	2.855	2.798	2.690	2.589	2.494	2.404	2.362	2.320	2.241	2.166	1.849	1.605
3.9927	3.7908	3.605	3.433	3.352	3.274	3.127	2.991	2.864	2.745	2.689	2.635	2.532	2.436	2.035	1.737
4.6229	4.3553	4.111	3.889	3.784	3.685	3.498	3.326	3.167	3.020	2.951	2.885	2.759	2.643	2.168	1.824
5.2064	4.8684	4.564	4.288	4.160	4.039	3.812	3.605	3.416	3.242	3.161	3.083	2.937	2.802	2.263	1.883
5.7466	5.3349	4.968	4.639	4.487	4.344	4.078	3.837	3.619	3.421	3.329	3.241	3.076	2.925	2.331	1.922
6.2469	5.7590	5.328	4.946	4.772	4.607	4.303	4.031	3.786	3.566	3.463	3.366	3.184	3.019	2.379	1.948
6.7101	6.1446	5.650	5.216	5.019	4.833	4.494	4.192	3.923	3.682	3.571	3.465	3.269	3.092	2.414	1.965
7.1390	6.4951	5.988	5.453	5.234	5.029	4.656	4.327	4.035	3.776	3.656	3.544	3.335	3.147	2.438	1.977
7.5361	6.8137	6.194	5.660	5.421	5.197	4.793	4.439	4.127	3.851	3.725	3.606	3.387	3.190	2.456	1.985
7.9038	7.1034	6.424	5.842	5.583	5.342	4.910	4.533	4.203	3.912	3.780	3.656	3.427	3.223	2.468	1.990
8.2442	7.3667	6.628	6.002	5.724	5.468	5.008	4.611	4.265	3.962	3.824	3.695	3.459	3.249	2.477	1.993
8.5595	7.6061	6.811	6.142	5.847	5.575	5.092	4.675	4.315	4.001	3.859	3.726	3.483	3.268	2.484	1.995
8.8514	7.8237	6.974	6.265	5.954	5.669	5.162	4.730	4.357	4.033	3.887	3.751	3.503	3.283	2.489	1.997
9.1216	8.0216	7.120	6.373	6.047	5.749	5.222	4.775	4.391	4.059	3.910	3.771	3.518	3.295	2.492	1.998
9.3719	8.2014	7.250	6.467	6.128	5.818	5.273	4.812	4.419	4.080	3.928	3.786	3.529	3.304	2.494	1.999
9.6036	8.3649	7.366	6.550	6.198	5.877	5.316	4.844	4.442	4.097	3.942	3.799	3.539	3.311	2.496	1.999
9.8181	8.5136	7.469	6.623	6.259	5.929	5.353	4.870	4.460	4.110	3.954	3.808	3.546	3.316	2.497	1.999
10.0168	8.6487	7.562	6.687	6.312	5.973	5.384	4.891	4.476	4.121	3.963	3.816	3.551	3.320	2.498	2.000
10.2007	8.7715	7.645	6.743	6.359	6.011	5.410	4.909	4.488	4.130	3.970	3.822	3.556	3.323	2.498	2.000
10.3711	8.8832	7.718	6.792	6.399	6.044	5.432	4.925	4.499	4.137	3.976	3.827	3.559	3.325	2.499	2.000
10.5288	8.9847	7.784	6.835	6.434	6.073	5.451	4.937	4.507	4.143	3.981	3.831	3.562	3.327	2.499	2.000
10.6748	9.0770	7.843	6.873	6.464	6.097	5.467	4.948	4.514	4.147	3.985	3.834	3.564	3.329	2.499	2.000
10.8100	9.1609	7.896	6.906	6.491	6.118	5.480	4.956	4.520	4.151	3.988	3.837	3.566	3.330	2.500	2.000
10.9352	9.2372	7.943	6.935	6.514	6.136	5.492	4.964	4.524	4.154	3.990	3.839	3.567	3.331	2.500	2.000
11.0511	9.3066	7.984	6.961	6.534	6.152	5.502	4.970	4.528	4.157	3.992	3.840	3.568	3.331	2.500	2.000
11.1584	9.3696	8.022	6.983	6.551	6.166	5.510	4.975	4.531	4.159	3.994	3.841	3.569	3.332	2.500	2.000
11.2578	9.4269	8.055	7.003	6.566	6.177	5.517	4.979	4.534	4.160	3.995	3.842	3.569	3.332	2.500	2.000
11.9246	9.7791	8.244	7.105	6.642	6.234	5.548	4.997	4.544	4.166	3.999	3.846	3.571	3.333	2.500	2.000
12.2335	9.9148	8.304	7.133	6.661	6.246	5.554	4.999	4.545	4.167	4.000	3.846	3.571	3.333	2.500	2.000

Note: To convert this table to values of an annuity in advance, take one less period and add 1.0000.

Appendix C

GRAPHS OF EARNINGS AND EARNINGS TRENDS

EARNINGS & EARNINGS TRENDS

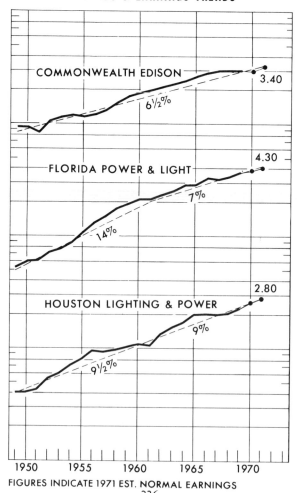

FIGURES INDICATE 1971 EST. NORMAL EARNINGS

EARNINGS & EARNINGS TRENDS

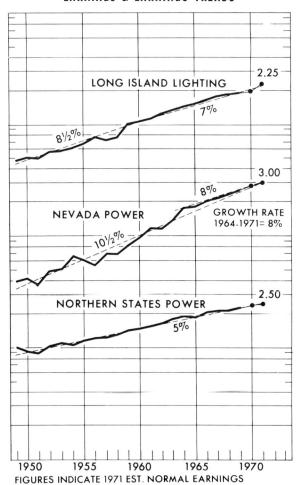

LONG ISLAND LIGHTING — 2.25

7%

8½%

NEVADA POWER — 3.00

8%

GROWTH RATE
1964-1971= 8%

10½%

NORTHERN STATES POWER — 2.50

5%

1950   1955   1960   1965   1970

FIGURES INDICATE 1971 EST. NORMAL EARNINGS

EARNINGS & EARNINGS TRENDS

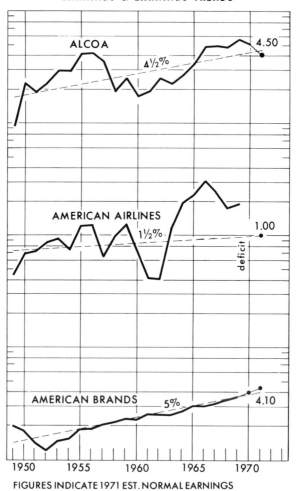

FIGURES INDICATE 1971 EST. NORMAL EARNINGS

EARNINGS & EARNINGS TRENDS

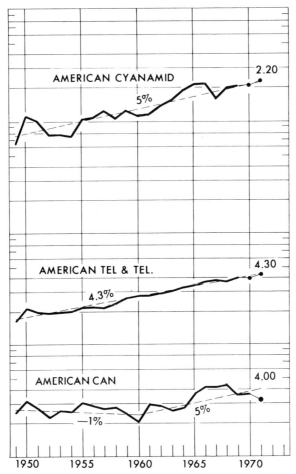

AMERICAN CYANAMID
5%
2.20

AMERICAN TEL & TEL.
4.3%
4.30

AMERICAN CAN
—1%
5%
4.00

1950   1955   1960   1965   1970

FIGURES INDICATE 1971 EST. NORMAL EARNINGS

EARNINGS & EARNINGS TRENDS

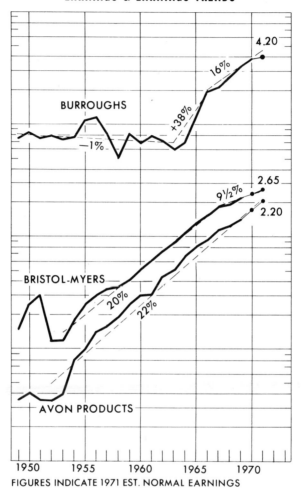

BURROUGHS

4.20

16%

+38%

−1%

2.65

9½%

2.20

BRISTOL-MYERS

20%

22%

AVON PRODUCTS

1950   1955   1960   1965   1970

FIGURES INDICATE 1971 EST. NORMAL EARNINGS

EARNINGS & EARNINGS TRENDS

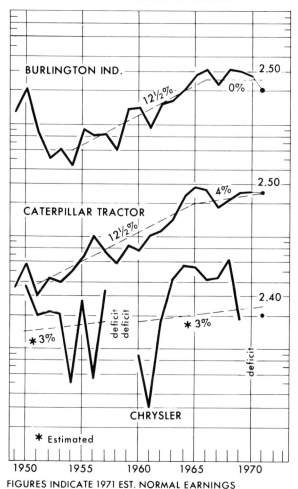

FIGURES INDICATE 1971 EST. NORMAL EARNINGS

EARNINGS & EARNINGS TRENDS

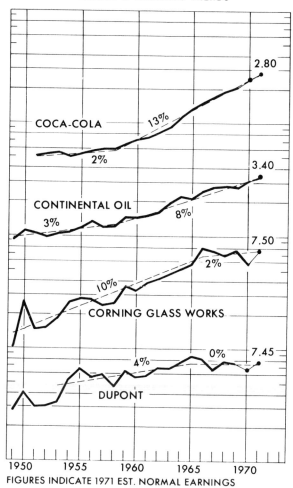

FIGURES INDICATE 1971 EST. NORMAL EARNINGS

EARNINGS & EARNINGS TRENDS

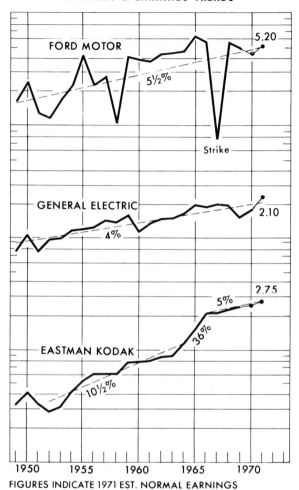

FIGURES INDICATE 1971 EST. NORMAL EARNINGS

EARNINGS & EARNINGS TRENDS

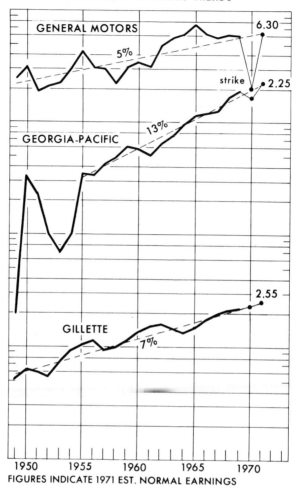

FIGURES INDICATE 1971 EST. NORMAL EARNINGS

EARNINGS & EARNINGS TRENDS

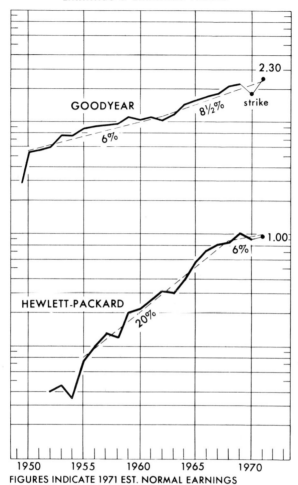

FIGURES INDICATE 1971 EST. NORMAL EARNINGS

EARNINGS & EARNINGS TRENDS

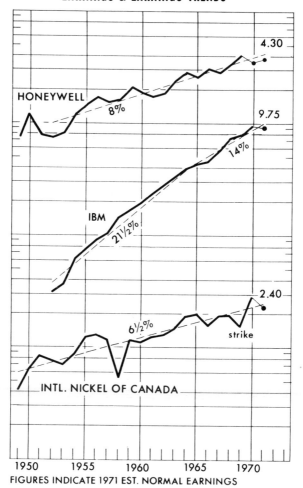

FIGURES INDICATE 1971 EST. NORMAL EARNINGS

EARNINGS & EARNINGS TRENDS

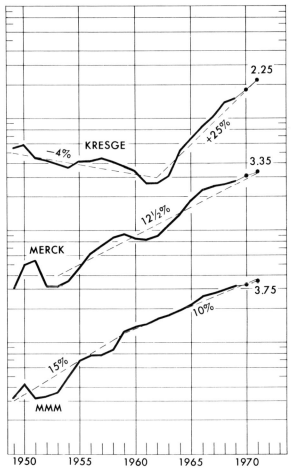

FIGURES INDICATE 1971 EST. NORMAL EARNINGS

EARNINGS & EARNINGS TRENDS

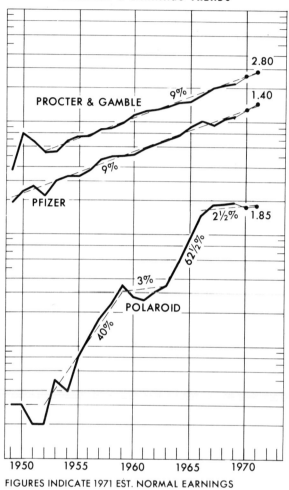

FIGURES INDICATE 1971 EST. NORMAL EARNINGS

EARNINGS & EARNINGS TRENDS

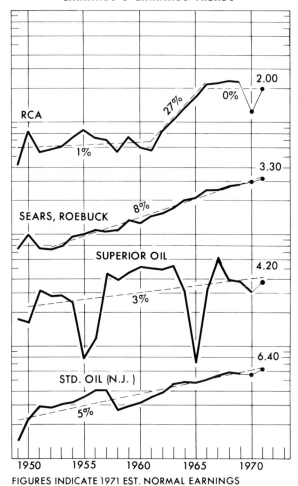

RCA

1%

27%

0%

2.00

SEARS, ROEBUCK

8%

3.30

SUPERIOR OIL

3%

4.20

STD. OIL (N.J.)

5%

6.40

1950   1955   1960   1965   1970

FIGURES INDICATE 1971 EST. NORMAL EARNINGS

EARNINGS & EARNINGS TRENDS

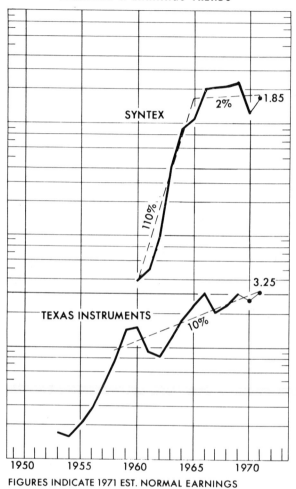

FIGURES INDICATE 1971 EST. NORMAL EARNINGS

EARNINGS & EARNINGS TRENDS

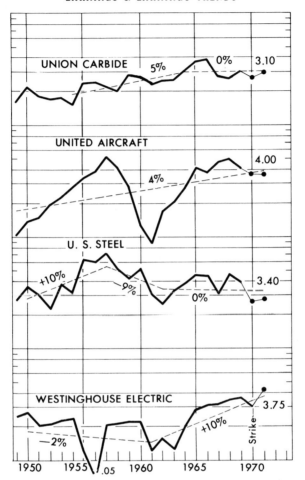

FIGURES INDICATE 1971 EST. NORMAL EARNINGS

EARNINGS & EARNINGS TRENDS

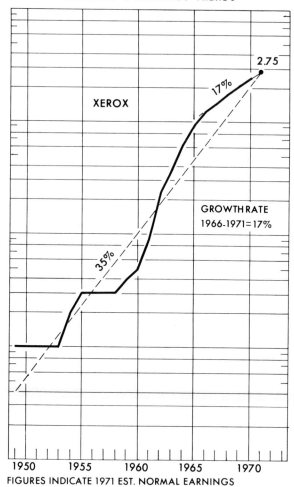

XEROX

2.75

17%

GROWTH RATE
1966-1971=17%

35%

1950   1955   1960   1965   1970

FIGURES INDICATE 1971 EST. NORMAL EARNINGS

Appendix D

THE STOCK VALUATOR—
INDUSTRIALS

77 tables for Industrials
5 sets: 7% to 10% and 12% Return

Industrials—Investment Values of Normal Earnings of $1 at 7% Return

Projected Earnings Growth Rate

1 %

YEARS CONST. GROWTH	2	4	6	8	YEARS SETTLING GROWTH 10	12	14	16	18	20
1	20.1	19.6	18.8	18.4	18.0	17.7	17.3	17.0	16.7	16.5
2	19.6	19.1	18.4	18.0	17.7	17.3	17.0	16.7	16.4	16.2
3	19.1	18.7	18.0	17.6	17.3	17.0	16.7	16.4	16.1	15.9
4	18.7	18.3	17.6	17.3	17.0	16.7	16.4	16.1	15.9	15.6
5	18.3	17.9	17.3	16.9	16.6	16.4	16.1	15.9	15.6	15.4
6	17.9	17.5	16.9	16.6	16.3	16.1	15.8	15.6	15.4	15.2
7	17.5	17.2	16.6	16.3	16.1	15.8	15.6	15.4	15.2	15.0
8	17.2	16.9	16.3	16.1	15.8	15.6	15.3	15.1	14.9	14.8
9	16.8	16.5	16.0	15.8	15.5	15.3	15.1	14.9	14.7	14.6
10	16.5	16.2	15.8	15.5	15.3	15.1	14.9	14.7	14.5	14.4
12	16.0	15.7	15.3	15.1	14.9	14.7	14.5	14.3	14.2	14.0
14	15.5	15.2	14.9	14.7	14.5	14.3	14.2	14.0	13.9	13.7
16	15.0	14.8	14.5	14.3	14.1	14.0	13.9	13.7	13.6	13.5
18	14.6	14.4	14.1	14.0	13.8	13.7	13.6	13.5	13.3	13.2
20	14.2	14.1	13.8	13.7	13.6	13.4	13.3	13.2	13.1	13.0
25	13.5	13.4	13.2	13.1	13.0	12.9	12.8	12.7	12.7	12.6

2 %

YEARS CONST. GROWTH	2	4	6	8	YEARS SETTLING GROWTH 10	12	14	16	18	20
1	20.4	20.1	19.6	19.3	19.0	18.8	18.5	18.3	18.1	17.9
2	20.1	19.8	19.3	19.0	18.7	18.5	18.3	18.1	17.9	17.7
3	19.8	19.5	19.0	18.7	18.5	18.3	18.0	17.8	17.6	17.5
4	19.5	19.2	18.7	18.5	18.2	18.0	17.8	17.6	17.4	17.3
5	19.2	18.9	18.5	18.2	18.0	17.8	17.6	17.4	17.2	17.1
6	18.9	18.7	18.2	18.0	17.8	17.6	17.4	17.2	17.1	16.9
7	18.6	18.4	18.0	17.8	17.6	17.4	17.2	17.0	16.9	16.7
8	18.4	18.2	17.8	17.6	17.4	17.2	17.0	16.9	16.7	16.6
9	18.2	17.9	17.6	17.4	17.2	17.0	16.9	16.7	16.6	16.4
10	17.9	17.7	17.4	17.2	17.0	16.8	16.7	16.5	16.4	16.3
12	17.5	17.3	17.0	16.8	16.7	16.5	16.4	16.2	16.1	16.0
14	17.1	16.9	16.7	16.5	16.4	16.2	16.1	16.0	15.9	15.7
16	16.8	16.6	16.3	16.2	16.1	16.C	15.8	15.7	15.6	15.5
18	16.5	16.3	16.1	15.9	15.8	15.7	15.6	15.5	15.4	15.3
20	16.2	16.0	15.8	15.7	15.6	15.5	15.4	15.3	15.2	15.1
25	15.5	15.4	15.3	15.2	15.1	15.0	14.9	14.9	14.8	14.7

7% Return Tables

YEARS CONST. GROWTH	3 % YEARS SETTLING GROWTH									
	2	4	6	8	10	12	14	16	18	20
1	20.8	20.6	20.3	20.2	20.1	19.9	19.8	19.7	19.5	19.4
2	20.6	20.5	20.2	20.0	19.9	19.8	19.7	19.5	19.4	19.3
3	20.5	20.3	20.0	19.9	19.8	19.6	19.5	19.4	19.3	19.2
4	20.3	20.1	19.9	19.8	19.6	19.5	19.4	19.3	19.2	19.1
5	20.1	20.0	19.8	19.6	19.5	19.4	19.3	19.2	19.1	19.0
6	20.0	19.9	19.6	19.5	19.4	19.3	19.2	19.1	19.0	18.9
7	19.9	19.7	19.5	19.4	19.3	19.2	19.1	19.0	18.9	18.8
8	19.7	19.6	19.4	19.3	19.2	19.1	19.0	18.9	18.8	18.7
9	19.6	19.5	19.3	19.2	19.0	18.9	18.9	18.8	18.7	18.6
10	19.5	19.3	19.1	19.0	18.9	18.8	18.8	18.7	18.6	18.5
12	19.2	19.1	18.9	18.8	18.7	18.7	18.6	18.5	18.4	18.3
14	19.0	18.9	18.7	18.6	18.6	18.5	18.4	18.3	18.2	18.2
16	18.8	18.7	18.6	18.5	18.4	18.3	18.2	18.2	18.1	18.0
18	18.6	18.5	18.4	18.3	18.2	18.2	18.1	18.0	18.0	17.9
20	18.4	18.4	18.2	18.1	18.1	18.0	18.0	17.9	17.8	17.8
25	18.1	18.0	17.9	17.8	17.8	17.7	17.7	17.6	17.6	17.5

YEARS CONST. GROWTH	4 % YEARS SETTLING GROWTH									
	2	4	6	8	10	12	14	16	18	20
1	21.1	21.1	21.1	21.1	21.1	21.1	21.1	21.1	21.1	21.1
2	21.1	21.1	21.1	21.1	21.1	21.1	21.1	21.1	21.1	21.1
3	21.1	21.1	21.1	21.1	21.1	21.1	21.1	21.1	21.1	21.1
4	21.1	21.1	21.1	21.1	21.1	21.1	21.1	21.1	21.1	21.1
5	21.1	21.1	21.1	21.1	21.1	21.1	21.1	21.1	21.1	21.1
6	21.1	21.1	21.1	21.1	21.1	21.1	21.1	21.1	21.1	21.1
7	21.1	21.1	21.1	21.1	21.1	21.1	21.1	21.1	21.1	21.1
8	21.1	21.1	21.1	21.1	21.1	21.1	21.1	21.1	21.1	21.1
9	21.1	21.1	21.1	21.1	21.1	21.1	21.1	21.1	21.1	21.1
10	21.1	21.1	21.1	21.1	21.1	21.1	21.1	21.1	21.1	21.1
12	21.1	21.1	21.1	21.1	21.1	21.1	21.1	21.1	21.1	21.1
14	21.1	21.1	21.1	21.1	21.1	21.1	21.1	21.1	21.1	21.1
16	21.1	21.1	21.1	21.1	21.1	21.1	21.1	21.1	21.1	21.1
18	21.1	21.1	21.1	21.1	21.1	21.1	21.1	21.1	21.1	21.1
20	21.1	21.1	21.1	21.1	21.1	21.1	21.1	21.1	21.1	21.1
25	21.1	21.1	21.1	21.1	21.1	21.1	21.1	21.1	21.1	21.1

YEARS CONST. GROWTH	5 % YEARS SETTLING GROWTH									
	2	4	6	8	10	12	14	16	18	20
1	21.5	21.7	22.0	22.2	22.3	22.5	22.6	22.8	22.9	23.0
2	21.7	21.9	22.2	22.3	22.5	22.6	22.8	22.9	23.1	23.2
3	21.9	22.0	22.3	22.5	22.6	22.8	22.9	23.1	23.2	23.3
4	22.0	22.2	22.5	22.6	22.8	22.9	23.1	23.2	23.4	23.5
5	22.2	22.4	22.6	22.8	22.9	23.1	23.2	23.4	23.5	23.6
6	22.4	22.5	22.8	22.9	23.1	23.2	23.4	23.5	23.6	23.8
7	22.5	22.7	23.0	23.1	23.2	23.4	23.5	23.6	23.8	23.9
8	22.7	22.8	23.1	23.2	23.4	23.5	23.7	23.8	23.9	24.0
9	22.8	23.0	23.3	23.4	23.5	23.7	23.8	23.9	24.0	24.2
10	23.0	23.1	23.4	23.5	23.7	23.8	23.9	24.1	24.2	24.3
12	23.3	23.4	23.7	23.8	23.9	24.1	24.2	24.3	24.4	24.5
14	23.6	23.7	23.9	24.1	24.2	24.3	24.4	24.6	24.7	24.8
16	23.9	24.0	24.2	24.3	24.5	24.6	24.7	24.8	24.9	25.0
18	24.1	24.2	24.5	24.6	24.7	24.8	24.9	25.0	25.1	25.2
20	24.4	24.5	24.7	24.8	24.9	25.0	25.1	25.2	25.3	25.4
25	25.0	25.1	25.3	25.4	25.5	25.6	25.7	25.8	25.9	25.9

7% Return Tables

6 % YEARS SETTLING GROWTH

YEARS CONST. GROWTH	2	4	6	8	10	12	14	16	18	20
1	21.9	22.2	22.9	23.2	23.5	23.9	24.2	24.5	24.8	25.1
2	22.2	22.6	23.2	23.6	23.9	24.2	24.5	24.8	25.2	25.5
3	22.6	23.0	23.6	23.9	24.2	24.6	24.9	25.2	25.5	25.8
4	23.0	23.3	23.9	24.2	24.6	24.9	25.2	25.5	25.8	26.1
5	23.3	23.7	24.2	24.6	24.9	25.2	25.5	25.8	26.1	26.4
6	23.7	24.0	24.6	24.9	25.2	25.6	25.9	26.2	26.5	26.8
7	24.0	24.3	24.9	25.3	25.6	25.9	26.2	26.5	26.8	27.1
8	24.3	24.7	25.3	25.6	25.9	26.2	26.5	26.8	27.1	27.4
9	24.7	25.0	25.6	25.9	26.2	26.5	26.8	27.1	27.4	27.7
10	25.0	25.3	25.9	26.2	26.5	26.8	27.1	27.4	27.7	28.0
12	25.7	26.0	26.6	26.9	27.2	27.5	27.8	28.1	28.3	28.6
14	26.3	26.6	27.2	27.5	27.8	28.1	28.4	28.7	28.9	29.2
16	27.0	27.3	27.8	28.1	28.4	28.7	29.0	29.3	29.5	29.8
18	27.6	27.9	28.4	28.7	29.0	29.3	29.6	29.8	30.1	30.4
20	28.2	28.5	29.0	29.3	29.6	29.9	30.1	30.4	30.7	30.9
25	29.7	30.0	30.5	30.7	31.0	31.3	31.5	31.8	32.0	32.3

7 % YEARS SETTLING GROWTH

YEARS CONST. GROWTH	2	4	6	8	10	12	14	16	18	20
1	22.3	22.8	23.8	24.3	24.8	25.4	25.9	26.4	26.9	27.4
2	22.8	23.4	24.3	24.9	25.4	25.9	26.4	27.0	27.5	28.0
3	23.4	23.9	24.9	25.4	25.9	26.5	27.0	27.5	28.0	28.5
4	23.9	24.5	25.4	26.0	26.5	27.0	27.6	28.1	28.6	29.1
5	24.5	25.0	26.0	26.5	27.1	27.6	28.1	28.6	29.2	29.7
6	25.0	25.6	26.5	27.1	27.6	28.1	28.7	29.2	29.7	30.2
7	25.6	26.1	27.1	27.6	28.2	28.7	29.2	29.7	30.3	30.8
8	26.1	26.7	27.7	28.2	28.7	29.3	29.8	30.3	30.8	31.3
9	26.7	27.2	28.2	28.7	29.3	29.8	30.3	30.9	31.4	31.9
10	27.3	27.8	28.8	29.3	29.8	30.4	30.9	31.4	31.9	32.4
12	28.4	28.9	29.9	30.4	31.0	31.5	32.0	32.5	33.0	33.6
14	29.5	30.0	31.0	31.5	32.1	32.6	33.1	33.6	34.2	34.7
16	30.6	31.1	32.1	32.6	33.2	33.7	34.2	34.8	35.3	35.8
18	31.7	32.3	33.2	33.8	34.3	34.8	35.3	35.9	36.4	36.9
20	32.8	33.4	34.3	34.9	35.4	35.9	36.5	37.0	37.5	38.0
25	35.6	36.1	37.1	37.6	38.2	38.7	39.2	39.8	40.3	40.8

8 % YEARS SETTLING GROWTH

YEARS CONST. GROWTH	2	4	6	8	10	12	14	16	18	20
1	22.6	23.4	24.7	25.5	26.2	27.0	27.7	28.5	29.2	30.0
2	23.4	24.1	25.5	26.2	27.0	27.7	28.5	29.3	30.0	30.8
3	24.1	24.9	26.2	27.0	27.8	28.5	29.3	30.1	30.9	31.6
4	24.9	25.7	27.0	27.8	28.6	29.4	30.1	30.9	31.7	32.5
5	25.7	26.5	27.8	28.6	29.4	30.2	31.0	31.7	32.5	33.3
6	26.5	27.2	28.6	29.4	30.2	31.0	31.8	32.6	33.4	34.2
7	27.3	28.0	29.4	30.2	31.0	31.8	32.6	33.4	34.2	35.0
8	28.0	28.8	30.3	31.1	31.9	32.7	33.5	34.3	35.1	35.9
9	28.9	29.7	31.1	31.9	32.7	33.5	34.3	35.1	35.9	36.8
10	29.7	30.5	31.9	32.7	33.5	34.4	35.2	36.0	36.8	37.6
12	31.3	32.1	33.6	34.4	35.3	36.1	36.9	37.8	38.6	39.4
14	33.0	33.8	35.3	36.2	37.0	37.9	38.7	39.6	40.4	41.3
16	34.7	35.5	37.1	37.9	38.8	39.7	40.5	41.4	42.3	43.1
18	36.4	37.3	38.8	39.7	40.6	41.5	42.4	43.3	44.1	45.0
20	38.2	39.1	40.7	41.6	42.5	43.4	44.3	45.2	46.1	47.0
25	42.8	43.7	45.4	46.3	47.2	48.2	49.1	50.1	51.0	51.9

7% **Return Tables**

YEARS CONST. GROWTH	9 % YEARS SETTLING GROWTH									
	2	4	6	8	10	12	14	16	18	20
1	23.0	24.0	25.7	26.7	27.6	28.7	29.7	30.7	31.7	32.8
2	24.0	24.9	26.7	27.7	28.7	29.7	30.8	31.8	32.8	33.9
3	24.9	25.9	27.7	28.7	29.8	30.8	31.9	32.9	34.0	35.1
4	25.9	26.9	28.8	29.8	30.8	31.9	33.0	34.1	35.1	36.2
5	27.0	28.0	29.8	30.9	31.9	33.0	34.1	35.2	36.3	37.5
6	28.0	29.0	30.9	32.0	33.1	34.2	35.3	36.4	37.5	38.7
7	29.0	30.1	32.0	33.1	34.2	35.3	36.5	37.6	38.8	39.9
8	30.1	31.2	33.1	34.3	35.4	36.5	37.7	38.8	40.0	41.2
9	31.2	32.3	34.3	35.4	36.6	37.7	38.9	40.1	41.3	42.5
10	32.3	33.4	35.5	36.6	37.8	39.0	40.2	41.4	42.6	43.8
12	34.6	35.8	37.9	39.1	40.3	41.5	42.8	44.0	45.3	46.6
14	37.0	38.2	40.4	41.6	42.9	44.1	45.4	46.7	48.1	49.4
16	39.4	40.7	42.9	44.2	45.6	46.9	48.2	49.6	50.9	52.3
18	42.0	43.3	45.6	47.0	48.3	49.7	51.1	52.5	53.9	55.3
20	44.6	46.0	48.4	49.8	51.2	52.7	54.1	55.6	57.0	58.5
25	51.7	53.2	55.9	57.4	58.9	60.5	62.1	63.7	65.3	66.9

YEARS CONST. GROWTH	10 % YEARS SETTLING GROWTH									
	2	4	6	8	10	12	14	16	18	20
1	23.4	24.6	26.7	27.9	29.2	30.5	31.8	33.1	34.5	35.8
2	24.6	25.8	27.9	29.2	30.5	31.8	33.2	34.5	35.9	37.4
3	25.8	27.0	29.2	30.6	31.9	33.2	34.6	36.0	37.5	38.9
4	27.0	28.3	30.6	31.9	33.3	34.7	36.1	37.6	39.0	40.5
5	28.3	29.6	32.0	33.3	34.7	36.2	37.6	39.1	40.6	42.2
6	29.6	30.9	33.4	34.8	36.2	37.7	39.2	40.7	42.3	43.9
7	30.9	32.3	34.8	36.3	37.8	39.3	40.8	42.4	44.0	45.6
8	32.3	33.7	36.3	37.8	39.3	40.9	42.5	44.1	45.7	47.4
9	33.8	35.2	37.8	39.4	41.0	42.6	44.2	45.9	47.5	49.3
10	35.2	36.7	39.4	41.0	42.6	44.3	45.9	47.7	49.4	51.2
12	38.3	39.8	42.7	44.4	46.1	47.8	49.6	51.4	53.2	55.1
14	41.5	43.2	46.2	48.0	49.8	51.6	53.5	55.4	57.3	59.3
16	44.9	46.7	49.9	51.7	53.6	55.6	57.6	59.6	61.6	63.7
18	48.5	50.4	53.7	55.7	57.7	59.8	61.9	64.0	66.2	68.4
20	52.3	54.3	57.8	59.9	62.1	64.2	66.4	68.7	71.0	73.3
25	62.8	65.0	69.2	71.6	74.0	76.5	79.0	81.6	84.2	86.9

YEARS CONST. GROWTH	11 % YEARS SETTLING GROWTH									
	2	4	6	8	10	12	14	16	18	20
1	23.8	25.2	27.7	29.2	30.8	32.4	34.0	35.7	37.4	39.2
2	25.2	26.6	29.3	30.8	32.4	34.1	35.8	37.5	39.3	41.2
3	26.6	28.1	30.9	32.5	34.2	35.9	37.6	39.5	41.3	43.2
4	28.1	29.7	32.5	34.2	35.9	37.7	39.6	41.4	43.4	45.4
5	29.7	31.3	34.2	36.0	37.8	39.6	41.5	43.5	45.5	47.6
6	31.3	33.0	36.0	37.8	39.7	41.6	43.6	45.6	47.7	49.8
7	33.0	34.7	37.9	39.8	41.7	43.7	45.7	47.8	50.0	52.2
8	34.7	36.5	39.8	41.8	43.8	45.8	47.9	50.1	52.4	54.7
9	36.5	38.4	41.8	43.8	45.9	48.0	50.2	52.5	54.8	57.2
10	38.4	40.3	43.9	46.0	48.1	50.3	52.6	55.0	57.4	59.8
12	42.3	44.4	48.2	50.5	52.8	55.2	57.7	60.2	62.8	65.4
14	46.6	48.8	52.9	55.4	57.9	60.4	63.1	65.8	68.6	71.4
16	51.2	53.6	58.0	60.6	63.3	66.1	68.9	71.8	74.8	77.9
18	56.1	58.7	63.4	66.2	69.1	72.1	75.2	78.3	81.6	84.9
20	61.4	64.2	69.3	72.3	75.4	78.6	81.9	85.3	88.8	92.4
25	76.5	79.8	86.0	89.6	93.3	97.2	101.2	105.2	109.4	113.7

7% Return Tables

12 %

YEARS CONST. GROWTH	2	4	6	8	10	12	14	16	18	20
1	24.2	25.8	28.8	30.6	32.5	34.4	36.4	38.5	40.7	42.9
2	25.8	27.5	3C.6	32.5	34.5	36.5	38.6	40.8	43.1	45.4
3	27.5	29.3	32.6	34.5	36.6	38.7	40.9	43.2	45.6	48.1
4	29.3	31.1	34.6	36.7	38.8	41.0	43.3	45.7	48.2	50.8
5	31.2	33.1	36.7	38.9	41.1	43.4	45.9	48.4	51.0	53.7
6	33.1	35.1	38.9	41.2	43.5	46.C	48.5	51.1	53.8	56.7
7	35.1	37.3	41.2	43.6	46.0	48.6	51.3	54.0	56.8	59.8
8	37.3	39.5	43.6	46.1	48.7	51.4	54.1	57.0	60.0	63.1
9	39.5	41.8	46.2	48.8	51.5	54.3	57.2	60.2	63.3	66.5
10	41.8	44.3	48.8	51.5	54.4	57.3	60.3	63.5	66.7	70.1
12	46.9	49.5	54.5	57.5	60.6	63.8	67.1	7C.6	74.1	77.8
14	52.3	55.3	60.7	64.0	67.4	70.9	74.5	78.3	82.2	86.3
16	58.4	61.6	67.5	71.1	74.8	78.7	82.7	86.8	91.1	95.6
18	65.0	68.5	75.0	78.9	83.0	87.2	91.6	96.1	100.8	105.7
20	72.2	76.C	83.2	87.5	91.9	96.6	101.4	106.3	111.5	116.8
25	93.4	98.2	107.2	112.6	118.2	124.C	130.1	136.3	142.8	149.5

13 %

YEARS CONST. GROWTH	2	4	6	8	10	12	14	16	18	20
1	24.6	26.4	29.9	32.1	34.3	36.6	39.0	41.6	44.2	47.0
2	26.5	28.4	32.1	34.3	36.7	39.1	41.7	44.4	47.2	50.1
3	28.4	30.5	34.4	36.7	39.2	41.8	44.5	47.4	50.3	53.4
4	30.5	32.7	36.8	39.3	41.9	44.6	47.5	5C.5	53.6	56.9
5	32.7	35.0	39.3	42.0	44.7	47.6	50.6	53.8	57.1	60.6
6	35.0	37.4	42.0	44.8	47.7	50.8	54.0	57.3	60.8	64.5
7	37.4	40.0	44.8	47.8	50.9	54.1	57.5	61.0	64.7	68.6
8	40.0	42.7	47.8	51.0	54.2	57.6	61.2	64.9	68.8	72.9
9	42.7	45.6	51.0	54.3	57.7	61.3	65.1	69.0	73.1	77.5
10	45.6	48.6	54.3	57.8	61.4	65.2	69.2	73.4	77.7	82.3
12	51.9	55.2	61.6	65.5	69.5	73.8	78.2	82.8	87.7	92.8
14	58.8	62.6	69.7	74.0	78.5	83.3	88.2	93.4	98.8	104.4
16	66.6	70.8	78.7	83.5	88.6	93.8	99.4	105.1	111.2	117.5
18	75.3	80.C	88.8	94.2	99.8	105.6	111.8	118.2	125.0	132.0
20	85.0	90.2	100.0	106.0	112.3	118.8	125.7	132.9	140.4	148.2
25	114.3	121.1	134.1	141.9	150.2	158.8	167.8	177.2	187.1	197.4

14 %

YEARS CONST. GROWTH	2	4	6	8	10	12	14	16	18	20
1	25.0	27.1	31.1	33.6	36.2	38.9	41.8	44.9	48.1	51.5
2	27.1	29.3	33.6	36.2	39.0	41.9	45.0	48.3	51.7	55.4
3	29.3	31.7	36.3	39.1	42.0	45.1	48.4	51.9	55.6	59.4
4	31.7	34.3	39.1	42.1	45.2	48.6	52.1	55.8	59.7	63.8
5	34.3	37.0	42.1	45.3	48.7	52.2	55.9	59.9	64.1	68.5
6	37.0	39.9	45.4	48.7	52.3	56.1	60.1	64.3	68.7	73.4
7	39.9	42.9	48.8	52.4	56.2	60.2	64.5	69.0	73.7	78.7
8	43.0	46.2	52.5	56.3	60.4	64.6	69.2	73.9	79.0	84.3
9	46.2	49.7	56.4	60.5	64.8	69.3	74.2	79.2	84.6	90.3
10	49.7	53.4	60.5	64.9	69.5	74.4	79.5	84.9	90.6	96.6
12	57.4	61.6	69.7	74.6	79.9	85.4	91.2	97.3	103.8	110.7
14	66.2	70.9	80.1	85.7	91.6	97.9	104.5	111.5	118.8	126.6
16	76.1	81.5	91.8	98.2	105.0	112.1	119.6	127.5	135.9	144.7
18	87.3	93.5	105.2	112.5	120.1	128.2	136.7	145.7	155.2	165.2
20	100.1	107.1	120.4	128.6	137.3	146.5	156.1	166.4	177.1	188.5
25	140.1	149.7	168.0	179.3	191.2	203.8	217.0	231.1	245.8	261.4

7% Return Tables

YEARS CONST. GROWTH	15 % YEARS SETTLING GROWTH									
	2	4	6	8	10	12	14	16	18	20
1	25.4	27.8	32.3	35.1	38.2	41.4	44.8	48.4	52.3	56.5
2	27.8	30.3	35.2	38.2	41.5	44.9	48.6	52.5	56.7	61.1
3	30.3	33.C	38.3	41.5	45.0	48.7	52.7	56.9	61.4	66.2
4	33.0	35.9	41.6	45.1	48.8	52.8	57.1	61.6	66.4	71.6
5	36.0	39.1	45.2	48.9	53.0	57.3	61.8	66.7	71.9	77.4
6	39.1	42.5	49.0	53.0	57.4	62.0	66.9	72.1	77.7	83.6
7	42.5	46.1	53.1	57.5	62.1	67.1	72.4	78.0	84.0	90.3
8	46.1	50.0	57.5	62.2	67.2	72.6	78.2	84.3	90.7	97.5
9	50.0	54.2	62.3	67.3	72.7	78.4	84.5	91.0	97.9	105.3
10	54.2	58.7	67.4	72.8	78.6	84.8	91.3	98.3	105.7	113.6
12	63.6	68.8	78.8	85.1	91.8	98.9	106.4	114.5	123.1	132.2
14	74.4	80.4	92.0	99.2	106.9	115.2	123.9	133.2	143.1	153.7
16	86.9	93.8	107.2	115.6	124.5	134.0	144.1	154.8	166.3	178.5
18	101.3	109.3	124.8	134.5	144.8	155.7	167.4	179.8	193.0	207.1
20	118.0	127.3	145.1	156.3	168.2	180.8	194.3	208.6	223.9	240.2
25	171.9	185.2	210.8	226.8	243.8	262.0	281.3	301.9	323.8	347.1

YEARS CONST. GROWTH	16 % YEARS SETTLING GROWTH									
	2	4	6	8	10	12	14	16	18	20
1	25.8	28.4	33.5	36.8	40.2	44.0	48.0	52.3	56.9	61.9
2	28.4	31.3	36.8	40.3	44.1	48.1	52.5	57.1	62.1	67.5
3	31.3	34.4	40.4	44.2	48.2	52.6	57.3	62.4	67.8	73.7
4	34.4	37.7	44.2	48.3	52.7	57.5	62.6	68.1	74.0	80.3
5	37.7	41.3	48.4	52.8	57.6	62.8	68.3	74.3	80.6	87.5
6	41.3	45.2	52.9	57.7	62.9	68.5	74.5	81.0	87.9	95.3
7	45.2	49.5	57.8	63.0	68.7	74.7	81.2	88.2	95.7	103.8
8	49.5	54.1	63.1	68.8	74.9	81.5	88.5	96.1	104.2	112.9
9	54.1	59.1	68.9	75.0	81.6	88.7	96.4	104.6	113.4	122.9
10	59.1	64.5	75.1	81.8	88.9	96.7	105.0	113.9	123.4	133.7
12	70.4	76.8	89.2	97.0	105.5	114.5	124.3	134.7	146.0	158.0
14	83.7	91.2	105.8	115.0	124.9	135.6	147.0	159.3	172.5	186.7
16	99.3	108.1	125.2	136.1	147.7	160.3	173.7	188.2	203.7	220.3
18	117.6	128.0	148.1	160.9	174.6	189.3	205.1	222.1	240.3	259.9
20	139.2	151.3	175.0	190.0	206.1	223.4	242.0	261.9	283.4	306.4
25	211.1	229.3	264.7	287.2	311.3	337.2	365.0	394.9	427.0	461.5

YEARS CONST. GROWTH	17 % YEARS SETTLING GROWTH									
	2	4	6	8	10	12	14	16	18	20
1	26.2	29.1	34.8	38.5	42.5	46.7	51.4	56.4	61.9	67.8
2	29.1	32.3	38.5	42.5	46.9	51.6	56.6	62.2	68.1	74.6
3	32.3	35.7	42.6	46.9	51.7	56.8	62.4	68.4	74.9	82.0
4	35.7	39.5	47.0	51.8	56.9	62.6	68.6	75.2	82.4	90.1
5	39.5	43.7	51.8	57.0	62.7	68.8	75.5	82.7	90.5	99.0
6	43.7	48.2	57.1	62.8	69.0	75.7	83.0	9C.9	99.4	108.7
7	48.2	53.1	62.9	69.1	75.9	83.2	91.2	99.8	109.1	119.2
8	53.1	58.5	69.2	76.0	83.4	91.4	100.1	109.6	119.8	130.8
9	58.5	64.4	76.1	83.6	91.7	100.4	109.9	120.2	131.4	143.5
10	64.4	70.9	83.6	91.8	100.7	110.2	120.6	131.9	144.1	157.3
12	77.9	85.7	100.9	110.7	121.3	132.7	145.2	158.6	173.2	189.0
14	94.1	103.3	121.6	133.3	145.9	159.6	174.5	190.6	208.1	226.9
16	113.4	124.5	146.3	160.2	175.4	191.8	2C9.5	228.8	249.7	272.3
18	136.6	149.8	175.8	192.5	210.6	230.2	251.5	274.5	299.4	326.4
20	164.2	180.0	211.1	231.1	252.7	276.2	301.6	329.1	359.0	391.2
25	259.3	284.0	332.7	363.9	397.7	434.3	474.0	517.1	563.7	614.2

7% Return Tables

YEARS CONST. GROWTH	18 % YEARS SETTLING GROWTH									
	2	4	6	8	10	12	14	16	18	20
1	26.7	29.8	36.2	40.3	44.8	49.7	55.1	60.9	67.3	74.3
2	29.8	33.3	40.3	44.9	49.8	55.2	61.1	67.6	74.7	82.4
3	33.3	37.2	44.9	49.9	55.4	61.3	67.9	75.0	82.8	91.3
4	37.2	41.4	49.9	55.4	61.5	68.1	75.3	83.1	91.7	101.1
5	41.4	46.1	55.5	61.6	68.2	75.5	83.4	92.1	101.6	112.0
6	46.1	51.3	61.6	68.3	75.7	83.7	92.4	102.0	112.5	123.9
7	51.3	57.0	68.4	75.8	83.9	92.7	102.4	112.9	124.5	137.1
8	57.0	63.3	75.9	84.0	92.9	102.7	113.3	125.0	137.7	151.6
9	63.3	70.2	84.1	93.1	102.9	113.6	125.4	138.2	152.3	167.6
10	70.2	77.9	93.2	103.1	113.9	125.8	138.7	152.9	168.3	185.2
12	86.3	95.6	114.2	126.2	139.4	153.8	169.6	186.8	205.6	226.2
14	105.8	117.2	139.8	154.4	170.4	188.0	207.1	228.1	251.0	276.0
16	129.6	143.4	170.9	188.7	208.2	229.5	252.8	278.3	306.1	336.5
18	158.5	175.3	208.7	230.4	254.1	280.0	308.4	339.4	373.2	410.2
20	193.7	214.1	254.8	281.1	309.9	341.5	375.9	413.6	454.8	499.7
25	318.6	351.8	418.2	461.2	508.2	559.6	615.8	677.3	744.4	817.8

YEARS CONST. GROWTH	19 % YEARS SETTLING GROWTH									
	2	4	6	8	10	12	14	16	18	20
1	27.1	30.6	37.6	42.2	47.2	52.8	59.0	65.8	73.3	81.5
2	30.6	34.4	42.2	47.3	52.9	59.1	66.0	73.6	81.9	91.1
3	34.4	38.7	47.3	53.0	59.3	66.2	73.8	82.2	91.5	101.7
4	38.7	43.4	53.1	59.4	66.4	74.0	82.5	91.9	102.2	113.5
5	43.4	48.7	59.4	66.5	74.2	82.8	92.2	102.6	114.0	126.7
6	48.7	54.6	66.5	74.3	83.0	92.5	102.9	114.5	127.2	141.3
7	54.6	61.2	74.4	83.1	92.7	103.2	114.9	127.8	141.9	157.5
8	61.1	68.4	83.2	92.8	103.5	115.2	128.2	142.5	158.3	175.6
9	68.4	76.5	92.9	103.6	115.5	128.6	143.0	158.9	176.4	195.7
10	76.5	85.5	103.7	115.7	128.9	143.4	159.5	177.1	196.6	218.1
12	95.5	106.7	129.2	144.0	160.3	178.3	198.1	220.0	244.1	270.6
14	119.0	132.8	160.7	179.0	199.1	221.4	245.9	273.0	302.8	335.6
16	148.1	165.2	199.6	222.2	247.2	274.7	305.1	338.5	375.4	416.0
18	184.0	205.2	247.8	275.8	306.6	340.7	378.2	419.6	465.2	515.5
20	228.5	254.7	307.4	342.0	380.1	422.3	468.7	519.9	576.3	638.4
25	391.4	435.9	525.6	584.4	649.4	721.0	800.0	887.1	983.1	1088.9

YEARS CONST. GROWTH	20 % YEARS SETTLING GROWTH									
	2	4	6	8	10	12	14	16	18	20
1	27.5	31.3	39.0	44.1	49.8	56.1	63.2	71.0	79.7	89.3
2	31.3	35.5	44.1	49.9	56.2	63.3	71.2	80.0	89.8	100.6
3	35.5	40.2	49.9	56.3	63.5	71.5	80.3	90.1	101.1	113.2
4	40.2	45.5	56.4	63.6	71.6	80.5	90.5	101.5	113.8	127.4
5	45.5	51.5	63.6	71.7	80.7	90.7	101.9	114.2	128.0	143.3
6	51.4	58.1	71.8	80.8	90.9	102.2	114.6	128.5	144.0	161.1
7	58.1	65.6	80.9	91.1	102.4	115.0	129.0	144.6	161.9	181.1
8	65.6	74.0	91.1	102.5	115.2	129.4	145.1	162.5	181.9	203.5
9	73.9	83.4	102.6	115.4	129.6	145.5	163.1	182.7	204.4	228.6
10	83.3	93.9	115.5	129.8	145.8	163.6	183.3	205.3	229.7	256.8
12	105.7	119.0	146.1	164.2	184.3	206.6	231.4	259.0	289.8	323.9
14	133.8	150.5	184.7	207.4	232.6	260.7	291.9	326.7	365.3	408.2
16	169.1	190.2	233.1	261.7	293.4	328.8	368.1	411.7	460.3	514.3
18	213.6	240.0	294.1	330.0	369.9	414.4	463.8	518.7	579.8	647.7
20	269.5	302.8	370.7	415.9	466.1	522.0	584.2	653.3	730.2	815.5
25	480.7	539.8	660.3	740.4	829.6	928.8	1039.0	1161.7	1298.0	1449.5

7% Return Tables

YEARS CONST. GROWTH	2	4	6	8	25 % YEARS SETTLING GROWTH 10	12	14	16	18	20
1	29.8	35.2	46.9	55.2	64.8	75.9	88.8	103.8	121.2	141.3
2	35.1	41.5	55.2	64.8	76.0	89.0	104.1	121.6	141.9	165.4
3	41.4	48.8	64.8	76.1	89.2	104.4	122.0	142.4	166.1	193.6
4	48.7	57.4	76.1	89.2	104.5	122.3	142.9	166.8	194.4	226.5
5	57.3	67.4	89.2	104.6	122.5	143.2	167.3	195.2	227.5	265.0
6	67.3	79.1	104.6	122.6	143.5	167.7	195.8	228.4	266.1	309.9
7	79.0	92.8	122.6	143.6	168.0	196.2	229.1	267.1	311.3	362.4
8	92.6	108.8	143.5	168.1	196.6	229.6	268.0	312.4	364.0	423.8
9	108.6	127.5	168.1	196.7	230.0	268.6	313.4	365.4	425.6	495.4
10	127.2	149.3	196.7	230.2	269.0	314.2	366.5	427.2	497.6	579.1
12	174.4	204.5	269.2	314.9	368.0	429.5	501.0	583.8	679.8	791.1
14	238.8	279.9	368.2	430.6	503.0	587.0	684.5	797.5	928.6	1080.4
16	326.7	382.7	503.3	588.4	687.2	801.9	934.9	1089.2	1268.0	1475.3
18	446.6	523.1	687.6	803.8	938.6	1095.1	1276.7	1487.2	1731.3	2014.2
20	610.3	714.7	939.2	1097.7	1281.8	1495.4	1743.2	2030.5	2363.6	2749.7
25	1330.5	1557.5	2046.1	2391.0	2791.5	3256.2	3795.4	4420.6	5145.4	5985.4

Industrials—Investment Values of Normal Earnings of $1 at 8% Return

Projected Earnings Growth Rate

YEARS CONST. GROWTH	2	4	6	8	1 % YEARS SETTLING GROWTH 10	12	14	16	18	20
1	15.1	14.8	14.2	13.9	13.7	13.4	13.2	13.0	12.8	12.6
2	14.7	14.4	13.9	13.7	13.4	13.2	13.0	12.8	12.6	12.4
3	14.4	14.1	13.6	13.4	13.2	13.0	12.8	12.6	12.4	12.3
4	14.1	13.8	13.4	13.2	12.9	12.7	12.6	12.4	12.2	12.1
5	13.8	13.6	13.1	12.9	12.7	12.6	12.4	12.2	12.1	11.9
6	13.6	13.3	12.9	12.7	12.5	12.4	12.2	12.1	11.9	11.8
7	13.3	13.1	12.7	12.5	12.4	12.2	12.0	11.9	11.8	11.7
8	13.1	12.9	12.5	12.3	12.2	12.0	11.9	11.8	11.6	11.5
9	12.9	12.7	12.3	12.2	12.0	11.9	11.8	11.6	11.5	11.4
10	12.7	12.5	12.2	12.0	11.9	11.7	11.6	11.5	11.4	11.3
12	12.3	12.1	11.9	11.7	11.6	11.5	11.4	11.3	11.2	11.1
14	12.0	11.8	11.6	11.5	11.4	11.3	11.2	11.1	11.0	10.9
16	11.7	11.6	11.3	11.2	11.2	11.1	11.0	10.9	10.8	10.8
18	11.4	11.3	11.1	11.1	11.0	10.9	10.8	10.8	10.7	10.6
20	11.2	11.1	11.0	10.9	10.8	10.7	10.7	10.6	10.6	10.5
25	10.8	10.7	10.6	10.5	10.5	10.4	10.4	10.4	10.3	10.3

YEARS CONST. GROWTH	2	4	6	8	2 % YEARS SETTLING GROWTH 10	12	14	16	18	20
1	15.3	15.1	14.7	14.5	14.4	14.2	14.0	13.9	13.7	13.6
2	15.1	14.9	14.5	14.3	14.2	14.0	13.9	13.7	13.6	13.5
3	14.9	14.7	14.3	14.2	14.0	13.9	13.7	13.6	13.5	13.3
4	14.7	14.5	14.2	14.0	13.8	13.7	13.6	13.4	13.3	13.2
5	14.5	14.3	14.0	13.8	13.7	13.6	13.4	13.3	13.2	13.1
6	14.3	14.1	13.8	13.7	13.5	13.4	13.3	13.2	13.1	13.0
7	14.1	13.9	13.7	13.5	13.4	13.3	13.2	13.1	13.0	12.9
8	13.9	13.8	13.5	13.4	13.3	13.2	13.1	13.0	12.9	12.8
9	13.8	13.6	13.4	13.3	13.2	13.0	12.9	12.8	12.8	12.7
10	13.6	13.5	13.3	13.1	13.0	12.9	12.8	12.7	12.7	12.6
12	13.3	13.2	13.0	12.9	12.8	12.7	12.6	12.6	12.5	12.4
14	13.1	13.0	12.8	12.7	12.6	12.6	12.5	12.4	12.3	12.3
16	12.9	12.8	12.6	12.5	12.5	12.4	12.3	12.3	12.2	12.1
18	12.7	12.6	12.5	12.4	12.3	12.2	12.2	12.1	12.1	12.0
20	12.5	12.4	12.3	12.2	12.2	12.1	12.1	12.0	12.0	11.9
25	12.2	12.1	12.0	11.9	11.9	11.9	11.8	11.8	11.7	11.7

8% Return Tables

3 %

YEARS CONST. GROWTH	\multicolumn{10}{c}{YEARS SETTLING GROWTH}
	2	4	6	8	10	12	14	16	18	20
1	15.6	15.5	15.3	15.2	15.1	15.0	14.9	14.8	14.8	14.7
2	15.5	15.4	15.2	15.1	15.0	14.9	14.8	14.7	14.7	14.6
3	15.4	15.3	15.3	15.0	14.9	14.8	14.7	14.7	14.6	14.5
4	15.3	15.2	15.0	14.9	14.8	14.7	14.7	14.6	14.5	14.5
5	15.2	15.1	14.9	14.8	14.7	14.6	14.6	14.5	14.4	14.4
6	15.1	15.0	14.8	14.7	14.6	14.6	14.5	14.4	14.4	14.3
7	15.0	14.9	14.7	14.6	14.6	14.5	14.4	14.4	14.3	14.3
8	14.9	14.8	14.6	14.6	14.5	14.4	14.4	14.3	14.3	14.2
9	14.8	14.7	14.6	14.5	14.4	14.4	14.3	14.2	14.2	14.1
10	14.7	14.6	14.5	14.4	14.4	14.3	14.2	14.2	14.1	14.1
12	14.5	14.5	14.4	14.3	14.2	14.2	14.1	14.1	14.0	14.0
14	14.4	14.3	14.2	14.2	14.1	14.1	14.0	14.0	13.9	13.9
16	14.3	14.2	14.1	14.1	14.0	14.0	13.9	13.9	13.9	13.8
18	14.2	14.1	14.0	14.0	13.9	13.9	13.8	13.8	13.8	13.7
20	14.0	14.0	13.9	13.9	13.8	13.8	13.8	13.7	13.7	13.7
25	13.8	13.8	13.7	13.7	13.7	13.6	13.6	13.6	13.5	13.5

4 %

YEARS CONST. GROWTH	\multicolumn{10}{c}{YEARS SETTLING GROWTH}
	2	4	6	8	10	12	14	16	18	20
1	15.9	15.9	15.9	15.9	15.9	15.9	15.9	15.9	15.9	15.9
2	15.9	15.9	15.9	15.9	15.9	15.9	15.9	15.9	15.9	15.9
3	15.9	15.9	15.9	15.9	15.9	15.9	15.9	15.9	15.9	15.9
4	15.9	15.9	15.9	15.9	15.9	15.9	15.9	15.9	15.9	15.9
5	15.9	15.9	15.9	15.9	15.9	15.9	15.9	15.9	15.9	15.9
6	15.9	15.9	15.9	15.9	15.9	15.9	15.9	15.9	15.9	15.9
7	15.9	15.9	15.9	15.9	15.9	15.9	15.9	15.9	15.9	15.9
8	15.9	15.9	15.9	15.9	15.9	15.9	15.9	15.9	15.9	15.9
9	15.9	15.9	15.9	15.9	15.9	15.9	15.9	15.9	15.9	15.9
10	15.9	15.9	15.9	15.9	15.9	15.9	15.9	15.9	15.9	15.9
12	15.9	15.9	15.9	15.9	15.9	15.9	15.9	15.9	15.9	15.9
14	15.9	15.9	15.9	15.9	15.9	15.9	15.9	15.9	15.9	15.9
16	15.9	15.9	15.9	15.9	15.9	15.9	15.9	15.9	15.9	15.9
18	15.9	15.9	15.9	15.9	15.9	15.9	15.9	15.9	15.9	15.9
20	15.9	15.9	15.9	15.9	15.9	15.9	15.9	15.9	15.9	15.9
25	15.9	15.9	15.9	15.9	15.9	15.9	15.9	15.9	15.9	15.9

5 %

YEARS CONST. GROWTH	\multicolumn{10}{c}{YEARS SETTLING GROWTH}
	2	4	6	8	10	12	14	16	18	20
1	16.1	16.2	16.5	16.6	16.7	16.8	16.9	17.0	17.1	17.2
2	16.3	16.4	16.6	16.7	16.8	16.9	17.0	17.1	17.2	17.3
3	16.4	16.5	16.7	16.8	16.9	17.0	17.1	17.2	17.3	17.4
4	16.5	16.6	16.8	16.9	17.0	17.1	17.2	17.3	17.4	17.4
5	16.6	16.7	16.9	17.0	17.1	17.2	17.3	17.4	17.5	17.5
6	16.7	16.8	17.0	17.1	17.2	17.3	17.4	17.5	17.5	17.6
7	16.8	16.9	17.1	17.2	17.3	17.4	17.5	17.6	17.6	17.7
8	16.9	17.0	17.2	17.3	17.4	17.5	17.6	17.6	17.7	17.8
9	17.0	17.1	17.3	17.4	17.5	17.6	17.6	17.7	17.8	17.9
10	17.1	17.2	17.4	17.5	17.6	17.7	17.7	17.8	17.9	17.9
12	17.3	17.4	17.6	17.7	17.7	17.8	17.9	18.0	18.0	18.1
14	17.5	17.6	17.8	17.8	17.9	18.0	18.0	18.1	18.2	18.2
16	17.7	17.8	17.9	18.0	18.1	18.1	18.2	18.3	18.3	18.4
18	17.9	17.9	18.1	18.1	18.2	18.3	18.3	18.4	18.4	18.5
20	18.0	18.1	18.2	18.3	18.3	18.4	18.5	18.5	18.6	18.6
25	18.4	18.4	18.5	18.6	18.6	18.7	18.7	18.8	18.8	18.9

8% Return Tables

YEARS CONST. GROWTH	6 % YEARS SETTLING GROWTH									
	2	4	6	8	10	12	14	16	18	20
1	16.4	16.6	17.1	17.3	17.5	17.8	18.0	18.2	18.4	18.6
2	16.6	16.9	17.3	17.6	17.8	18.0	18.2	18.4	18.6	18.8
3	16.9	17.1	17.6	17.8	18.0	18.2	18.4	18.6	18.8	19.0
4	17.1	17.4	17.8	18.0	18.2	18.4	18.7	18.8	19.0	19.2
5	17.4	17.6	18.0	18.2	18.5	18.7	18.9	19.1	19.2	19.4
6	17.6	17.9	18.3	18.5	18.7	18.9	19.1	19.3	19.5	19.6
7	17.9	18.1	18.5	18.7	18.9	19.1	19.3	19.5	19.7	19.8
8	18.1	18.3	18.7	18.9	19.1	19.3	19.5	19.7	19.9	20.0
9	18.3	18.5	18.9	19.1	19.3	19.5	19.7	19.9	20.0	20.2
10	18.5	18.8	19.1	19.3	19.5	19.7	19.9	20.1	20.2	20.4
12	19.0	19.2	19.5	19.7	19.9	20.1	20.3	20.4	20.6	20.8
14	19.4	19.6	19.9	20.1	20.3	20.5	20.6	20.8	21.0	21.1
16	19.8	20.0	20.3	20.5	20.7	20.8	21.0	21.1	21.3	21.5
18	20.2	20.4	20.7	20.8	21.0	21.2	21.3	21.5	21.6	21.8
20	20.5	20.7	21.0	21.2	21.4	21.5	21.7	21.8	22.0	22.1
25	21.4	21.6	21.9	22.0	22.2	22.3	22.4	22.6	22.7	22.8

YEARS CONST. GROWTH	7 % YEARS SETTLING GROWTH									
	2	4	6	8	10	12	14	16	18	20
1	16.7	17.0	17.7	18.1	18.5	18.8	19.2	19.5	19.8	20.2
2	17.1	17.4	18.1	18.5	18.8	19.2	19.5	19.9	20.2	20.5
3	17.4	17.8	18.5	18.8	19.2	19.6	19.9	20.2	20.6	20.9
4	17.8	18.2	18.9	19.2	19.6	19.9	20.3	20.6	20.9	21.2
5	18.2	18.6	19.2	19.6	19.9	20.3	20.6	20.9	21.3	21.6
6	18.6	19.0	19.6	20.0	20.3	20.6	21.0	21.3	21.6	21.9
7	19.0	19.3	20.0	20.3	20.7	21.0	21.3	21.7	22.0	22.3
8	19.3	19.7	20.3	20.7	21.0	21.4	21.7	22.0	22.3	22.6
9	19.7	20.1	20.7	21.0	21.4	21.7	22.0	22.3	22.7	23.0
10	20.1	20.4	21.1	21.4	21.7	22.1	22.4	22.7	23.0	23.3
12	20.8	21.1	21.8	22.1	22.4	22.7	23.1	23.4	23.7	24.0
14	21.5	21.9	22.4	22.8	23.1	23.4	23.7	24.0	24.3	24.6
16	22.2	22.5	23.1	23.4	23.8	24.1	24.4	24.7	25.0	25.2
18	22.9	23.2	23.8	24.1	24.4	24.7	25.0	25.3	25.6	25.9
20	23.6	23.9	24.4	24.8	25.1	25.4	25.6	25.9	26.2	26.5
25	25.2	25.5	26.0	26.3	26.6	26.9	27.2	27.4	27.7	28.0

YEARS CONST. GROWTH	8 % YEARS SETTLING GROWTH									
	2	4	6	8	10	12	14	16	18	20
1	16.9	17.5	18.4	18.9	19.4	19.9	20.4	20.9	21.4	21.9
2	17.5	18.0	18.9	19.4	19.9	20.4	20.9	21.4	21.9	22.4
3	18.0	18.5	19.4	20.0	20.5	21.0	21.5	22.0	22.5	22.9
4	18.5	19.0	20.0	20.5	21.0	21.5	22.0	22.5	23.0	23.5
5	19.1	19.6	20.5	21.0	21.5	22.0	22.5	23.0	23.5	24.0
6	19.6	20.1	21.0	21.6	22.1	22.6	23.1	23.6	24.1	24.5
7	20.1	20.6	21.6	22.1	22.6	23.1	23.6	24.1	24.6	25.1
8	20.6	21.2	22.1	22.6	23.1	23.6	24.1	24.6	25.1	25.6
9	21.2	21.7	22.6	23.2	23.7	24.2	24.7	25.2	25.7	26.1
10	21.7	22.2	23.2	23.7	24.2	24.7	25.2	25.7	26.2	26.7
12	22.8	23.3	24.2	24.7	25.3	25.8	26.3	26.8	27.2	27.7
14	23.8	24.4	25.3	25.8	26.3	26.8	27.3	27.8	28.3	28.8
16	24.9	25.4	26.4	26.9	27.4	27.9	28.4	28.9	29.4	29.9
18	26.0	26.5	27.4	27.9	28.4	29.0	29.5	29.9	30.4	30.9
20	27.0	27.6	28.5	29.0	29.5	30.0	30.5	31.0	31.5	32.0
25	29.7	30.2	31.1	31.7	32.2	32.7	33.2	33.7	34.2	34.6

8% Return Tables

YEARS CONST. GROWTH	2	4	6	8	10	12	14	16	18	20
					9 % YEARS SETTLING GROWTH					
1	17.2	17.5	19.1	19.8	20.4	21.1	21.8	22.4	23.1	23.8
2	17.9	18.6	19.8	20.5	21.1	21.8	22.5	23.2	23.8	24.5
3	18.6	19.3	20.5	21.2	21.9	22.5	23.2	23.9	24.6	25.3
4	19.3	20.0	21.2	21.9	22.6	23.3	24.0	24.7	25.3	26.0
5	20.0	20.7	21.9	22.6	23.3	24.0	24.7	25.4	26.1	26.8
6	20.7	21.4	22.6	23.3	24.1	24.8	25.5	26.2	26.9	27.6
7	21.4	22.1	23.4	24.1	24.8	25.5	26.2	26.9	27.6	28.3
8	22.1	22.8	24.1	24.8	25.6	26.3	27.0	27.7	28.4	29.1
9	22.8	23.6	24.9	25.6	26.3	27.0	27.8	28.5	29.2	29.9
10	23.6	24.3	25.6	26.4	27.1	27.8	28.5	29.3	30.0	30.7
12	25.1	25.8	27.1	27.9	28.6	29.4	30.1	30.9	31.6	32.3
14	26.6	27.3	28.7	29.5	30.2	31.0	31.7	32.5	33.2	34.0
16	28.1	28.9	30.3	31.1	31.8	32.6	33.4	34.2	34.9	35.7
18	29.7	30.5	31.9	32.7	33.5	34.3	35.1	35.8	36.6	37.4
20	31.3	32.1	33.5	34.4	35.2	36.0	36.8	37.6	38.4	39.1
25	35.5	36.3	37.8	38.6	39.5	40.3	41.2	42.0	42.8	43.7

YEARS CONST. GROWTH	2	4	6	8	10	12	14	16	18	20
					10 % YEARS SETTLING GROWTH					
1	17.5	18.3	19.8	20.6	21.5	22.4	23.2	24.1	25.0	25.9
2	18.3	19.2	20.7	21.5	22.4	23.3	24.2	25.1	25.9	26.8
3	19.2	20.0	21.6	22.4	23.3	24.2	25.1	26.0	26.9	27.9
4	20.0	20.9	22.5	23.4	24.3	25.2	26.1	27.0	28.0	28.9
5	20.9	21.8	23.4	24.3	25.2	26.2	27.1	28.0	29.0	29.9
6	21.8	22.7	24.3	25.3	26.2	27.2	28.1	29.1	30.0	31.0
7	22.7	23.7	25.3	26.3	27.2	28.2	29.1	30.1	31.1	32.1
8	23.7	24.6	26.3	27.3	28.2	29.2	30.2	31.2	32.2	33.2
9	24.6	25.6	27.3	28.3	29.3	30.3	31.3	32.3	33.3	34.3
10	25.6	26.6	28.3	29.3	30.3	31.3	32.4	33.4	34.4	35.5
12	27.6	28.6	30.4	31.4	32.5	33.5	34.6	35.7	36.7	37.8
14	29.6	30.7	32.6	33.6	34.7	35.8	36.9	38.0	39.1	40.3
16	31.8	32.9	34.8	35.9	37.1	38.2	39.3	40.5	41.6	42.8
18	34.0	35.1	37.1	38.3	39.5	40.7	41.8	43.0	44.2	45.4
20	36.3	37.5	39.6	40.8	42.0	43.2	44.4	45.7	46.9	48.2
25	42.4	43.7	46.0	47.3	48.7	50.0	51.4	52.7	54.1	55.4

YEARS CONST. GROWTH	2	4	6	8	10	12	14	16	18	20
					11 % YEARS SETTLING GROWTH					
1	17.8	18.7	20.5	21.6	22.6	23.7	24.8	25.9	27.0	28.1
2	18.8	19.8	21.6	22.7	23.8	24.9	26.0	27.1	28.3	29.4
3	19.8	20.8	22.7	23.8	24.9	26.0	27.2	28.4	29.5	30.7
4	20.8	21.9	23.8	25.0	26.1	27.3	28.4	29.6	30.9	32.1
5	21.9	23.0	25.0	26.2	27.3	28.5	29.7	31.0	32.2	33.5
6	23.0	24.1	26.2	27.4	28.6	29.8	31.1	32.3	33.6	34.9
7	24.2	25.3	27.4	28.6	29.9	31.1	32.4	33.7	35.0	36.4
8	25.3	26.5	28.7	29.9	31.2	32.5	33.8	35.2	36.5	37.9
9	26.5	27.7	30.0	31.3	32.6	33.9	35.3	36.6	38.0	39.5
10	27.8	29.0	31.3	32.6	34.0	35.4	36.7	38.2	39.6	41.0
12	30.3	31.7	34.1	35.5	36.9	38.4	39.8	41.3	42.8	44.4
14	33.1	34.5	37.0	38.5	40.0	41.5	43.1	44.7	46.3	47.9
16	35.9	37.4	40.1	41.7	43.3	44.9	46.5	48.2	49.9	51.6
18	39.0	40.5	43.4	45.0	46.7	48.4	50.2	51.9	53.7	55.5
20	42.2	43.8	46.8	48.6	50.4	52.2	54.0	55.9	57.7	59.7
25	51.0	52.9	56.4	58.4	60.4	62.5	64.6	66.7	68.9	71.1

8% Return Tables

YEARS CONST. GROWTH	12 % YEARS SETTLING GROWTH									
	2	4	6	8	10	12	14	16	18	20
1	18.1	19.2	21.3	22.5	23.8	25.1	26.5	27.8	29.2	30.7
2	19.2	20.4	22.6	23.9	25.2	26.5	27.9	29.3	30.8	32.3
3	20.4	21.6	23.9	25.2	26.6	28.0	29.4	30.9	32.4	34.0
4	21.7	22.9	25.3	26.7	28.1	29.5	31.0	32.5	34.1	35.7
5	22.9	24.3	26.7	28.1	29.6	31.1	32.7	34.2	35.9	37.5
6	24.3	25.7	28.2	29.7	31.2	32.8	34.4	36.0	37.7	39.4
7	25.7	27.1	29.7	31.3	32.8	34.5	36.1	37.8	39.6	41.3
8	27.1	28.6	31.3	32.9	34.5	36.2	37.9	39.7	41.5	43.4
9	28.6	30.1	33.0	34.6	36.3	38.1	39.8	41.7	43.5	45.5
10	30.2	31.7	34.7	36.4	38.1	39.9	41.8	43.7	45.6	47.6
12	33.4	35.1	38.3	40.1	42.0	44.0	45.9	48.0	50.1	52.2
14	36.9	38.8	42.1	44.1	46.2	48.3	50.4	52.6	54.8	57.1
16	40.7	42.7	46.3	48.5	50.7	52.9	55.2	57.6	60.0	62.5
18	44.8	46.9	50.8	53.1	55.5	57.9	60.4	62.9	65.5	68.2
20	49.2	51.4	55.6	58.1	60.7	63.3	65.9	68.6	71.4	74.3
25	61.6	64.3	69.4	72.3	75.4	78.5	81.7	85.0	88.3	91.7

YEARS CONST. GROWTH	13 % YEARS SETTLING GROWTH									
	2	4	6	8	10	12	14	16	18	20
1	18.3	19.7	22.1	23.6	25.1	26.6	28.2	29.9	31.6	33.4
2	19.7	21.0	23.6	25.1	26.7	28.3	30.0	31.8	33.6	35.4
3	21.1	22.5	25.2	26.8	28.4	30.1	31.9	33.7	35.6	37.5
4	22.5	24.0	26.8	28.5	30.2	32.0	33.8	35.8	37.7	39.8
5	24.0	25.6	28.5	30.3	32.1	34.0	35.9	37.9	39.9	42.1
6	25.6	27.3	30.3	32.2	34.1	36.0	38.0	40.1	42.3	44.5
7	27.3	29.0	32.2	34.1	36.1	38.2	40.3	42.5	44.7	47.0
8	29.0	30.8	34.2	36.2	38.3	40.4	42.6	44.9	47.3	49.7
9	30.8	32.7	36.2	38.3	40.5	42.7	45.1	47.4	49.9	52.5
10	32.7	34.7	38.4	40.6	42.9	45.2	47.6	50.1	52.7	55.4
12	36.8	39.0	43.0	45.4	47.9	50.5	53.1	55.8	58.7	61.6
14	41.3	43.6	48.1	50.7	53.4	56.2	59.1	62.1	65.2	68.4
16	46.2	48.8	53.6	56.5	59.4	62.5	65.7	69.0	72.4	75.9
18	51.5	54.4	59.6	62.8	66.0	69.4	72.9	76.5	80.2	84.0
20	57.4	60.5	66.3	69.7	73.3	77.0	80.8	84.7	88.8	93.0
25	74.6	78.4	85.7	90.0	94.5	99.1	103.9	108.8	113.9	119.2

YEARS CONST. GROWTH	14 % YEARS SETTLING GROWTH									
	2	4	6	8	10	12	14	16	18	20
1	18.6	20.1	22.9	24.6	26.4	28.2	30.2	32.2	34.2	36.4
2	20.1	21.7	24.7	26.5	28.3	30.3	32.3	34.4	36.6	38.9
3	21.7	23.4	26.5	28.4	30.4	32.4	34.6	36.8	39.1	41.5
4	23.4	25.1	28.4	30.4	32.5	34.7	36.9	39.3	41.8	44.3
5	25.2	27.0	30.5	32.6	34.8	37.1	39.5	41.9	44.5	47.2
6	27.0	29.0	32.6	34.9	37.2	39.6	42.1	44.7	47.5	50.3
7	29.0	31.0	34.9	37.3	39.7	42.3	44.9	47.7	50.6	53.6
8	31.1	33.2	37.3	39.8	42.4	45.1	47.9	50.8	53.9	57.0
9	33.3	35.5	39.9	42.5	45.2	48.1	51.0	54.1	57.3	60.7
10	35.6	38.0	42.6	45.3	48.2	51.2	54.3	57.6	61.0	64.5
12	40.6	43.3	48.4	51.4	54.6	58.0	61.5	65.1	68.9	72.8
14	46.2	49.2	54.9	58.3	61.8	65.6	69.4	73.5	77.7	82.1
16	52.4	55.7	62.1	65.9	69.9	74.0	78.3	82.8	87.5	92.4
18	59.4	63.1	70.1	74.4	78.8	83.4	88.2	93.3	98.5	104.0
20	67.1	71.2	79.1	83.8	88.8	93.9	99.3	104.9	110.7	116.8
25	90.5	95.9	106.2	112.4	118.9	125.7	132.7	140.0	147.7	155.6

8% Return Tables

15 %

YEARS CONST. GROWTH	2	4	6	8	YEARS SETTLING GROWTH 10	12	14	16	18	20
1	18.9	20.6	23.8	25.7	27.8	29.9	32.2	34.6	37.1	39.7
2	20.6	22.4	25.8	27.9	30.0	32.3	34.7	37.3	40.0	42.8
3	22.4	24.3	27.9	30.1	32.4	34.9	37.5	40.2	43.0	46.0
4	24.3	26.3	30.2	32.5	35.0	37.6	40.3	43.2	46.2	49.4
5	26.3	28.5	32.6	35.1	37.7	40.5	43.4	46.5	49.7	53.1
6	28.5	30.8	35.1	37.8	40.6	43.6	46.7	49.9	53.4	57.0
7	30.8	33.2	37.9	40.7	43.7	46.9	50.2	53.6	57.3	61.1
8	33.3	35.8	40.8	43.8	47.0	50.3	53.9	57.6	61.5	65.6
9	35.9	38.6	43.9	47.1	50.5	54.1	57.8	61.8	65.9	70.3
10	38.7	41.6	47.2	50.6	54.2	58.0	62.0	66.2	70.6	75.3
12	44.8	48.1	54.4	58.3	62.4	66.7	71.2	76.0	81.0	86.3
14	51.7	55.5	62.7	67.1	71.7	76.6	81.7	87.1	92.8	98.8
16	59.6	63.8	72.0	77.0	82.3	87.8	93.6	99.7	106.2	112.9
18	68.5	73.3	82.6	88.2	94.2	100.5	107.1	114.0	121.3	129.0
20	78.6	84.1	94.6	101.0	107.7	114.9	122.3	130.2	138.5	147.2
25	110.1	117.6	132.0	140.8	150.1	159.8	170.0	180.8	192.1	204.0

16 %

YEARS CONST. GROWTH	2	4	6	8	YEARS SETTLING GROWTH 10	12	14	16	18	20
1	19.2	21.1	24.7	26.9	29.2	31.7	34.4	37.2	40.2	43.4
2	21.1	23.1	26.9	29.3	31.9	34.5	37.4	40.4	43.6	47.0
3	23.1	25.2	29.4	31.9	34.7	37.5	40.6	43.9	47.3	51.0
4	25.3	27.6	32.0	34.9	37.7	40.8	44.1	47.6	51.2	55.2
5	27.6	30.0	34.8	37.8	40.9	44.2	47.8	51.5	55.5	59.7
6	30.1	32.7	37.8	41.0	44.4	48.0	51.8	55.8	60.0	64.6
7	32.7	35.6	41.1	44.5	48.1	52.0	56.0	60.4	64.9	69.8
8	35.6	38.7	44.6	48.2	52.1	56.2	60.6	65.3	70.2	75.4
9	38.7	42.0	48.3	52.3	56.4	60.9	65.6	70.5	75.8	81.4
10	42.0	45.5	52.3	56.6	61.1	65.8	70.9	76.2	81.9	87.9
12	49.4	53.4	61.3	66.2	71.4	76.8	82.7	88.8	95.4	102.3
14	57.9	62.6	71.7	77.3	83.2	89.6	96.3	103.4	111.0	119.0
16	67.7	73.1	83.6	90.1	97.0	104.3	112.0	120.2	128.9	138.2
18	79.0	85.3	97.3	104.8	112.8	121.2	130.1	139.6	149.7	160.3
20	92.1	99.3	113.2	121.9	131.0	140.7	151.0	162.0	173.6	185.9
25	134.2	144.5	164.4	176.8	189.9	203.7	218.5	234.1	250.7	268.3

17 %

YEARS CONST. GROWTH	2	4	6	8	YEARS SETTLING GROWTH 10	12	14	16	18	20
1	19.5	21.6	25.6	28.1	30.8	33.7	36.8	40.0	43.6	47.3
2	21.6	23.8	28.2	30.9	33.8	36.9	40.2	43.8	47.6	51.7
3	23.8	26.2	30.9	33.9	37.0	40.4	44.0	47.9	52.0	56.5
4	26.3	28.9	33.9	37.1	40.6	44.2	48.1	52.3	56.8	61.6
5	28.9	31.7	37.2	40.7	44.4	48.3	52.6	57.1	62.0	67.2
6	31.7	34.8	40.7	44.5	48.5	52.8	57.4	62.3	67.6	73.2
7	34.8	38.1	44.6	48.6	53.0	57.6	62.6	67.9	73.6	79.7
8	38.1	41.7	48.7	53.1	57.8	62.9	68.3	74.0	80.2	86.8
9	41.7	45.6	53.2	58.0	63.1	68.5	74.4	80.6	87.3	94.5
10	45.6	49.9	58.1	63.2	68.8	74.7	81.0	87.8	95.0	102.8
12	54.5	59.4	69.1	75.1	81.6	88.6	96.0	103.9	112.4	121.5
14	64.8	70.6	82.0	89.1	96.7	104.8	113.6	122.9	132.9	143.5
16	77.0	83.8	97.1	105.4	114.4	123.9	134.2	145.1	156.8	169.4
18	91.3	99.2	114.9	124.7	135.1	146.4	158.4	171.2	185.0	199.7
20	108.0	117.4	135.7	147.2	159.5	172.7	186.8	201.9	218.0	235.2
25	163.7	177.7	205.1	222.2	240.6	260.2	281.3	303.8	327.8	353.6

8% Return Tables

YEARS CONST. GROWTH	18 % YEARS SETTLING GROWTH									
	2	4	6	8	10	12	14	16	18	20
1	19.8	22.1	26.5	29.4	32.4	35.7	39.3	43.1	47.2	51.7
2	22.1	24.6	29.4	32.5	35.8	39.4	43.3	47.5	52.0	56.9
3	24.6	27.3	32.6	35.9	39.6	43.5	47.8	52.3	57.3	62.6
4	27.3	30.2	36.0	39.7	43.7	48.0	52.6	57.6	63.0	68.8
5	30.2	33.4	39.8	43.8	48.1	52.8	57.9	63.4	69.3	75.6
6	33.4	36.9	43.9	48.3	53.0	58.1	63.7	69.7	76.1	83.0
7	37.0	40.8	48.4	53.2	58.3	64.0	70.0	76.5	83.6	91.2
8	40.8	45.0	53.3	58.5	64.2	70.3	76.9	84.0	91.7	100.0
9	45.0	49.6	58.6	64.3	70.5	77.2	84.4	92.2	100.6	109.7
10	49.6	54.6	64.5	70.7	77.5	84.8	92.7	101.2	110.4	120.3
12	60.1	66.1	77.8	85.3	93.4	102.1	111.5	121.7	132.7	144.5
14	72.6	79.7	93.8	102.7	112.4	122.8	134.0	146.2	159.2	173.4
16	87.6	96.1	112.9	123.5	135.0	147.5	160.9	175.4	191.0	207.8
18	105.5	115.6	135.6	148.3	162.1	176.9	192.9	210.2	228.9	249.0
20	126.8	138.9	162.8	178.0	194.4	212.1	231.2	251.9	274.1	298.1
25	199.9	218.8	256.0	279.7	305.2	332.8	362.6	394.7	429.3	466.7

YEARS CONST. GROWTH	19 % YEARS SETTLING GROWTH									
	2	4	6	8	10	12	14	16	18	20
1	20.2	22.6	27.5	30.7	34.1	37.9	41.9	46.4	51.2	56.5
2	22.6	25.3	30.7	34.2	38.0	42.1	46.6	51.5	56.8	62.6
3	25.3	28.3	34.3	38.1	42.3	46.8	51.8	57.2	63.1	69.4
4	28.3	31.6	38.2	42.4	47.0	52.0	57.5	63.4	69.9	76.9
5	31.6	35.3	42.5	47.1	52.2	57.7	63.8	70.3	77.4	85.2
6	35.3	39.3	47.2	52.4	58.0	64.0	70.7	77.9	85.7	94.3
7	39.3	43.7	52.5	58.1	64.3	71.0	78.3	86.2	94.9	104.3
8	43.7	48.5	58.2	64.4	71.2	78.6	86.7	95.4	104.9	115.3
9	48.6	53.9	64.6	71.4	78.9	87.0	95.9	105.5	116.0	127.5
10	53.9	59.8	71.5	79.1	87.3	96.3	106.1	116.7	128.3	140.9
12	66.3	73.5	87.7	96.9	106.9	117.8	129.7	142.6	156.6	171.9
14	81.4	90.1	107.4	118.5	130.7	143.9	158.3	173.9	191.0	209.5
16	99.7	110.2	131.2	144.8	159.5	175.6	193.0	212.1	232.7	255.3
18	121.9	134.7	160.2	176.6	194.5	214.0	235.2	258.3	283.4	310.8
20	148.8	164.4	195.4	215.3	237.0	260.7	286.4	314.5	345.0	379.2
25	244.3	269.5	319.8	352.2	387.5	425.9	467.8	513.3	562.8	616.7

YEARS CONST. GROWTH	20 % YEARS SETTLING GROWTH									
	2	4	6	8	10	12	14	16	18	20
1	20.5	23.1	28.5	32.1	35.9	40.2	44.8	49.9	55.5	61.7
2	23.1	26.1	32.1	36.0	40.3	45.0	50.2	55.9	62.1	69.0
3	26.1	29.4	36.1	40.4	45.2	50.4	56.2	62.5	69.4	77.0
4	29.4	33.1	40.5	45.0	50.6	56.4	62.8	69.8	77.5	86.0
5	33.1	37.2	45.4	50.8	56.6	63.1	70.2	78.0	86.6	95.9
6	37.2	41.7	50.9	56.8	63.3	70.5	78.4	87.1	96.6	107.0
7	41.7	46.7	56.9	63.5	70.8	78.8	87.5	97.2	107.7	119.3
8	46.8	52.3	63.6	71.0	79.1	87.9	97.7	108.4	120.1	133.0
9	52.4	58.6	71.1	79.3	88.2	98.1	108.9	120.8	133.8	148.1
10	58.6	65.5	79.4	88.5	98.5	109.4	121.4	134.6	149.1	165.0
12	73.2	81.7	98.9	110.1	122.4	135.9	150.8	167.0	184.9	204.5
14	91.2	101.7	122.9	136.8	152.0	168.6	187.0	207.1	229.2	253.4
16	113.4	126.4	152.6	169.7	188.5	209.1	231.7	256.5	283.8	313.7
18	140.9	156.9	189.3	210.4	233.5	258.9	286.9	317.5	351.2	388.1
20	174.8	194.6	234.5	260.5	289.1	320.5	355.0	392.9	434.4	480.0
25	298.5	332.0	399.7	443.8	492.2	545.4	603.8	667.8	738.2	815.3

8% Return Tables

YEARS CONST. GROWTH	25 % YEARS SETTLING GROWTH									
	2	4	6	8	10	12	14	16	18	20
1	22.1	26.0	34.2	39.8	46.4	53.8	62.4	72.1	83.3	96.1
2	25.9	30.4	39.9	46.5	54.0	62.7	72.5	83.9	96.8	111.6
3	30.4	35.5	46.5	54.2	62.9	72.9	84.3	97.4	112.4	129.5
4	35.5	41.5	54.2	63.0	73.1	84.7	97.9	113.1	130.4	150.3
5	41.5	48.4	63.1	73.3	85.0	98.4	113.7	131.3	151.3	174.3
6	48.3	56.3	73.4	85.2	98.7	114.2	132.0	152.3	175.5	202.1
7	56.3	65.6	85.3	99.0	114.6	132.6	153.1	176.6	203.5	234.3
8	65.5	76.3	99.1	114.9	133.0	153.8	177.6	204.8	235.9	271.5
9	76.2	88.6	115.1	133.4	154.3	178.4	205.9	237.4	273.4	314.6
10	88.6	102.9	133.5	154.7	179.0	206.8	238.6	275.1	316.8	364.4
12	119.4	138.6	179.6	208.0	240.5	277.8	320.5	369.3	425.1	489.0
14	160.7	186.5	241.4	279.4	323.0	372.9	430.0	495.4	570.2	655.8
16	216.1	250.6	324.2	375.1	433.5	500.3	576.9	664.4	764.7	879.3
18	290.2	336.5	435.0	503.3	581.4	671.0	773.5	890.8	1025.1	1178.6
20	389.5	451.5	583.6	674.9	779.7	899.6	1037.0	1194.1	1374.0	1579.7
25	811.5	940.2	1214.5	1404.3	1621.8	1870.9	2156.2	2482.6	2856.2	3283.4

Industrials—Investment Values of Normal Earnings of $1 at 9% Return

Projected Earnings Growth Rate

YEARS CONST. GROWTH	1 % YEARS SETTLING GROWTH									
	2	4	6	8	10	12	14	16	18	20
1	12.1	11.8	11.4	11.2	11.0	10.9	10.7	10.6	10.4	10.3
2	11.8	11.6	11.2	11.0	10.9	10.7	10.6	10.4	10.3	10.2
3	11.6	11.4	11.0	10.8	10.7	10.5	10.4	10.3	10.2	10.1
4	11.4	11.2	10.8	10.7	10.5	10.4	10.3	10.1	10.0	9.9
5	11.2	11.0	10.7	10.5	10.4	10.2	10.1	10.0	9.9	9.8
6	11.0	10.8	10.5	10.4	10.2	10.1	10.0	9.9	9.8	9.7
7	10.8	10.6	10.4	10.2	10.1	10.0	9.9	9.8	9.7	9.6
8	10.6	10.5	10.2	10.1	10.0	9.9	9.8	9.7	9.6	9.6
9	10.5	10.3	10.1	10.0	9.9	9.8	9.7	9.6	9.5	9.5
10	10.3	10.2	10.0	9.9	9.8	9.7	9.6	9.5	9.5	9.4
12	10.1	9.9	9.8	9.7	9.6	9.5	9.5	9.4	9.3	9.3
14	9.8	9.7	9.6	9.5	9.4	9.4	9.3	9.3	9.2	9.2
16	9.6	9.6	9.4	9.4	9.3	9.2	9.2	9.2	9.1	9.1
18	9.5	9.4	9.3	9.2	9.2	9.1	9.1	9.1	9.0	9.0
20	9.3	9.3	9.2	9.1	9.1	9.0	9.0	9.0	8.9	8.9
25	9.1	9.0	9.0	8.9	8.9	8.9	8.8	8.8	8.8	8.8

YEARS CONST. GROWTH	2 % YEARS SETTLING GROWTH									
	2	4	6	8	10	12	14	16	18	20
1	12.3	12.1	11.8	11.7	11.6	11.4	11.3	11.2	11.1	11.0
2	12.1	12.0	11.7	11.6	11.4	11.3	11.2	11.1	11.0	10.9
3	11.9	11.8	11.5	11.4	11.3	11.2	11.1	11.0	10.9	10.8
4	11.8	11.6	11.4	11.3	11.2	11.1	11.0	10.9	10.8	10.8
5	11.6	11.5	11.3	11.2	11.1	11.0	10.9	10.8	10.7	10.7
6	11.5	11.4	11.2	11.1	11.0	10.9	10.8	10.7	10.7	10.6
7	11.4	11.3	11.1	11.0	10.9	10.8	10.7	10.7	10.6	10.5
8	11.3	11.1	11.0	10.9	10.8	10.7	10.6	10.6	10.5	10.5
9	11.1	11.0	10.9	10.8	10.7	10.6	10.6	10.5	10.4	10.4
10	11.0	10.9	10.8	10.7	10.6	10.6	10.5	10.4	10.4	10.3
12	10.8	10.8	10.6	10.5	10.5	10.4	10.4	10.3	10.3	10.2
14	10.7	10.6	10.5	10.4	10.4	10.3	10.3	10.2	10.2	10.1
16	10.5	10.5	10.4	10.3	10.3	10.2	10.2	10.1	10.1	10.1
18	10.4	10.3	10.2	10.2	10.2	10.1	10.1	10.0	10.0	10.0
20	10.3	10.2	10.2	10.1	10.1	10.0	10.0	10.0	9.9	9.9
25	10.1	10.0	10.0	9.9	9.9	9.9	9.9	9.8	9.8	9.8

9% Return Tables

YEARS CONST. GROWTH	3 % YEARS SETTLING GROWTH									
	2	4	6	8	10	12	14	16	18	20
1	12.5	12.4	12.3	12.2	12.1	12.C	12.0	11.9	11.9	11.8
2	12.4	12.3	12.2	12.1	12.0	12.C	11.9	11.9	11.8	11.8
3	12.3	12.2	12.1	12.C	11.9	11.9	11.9	11.8	11.8	11.7
4	12.2	12.2	12.0	12.C	11.9	11.9	11.8	11.8	11.7	11.7
5	12.2	12.1	12.0	11.9	11.8	11.8	11.7	11.7	11.7	11.6
6	12.1	12.C	11.9	11.8	11.8	11.7	11.7	11.7	11.6	11.6
7	12.0	11.9	11.8	11.8	11.7	11.7	11.6	11.6	11.6	11.5
8	11.9	11.9	11.8	11.7	11.7	11.6	11.6	11.6	11.5	11.5
9	11.9	11.8	11.7	11.7	11.6	11.6	11.6	11.5	11.5	11.5
10	11.8	11.8	11.7	11.6	11.6	11.6	11.5	11.5	11.5	11.4
12	11.7	11.7	11.6	11.5	11.5	11.5	11.4	11.4	11.4	11.4
14	11.6	11.6	11.5	11.5	11.4	11.4	11.4	11.3	11.3	11.3
16	11.5	11.5	11.4	11.4	11.4	11.3	11.3	11.3	11.3	11.2
18	11.5	11.4	11.4	11.3	11.3	11.3	11.3	11.2	11.2	11.2
20	11.4	11.4	11.3	11.3	11.3	11.2	11.2	11.2	11.2	11.2
25	11.2	11.2	11.2	11.2	11.1	11.1	11.1	11.1	11.1	11.1

YEARS CONST. GROWTH	4 % YEARS SETTLING GROWTH									
	2	4	6	8	10	12	14	16	18	20
1	12.7	12.7	12.7	12.7	12.7	12.7	12.7	12.7	12.7	12.7
2	12.7	12.7	12.7	12.7	12.7	12.7	12.7	12.7	12.7	12.7
3	12.7	12.7	12.7	12.7	12.7	12.7	12.7	12.7	12.7	12.7
4	12.7	12.7	12.7	12.7	12.7	12.7	12.7	12.7	12.7	12.7
5	12.7	12.7	12.7	12.7	12.7	12.7	12.7	12.7	12.7	12.7
6	12.7	12.7	12.7	12.7	12.7	12.7	12.7	12.7	12.7	12.7
7	12.7	12.7	12.7	12.7	12.7	12.7	12.7	12.7	12.7	12.7
8	12.7	12.7	12.7	12.7	12.7	12.7	12.7	12.7	12.7	12.7
9	12.7	12.7	12.7	12.7	12.7	12.7	12.7	12.7	12.7	12.7
10	12.7	12.7	12.7	12.7	12.7	12.7	12.7	12.7	12.7	12.7
12	12.7	12.7	12.7	12.7	12.7	12.7	12.7	12.7	12.7	12.7
14	12.7	12.7	12.7	12.7	12.7	12.7	12.7	12.7	12.7	12.7
16	12.7	12.7	12.7	12.7	12.7	12.7	12.7	12.7	12.7	12.7
18	12.7	12.7	12.7	12.7	12.7	12.7	12.7	12.7	12.7	12.7
20	12.7	12.7	12.7	12.7	12.7	12.7	12.7	12.7	12.7	12.7
25	12.7	12.7	12.7	12.7	12.7	12.7	12.7	12.7	12.7	12.7

YEARS CONST. GROWTH	5 % YEARS SETTLING GROWTH									
	2	4	6	8	10	12	14	16	18	20
1	12.9	13.C	13.1	13.2	13.3	13.4	13.4	13.5	13.6	13.6
2	13.0	13.1	13.2	13.3	13.4	13.5	13.5	13.6	13.6	13.7
3	13.1	13.2	13.3	13.4	13.5	13.5	13.6	13.7	13.7	13.8
4	13.2	13.3	13.4	13.5	13.5	13.6	13.7	13.7	13.8	13.8
5	13.3	13.3	13.5	13.5	13.6	13.7	13.7	13.8	13.8	13.9
6	13.3	13.4	13.5	13.6	13.7	13.7	13.8	13.9	13.9	14.0
7	13.4	13.5	13.6	13.7	13.7	13.8	13.9	13.9	14.0	14.0
8	13.5	13.6	13.7	13.7	13.8	13.9	13.9	14.0	14.0	14.1
9	13.6	13.6	13.8	13.8	13.9	13.9	14.0	14.0	14.1	14.1
10	13.6	13.7	13.8	13.9	13.9	14.C	14.0	14.1	14.1	14.2
12	13.8	13.8	13.9	14.0	14.0	14.1	14.1	14.2	14.2	14.3
14	13.9	14.C	14.1	14.1	14.1	14.2	14.2	14.3	14.3	14.4
16	14.0	14.1	14.2	14.2	14.2	14.3	14.3	14.4	14.4	14.4
18	14.1	14.2	14.3	14.3	14.3	14.4	14.4	14.5	14.5	14.5
20	14.2	14.3	14.3	14.4	14.4	14.5	14.5	14.5	14.6	14.6
25	14.4	14.5	14.5	14.6	14.6	14.6	14.7	14.7	14.7	14.7

9% Return Tables

YEARS CONST. GROWTH	2	4	6	8	6 % YEARS SETTLING GROWTH 10	12	14	16	18	20
1	13.1	13.3	13.6	13.8	13.9	14.1	14.3	14.4	14.5	14.7
2	13.3	13.5	13.8	14.0	14.1	14.3	14.4	14.6	14.7	14.8
3	13.5	13.7	14.0	14.1	14.3	14.4	14.6	14.7	14.9	15.0
4	13.7	13.8	14.1	14.3	14.5	14.6	14.7	14.9	15.0	15.1
5	13.8	14.0	14.3	14.5	14.6	14.8	14.9	15.0	15.1	15.3
6	14.0	14.2	14.5	14.6	14.8	14.9	15.0	15.2	15.3	15.4
7	14.2	14.4	14.6	14.8	14.9	15.0	15.2	15.3	15.4	15.5
8	14.4	14.5	14.8	14.9	15.1	15.2	15.3	15.4	15.6	15.7
9	14.5	14.7	14.9	15.1	15.2	15.3	15.4	15.6	15.7	15.8
10	14.7	14.8	15.1	15.2	15.3	15.5	15.6	15.7	15.8	15.9
12	15.0	15.1	15.4	15.5	15.6	15.7	15.8	15.9	16.0	16.1
14	15.3	15.4	15.6	15.7	15.9	16.0	16.1	16.2	16.3	16.4
16	15.5	15.7	15.9	16.0	16.1	16.2	16.3	16.4	16.5	16.6
18	15.8	15.9	16.1	16.2	16.3	16.4	16.5	16.6	16.7	16.8
20	16.0	16.1	16.3	16.4	16.5	16.6	16.7	16.8	16.9	17.0
25	16.6	16.7	16.8	16.9	17.0	17.1	17.2	17.2	17.3	17.4

YEARS CONST. GROWTH	2	4	6	8	7 % YEARS SETTLING GROWTH 10	12	14	16	18	20
1	13.3	13.6	14.1	14.4	14.6	14.9	15.1	15.4	15.6	15.8
2	13.6	13.9	14.4	14.6	14.9	15.2	15.4	15.6	15.9	16.1
3	13.9	14.2	14.7	14.9	15.2	15.4	15.7	15.9	16.1	16.3
4	14.2	14.5	14.9	15.2	15.4	15.7	15.9	16.1	16.4	16.6
5	14.5	14.7	15.2	15.5	15.7	15.9	16.2	16.4	16.6	16.8
6	14.7	15.0	15.5	15.7	16.0	16.2	16.4	16.6	16.8	17.0
7	15.0	15.3	15.7	16.0	16.2	16.4	16.7	16.9	17.1	17.3
8	15.3	15.5	16.0	16.2	16.5	16.7	16.9	17.1	17.3	17.5
9	15.5	15.8	16.2	16.5	16.7	16.9	17.1	17.3	17.5	17.7
10	15.8	16.1	16.5	16.7	16.9	17.1	17.4	17.6	17.8	17.9
12	16.3	16.5	17.0	17.2	17.4	17.6	17.8	18.0	18.2	18.4
14	16.8	17.0	17.4	17.6	17.8	18.0	18.2	18.4	18.6	18.8
16	17.3	17.5	17.9	18.1	18.3	18.5	18.6	18.8	19.0	19.2
18	17.7	17.9	18.3	18.5	18.7	18.9	19.0	19.2	19.4	19.5
20	18.1	18.3	18.7	18.9	19.1	19.3	19.4	19.6	19.8	19.9
25	19.2	19.3	19.7	19.8	20.0	20.2	20.3	20.5	20.6	20.8

YEARS CONST. GROWTH	2	4	6	8	8 % YEARS SETTLING GROWTH 10	12	14	16	18	20
1	13.5	13.9	14.6	15.0	15.4	15.7	16.1	16.4	16.7	17.1
2	13.9	14.3	15.0	15.4	15.7	16.1	16.5	16.8	17.1	17.5
3	14.3	14.7	15.4	15.8	16.1	16.5	16.8	17.2	17.5	17.8
4	14.7	15.1	15.8	16.2	16.5	16.9	17.2	17.5	17.9	18.2
5	15.1	15.5	16.2	16.5	16.9	17.2	17.6	17.9	18.2	18.6
6	15.5	15.9	16.6	16.9	17.3	17.6	17.9	18.3	18.6	18.9
7	15.9	16.3	16.9	17.3	17.6	18.0	18.3	18.6	19.0	19.3
8	16.3	16.7	17.3	17.7	18.0	18.3	18.7	19.0	19.3	19.6
9	16.7	17.0	17.7	18.0	18.4	18.7	19.0	19.4	19.7	20.0
10	17.0	17.4	18.0	18.4	18.7	19.1	19.4	19.7	20.0	20.3
12	17.8	18.1	18.8	19.1	19.5	19.8	20.1	20.4	20.7	21.0
14	18.5	18.9	19.5	19.8	20.2	20.5	20.8	21.1	21.4	21.7
16	19.2	19.6	20.2	20.5	20.8	21.2	21.5	21.8	22.1	22.3
18	19.9	20.3	20.9	21.2	21.5	21.8	22.1	22.4	22.7	23.0
20	20.6	21.0	21.6	21.9	22.2	22.5	22.8	23.1	23.4	23.6
25	22.3	22.6	23.2	23.5	23.8	24.1	24.4	24.6	24.9	25.2

9% Return Tables

YEARS CONST. GROWTH	9 % YEARS SETTLING GROWTH									
	2	4	6	8	10	12	14	16	18	20
1	13.7	14.2	15.1	15.6	16.1	16.6	17.1	17.5	18.0	18.5
2	14.2	14.7	15.6	16.1	16.6	17.1	17.6	18.1	18.5	19.0
3	14.8	15.3	16.2	16.7	17.2	17.6	18.1	18.6	19.0	19.5
4	15.3	15.8	16.7	17.2	17.7	18.2	18.6	19.1	19.6	20.0
5	15.8	16.3	17.2	17.7	18.2	18.7	19.1	19.6	20.1	20.5
6	16.3	16.8	17.7	18.2	18.7	19.2	19.7	20.1	20.6	21.1
7	16.8	17.3	18.2	18.7	19.2	19.7	20.2	20.7	21.1	21.6
8	17.4	17.9	18.8	19.3	19.7	20.2	20.7	21.2	21.6	22.1
9	17.9	18.4	19.3	19.8	20.3	20.7	21.2	21.7	22.2	22.6
10	18.4	18.9	19.8	20.3	20.8	21.3	21.7	22.2	22.7	23.1
12	19.4	19.9	20.8	21.3	21.8	22.3	22.8	23.3	23.7	24.2
14	20.5	21.0	21.9	22.4	22.9	23.3	23.8	24.3	24.8	25.2
16	21.5	22.0	22.9	23.4	23.9	24.4	24.9	25.3	25.8	26.2
18	22.5	23.1	24.0	24.4	24.9	25.4	25.9	26.4	26.8	27.3
20	23.6	24.1	25.0	25.5	26.0	26.5	26.9	27.4	27.9	28.3
25	26.2	26.7	27.6	28.1	28.6	29.1	29.5	30.0	30.5	30.9

YEARS CONST. GROWTH	10 % YEARS SETTLING GROWTH									
	2	4	6	8	10	12	14	16	18	20
1	13.9	14.6	15.7	16.3	16.9	17.5	18.1	18.8	19.4	20.0
2	14.6	15.2	16.3	16.9	17.6	18.2	18.8	19.4	20.0	20.7
3	15.2	15.9	17.0	17.6	18.2	18.9	19.5	20.1	20.7	21.3
4	15.9	16.5	17.6	18.3	18.9	19.6	20.2	20.8	21.4	22.1
5	16.5	17.2	18.3	19.0	19.6	20.2	20.9	21.5	22.1	22.8
6	17.2	17.8	19.0	19.6	20.3	20.9	21.6	22.2	22.8	23.5
7	17.8	18.5	19.7	20.3	21.0	21.6	22.3	22.9	23.6	24.2
8	18.5	19.2	20.4	21.0	21.7	22.3	23.0	23.6	24.3	24.9
9	19.2	19.8	21.0	21.7	22.4	23.0	23.7	24.4	25.0	25.7
10	19.9	20.5	21.7	22.4	23.1	23.8	24.4	25.1	25.8	26.4
12	21.2	21.9	23.2	23.9	24.5	25.2	25.9	26.6	27.2	27.9
14	22.7	23.4	24.6	25.3	26.0	26.7	27.4	28.1	28.8	29.4
16	24.1	24.8	26.1	26.8	27.5	28.2	28.9	29.6	30.3	31.0
18	25.6	26.3	27.6	28.3	29.0	29.8	30.5	31.2	31.9	32.6
20	27.0	27.8	29.1	29.8	30.6	31.3	32.0	32.8	33.5	34.2
25	30.9	31.7	33.0	33.8	34.6	35.4	36.1	36.9	37.6	38.4

YEARS CONST. GROWTH	11 % YEARS SETTLING GROWTH									
	2	4	6	8	10	12	14	16	18	20
1	14.2	14.9	16.2	17.0	17.8	18.5	19.3	20.1	20.8	21.6
2	14.9	15.7	17.0	17.8	18.6	19.4	20.1	20.9	21.7	22.5
3	15.7	16.4	17.8	18.6	19.4	20.2	21.0	21.8	22.6	23.4
4	16.5	17.2	18.7	19.5	20.3	21.1	21.9	22.7	23.5	24.3
5	17.3	18.1	19.5	20.3	21.1	22.0	22.8	23.6	24.4	25.3
6	18.1	18.9	20.3	21.2	22.0	22.9	23.7	24.5	25.4	26.2
7	18.9	19.7	21.2	22.1	22.9	23.8	24.6	25.5	26.4	27.2
8	19.7	20.6	22.1	23.0	23.8	24.7	25.6	26.4	27.3	28.2
9	20.6	21.5	23.0	23.9	24.8	25.6	26.5	27.4	28.3	29.2
10	21.5	22.3	23.9	24.8	25.7	26.6	27.5	28.4	29.3	30.3
12	23.3	24.2	25.8	26.7	27.7	28.6	29.5	30.5	31.4	32.4
14	25.1	26.1	27.8	28.7	29.7	30.7	31.6	32.6	33.6	34.6
16	27.1	28.0	29.8	30.8	31.8	32.8	33.8	34.8	35.8	36.9
18	29.1	30.1	31.9	32.9	34.0	35.0	36.1	37.1	38.2	39.2
20	31.1	32.2	34.1	35.1	36.2	37.3	38.4	39.5	40.6	41.7
25	36.7	37.8	39.9	41.1	42.2	43.4	44.6	45.8	47.0	48.2

9% Return Tables

YEARS CONST. GROWTH	2	4	6	8	12 % YEARS SETTLING GROWTH 10	12	14	16	18	20
1	14.4	15.2	16.8	17.7	18.6	19.6	20.5	21.5	22.4	23.4
2	15.3	16.1	17.8	18.7	19.6	20.6	21.6	22.6	23.5	24.6
3	16.2	17.1	18.7	19.7	20.7	21.7	22.6	23.7	24.7	25.7
4	17.1	18.0	19.7	20.7	21.7	22.7	23.8	24.8	25.8	26.9
5	18.0	19.0	20.8	21.8	22.8	23.8	24.9	26.0	27.0	28.1
6	19.0	20.0	21.8	22.9	23.9	25.0	26.1	27.2	28.3	29.4
7	20.0	21.0	22.9	24.0	25.1	26.2	27.3	28.4	29.5	30.7
8	21.1	22.1	24.0	25.1	26.2	27.4	28.5	29.7	30.8	32.0
9	22.1	23.2	25.2	26.3	27.4	28.6	29.8	31.0	32.2	33.4
10	23.2	24.3	26.3	27.5	28.7	29.9	31.1	32.3	33.5	34.8
12	25.5	26.7	28.8	30.0	31.3	32.5	33.8	35.1	36.4	37.7
14	27.9	29.1	31.4	32.7	34.0	35.3	36.6	38.0	39.4	40.8
16	30.4	31.7	34.1	35.5	36.9	38.3	39.7	41.1	42.6	44.0
18	33.1	34.5	37.0	38.4	39.9	41.4	42.9	44.4	45.9	47.5
20	35.9	37.4	40.0	41.6	43.1	44.7	46.2	47.8	49.5	51.1
25	43.7	45.4	48.4	50.2	51.9	53.7	55.5	57.4	59.2	61.1

YEARS CONST. GROWTH	2	4	6	8	13 % YEARS SETTLING GROWTH 10	12	14	16	18	20
1	14.6	15.6	17.4	18.5	19.6	20.7	21.8	23.0	24.2	25.4
2	15.6	16.6	18.5	19.6	20.8	21.9	23.1	24.3	25.6	26.8
3	16.7	17.7	19.7	20.8	22.0	23.2	24.4	25.7	27.0	28.3
4	17.7	18.8	20.9	22.1	23.3	24.5	25.8	27.1	28.4	29.8
5	18.9	20.0	22.1	23.4	24.6	25.9	27.2	28.6	29.9	31.3
6	20.0	21.2	23.4	24.7	26.0	27.3	28.7	30.1	31.5	33.0
7	21.2	22.5	24.7	26.1	27.4	28.8	30.2	31.7	33.1	34.6
8	22.5	23.8	26.1	27.5	28.9	30.3	31.8	33.3	34.8	36.4
9	23.8	25.1	27.5	29.0	30.4	31.9	33.4	35.0	36.6	38.2
10	25.1	26.5	29.0	30.5	32.0	33.6	35.1	36.8	38.4	40.1
12	28.0	29.4	32.2	33.8	35.4	37.0	38.7	40.5	42.2	44.0
14	31.0	32.6	35.5	37.2	39.0	40.8	42.6	44.4	46.3	48.3
16	34.3	36.0	39.1	41.0	42.9	44.8	46.7	48.7	50.8	52.9
18	37.8	39.6	43.0	45.0	47.0	49.1	51.2	53.3	55.5	57.8
20	41.6	43.6	47.2	49.3	51.5	53.7	56.0	58.3	60.6	63.1
25	52.4	54.7	59.1	61.6	64.2	66.9	69.6	72.3	75.2	78.0

YEARS CONST. GROWTH	2	4	6	8	14 % YEARS SETTLING GROWTH 10	12	14	16	18	20
1	14.8	15.9	18.0	19.3	20.6	21.9	23.3	24.7	26.1	27.6
2	16.0	17.1	19.3	20.6	22.0	23.4	24.8	26.2	27.8	29.3
3	17.2	18.4	20.7	22.0	23.4	24.9	26.4	27.9	29.5	31.1
4	18.4	19.7	22.1	23.5	25.0	26.5	28.0	29.7	31.3	33.0
5	19.7	21.1	23.6	25.1	26.6	28.2	29.8	31.5	33.2	35.0
6	21.1	22.5	25.1	26.7	28.3	29.9	31.6	33.4	35.2	37.0
7	22.5	24.0	26.7	28.4	30.0	31.8	33.5	35.4	37.3	39.2
8	24.0	25.5	28.4	30.1	31.9	33.7	35.5	37.5	39.4	41.5
9	25.6	27.2	30.2	32.0	33.8	35.7	37.6	39.6	41.7	43.8
10	27.2	28.9	32.0	33.9	35.8	37.8	39.8	41.9	44.1	46.3
12	30.7	32.5	36.0	38.0	40.1	42.3	44.5	46.8	49.2	51.6
14	34.5	36.5	40.3	42.5	44.8	47.2	49.6	52.1	54.7	57.4
16	38.7	40.9	45.0	47.5	50.0	52.6	55.2	58.0	60.8	63.7
18	43.3	45.7	50.2	52.9	55.6	58.4	61.3	64.3	67.4	70.6
20	48.3	50.9	55.8	58.8	61.8	64.9	68.0	71.3	74.7	78.2
25	63.0	66.2	72.4	76.1	79.8	83.7	87.7	91.8	96.0	100.4

9% Return Tables

YEARS CONST. GROWTH	15 % YEARS SETTLING GROWTH									
	2	4	6	8	10	12	14	16	18	20
1	15.1	16.3	18.7	20.1	21.6	23.2	24.8	26.4	28.2	30.0
2	16.3	17.7	20.2	21.7	23.3	24.9	26.6	28.3	30.2	32.1
3	17.7	19.1	21.7	23.3	25.0	26.7	28.5	30.3	32.3	34.3
4	19.1	20.6	23.4	25.1	26.8	28.6	30.5	32.5	34.5	36.6
5	20.6	22.2	25.1	26.9	28.7	30.6	32.6	34.7	36.8	39.1
6	22.2	23.8	27.0	28.8	30.8	32.8	34.9	37.1	39.3	41.7
7	23.9	25.6	28.9	30.9	32.9	35.0	37.3	39.5	41.9	44.4
8	25.5	27.5	30.9	33.0	35.2	37.4	39.8	42.2	44.7	47.3
9	27.5	29.4	33.1	35.3	37.6	39.9	42.4	44.9	47.6	50.4
10	29.5	31.5	35.4	37.7	40.1	42.6	45.2	47.9	50.7	53.6
12	33.7	36.0	40.3	42.9	45.5	48.3	51.2	54.2	57.3	60.6
14	38.5	41.0	45.8	48.6	51.6	54.7	57.9	61.3	64.8	68.4
16	43.7	46.5	51.9	55.1	58.4	61.8	65.4	69.1	73.0	77.0
18	49.6	52.7	58.7	62.2	65.9	69.7	73.7	77.9	82.2	86.7
20	56.1	59.6	66.2	70.2	74.3	78.6	83.0	87.6	92.4	97.4
25	75.9	80.5	89.1	94.3	99.6	105.2	111.0	117.1	123.3	129.8

YEARS CONST. GROWTH	16 % YEARS SETTLING GROWTH									
	2	4	6	8	10	12	14	16	18	20
1	15.3	16.7	19.4	21.0	22.7	24.5	26.4	28.3	30.4	32.6
2	16.7	18.2	21.1	22.8	24.6	26.5	28.5	30.6	32.8	35.1
3	18.2	19.8	22.8	24.7	26.6	28.7	30.8	33.0	35.3	37.8
4	19.8	21.5	24.8	26.7	28.8	30.9	33.2	35.6	38.0	40.6
5	21.5	23.3	26.8	28.9	31.1	33.4	35.8	38.3	40.9	43.7
6	23.4	25.3	28.9	31.2	33.5	35.9	38.5	41.2	44.0	46.9
7	25.3	27.3	31.2	33.6	36.1	38.7	41.4	44.3	47.3	50.4
8	27.4	29.5	33.7	36.2	38.8	41.6	44.5	47.6	50.7	54.1
9	29.6	31.9	36.3	39.0	41.8	44.7	47.8	51.0	54.4	58.0
10	31.9	34.4	39.1	41.9	44.9	48.0	51.3	54.8	58.4	62.2
12	37.0	39.8	45.1	48.4	51.8	55.3	59.0	62.9	67.0	71.3
14	42.9	46.0	52.0	55.7	59.5	63.6	67.8	72.2	76.8	81.7
16	49.5	53.0	59.8	64.0	68.3	72.9	77.7	82.7	87.9	93.4
18	56.9	61.0	68.7	73.4	78.3	83.5	88.9	94.5	100.5	106.7
20	65.4	69.9	78.7	84.0	89.6	95.4	101.6	108.0	114.7	121.7
25	91.6	98.0	109.9	117.2	124.8	132.8	141.1	149.9	159.1	168.7

YEARS CONST. GROWTH	17 % YEARS SETTLING GROWTH									
	2	4	6	8	10	12	14	16	18	20
1	15.5	17.1	20.1	21.9	23.9	25.9	28.1	30.4	32.8	35.4
2	17.1	18.7	22.0	23.9	26.0	28.2	30.6	33.1	35.7	38.4
3	18.8	20.6	24.0	26.1	28.4	30.8	33.3	35.9	38.7	41.7
4	20.6	22.5	26.2	28.5	30.9	33.4	36.1	39.0	42.0	45.2
5	22.5	24.6	28.6	31.0	33.6	36.3	39.2	42.3	45.5	48.9
6	24.6	26.8	31.1	33.7	36.5	39.4	42.5	45.8	49.3	52.9
7	26.8	29.2	33.8	36.6	39.6	42.7	46.1	49.6	53.3	57.2
8	29.2	31.8	36.7	39.7	42.9	46.3	49.9	53.7	57.7	61.9
9	31.8	34.5	39.8	43.1	46.5	50.1	54.0	58.0	62.3	66.8
10	34.6	37.5	43.2	46.7	50.3	54.2	58.4	62.7	67.3	72.2
12	40.7	44.1	50.6	54.6	58.9	63.4	68.1	73.2	78.5	84.1
14	47.8	51.7	59.2	63.9	68.8	73.9	79.4	85.2	91.3	97.7
16	56.0	60.5	69.1	74.5	80.1	86.1	92.4	99.0	106.1	113.5
18	65.4	70.6	80.5	86.7	93.2	100.1	107.3	115.0	123.1	131.7
20	76.2	82.2	93.7	100.8	108.3	116.2	124.5	133.4	142.7	152.6
25	111.1	119.6	136.0	146.1	156.7	168.0	180.0	192.5	205.9	219.9

9% Return Tables

18 %

YEARS CONST. GROWTH	\(2\)	4	6	8	YEARS SETTLING GROWTH 10	12	14	16	18	20
1	15.8	17.5	20.8	22.9	25.1	27.4	29.9	32.6	35.5	38.5
2	17.5	19.3	22.9	25.2	27.6	30.1	32.8	35.7	38.8	42.1
3	19.3	21.3	25.2	27.7	30.2	33.0	36.0	39.1	42.4	46.0
4	21.4	23.5	27.7	30.4	33.2	36.2	39.3	42.7	46.4	50.2
5	23.5	25.9	30.4	33.3	36.3	39.6	43.0	46.7	50.6	54.8
6	25.9	28.4	33.4	36.5	39.7	43.2	47.0	51.0	55.2	59.7
7	28.5	31.2	36.6	39.9	43.4	47.2	51.3	55.6	60.2	65.1
8	31.2	34.2	40.0	43.6	47.5	51.6	55.9	60.6	65.6	70.9
9	34.2	37.4	43.7	47.6	51.8	56.2	61.0	66.0	71.4	77.2
10	37.5	40.9	47.7	52.0	56.5	61.3	66.4	71.9	77.7	83.9
12	44.6	48.9	56.8	61.8	67.1	72.7	78.7	85.1	92.0	99.3
14	53.4	58.1	67.5	73.3	79.5	86.1	93.1	100.7	108.7	117.2
16	63.4	69.0	79.9	86.8	94.0	101.8	110.0	118.8	128.2	138.2
18	75.2	81.7	94.6	102.5	111.1	120.1	129.8	140.1	151.1	162.9
20	89.0	96.7	111.7	121.1	131.0	141.7	153.0	165.1	178.0	191.7
25	134.8	146.2	168.6	182.5	197.3	213.1	230.0	248.0	267.2	287.6

19 %

YEARS CONST. GROWTH	2	4	6	8	YEARS SETTLING GROWTH 10	12	14	16	18	20
1	16.0	17.9	21.5	23.8	26.3	29.0	31.9	35.0	38.3	41.9
2	17.9	19.9	23.9	26.4	29.2	32.1	35.2	38.6	42.3	46.2
3	19.9	22.1	26.5	29.3	32.2	35.4	38.9	42.6	46.5	50.8
4	22.2	24.6	29.4	32.4	35.6	39.1	42.9	46.9	51.2	55.9
5	24.6	27.2	32.5	35.8	39.3	43.1	47.2	51.6	56.3	61.4
6	27.3	30.1	35.8	39.4	43.3	47.5	51.9	56.8	61.9	67.5
7	30.2	33.3	39.5	43.5	47.7	52.2	57.1	62.4	68.0	74.1
8	33.4	36.8	43.6	47.9	52.5	57.4	62.8	68.5	74.7	81.3
9	36.8	40.6	48.0	52.7	57.7	63.1	68.9	75.2	81.9	89.1
10	40.6	44.7	52.8	57.9	63.4	69.3	75.7	82.5	89.8	97.7
12	49.3	54.1	63.8	69.9	76.4	83.5	91.0	99.2	107.9	117.3
14	59.6	65.4	76.9	84.2	92.0	100.4	109.4	119.1	129.5	140.7
16	71.9	78.8	92.5	101.2	110.5	120.5	131.2	142.8	155.2	168.6
18	86.5	94.8	111.1	121.4	132.5	144.4	157.3	171.0	185.9	201.8
20	104.0	113.8	133.3	145.6	158.8	173.0	188.3	204.7	222.4	241.4
25	163.7	179.0	209.2	228.3	248.8	270.8	294.5	320.0	347.4	376.8

20 %

YEARS CONST. GROWTH	2	4	6	8	YEARS SETTLING GROWTH 10	12	14	16	18	20
1	16.2	18.3	22.3	24.9	27.7	30.7	34.0	37.6	41.4	45.6
2	18.3	20.5	24.9	27.8	30.9	34.2	37.8	41.8	46.0	50.6
3	20.5	23.0	27.9	31.0	34.4	38.1	42.1	46.4	51.1	56.1
4	23.0	25.7	31.1	34.5	38.3	42.3	46.7	51.5	56.6	62.2
5	25.7	28.7	34.6	38.4	42.5	47.0	51.8	57.1	62.7	68.9
6	28.7	32.0	38.5	42.7	47.2	52.1	57.4	63.2	69.5	76.2
7	32.0	35.6	42.8	47.4	52.4	57.8	63.6	70.0	76.9	84.3
8	35.6	39.6	47.5	52.6	58.1	64.0	70.5	77.5	85.0	93.2
9	39.6	44.0	52.7	58.3	64.3	70.9	78.0	85.7	94.0	103.1
10	44.0	48.8	58.4	64.6	71.2	78.4	86.2	94.7	103.9	113.9
12	54.2	60.0	71.7	79.1	87.1	95.9	105.4	115.6	126.8	138.8
14	66.5	73.6	87.7	96.7	106.5	117.1	128.5	141.0	154.5	169.1
16	81.5	90.0	107.1	118.0	129.9	142.7	156.6	171.7	188.1	205.8
18	99.6	110.0	130.7	143.9	158.2	173.8	190.7	209.0	228.8	250.3
20	121.6	134.1	159.2	175.2	192.6	211.5	232.0	254.1	278.2	304.2
25	199.0	219.3	259.9	285.9	314.0	344.5	377.6	413.5	452.3	494.4

9% Return Tables

YEARS CONST. GROWTH	2	4	6	8	25 % YEARS SETTLING GROWTH 10	12	14	16	18	20
1	17.5	20.4	26.6	30.7	35.5	40.8	46.8	53.6	61.3	70.0
2	20.4	23.8	30.8	35.6	41.0	47.1	54.1	61.9	70.7	80.7
3	23.8	27.6	35.7	41.2	47.4	54.4	62.3	71.3	81.4	92.9
4	27.6	32.0	41.3	47.6	54.7	62.7	71.8	82.1	93.7	106.9
5	32.0	37.1	47.7	54.9	63.1	72.3	82.7	94.5	107.9	122.9
6	37.1	42.9	55.1	63.3	72.7	83.3	95.2	108.8	124.0	141.3
7	42.9	49.5	63.5	73.0	83.7	95.9	109.6	125.1	142.6	162.4
8	49.5	57.1	73.2	84.0	96.4	110.3	126.0	143.8	163.9	186.6
9	57.1	65.9	84.3	96.7	110.9	126.8	144.9	165.3	188.3	214.3
10	65.9	75.9	97.0	111.3	127.5	145.8	166.5	189.9	216.3	246.1
12	87.4	100.5	128.3	147.1	168.4	192.5	219.7	250.5	285.2	324.5
14	115.7	133.0	169.5	194.2	222.2	253.9	289.7	330.2	375.9	427.5
16	152.9	175.7	223.7	256.2	293.0	334.7	381.8	435.0	495.1	562.9
18	201.9	231.8	294.9	337.7	386.2	440.9	502.9	572.8	651.9	741.1
20	266.2	305.6	388.6	444.9	508.6	580.6	662.1	754.1	858.0	975.4
25	530.5	608.5	773.1	884.8	1011.1	1154.0	1315.6	1498.1	1704.2	1936.9

Industrials—Investment Values of Normal Earnings of $1 at 10% Return

Projected Earnings Growth Rate

YEARS CONST. GROWTH	2	4	6	8	1 % YEARS SETTLING GROWTH 10	12	14	16	18	20
1	10.1	9.9	9.6	9.4	9.3	9.2	9.0	8.9	8.8	8.8
2	9.9	9.7	9.4	9.3	9.1	9.0	8.9	8.8	8.7	8.7
3	9.7	9.5	9.3	9.1	9.0	8.9	8.8	8.7	8.6	8.6
4	9.5	9.4	9.1	9.0	8.9	8.8	8.7	8.6	8.5	8.5
5	9.4	9.2	9.0	8.9	8.8	8.7	8.6	8.5	8.5	8.4
6	9.2	9.1	8.9	8.8	8.7	8.6	8.5	8.5	8.4	8.3
7	9.1	9.0	8.8	8.7	8.6	8.5	8.4	8.4	8.3	8.3
8	9.0	8.8	8.7	8.6	8.5	8.4	8.4	8.3	8.3	8.2
9	8.8	8.7	8.6	8.5	8.4	8.4	8.3	8.2	8.2	8.2
10	8.7	8.6	8.5	8.4	8.4	8.3	8.2	8.2	8.1	8.1
12	8.5	8.5	8.3	8.3	8.2	8.2	8.1	8.1	8.1	8.0
14	8.4	8.3	8.2	8.2	8.1	8.1	8.0	8.0	8.0	7.9
16	8.3	8.2	8.1	8.1	8.0	8.0	8.0	7.9	7.9	7.9
18	8.1	8.1	8.0	8.0	8.0	7.9	7.9	7.9	7.8	7.8
20	8.1	8.0	7.9	7.9	7.9	7.9	7.8	7.8	7.8	7.8

YEARS CONST. GROWTH	2	4	6	8	2 % YEARS SETTLING GROWTH 10	12	14	16	18	20
1	10.3	10.1	9.9	9.8	9.7	9.6	9.5	9.4	9.4	9.3
2	10.1	10.0	9.8	9.7	9.6	9.5	9.4	9.4	9.3	9.2
3	10.0	9.9	9.7	9.6	9.5	9.4	9.3	9.3	9.2	9.2
4	9.9	9.8	9.6	9.5	9.4	9.3	9.3	9.2	9.2	9.1
5	9.7	9.6	9.5	9.4	9.3	9.3	9.2	9.1	9.1	9.0
6	9.6	9.5	9.4	9.3	9.3	9.2	9.1	9.1	9.0	9.0
7	9.5	9.5	9.3	9.2	9.2	9.1	9.1	9.0	9.0	8.9
8	9.5	9.4	9.2	9.2	9.1	9.1	9.0	9.0	8.9	8.9
9	9.4	9.3	9.2	9.1	9.1	9.0	9.0	8.9	8.9	8.8
10	9.3	9.2	9.1	9.1	9.0	9.0	8.9	8.9	8.8	8.8
12	9.2	9.1	9.0	8.9	8.9	8.9	8.8	8.8	8.8	8.7
14	9.0	9.0	8.9	8.9	8.8	8.8	8.8	8.7	8.7	8.7
16	8.9	8.9	8.8	8.8	8.7	8.7	8.7	8.7	8.6	8.6
18	8.8	8.8	8.7	8.7	8.7	8.7	8.6	8.6	8.6	8.6
20	8.8	8.7	8.7	8.7	8.6	8.6	8.6	8.6	8.6	8.5

10% Return Tables

3 %

YEARS CONST. GROWTH	2	4	6	8	10	12	14	16	18	20
					YEARS SETTLING GROWTH					
1	10.4	10.3	10.2	10.2	10.1	10.1	10.0	10.0	9.9	9.9
2	10.3	10.3	10.2	10.1	10.1	10.0	10.0	9.9	9.9	9.9
3	10.3	10.2	10.2	10.1	10.0	10.0	9.9	9.9	9.9	9.8
4	10.2	10.2	10.1	10.0	10.0	9.9	9.9	9.9	9.8	9.8
5	10.2	10.1	10.0	10.0	9.9	9.9	9.9	9.8	9.8	9.8
6	10.1	10.0	10.0	9.9	9.9	9.8	9.8	9.8	9.8	9.7
7	10.0	10.0	9.9	9.9	9.8	9.8	9.8	9.8	9.7	9.7
8	10.0	9.9	9.9	9.8	9.8	9.8	9.7	9.7	9.7	9.7
9	9.9	9.9	9.8	9.8	9.8	9.7	9.7	9.7	9.7	9.7
10	9.9	9.9	9.8	9.8	9.7	9.7	9.7	9.7	9.6	9.6
12	9.8	9.8	9.7	9.7	9.7	9.7	9.6	9.6	9.6	9.6
14	9.8	9.7	9.7	9.7	9.6	9.6	9.6	9.6	9.6	9.5
16	9.7	9.7	9.6	9.6	9.6	9.6	9.6	9.5	9.5	9.5
18	9.6	9.6	9.6	9.6	9.5	9.5	9.5	9.5	9.5	9.5
20	9.6	9.6	9.5	9.5	9.5	9.5	9.5	9.5	9.5	9.5

4 %

YEARS CONST. GROWTH	2	4	6	8	10	12	14	16	18	20
					YEARS SETTLING GROWTH					
1	10.6	10.6	10.6	10.6	10.6	10.6	10.6	10.6	10.6	10.6
2	10.6	10.6	10.6	10.6	10.6	10.6	10.6	10.6	10.6	10.6
3	10.6	10.6	10.6	10.6	10.6	10.6	10.6	10.6	10.6	10.6
4	10.6	10.6	10.6	10.6	10.6	10.6	10.6	10.6	10.6	10.6
5	10.6	10.6	10.6	10.6	10.6	10.6	10.6	10.6	10.6	10.6
6	10.6	10.6	10.6	10.6	10.6	10.6	10.6	10.6	10.6	10.6
7	10.6	10.6	10.6	10.6	10.6	10.6	10.6	10.6	10.6	10.6
8	10.6	10.6	10.6	10.6	10.6	10.6	10.6	10.6	10.6	10.6
9	10.6	10.6	10.6	10.6	10.6	10.6	10.6	10.6	10.6	10.6
10	10.6	10.6	10.6	10.6	10.6	10.6	10.6	10.6	10.6	10.6
12	10.6	10.6	10.6	10.6	10.6	10.6	10.6	10.6	10.6	10.6
14	10.6	10.6	10.6	10.6	10.6	10.6	10.6	10.6	10.6	10.6
16	10.6	10.6	10.6	10.6	10.6	10.6	10.6	10.6	10.6	10.6
18	10.6	10.6	10.6	10.6	10.6	10.6	10.6	10.6	10.6	10.6
20	10.6	10.6	10.6	10.6	10.6	10.6	10.6	10.6	10.6	10.6

5 %

YEARS CONST. GROWTH	2	4	6	8	10	12	14	16	18	20
					YEARS SETTLING GROWTH					
1	10.7	10.8	10.9	11.0	11.1	11.1	11.2	11.2	11.3	11.3
2	10.8	10.9	11.0	11.1	11.1	11.2	11.2	11.3	11.3	11.4
3	10.9	11.0	11.1	11.1	11.2	11.2	11.3	11.3	11.4	11.4
4	11.0	11.0	11.1	11.2	11.2	11.3	11.3	11.4	11.4	11.4
5	11.0	11.1	11.2	11.2	11.3	11.3	11.4	11.4	11.5	11.5
6	11.1	11.1	11.2	11.3	11.3	11.4	11.4	11.5	11.5	11.5
7	11.1	11.2	11.3	11.3	11.4	11.4	11.4	11.5	11.5	11.6
8	11.2	11.3	11.3	11.4	11.4	11.5	11.5	11.5	11.6	11.6
9	11.3	11.3	11.4	11.4	11.5	11.5	11.5	11.6	11.6	11.6
10	11.3	11.4	11.4	11.5	11.5	11.6	11.6	11.6	11.6	11.7
12	11.4	11.4	11.5	11.6	11.6	11.6	11.7	11.7	11.7	11.7
14	11.5	11.5	11.6	11.6	11.7	11.7	11.7	11.8	11.8	11.8
16	11.6	11.6	11.6	11.7	11.7	11.8	11.8	11.8	11.8	11.9
18	11.6	11.7	11.7	11.8	11.8	11.8	11.8	11.9	11.9	11.9
20	11.7	11.7	11.8	11.8	11.8	11.9	11.9	11.9	11.9	11.9

10% Return Tables

YEARS CONST. GROWTH	2	4	6	8	10	12	14	16	18	20
					6 % YEARS SETTLING GROWTH					
1	10.9	11.0	11.3	11.4	11.6	11.7	11.8	11.9	12.0	12.1
2	11.1	11.2	11.4	11.6	11.7	11.8	11.9	12.0	12.1	12.2
3	11.2	11.3	11.6	11.7	11.8	11.9	12.0	12.1	12.2	12.3
4	11.3	11.5	11.7	11.8	11.9	12.0	12.1	12.2	12.3	12.4
5	11.5	11.6	11.8	11.9	12.1	12.2	12.3	12.3	12.4	12.5
6	11.6	11.7	12.0	12.1	12.2	12.3	12.4	12.4	12.5	12.6
7	11.7	11.9	12.1	12.2	12.3	12.4	12.5	12.5	12.6	12.7
8	11.9	12.0	12.2	12.3	12.4	12.5	12.6	12.6	12.7	12.8
9	12.0	12.1	12.3	12.4	12.5	12.6	12.7	12.7	12.8	12.9
10	12.1	12.2	12.4	12.5	12.6	12.7	12.7	12.8	12.9	13.0
12	12.3	12.4	12.6	12.7	12.8	12.8	12.9	13.0	13.1	13.1
14	12.5	12.6	12.8	12.9	12.9	13.0	13.1	13.1	13.2	13.3
16	12.7	12.8	12.9	13.0	13.1	13.2	13.2	13.3	13.3	13.4
18	12.9	13.0	13.1	13.2	13.2	13.3	13.4	13.4	13.5	13.5
20	13.0	13.1	13.2	13.3	13.4	13.4	13.5	13.5	13.6	13.6

YEARS CONST. GROWTH	2	4	6	8	10	12	14	16	18	20
					7 % YEARS SETTLING GROWTH-					
1	11.1	11.3	11.7	11.9	12.1	12.3	12.5	12.6	12.8	13.0
2	11.3	11.5	11.9	12.1	12.3	12.5	12.7	12.8	13.0	13.1
3	11.5	11.7	12.1	12.3	12.5	12.7	12.9	13.0	13.2	13.3
4	11.8	12.0	12.3	12.5	12.7	12.9	13.0	13.2	13.4	13.5
5	12.0	12.2	12.5	12.7	12.9	13.1	13.2	13.4	13.5	13.7
6	12.2	12.4	12.7	12.9	13.1	13.2	13.4	13.6	13.7	13.8
7	12.4	12.6	12.9	13.1	13.3	13.4	13.6	13.7	13.9	14.0
8	12.6	12.8	13.1	13.3	13.4	13.6	13.7	13.9	14.0	14.2
9	12.8	13.0	13.3	13.5	13.6	13.8	13.9	14.0	14.2	14.3
10	13.0	13.2	13.5	13.6	13.8	13.9	14.1	14.2	14.3	14.5
12	13.3	13.5	13.8	14.0	14.1	14.2	14.4	14.4	14.6	14.7
14	13.7	13.8	14.1	14.3	14.4	14.5	14.7	14.8	14.9	15.0
16	14.0	14.2	14.4	14.6	14.7	14.8	14.9	15.1	15.2	15.3
18	14.3	14.5	14.7	14.8	15.0	15.1	15.2	15.3	15.4	15.5
20	14.6	14.7	15.0	15.1	15.2	15.3	15.4	15.5	15.6	15.7

YEARS CONST. GROWTH	2	4	6	8	10	12	14	16	18	20
					8 % YEARS SETTLING GROWTH					
1	11.2	11.5	12.1	12.4	12.7	12.9	13.2	13.4	13.7	13.9
2	11.6	11.9	12.4	12.7	13.0	13.2	13.5	13.7	14.0	14.2
3	11.9	12.2	12.7	13.0	13.2	13.5	13.8	14.0	14.2	14.5
4	12.2	12.5	13.0	13.3	13.5	13.8	14.0	14.3	14.5	14.7
5	12.5	12.8	13.3	13.5	13.8	14.1	14.3	14.5	14.8	15.0
6	12.8	13.1	13.6	13.8	14.1	14.3	14.6	14.8	15.0	15.2
7	13.1	13.4	13.8	14.1	14.4	14.6	14.8	15.1	15.3	15.5
8	13.4	13.6	14.1	14.4	14.6	14.9	15.1	15.3	15.5	15.7
9	13.6	13.9	14.4	14.6	14.9	15.1	15.3	15.6	15.8	16.0
10	13.9	14.2	14.7	14.9	15.1	15.4	15.6	15.8	16.0	16.2
12	14.5	14.7	15.2	15.4	15.6	15.9	16.1	16.3	16.5	16.7
14	15.0	15.2	15.7	15.9	16.1	16.3	16.5	16.7	16.9	17.1
16	15.5	15.7	16.1	16.4	16.6	16.8	17.0	17.2	17.4	17.5
18	16.0	16.2	16.6	16.8	17.0	17.2	17.4	17.6	17.8	17.9
20	16.4	16.7	17.0	17.3	17.4	17.6	17.8	18.0	18.2	18.3

10% Return Tables

9%

YEARS CONST. GROWTH	2	4	6	8	10	12	14	16	18	20
1	11.4	11.8	12.5	12.9	13.2	13.6	14.0	14.3	14.6	15.0
2	11.8	12.2	12.9	13.3	13.6	14.0	14.3	14.7	15.0	15.3
3	12.2	12.6	13.3	13.7	14.0	14.4	14.7	15.1	15.4	15.7
4	12.6	13.0	13.7	14.1	14.4	14.8	15.1	15.4	15.8	16.1
5	13.0	13.4	14.1	14.4	14.8	15.1	15.5	15.8	16.1	16.5
6	13.4	13.8	14.5	14.8	15.2	15.5	15.9	16.2	16.5	16.8
7	13.8	14.2	14.8	15.2	15.6	15.9	16.2	16.6	16.9	17.2
8	14.2	14.6	15.2	15.6	15.9	16.3	16.6	16.9	17.2	17.5
9	14.6	15.0	15.6	16.0	16.3	16.6	17.0	17.3	17.6	17.9
10	15.0	15.3	16.0	16.3	16.7	17.0	17.3	17.6	17.9	18.2
12	15.7	16.1	16.7	17.1	17.4	17.7	18.0	18.3	18.6	18.9
14	16.5	16.8	17.4	17.8	18.1	18.4	18.7	19.0	19.3	19.6
16	17.2	17.5	18.1	18.5	18.8	19.1	19.4	19.7	20.0	20.3
18	17.9	18.2	18.8	19.2	19.5	19.8	20.1	20.4	20.7	20.9
20	18.6	18.9	19.5	19.8	20.1	20.4	20.7	21.0	21.3	21.6

10%

YEARS CONST. GROWTH	2	4	6	8	10	12	14	16	18	20
1	11.6	12.1	12.9	13.4	13.9	14.3	14.8	15.2	15.7	16.1
2	12.1	12.6	13.4	13.9	14.4	14.8	15.3	15.7	16.2	16.6
3	12.6	13.1	13.9	14.4	14.9	15.3	15.8	16.2	16.7	17.1
4	13.1	13.6	14.4	14.9	15.4	15.8	16.3	16.7	17.2	17.6
5	13.6	14.1	14.9	15.4	15.9	16.3	16.8	17.2	17.7	18.1
6	14.1	14.6	15.4	15.9	16.4	16.8	17.3	17.7	18.2	18.6
7	14.6	15.1	15.9	16.4	16.9	17.3	17.8	18.2	18.7	19.1
8	15.1	15.6	16.4	16.9	17.4	17.8	18.3	18.7	19.2	19.6
9	15.6	16.1	16.9	17.4	17.9	18.3	18.8	19.2	19.7	20.1
10	16.1	16.6	17.4	17.9	18.4	18.8	19.3	19.7	20.2	20.6
12	17.1	17.6	18.4	18.9	19.4	19.9	20.3	20.8	21.2	21.6
14	18.1	18.6	19.4	19.9	20.4	20.9	21.3	21.8	22.2	22.6
16	19.1	19.6	20.5	20.9	21.4	21.9	22.3	22.8	23.2	23.6
18	20.1	20.6	21.5	21.9	22.4	22.9	23.3	23.8	24.2	24.6
20	21.1	21.6	22.5	22.9	23.4	23.9	24.3	24.8	25.2	25.6

11%

YEARS CONST. GROWTH	2	4	6	8	10	12	14	16	18	20
1	11.7	12.3	13.4	14.0	14.5	15.1	15.7	16.2	16.8	17.3
2	12.3	12.9	14.0	14.6	15.2	15.7	16.3	16.9	17.4	18.0
3	12.9	13.5	14.6	15.2	15.8	16.4	16.9	17.5	18.1	18.6
4	13.6	14.2	15.2	15.8	16.4	17.0	17.6	18.2	18.7	19.3
5	14.2	14.8	15.9	16.5	17.1	17.6	18.2	18.8	19.4	20.0
6	14.8	15.4	16.5	17.1	17.7	18.3	18.9	19.5	20.1	20.6
7	15.4	16.0	17.1	17.7	18.4	19.0	19.6	20.1	20.7	21.3
8	16.0	16.7	17.8	18.4	19.0	19.6	20.2	20.8	21.4	22.0
9	16.7	17.3	18.4	19.1	19.7	20.3	20.9	21.5	22.1	22.7
10	17.3	18.0	19.1	19.7	20.3	21.0	21.6	22.2	22.8	23.4
12	18.6	19.3	20.4	21.1	21.7	22.3	23.0	23.6	24.2	24.8
14	20.0	20.6	21.8	22.4	23.1	23.7	24.4	25.0	25.6	26.2
16	21.3	22.0	23.2	23.8	24.5	25.1	25.8	26.4	27.1	27.7
18	22.7	23.4	24.6	25.2	25.9	26.6	27.3	27.9	28.6	29.2
20	24.1	24.8	26.0	26.7	27.4	28.1	28.7	29.4	30.1	30.7

10% Return Tables

12 %

YEARS CONST. GROWTH	2	4	6	8	YEARS SETTLING GROWTH 10	12	14	16	18	20
1	11.9	12.6	13.8	14.5	15.2	15.9	16.6	17.3	18.0	18.7
2	12.6	13.3	14.6	15.3	16.0	16.7	17.4	18.1	18.8	19.5
3	13.3	14.0	15.3	16.0	16.7	17.5	18.2	18.9	19.6	20.4
4	14.1	14.8	16.1	16.8	17.5	18.3	19.0	19.7	20.5	21.2
5	14.8	15.5	16.8	17.6	18.3	19.1	19.8	20.6	21.3	22.1
6	15.5	16.3	17.6	18.4	19.1	19.9	20.7	21.4	22.2	23.0
7	16.3	17.1	18.4	19.2	20.0	20.7	21.5	22.3	23.1	23.9
8	17.1	17.8	19.2	20.0	20.8	21.6	22.4	23.2	24.0	24.8
9	17.9	18.6	20.1	20.9	21.7	22.5	23.3	24.1	24.9	25.7
10	18.7	19.5	20.9	21.7	22.5	23.4	24.2	25.0	25.8	26.6
12	20.3	21.1	22.6	23.5	24.3	25.2	26.0	26.9	27.7	28.6
14	22.0	22.9	24.4	25.3	26.2	27.1	28.0	28.8	29.7	30.6
16	23.8	24.7	26.3	27.2	28.1	29.0	30.0	30.9	31.8	32.7
18	25.6	26.6	28.2	29.2	30.1	31.1	32.0	33.0	33.9	34.9
20	27.6	28.5	30.2	31.2	32.2	33.2	34.2	35.1	36.1	37.1

13 %

YEARS CONST. GROWTH	2	4	6	8	YEARS SETTLING GROWTH 10	12	14	16	18	20
1	12.1	12.9	14.3	15.1	16.0	16.8	17.6	18.5	19.3	20.2
2	12.9	13.7	15.2	16.0	16.9	17.7	18.6	19.4	20.3	21.2
3	13.7	14.5	16.1	16.9	17.8	18.7	19.6	20.4	21.4	22.3
4	14.6	15.4	17.0	17.8	18.7	19.6	20.6	21.5	22.4	23.3
5	15.4	16.3	17.9	18.8	19.7	20.6	21.6	22.5	23.5	24.4
6	16.3	17.2	18.8	19.8	20.7	21.7	22.6	23.6	24.6	25.6
7	17.2	18.1	19.8	20.8	21.8	22.7	23.7	24.7	25.7	26.7
8	18.2	19.1	20.8	21.8	22.8	23.8	24.8	25.9	26.9	27.9
9	19.1	20.1	21.9	22.9	23.9	24.9	26.0	27.0	28.1	29.2
10	20.1	21.1	22.9	24.0	25.0	26.1	27.2	28.2	29.3	30.4
12	22.2	23.2	25.2	26.3	27.4	28.5	29.6	30.8	31.9	33.1
14	24.4	25.5	27.5	28.7	29.8	31.0	32.2	33.4	34.6	35.8
16	26.7	27.8	30.0	31.2	32.4	33.7	34.9	36.2	37.5	38.8
18	29.1	30.3	32.6	33.9	35.2	36.5	37.8	39.2	40.5	41.9
20	31.6	32.9	35.3	36.7	38.1	39.4	40.8	42.3	43.7	45.1

14 %

YEARS CONST. GROWTH	2	4	6	8	YEARS SETTLING GROWTH 10	12	14	16	18	20
1	12.3	13.2	14.8	15.8	16.7	17.7	18.7	19.7	20.8	21.8
2	13.2	14.1	15.8	16.8	17.8	18.8	19.8	20.9	22.0	23.1
3	14.1	15.1	16.8	17.9	18.9	20.0	21.0	22.1	23.2	24.4
4	15.1	16.1	17.9	19.0	20.0	21.1	22.2	23.4	24.5	25.7
5	16.1	17.1	19.0	20.1	21.2	22.4	23.5	24.7	25.9	27.1
6	17.1	18.2	20.2	21.3	22.5	23.6	24.8	26.0	27.3	28.6
7	18.2	19.3	21.3	22.5	23.7	24.9	26.2	27.5	28.7	30.1
8	19.3	20.5	22.6	23.8	25.0	26.3	27.6	28.9	30.2	31.6
9	20.5	21.7	23.9	25.1	26.4	27.7	29.1	30.4	31.8	33.2
10	21.7	22.9	25.2	26.5	27.8	29.2	30.6	32.0	33.4	34.9
12	24.3	25.6	28.0	29.4	30.8	32.3	33.8	35.3	36.8	38.4
14	27.0	28.4	31.0	32.5	34.0	35.6	37.2	38.8	40.5	42.2
16	29.9	31.4	34.2	35.8	37.5	39.2	40.9	42.6	44.4	46.2
18	33.1	34.7	37.7	39.4	41.2	43.0	44.8	46.7	48.6	50.6
20	36.4	38.2	41.4	43.3	45.2	47.1	49.1	51.1	53.2	55.2

10% Return Tables

| YEARS CONST. GROWTH | | | | | 15 %
YEARS SETTLING GROWTH | | | | | |
|---|---|---|---|---|---|---|---|---|---|---|
| | 2 | 4 | 6 | 8 | 10 | 12 | 14 | 16 | 18 | 20 |
| 1 | 12.5 | 13.5 | 15.3 | 16.4 | 17.5 | 18.7 | 19.9 | 21.1 | 22.3 | 23.6 |
| 2 | 13.5 | 14.5 | 16.5 | 17.6 | 18.8 | 20.0 | 21.2 | 22.5 | 23.8 | 25.1 |
| 3 | 14.5 | 15.6 | 17.7 | 18.8 | 20.1 | 21.3 | 22.6 | 24.0 | 25.3 | 26.7 |
| 4 | 15.6 | 16.8 | 18.9 | 20.2 | 21.4 | 22.8 | 24.1 | 25.5 | 26.9 | 28.4 |
| 5 | 16.8 | 18.0 | 20.2 | 21.5 | 22.9 | 24.2 | 25.6 | 27.1 | 28.6 | 30.1 |
| 6 | 18.0 | 19.3 | 21.6 | 22.9 | 24.3 | 25.8 | 27.3 | 28.8 | 30.3 | 31.9 |
| 7 | 19.3 | 20.6 | 23.0 | 24.4 | 25.9 | 27.4 | 28.9 | 30.5 | 32.2 | 33.8 |
| 8 | 20.6 | 22.0 | 24.5 | 26.0 | 27.5 | 29.1 | 30.7 | 32.4 | 34.1 | 35.8 |
| 9 | 22.0 | 23.4 | 26.1 | 27.6 | 29.2 | 30.9 | 32.5 | 34.3 | 36.1 | 37.9 |
| 10 | 23.4 | 24.9 | 27.7 | 29.3 | 31.0 | 32.7 | 34.5 | 36.3 | 38.1 | 40.1 |
| 12 | 26.5 | 28.1 | 31.2 | 33.0 | 34.8 | 36.7 | 38.6 | 40.6 | 42.6 | 44.7 |
| 14 | 29.9 | 31.7 | 35.0 | 36.9 | 38.9 | 41.0 | 43.1 | 45.3 | 47.5 | 49.8 |
| 16 | 33.6 | 35.5 | 39.1 | 41.3 | 43.5 | 45.7 | 48.0 | 50.4 | 52.8 | 55.3 |
| 18 | 37.6 | 39.7 | 43.7 | 46.0 | 48.4 | 50.9 | 53.4 | 56.0 | 58.6 | 61.4 |
| 20 | 42.1 | 44.4 | 48.7 | 51.2 | 53.8 | 56.5 | 59.3 | 62.1 | 65.0 | 68.0 |

| YEARS CONST. GROWTH | | | | | 16 %
YEARS SETTLING GROWTH | | | | | |
|---|---|---|---|---|---|---|---|---|---|---|
| | 2 | 4 | 6 | 8 | 10 | 12 | 14 | 16 | 18 | 20 |
| 1 | 12.7 | 13.8 | 15.8 | 17.1 | 18.4 | 19.7 | 21.1 | 22.5 | 24.0 | 25.6 |
| 2 | 13.8 | 14.9 | 17.1 | 18.5 | 19.8 | 21.2 | 22.7 | 24.2 | 25.8 | 27.4 |
| 3 | 15.0 | 16.2 | 18.5 | 19.9 | 21.3 | 22.8 | 24.4 | 26.0 | 27.6 | 29.3 |
| 4 | 16.2 | 17.5 | 20.0 | 21.4 | 22.9 | 24.5 | 26.1 | 27.8 | 29.5 | 31.4 |
| 5 | 17.5 | 18.9 | 21.5 | 23.0 | 24.6 | 26.3 | 28.0 | 29.8 | 31.6 | 33.5 |
| 6 | 18.9 | 20.4 | 23.1 | 24.7 | 26.4 | 28.1 | 30.0 | 31.8 | 33.8 | 35.8 |
| 7 | 20.4 | 21.9 | 24.8 | 26.5 | 28.3 | 30.1 | 32.0 | 34.0 | 36.0 | 38.1 |
| 8 | 22.0 | 23.6 | 26.6 | 28.4 | 30.3 | 32.2 | 34.2 | 36.3 | 38.4 | 40.7 |
| 9 | 23.6 | 25.3 | 28.5 | 30.4 | 32.3 | 34.4 | 36.5 | 38.7 | 41.0 | 43.3 |
| 10 | 25.3 | 27.1 | 30.5 | 32.5 | 34.5 | 36.7 | 38.9 | 41.2 | 43.6 | 46.1 |
| 12 | 29.0 | 31.0 | 34.8 | 37.0 | 39.3 | 41.7 | 44.2 | 46.8 | 49.4 | 52.2 |
| 14 | 33.2 | 35.4 | 39.6 | 42.0 | 44.6 | 47.3 | 50.0 | 52.9 | 55.9 | 58.9 |
| 16 | 37.8 | 40.3 | 44.9 | 47.7 | 50.5 | 53.5 | 56.5 | 59.7 | 63.0 | 66.4 |
| 18 | 42.9 | 45.7 | 50.8 | 53.9 | 57.1 | 60.4 | 63.8 | 67.3 | 71.0 | 74.8 |
| 20 | 48.6 | 51.7 | 57.4 | 60.8 | 64.4 | 68.0 | 71.8 | 75.8 | 79.8 | 84.0 |

| YEARS CONST. GROWTH | | | | | 17 %
YEARS SETTLING GROWTH | | | | | |
|---|---|---|---|---|---|---|---|---|---|---|
| | 2 | 4 | 6 | 8 | 10 | 12 | 14 | 16 | 18 | 20 |
| 1 | 12.8 | 14.1 | 16.4 | 17.8 | 19.3 | 20.8 | 22.4 | 24.1 | 25.9 | 27.7 |
| 2 | 14.1 | 15.4 | 17.9 | 19.4 | 20.9 | 22.6 | 24.3 | 26.1 | 27.9 | 29.9 |
| 3 | 15.4 | 16.8 | 19.4 | 21.0 | 22.7 | 24.4 | 26.2 | 28.1 | 30.1 | 32.2 |
| 4 | 16.8 | 18.3 | 21.1 | 22.8 | 24.6 | 26.4 | 28.3 | 30.4 | 32.5 | 34.7 |
| 5 | 18.3 | 19.9 | 22.9 | 24.7 | 26.5 | 28.5 | 30.8 | 32.9 | 35.2 | 37.6 | 40.1 |
| 6 | 19.9 | 21.6 | 24.7 | 26.7 | 28.7 | 30.8 | 32.9 | 35.2 | 37.6 | 40.1 |
| 7 | 21.6 | 23.4 | 26.7 | 28.8 | 30.9 | 33.1 | 35.5 | 37.9 | 40.4 | 43.1 |
| 8 | 23.4 | 25.3 | 28.9 | 31.0 | 33.3 | 35.7 | 38.1 | 40.7 | 43.4 | 46.2 |
| 9 | 25.3 | 27.3 | 31.1 | 33.4 | 35.8 | 38.4 | 41.0 | 43.7 | 46.6 | 49.6 |
| 10 | 27.3 | 29.5 | 33.5 | 36.0 | 38.6 | 41.2 | 44.0 | 47.0 | 50.0 | 53.2 |
| 12 | 31.8 | 34.2 | 38.8 | 41.6 | 44.5 | 47.5 | 50.7 | 54.0 | 57.5 | 61.1 |
| 14 | 36.9 | 39.6 | 44.8 | 47.9 | 51.2 | 54.7 | 58.2 | 62.0 | 65.9 | 70.0 |
| 16 | 42.6 | 45.7 | 51.6 | 55.1 | 58.8 | 62.7 | 66.8 | 71.0 | 75.4 | 80.0 |
| 18 | 49.1 | 52.5 | 59.2 | 63.2 | 67.4 | 71.8 | 76.4 | 81.2 | 86.2 | 91.4 |
| 20 | 56.4 | 60.3 | 67.9 | 72.4 | 77.2 | 82.1 | 87.3 | 92.7 | 98.4 | 104.3 |

10% Return Tables

18 %

YEARS CONST. GROWTH	YEARS SETTLING GROWTH									
	2	4	6	8	10	12	14	16	18	20
1	13.0	14.4	17.0	18.5	20.2	22.0	23.8	25.8	27.8	30.0
2	14.4	15.8	18.6	20.3	22.1	24.0	26.0	28.1	30.3	32.6
3	15.9	17.4	20.4	22.2	24.1	26.2	28.3	30.5	32.9	35.4
4	17.4	19.1	22.3	24.2	26.3	28.5	30.8	33.2	35.7	38.4
5	19.1	20.9	24.3	26.4	28.6	31.0	33.4	36.0	38.7	41.6
6	20.9	22.8	26.5	28.8	31.1	33.6	36.3	39.0	41.9	45.0
7	22.9	24.9	28.8	31.3	33.8	36.5	39.3	42.3	45.4	48.7
8	24.9	27.1	31.4	33.9	36.7	39.6	42.6	45.8	49.1	52.7
9	27.2	29.5	34.1	36.8	39.8	42.8	46.1	49.5	53.1	56.9
10	29.6	32.1	36.9	39.9	43.1	46.4	49.9	53.5	57.4	61.5
12	34.9	37.8	43.4	46.8	50.4	54.2	58.2	62.5	66.9	71.6
14	41.0	44.3	50.8	54.7	58.9	63.3	67.9	72.7	77.9	83.3
16	48.0	51.9	59.3	63.8	68.6	73.7	79.0	84.6	90.5	96.7
18	56.1	60.5	69.1	74.3	79.8	85.6	91.8	98.2	105.0	112.1
20	65.5	70.5	80.4	86.4	92.7	99.4	106.4	113.9	121.7	129.9

19 %

YEARS CONST. GROWTH	YEARS SETTLING GROWTH									
	2	4	6	8	10	12	14	16	18	20
1	13.2	14.7	17.6	19.3	21.2	23.2	25.3	27.6	30.0	32.5
2	14.7	16.3	19.4	21.3	23.3	25.5	27.8	30.3	32.9	35.6
3	16.3	18.0	21.4	23.5	25.7	28.0	30.5	33.1	35.9	38.9
4	18.1	19.9	23.5	25.8	28.2	30.7	33.4	36.3	39.3	42.5
5	19.9	21.9	25.9	28.3	30.9	33.6	36.5	39.6	42.9	46.4
6	22.0	24.2	28.4	31.0	33.8	36.8	39.9	43.3	46.8	50.6
7	24.2	26.5	31.1	34.0	37.0	40.2	43.6	47.2	51.1	55.1
8	26.6	29.1	34.1	37.2	40.4	43.9	47.6	51.5	55.6	60.1
9	29.2	31.9	37.3	40.6	44.1	47.9	51.9	56.1	60.6	65.4
10	31.9	34.9	40.7	44.3	48.1	52.2	56.5	61.1	66.0	71.1
12	38.2	41.7	48.5	52.7	57.2	61.9	67.0	72.4	78.1	84.1
14	45.6	49.7	57.6	62.5	67.8	73.3	79.3	85.5	92.2	99.3
16	54.2	59.0	68.3	74.0	80.2	86.7	93.6	100.9	108.7	117.0
18	64.3	69.8	80.8	87.5	94.7	102.3	110.4	119.0	128.1	137.8
20	76.1	82.6	95.4	103.3	111.6	120.6	130.0	140.1	150.8	162.1

20 %

YEARS CONST. GROWTH	YEARS SETTLING GROWTH									
	2	4	6	8	10	12	14	16	18	20
1	13.4	15.0	18.2	20.1	22.2	24.5	26.9	29.5	32.3	35.3
2	15.0	16.8	20.2	22.4	24.7	27.1	29.8	32.6	35.7	38.9
3	16.8	18.7	22.4	24.8	27.3	30.0	32.9	36.0	39.3	42.8
4	18.7	20.8	24.9	27.4	30.2	33.1	36.3	39.7	43.3	47.1
5	20.8	23.1	27.5	30.3	33.3	36.5	40.0	43.7	47.6	51.8
6	23.1	25.6	30.4	33.5	36.7	40.3	44.0	48.0	52.3	56.9
7	25.6	28.3	33.6	36.9	40.5	44.3	48.4	52.8	57.5	62.5
8	28.3	31.3	37.0	40.7	44.6	48.7	53.2	58.0	63.1	68.6
9	31.3	34.5	40.8	44.8	49.0	53.6	58.4	63.6	69.2	75.2
10	34.5	38.0	44.9	49.2	53.9	58.8	64.1	69.8	75.9	82.4
12	41.9	46.1	54.3	59.4	64.9	70.8	77.2	83.9	91.2	98.9
14	50.7	55.7	65.4	71.5	78.1	85.1	92.6	100.7	109.3	118.6
16	61.2	67.1	78.7	86.0	93.8	102.1	111.1	120.7	130.9	141.9
18	73.7	80.7	94.5	103.1	112.4	122.4	133.0	144.4	156.7	169.7
20	88.5	96.8	113.3	123.6	134.6	146.5	159.1	172.7	187.3	202.8

10% Return Tables

YEARS CONST. GROWTH	\multicolumn{10}{c}{25 % YEARS SETTLING GROWTH}

YEARS CONST. GROWTH	2	4	6	8	10	12	14	16	18	20
1	14.4	16.7	21.5	24.7	28.3	32.3	36.7	41.7	47.2	53.4
2	16.7	19.4	24.8	28.4	32.5	37.0	42.1	47.7	54.0	61.0
3	19.4	22.3	28.5	32.7	37.3	42.4	48.2	54.6	61.7	69.7
4	22.4	25.7	32.8	37.5	42.7	48.5	55.1	62.4	70.5	79.5
5	25.8	29.6	37.6	42.9	48.9	55.5	62.9	71.2	80.4	90.7
6	29.6	34.0	43.1	49.1	55.9	63.4	71.9	81.3	91.7	103.4
7	34.0	39.0	49.3	56.2	63.9	72.4	82.0	92.7	104.6	117.9
8	39.0	44.7	56.4	64.2	72.9	82.7	93.6	105.7	119.2	134.3
9	44.7	51.1	64.4	73.3	83.2	94.3	106.7	120.5	135.8	153.0
10	51.2	58.4	73.6	83.7	94.9	107.5	121.6	137.2	154.7	174.2
12	66.8	76.2	95.8	108.8	123.3	139.6	157.7	178.0	200.5	225.7
14	87.0	99.1	124.4	141.2	160.0	181.0	204.4	230.6	259.7	292.2
16	113.1	128.7	161.4	183.1	207.4	234.5	264.7	298.5	336.1	378.1
18	146.8	167.0	209.2	237.2	268.5	303.5	342.6	386.2	434.7	489.0
20	190.4	216.4	270.9	307.1	347.5	392.7	443.1	499.4	562.1	632.2

Industrials—Investment Values of Normal Earnings of $1 at 12% Return

Projected Earnings Growth Rate

YEARS CONST. GROWTH	2	4	6	8	1 % YEARS SETTLING GROWTH 10	12	14	16	18	20
1	7.6	7.5	7.3	7.2	7.1	7.0	6.9	6.9	6.8	6.8
2	7.5	7.3	7.2	7.1	7.0	6.9	6.9	6.8	6.8	6.7
3	7.3	7.2	7.1	7.0	6.9	6.8	6.8	6.7	6.7	6.7
4	7.2	7.1	7.0	6.9	6.8	6.8	6.7	6.7	6.6	6.6
5	7.1	7.0	6.9	6.8	6.8	6.7	6.7	6.6	6.6	6.6
6	7.0	6.9	6.8	6.8	6.7	6.7	6.6	6.6	6.6	6.5
7	6.9	6.9	6.8	6.7	6.7	6.6	6.6	6.5	6.5	6.5
8	6.9	6.8	6.7	6.7	6.6	6.6	6.5	6.5	6.5	6.5
9	6.8	6.7	6.7	6.6	6.6	6.5	6.5	6.5	6.5	6.4
10	6.7	6.7	6.6	6.6	6.5	6.5	6.5	6.4	6.4	6.4
12	6.6	6.6	6.5	6.5	6.5	6.4	6.4	6.4	6.4	6.4
14	6.5	6.5	6.5	6.4	6.4	6.4	6.4	6.4	6.3	6.3
16	6.5	6.4	6.4	6.4	6.4	6.3	6.3	6.3	6.3	6.3
18	6.4	6.4	6.4	6.3	6.3	6.3	6.3	6.3	6.3	6.3
20	6.4	6.4	6.3	6.3	6.3	6.3	6.3	6.3	6.3	6.3

YEARS CONST. GROWTH	2	4	6	8	2 % YEARS SETTLING GROWTH 10	12	14	16	18	20
1	7.7	7.6	7.5	7.4	7.3	7.3	7.2	7.2	7.2	7.1
2	7.6	7.5	7.4	7.3	7.3	7.2	7.2	7.1	7.1	7.1
3	7.5	7.5	7.3	7.3	7.2	7.2	7.1	7.1	7.1	7.0
4	7.5	7.4	7.3	7.2	7.2	7.1	7.1	7.1	7.0	7.0
5	7.4	7.3	7.2	7.2	7.1	7.1	7.1	7.0	7.0	7.0
6	7.3	7.3	7.2	7.1	7.1	7.0	7.0	7.0	7.0	6.9
7	7.3	7.2	7.1	7.1	7.0	7.0	7.0	7.0	6.9	6.9
8	7.2	7.1	7.1	7.0	7.0	7.0	7.0	6.9	6.9	6.9
9	7.1	7.1	7.0	7.0	7.0	6.9	6.9	6.9	6.9	6.9
10	7.1	7.1	7.0	7.0	6.9	6.9	6.9	6.9	6.9	6.8
12	7.0	7.0	6.9	6.9	6.9	6.9	6.9	6.8	6.8	6.8
14	7.0	6.9	6.9	6.9	6.8	6.8	6.8	6.8	6.8	6.8
16	6.9	6.9	6.8	6.8	6.8	6.8	6.8	6.8	6.8	6.8
18	6.9	6.8	6.8	6.8	6.8	6.8	6.8	6.8	6.7	6.7
20	6.8	6.8	6.8	6.8	6.8	6.7	6.7	6.7	6.7	6.7

12% Return Tables

YEARS CONST. GROWTH	2	4	6	8	3 % YEARS SETTLING GROWTH 10	12	14	16	18	20
1	7.8	7.8	7.7	7.7	7.6	7.6	7.6	7.6	7.5	7.5
2	7.8	7.7	7.7	7.6	7.6	7.6	7.5	7.5	7.5	7.5
3	7.7	7.7	7.6	7.6	7.6	7.5	7.5	7.5	7.5	7.5
4	7.7	7.6	7.6	7.6	7.5	7.5	7.5	7.5	7.5	7.4
5	7.6	7.6	7.6	7.5	7.5	7.5	7.5	7.5	7.4	7.4
6	7.6	7.6	7.5	7.5	7.5	7.5	7.5	7.4	7.4	7.4
7	7.6	7.6	7.5	7.5	7.5	7.4	7.4	7.4	7.4	7.4
8	7.6	7.5	7.5	7.5	7.4	7.4	7.4	7.4	7.4	7.4
9	7.5	7.5	7.5	7.4	7.4	7.4	7.4	7.4	7.4	7.4
10	7.5	7.5	7.4	7.4	7.4	7.4	7.4	7.4	7.4	7.4
12	7.5	7.4	7.4	7.4	7.4	7.4	7.4	7.4	7.4	7.4
14	7.4	7.4	7.4	7.4	7.4	7.3	7.3	7.3	7.3	7.3
16	7.4	7.4	7.4	7.3	7.3	7.3	7.3	7.3	7.3	7.3
18	7.4	7.3	7.3	7.3	7.3	7.3	7.3	7.3	7.3	7.3
20	7.3	7.3	7.3	7.3	7.3	7.3	7.3	7.3	7.3	7.3

YEARS CONST. GROWTH	2	4	6	8	4 % YEARS SETTLING GROWTH 10	12	14	16	18	20
1	7.9	7.9	7.9	7.9	7.9	7.9	7.9	7.9	7.9	7.9
2	7.9	7.9	7.9	7.9	7.9	7.9	7.9	7.9	7.9	7.9
3	7.9	7.9	7.9	7.9	7.9	7.9	7.9	7.9	7.9	7.9
4	7.9	7.9	7.9	7.9	7.9	7.9	7.9	7.9	7.9	7.9
5	7.9	7.9	7.9	7.9	7.9	7.9	7.9	7.9	7.9	7.9
6	7.9	7.9	7.9	7.9	7.9	7.9	7.9	7.9	7.9	7.9
7	7.9	7.9	7.9	7.9	7.9	7.9	7.9	7.9	7.9	7.9
8	7.9	7.9	7.9	7.9	7.9	7.9	7.9	7.9	7.9	7.9
9	7.9	7.9	7.9	7.9	7.9	7.9	7.9	7.9	7.9	7.9
10	7.9	7.9	7.9	7.9	7.9	7.9	7.9	7.9	7.9	7.9
12	7.9	7.9	7.9	7.9	7.9	7.9	7.9	7.9	7.9	7.9
14	7.9	7.9	7.9	7.9	7.9	7.9	7.9	7.9	7.9	7.9
16	7.9	7.9	7.9	7.9	7.9	7.9	7.9	7.9	7.9	7.9
18	7.9	7.9	7.9	7.9	7.9	7.9	7.9	7.9	7.9	7.9
20	7.9	7.9	7.9	7.9	7.9	7.9	7.9	7.9	7.9	7.9

YEARS CONST. GROWTH	2	4	6	8	5 % YEARS SETTLING GROWTH 10	12	14	16	18	20
1	8.0	8.1	8.2	8.2	8.2	8.3	8.3	8.3	8.4	8.4
2	8.1	8.1	8.2	8.3	8.3	8.3	8.3	8.4	8.4	8.4
3	8.1	8.2	8.3	8.3	8.3	8.4	8.4	8.4	8.4	8.4
4	8.2	8.2	8.3	8.3	8.4	8.4	8.4	8.4	8.5	8.5
5	8.2	8.3	8.3	8.4	8.4	8.4	8.4	8.5	8.5	8.5
6	8.3	8.3	8.4	8.4	8.4	8.4	8.5	8.5	8.5	8.5
7	8.3	8.3	8.4	8.4	8.4	8.5	8.5	8.5	8.5	8.5
8	8.3	8.4	8.4	8.4	8.5	8.5	8.5	8.5	8.5	8.6
9	8.4	8.4	8.4	8.5	8.5	8.5	8.5	8.5	8.6	8.6
10	8.4	8.4	8.5	8.5	8.5	8.5	8.6	8.6	8.6	8.6
12	8.5	8.5	8.5	8.5	8.6	8.6	8.6	8.6	8.6	8.6
14	8.5	8.5	8.6	8.6	8.6	8.6	8.6	8.6	8.6	8.7
16	8.5	8.6	8.6	8.6	8.6	8.6	8.7	8.7	8.7	8.7
18	8.6	8.6	8.6	8.6	8.7	8.7	8.7	8.7	8.7	8.7
20	8.6	8.6	8.7	8.7	8.7	8.7	8.7	8.7	8.7	8.7

12% Return Tables

6 %

YEARS CONST. GROWTH	2	4	6	8	YEARS SETTLING GROWTH 10	12	14	16	18	20
1	8.2	8.3	8.4	8.5	8.6	8.7	8.7	8.8	8.8	8.9
2	8.3	8.4	8.5	8.6	8.7	8.7	8.8	8.9	8.9	9.0
3	8.4	8.4	8.6	8.7	8.7	8.8	8.9	8.9	9.0	9.0
4	8.5	8.5	8.7	8.7	8.8	8.9	8.9	9.0	9.0	9.1
5	8.5	8.6	8.8	8.8	8.9	8.9	9.0	9.0	9.1	9.1
6	8.6	8.7	8.8	8.9	8.9	9.0	9.1	9.1	9.1	9.2
7	8.7	8.8	8.9	9.0	9.0	9.1	9.1	9.2	9.2	9.2
8	8.8	8.8	9.0	9.0	9.1	9.1	9.2	9.2	9.2	9.3
9	8.8	8.9	9.0	9.1	9.1	9.2	9.2	9.3	9.3	9.3
10	8.9	9.0	9.1	9.1	9.2	9.2	9.3	9.3	9.3	9.4
12	9.0	9.1	9.2	9.2	9.3	9.3	9.3	9.4	9.4	9.4
14	9.2	9.2	9.3	9.3	9.4	9.4	9.4	9.5	9.5	9.5
16	9.2	9.3	9.4	9.4	9.4	9.5	9.5	9.5	9.5	9.6
18	9.3	9.4	9.4	9.5	9.5	9.5	9.6	9.6	9.6	9.6
20	9.4	9.5	9.5	9.5	9.6	9.6	9.6	9.6	9.7	9.7

7 %

YEARS CONST. GROWTH	2	4	6	8	YEARS SETTLING GROWTH 10	12	14	16	18	20
1	8.3	8.4	8.7	8.8	8.9	9.0	9.2	9.3	9.3	9.4
2	8.4	8.6	8.8	8.9	9.1	9.2	9.3	9.4	9.5	9.5
3	8.6	8.7	9.0	9.1	9.2	9.3	9.4	9.5	9.6	9.6
4	8.7	8.9	9.1	9.2	9.3	9.4	9.5	9.6	9.7	9.7
5	8.9	9.0	9.2	9.3	9.4	9.5	9.6	9.7	9.8	9.8
6	9.0	9.1	9.3	9.4	9.5	9.6	9.7	9.8	9.9	9.9
7	9.1	9.2	9.4	9.5	9.6	9.7	9.8	9.9	9.9	10.0
8	9.2	9.4	9.5	9.6	9.7	9.8	9.9	10.0	10.0	10.1
9	9.4	9.5	9.6	9.7	9.8	9.9	10.0	10.0	10.1	10.2
10	9.5	9.6	9.7	9.8	9.9	10.0	10.1	10.1	10.2	10.2
12	9.7	9.8	9.9	10.0	10.1	10.2	10.2	10.3	10.3	10.4
14	9.9	10.0	10.1	10.2	10.2	10.3	10.4	10.4	10.5	10.5
16	10.0	10.1	10.2	10.3	10.4	10.4	10.5	10.5	10.6	10.6
18	10.2	10.3	10.4	10.4	10.5	10.6	10.6	10.7	10.7	10.7
20	10.3	10.4	10.5	10.6	10.6	10.7	10.7	10.8	10.8	10.8

8 %

YEARS CONST. GROWTH	2	4	6	8	YEARS SETTLING GROWTH 10	12	14	16	18	20
1	8.4	8.6	8.9	9.1	9.3	9.5	9.6	9.8	9.9	10.0
2	8.6	8.8	9.1	9.3	9.5	9.6	9.8	9.9	10.1	10.2
3	8.8	9.0	9.3	9.5	9.7	9.8	10.0	10.1	10.2	10.3
4	9.0	9.2	9.5	9.7	9.8	10.0	10.1	10.3	10.4	10.5
5	9.2	9.4	9.7	9.9	10.0	10.1	10.3	10.4	10.5	10.6
6	9.4	9.6	9.9	10.0	10.2	10.3	10.4	10.5	10.7	10.8
7	9.6	9.7	10.0	10.2	10.3	10.4	10.6	10.7	10.8	10.9
8	9.8	9.9	10.2	10.3	10.5	10.6	10.7	10.8	10.9	11.0
9	9.9	10.1	10.3	10.5	10.6	10.7	10.8	11.0	11.1	11.2
10	10.1	10.2	10.5	10.6	10.7	10.9	11.0	11.1	11.2	11.3
12	10.4	10.5	10.8	10.9	11.0	11.1	11.2	11.3	11.4	11.5
14	10.7	10.8	11.0	11.1	11.2	11.4	11.4	11.5	11.6	11.7
16	10.9	11.1	11.3	11.4	11.5	11.6	11.7	11.7	11.8	11.9
18	11.2	11.3	11.5	11.6	11.7	11.8	11.9	11.9	12.0	12.1
20	11.4	11.5	11.7	11.8	11.9	12.0	12.0	12.1	12.2	12.2

12% Return Tables

YEARS CONST. GROWTH	2	4	6	8	9 % YEARS SETTLING GROWTH 10	12	14	16	18	20
1	8.5	8.8	9.2	9.5	9.7	9.9	10.1	10.3	10.5	10.7
2	8.8	9.0	9.5	9.7	9.9	10.1	10.4	10.5	10.7	10.9
3	9.1	9.3	9.7	10.0	10.2	10.4	10.6	10.8	10.9	11.1
4	9.3	9.6	10.0	10.2	10.4	10.6	10.8	11.0	11.2	11.3
5	9.6	9.8	10.2	10.4	10.6	10.8	11.0	11.2	11.4	11.5
6	9.8	10.0	10.4	10.7	10.9	11.0	11.2	11.4	11.6	11.7
7	10.1	10.3	10.7	10.9	11.1	11.3	11.4	11.6	11.8	11.9
8	10.3	10.5	10.9	11.1	11.3	11.5	11.6	11.8	11.9	12.1
9	10.5	10.7	11.1	11.3	11.5	11.7	11.8	12.0	12.1	12.3
10	10.7	11.0	11.3	11.5	11.7	11.8	12.0	12.2	12.3	12.5
12	11.2	11.4	11.7	11.9	12.1	12.2	12.4	12.5	12.7	12.8
14	11.6	11.8	12.1	12.3	12.4	12.6	12.7	12.9	13.0	13.1
16	12.0	12.1	12.4	12.6	12.8	12.9	13.0	13.2	13.3	13.4
18	12.3	12.5	12.8	12.9	13.1	13.2	13.3	13.5	13.6	13.7
20	12.7	12.8	13.1	13.2	13.4	13.5	13.6	13.8	13.9	14.0

YEARS CONST. GROWTH	2	4	6	8	10 % YEARS SETTLING GROWTH 10	12	14	16	18	20
1	8.6	8.9	9.5	9.8	10.1	10.4	10.6	10.9	11.2	11.4
2	9.0	9.3	9.8	10.1	10.4	10.7	11.0	11.2	11.4	11.7
3	9.3	9.6	10.2	10.4	10.7	11.0	11.2	11.5	11.7	12.0
4	9.6	9.9	10.5	10.8	11.0	11.3	11.5	11.8	12.0	12.2
5	9.9	10.2	10.8	11.1	11.3	11.6	11.8	12.1	12.3	12.5
6	10.3	10.6	11.1	11.3	11.6	11.9	12.1	12.3	12.6	12.8
7	10.6	10.9	11.4	11.6	11.9	12.1	12.4	12.6	12.8	13.1
8	10.9	11.2	11.7	11.9	12.2	12.4	12.7	12.9	13.1	13.3
9	11.2	11.5	11.9	12.2	12.5	12.7	12.9	13.2	13.4	13.6
10	11.5	11.7	12.2	12.5	12.7	13.0	13.2	13.4	13.6	13.8
12	12.0	12.3	12.8	13.0	13.3	13.5	13.7	13.9	14.1	14.3
14	12.6	12.8	13.3	13.5	13.8	14.0	14.2	14.4	14.6	14.8
16	13.1	13.4	13.8	14.0	14.3	14.5	14.7	14.9	15.1	15.2
18	13.6	13.9	14.3	14.5	14.7	14.9	15.1	15.3	15.5	15.7
20	14.1	14.4	14.8	15.0	15.2	15.4	15.6	15.8	15.9	16.1

YEARS CONST. GROWTH	2	4	6	8	11 % YEARS SETTLING GROWTH 10	12	14	16	18	20
1	8.7	9.1	9.8	10.2	10.5	10.9	11.2	11.5	11.9	12.2
2	9.1	9.5	10.2	10.6	10.9	11.3	11.6	11.9	12.2	12.5
3	9.5	9.9	10.6	11.0	11.3	11.6	12.0	12.3	12.6	12.9
4	9.9	10.3	11.0	11.3	11.7	12.0	12.4	12.7	13.0	13.3
5	10.3	10.7	11.4	11.7	12.1	12.4	12.7	13.0	13.3	13.6
6	10.7	11.1	11.8	12.1	12.4	12.8	13.1	13.4	13.7	14.0
7	11.1	11.5	12.1	12.5	12.8	13.1	13.5	13.8	14.1	14.4
8	11.5	11.9	12.5	12.8	13.2	13.5	13.8	14.1	14.4	14.7
9	11.9	12.2	12.9	13.2	13.5	13.9	14.2	14.5	14.8	15.1
10	12.3	12.6	13.2	13.6	13.9	14.2	14.5	14.8	15.1	15.4
12	13.0	13.3	14.0	14.3	14.6	14.9	15.2	15.5	15.8	16.1
14	13.7	14.1	14.7	15.0	15.3	15.6	15.9	16.2	16.5	16.8
16	14.4	14.8	15.4	15.7	16.0	16.3	16.6	16.9	17.2	17.4
18	15.1	15.5	16.1	16.4	16.7	17.0	17.3	17.5	17.8	18.1
20	15.8	16.2	16.7	17.0	17.3	17.6	17.9	18.2	18.5	18.7

12% Return Tables

12 %

YEARS CONST. GROWTH	\multicolumn{10}{c}{YEARS SETTLING GROWTH}
	2	4	6	8	10	12	14	16	18	20
1	8.9	9.3	10.1	10.6	11.0	11.4	11.8	12.2	12.6	13.0
2	9.3	9.8	10.6	11.0	11.4	11.9	12.3	12.7	13.1	13.5
3	9.8	10.2	11.0	11.5	11.9	12.3	12.7	13.1	13.5	13.9
4	10.2	10.7	11.5	11.9	12.4	12.8	13.2	13.6	14.0	14.4
5	10.7	11.2	12.0	12.4	12.8	13.3	13.7	14.1	14.5	14.9
6	11.2	11.6	12.4	12.9	13.3	13.7	14.1	14.5	14.9	15.3
7	11.6	12.1	12.9	13.3	13.8	14.2	14.6	15.0	15.4	15.8
8	12.1	12.6	13.4	13.8	14.2	14.7	15.1	15.5	15.9	16.2
9	12.6	13.0	13.8	14.3	14.7	15.1	15.5	15.9	16.3	16.7
10	13.0	13.5	14.3	14.7	15.2	15.6	16.0	16.4	16.8	17.2
12	14.0	14.4	15.2	15.7	16.1	16.5	16.9	17.3	17.7	18.1
14	14.9	15.3	16.1	16.6	17.0	17.4	17.8	18.2	18.6	19.0
16	15.8	16.3	17.1	17.5	17.9	18.4	18.8	19.2	19.6	20.0
18	16.7	17.2	18.0	18.4	18.9	19.3	19.7	20.1	20.5	20.9
20	17.7	18.1	18.9	19.4	19.8	20.2	20.6	21.0	21.4	21.8

13 %

YEARS CONST. GROWTH	\multicolumn{10}{c}{YEARS SETTLING GROWTH}
	2	4	6	8	10	12	14	16	18	20
1	9.0	9.5	10.4	11.0	11.5	12.0	12.5	13.0	13.4	13.9
2	9.5	10.1	11.0	11.5	12.0	12.5	13.0	13.5	14.0	14.5
3	10.1	10.6	11.6	12.1	12.6	13.1	13.6	14.1	14.6	15.1
4	10.6	11.2	12.1	12.6	13.2	13.7	14.2	14.7	15.2	15.7
5	11.2	11.7	12.7	13.2	13.7	14.3	14.8	15.3	15.8	16.3
6	11.7	12.3	13.3	13.8	14.3	14.9	15.4	15.9	16.4	16.9
7	12.3	12.9	13.8	14.4	14.9	15.5	16.0	16.5	17.0	17.5
8	12.9	13.4	14.4	15.0	15.5	16.0	16.6	17.1	17.6	18.1
9	13.4	14.0	15.0	15.6	16.1	16.7	17.2	17.7	18.2	18.7
10	14.0	14.6	15.6	16.2	16.7	17.3	17.8	18.3	18.9	19.4
12	15.2	15.8	16.8	17.4	17.9	18.5	19.0	19.6	20.1	20.6
14	16.4	17.0	18.0	18.6	19.2	19.7	20.3	20.9	21.4	21.9
16	17.6	18.2	19.3	19.9	20.5	21.0	21.6	22.2	22.7	23.3
18	18.9	19.5	20.5	21.1	21.7	22.3	22.9	23.5	24.0	24.6
20	20.1	20.7	21.8	22.4	23.1	23.7	24.2	24.8	25.4	26.0

14 %

YEARS CONST. GROWTH	\multicolumn{10}{c}{YEARS SETTLING GROWTH}
	2	4	6	8	10	12	14	16	18	20
1	9.1	9.7	10.8	11.4	12.0	12.6	13.2	13.8	14.3	14.9
2	9.7	10.3	11.4	12.0	12.6	13.2	13.8	14.4	15.0	15.6
3	10.4	11.0	12.1	12.7	13.3	13.9	14.5	15.2	15.8	16.4
4	11.0	11.6	12.7	13.4	14.0	14.6	15.3	15.9	16.5	17.1
5	11.6	12.3	13.4	14.1	14.7	15.3	16.0	16.6	17.2	17.9
6	12.3	12.9	14.1	14.8	15.4	16.1	16.7	17.3	18.0	18.6
7	13.0	13.6	14.8	15.5	16.1	16.8	17.5	18.1	18.8	19.4
8	13.6	14.3	15.5	16.2	16.9	17.5	18.2	18.9	19.5	20.2
9	14.3	15.0	16.2	16.9	17.6	18.3	19.0	19.7	20.3	21.0
10	15.0	15.7	17.0	17.7	18.4	19.1	19.8	20.5	21.2	21.8
12	16.5	17.2	18.5	19.2	20.0	20.7	21.4	22.1	22.8	23.5
14	18.0	18.7	20.1	20.8	21.6	22.3	23.1	23.8	24.6	25.3
16	19.5	20.3	21.7	22.5	23.3	24.0	24.8	25.6	26.3	27.1
18	21.1	21.9	23.4	24.2	25.0	25.8	26.6	27.4	28.2	29.0
20	22.8	23.6	25.1	26.0	26.8	27.6	28.5	29.3	30.1	30.9

12% Return Tables

YEARS CONST. GROWTH	2	4	6	8	15 % YEARS SETTLING GROWTH 10	12	14	16	18	20
1	9.2	9.5	11.1	11.8	12.5	13.2	13.9	14.6	15.3	16.0
2	9.9	10.6	11.9	12.6	13.3	14.0	14.7	15.4	16.2	16.9
3	10.6	11.3	12.6	13.3	14.1	14.8	15.5	16.3	17.0	17.8
4	11.4	12.1	13.4	14.1	14.9	15.6	16.4	17.2	17.9	18.7
5	12.1	12.8	14.2	15.0	15.7	16.5	17.3	18.1	18.8	19.6
6	12.9	13.6	15.0	15.8	16.6	17.4	18.2	19.0	19.8	20.6
7	13.6	14.4	15.8	16.7	17.5	18.3	19.1	19.9	20.7	21.6
8	14.5	15.2	16.7	17.5	18.4	19.2	20.1	20.9	21.7	22.6
9	15.3	16.1	17.6	18.5	19.3	20.2	21.0	21.9	22.8	23.6
10	16.1	17.0	18.5	19.4	20.3	21.1	22.0	22.9	23.8	24.7
12	17.9	18.8	20.4	21.3	22.3	23.2	24.1	25.1	26.0	26.9
14	19.7	20.7	22.4	23.4	24.3	25.3	26.3	27.3	28.3	29.3
16	21.7	22.7	24.5	25.5	26.6	27.6	28.6	29.7	30.7	31.8
18	23.8	24.8	26.7	27.8	28.9	30.0	31.1	32.2	33.3	34.4
20	26.0	27.0	29.1	30.2	31.3	32.5	33.6	34.8	36.0	37.1

YEARS CONST. GROWTH	2	4	6	8	16 % YEARS SETTLING GROWTH 10	12	14	16	18	20
1	9.4	10.1	11.5	12.3	13.1	13.9	14.7	15.5	16.3	17.2
2	10.1	10.9	12.3	13.1	14.0	14.8	15.6	16.5	17.4	18.2
3	10.9	11.7	13.2	14.0	14.9	15.7	16.6	17.5	18.4	19.3
4	11.7	12.6	14.1	15.0	15.8	16.7	17.6	18.6	19.5	20.4
5	12.6	13.4	15.0	15.9	16.8	17.8	18.7	19.7	20.6	21.6
6	13.5	14.3	16.0	16.9	17.9	18.8	19.8	20.8	21.8	22.8
7	14.4	15.3	17.0	18.0	18.9	19.9	20.9	22.0	23.0	24.0
8	15.3	16.3	18.0	19.0	20.0	21.1	22.1	23.2	24.2	25.3
9	16.3	17.3	19.1	20.1	21.2	22.3	23.3	24.4	25.5	26.7
10	17.3	18.3	20.2	21.3	22.4	23.5	24.6	25.7	26.9	28.0
12	19.4	20.5	22.5	23.7	24.9	26.1	27.3	28.5	29.7	30.9
14	21.7	22.9	25.0	26.3	27.5	28.8	30.1	31.4	32.7	34.1
16	24.2	25.4	27.7	29.1	30.4	31.8	33.2	34.6	36.0	37.4
18	26.8	28.1	30.6	32.1	33.5	35.0	36.4	37.9	39.5	41.0
20	29.6	31.1	33.7	35.3	36.8	38.4	40.0	41.6	43.2	44.9

YEARS CONST. GROWTH	2	4	6	8	17 % YEARS SETTLING GROWTH 10	12	14	16	18	20
1	9.5	10.3	11.9	12.7	13.6	14.6	15.5	16.5	17.5	18.5
2	10.3	11.2	12.8	13.7	14.7	15.6	16.6	17.6	18.7	19.7
3	11.2	12.1	13.8	14.8	15.7	16.8	17.8	18.8	19.9	21.0
4	12.1	13.1	14.8	15.8	16.9	17.9	19.0	20.1	21.2	22.4
5	13.1	14.1	15.9	17.0	18.0	19.1	20.3	21.4	22.6	23.8
6	14.1	15.1	17.0	18.1	19.3	20.4	21.6	22.8	24.0	25.3
7	15.2	16.2	18.2	19.4	20.5	21.7	23.0	24.2	25.5	26.8
8	16.3	17.4	19.4	20.6	21.9	23.1	24.4	25.7	27.1	28.4
9	17.4	18.5	20.7	22.0	23.3	24.6	25.9	27.3	28.7	30.1
10	18.6	19.8	22.1	23.4	24.7	26.1	27.5	28.9	30.4	31.9
12	21.1	22.5	24.9	26.4	27.8	29.3	30.9	32.4	34.0	35.7
14	23.9	25.4	28.1	29.6	31.2	32.9	34.5	36.3	38.0	39.8
16	27.0	28.5	31.5	33.2	34.9	36.7	38.6	40.4	42.3	44.3
18	30.3	32.0	35.2	37.1	39.0	40.9	42.9	45.0	47.0	49.1
20	33.9	35.8	39.3	41.3	43.4	45.5	47.7	49.9	52.2	54.5

12% Return Tables

YEARS CONST. GROWTH	18 % YEARS SETTLING GROWTH									
	2	4	6	8	10	12	14	16	18	20
1	9.6	10.5	12.2	13.2	14.3	15.3	16.4	17.5	18.7	19.9
2	10.6	11.5	13.3	14.4	15.4	16.6	17.7	18.9	20.1	21.4
3	11.5	12.5	14.4	15.5	16.7	17.8	19.1	20.3	21.6	22.9
4	12.6	13.6	15.6	16.8	18.0	19.2	20.5	21.8	23.2	24.5
5	13.6	14.7	16.8	18.1	19.3	20.7	22.0	23.4	24.8	26.3
6	14.8	15.9	18.2	19.5	20.8	22.2	23.6	25.0	26.5	28.1
7	16.0	17.2	19.5	20.9	22.3	23.8	25.3	26.8	28.4	30.0
8	17.2	18.5	21.0	22.4	23.9	25.4	27.0	28.6	30.3	32.0
9	18.6	19.9	22.5	24.0	25.6	27.2	28.9	30.6	32.3	34.1
10	20.0	21.4	24.1	25.7	27.4	29.1	30.8	32.6	34.5	36.4
12	23.0	24.6	27.6	29.4	31.2	33.1	35.1	37.1	39.1	41.2
14	26.4	28.2	31.5	33.5	35.5	37.6	39.8	42.0	44.2	46.6
16	30.1	32.1	35.8	38.0	40.3	42.6	45.0	47.4	49.9	52.6
18	34.3	36.5	40.6	43.0	45.5	48.1	50.8	53.5	56.3	59.2
20	38.9	41.3	45.9	48.6	51.4	54.2	57.2	60.2	63.3	66.5

YEARS CONST. GROWTH	19 % YEARS SETTLING GROWTH									
	2	4	6	8	10	12	14	16	18	20
1	9.8	10.7	12.6	13.7	14.9	16.1	17.4	18.7	20.0	21.4
2	10.8	11.8	13.8	15.0	16.2	17.5	18.9	20.2	21.7	23.2
3	11.9	13.0	15.1	16.3	17.7	19.0	20.4	21.9	23.4	25.0
4	13.0	14.2	16.4	17.8	19.2	20.6	22.1	23.7	25.3	27.0
5	14.2	15.4	17.8	19.3	20.8	22.3	23.9	25.5	27.3	29.0
6	15.5	16.8	19.4	20.9	22.4	24.1	25.8	27.5	29.4	31.3
7	16.9	18.3	21.0	22.6	24.3	26.0	27.8	29.7	31.6	33.6
8	18.3	19.8	22.7	24.4	26.2	28.0	29.9	31.9	34.0	36.1
9	19.8	21.4	24.5	26.3	28.2	30.2	32.2	34.3	36.5	38.8
10	21.5	23.2	26.4	28.4	30.4	32.4	34.6	36.8	39.2	41.6
12	25.1	27.0	30.7	32.8	35.1	37.4	39.9	42.4	45.0	47.8
14	29.1	31.3	35.4	37.9	40.4	43.1	45.8	48.7	51.7	54.7
16	33.7	36.1	40.8	43.6	46.5	49.5	52.6	55.8	59.2	62.6
18	38.9	41.6	46.9	50.0	53.3	56.7	60.2	63.8	67.6	71.5
20	44.7	47.8	53.8	57.3	61.0	64.8	68.8	72.9	77.1	81.6

YEARS CONST. GROWTH	20 % YEARS SETTLING GROWTH									
	2	4	6	8	10	12	14	16	18	20
1	9.9	11.0	13.0	14.3	15.6	17.0	18.4	19.9	21.4	23.1
2	11.0	12.1	14.4	15.7	17.1	18.6	20.1	21.7	23.4	25.1
3	12.2	13.4	15.8	17.2	18.7	20.3	21.9	23.6	25.4	27.3
4	13.4	14.7	17.3	18.8	20.4	22.1	23.9	25.7	27.6	29.6
5	14.8	16.2	18.9	20.6	22.3	24.1	26.0	27.9	30.0	32.1
6	16.2	17.7	20.7	22.4	24.3	26.2	28.2	30.3	32.5	34.8
7	17.8	19.4	22.5	24.4	26.4	28.4	30.6	32.9	35.2	37.7
8	19.4	21.2	24.5	26.5	28.7	30.9	33.2	35.6	38.1	40.8
9	21.2	23.1	26.7	28.8	31.1	33.5	35.9	38.5	41.3	44.1
10	23.1	25.1	29.0	31.3	33.7	36.2	38.9	41.7	44.6	47.6
12	27.3	29.6	34.0	36.7	39.5	42.4	45.5	48.7	52.0	55.5
14	32.2	34.8	39.9	42.9	46.1	49.5	53.0	56.7	60.5	64.5
16	37.8	40.8	46.6	50.1	53.8	57.6	61.6	65.8	70.2	74.9
18	44.2	47.6	54.3	58.3	62.5	66.9	71.6	76.4	81.4	86.7
20	51.5	55.4	63.1	67.8	72.6	77.7	83.0	88.5	94.3	100.4

12% Return Tables

YEARS CONST. GROWTH	2	4	6	8	25 % YEARS SETTLING GROWTH 10	12	14	16	18	20
1	10.6	12.1	15.3	17.3	19.5	21.9	24.5	27.4	30.5	33.9
2	12.2	13.9	17.4	19.7	22.1	24.8	27.7	30.9	34.4	38.1
3	13.9	15.9	19.8	22.3	25.0	28.0	31.3	34.8	38.7	42.9
4	15.9	18.0	22.4	25.2	28.3	31.6	35.3	39.2	43.5	48.2
5	18.1	20.5	25.4	28.5	31.9	35.7	39.7	44.1	48.9	54.2
6	20.5	23.2	28.7	32.2	36.0	40.1	44.7	49.6	55.0	60.8
7	23.3	26.2	32.3	36.2	40.5	45.1	50.2	55.7	61.7	68.2
8	26.3	29.6	36.4	40.8	45.5	50.7	56.4	62.5	69.2	76.5
9	29.7	33.4	41.0	45.9	51.2	57.0	63.2	70.1	77.6	85.7
10	33.5	37.6	46.1	51.5	57.5	63.9	70.9	78.6	86.9	96.0
12	42.5	47.6	58.2	64.9	72.3	80.3	89.1	98.6	109.0	120.3
14	53.6	60.0	73.2	81.6	90.8	100.8	111.7	123.6	136.5	150.6
16	67.5	75.5	91.9	102.4	113.8	126.3	139.9	154.6	170.7	188.3
18	84.9	94.8	115.2	128.3	142.5	158.0	174.9	193.4	213.4	235.2
20	106.4	118.8	144.3	160.5	178.2	197.6	218.6	241.6	266.6	293.7

NOTE ON CONSTRUCTION OF TABLES

THE TABLES ARE REPRODUCED from the output of a computer program which measures value by the Present Worth method.

The major difference from other somewhat similar programs is the reduction of the number of necessary assumptions by including the relationship of the dividend payout to the growth of earnings.

As explained in considerable detail in Chapter 3 under the subtitle "The Hypothetical or Normal Dividend," this relationship was estimated by correlating exhaustive data on payout and earnings growth. Thus the tables take into account the varying dividend policies as a corporation's growth rate slows and its need for a rapid buildup in its capital becomes less urgent.

For example, typical theoretical payout ratios for Industrials are as follows:

Earnings Growth Rate	Dividend Payout Ratio
30%	26%
20	36
10	50
4 (assumed infinitum growth rate)	61

Index

Index

Guild, Samuel Eliot, 134, 142, 181–82, 184–85, 187, 189, 191, 198

H

Hahn, Albert, 109 n
Hammond, Bill, 187
Harvard Business Review, 188–89
Harvard Club of New York, 2
Harvard Law School, 3–4
Heard, Stephen, 185
Heilbroner, Robert L., 101 n
Heim, Robert, 4
Helmer, Borden, 190
Hewlett-Packard earnings and earnings trends, 245
Holland shipbuilding production, 154
Homer, Sidney, 88
Houston Lighting & Power earnings and earnings trends, 236
Hultgren, Thor, 205
Hypothetical dividends, 201–3, 206

I

IBM, 161, 176–78
earnings and earnings trends, 246
elimination from Dow-Jones Industrial Average, 28
replacement by American Tel. & Tel., 29
Incorporation laws, 15
Index of Confidence, 124–25
Indexes; see Stock market indexes *or specific type*
Indexes of business activity, stock prices, commodity prices and, 108–9
Indicator Digest, 36
Indicators; see also Stock market indexes
lagging, 107
leading, 108
Industrial revolution, 16, 150
Industrial stock averages, 26–29; see also Dow-Jones Industrial Average (DJIA)
Industrials—stock valuator; see Stock Valuator—Industrials
Inflation, 81–82, 96, 99, 118, 145, 161, 203–4
Inland Steel, 48
"Insider" trading, 108
Inspector General, The, 93
Institute of Chartered Financial Analysts, The, 6
Institutional investments, 150
Institutional investors, 23–24
Interest rates
catalyst between political environment and trends in, 88
compound, 233
cycles in, 87–88
fluctuations in, 106–7
stock prices and, 106–7
Internal Revenue Code, 143

Intl. Nickel of Canada earnings and earnings trends, 246
International trade, comparative advantage principle in, 154
Investment analysis
economic change, significance of, awareness of, 43
skill required for, 43
specialization in, 43
Investment companies, flowering of, 80
Investment laws, changes in, 80
Investment multiplier and fiscal policy, 99–100
Investment return, 186
Investments in industrials—stock valuator; see Stock Valuator—Industrials
Italy
automobile production, 153
shipbuilding production, 154

J

Japan's shipbuilding production, 154
Jefferson, Thomas, 157
Johnson, Lyndon B., 101
Joint stock companies, 12–15
Jones & Laughlin, 48
Journal of Finance, The, 183, 186
Journal of Institute of Actuaries, and Assurance Magazine, 184
Juglar, 111

K

Kahn, R. F., 100
Kennedy, John F., 53–54, 138, 161
Keppel, Frederick Paul, 146
Keran, Michael W., 201 n
Keynes, John Maynard, 46 n, 99–101
Keynesian revolution, 101–2
King, Benjamin F., 116
King, Willford I., 201 n
Kitchin, 111
Knudsen, Semon, 22
Kondratieff, 111
Korean War, 54
Kresge earnings and earnings trends, 247
Kulp, Abe, 146
Kuznets, 102, 111–12

L

Lagging indicators, 107
Larner, Robert J., 18 n
Law of increasing stock values and income return, 104
Laissez-faire, 157–58
Lamont, Thomas, 113
Leading indicators, 108
Least squares method, 136, 197, 202
Levy, Paul, 115
Levy, Robert A., 120

This book has been set in 10 point Electra, leaded 2 points. Part numbers and titles are 24 point Scotch Roman and 24 point Scotch Roman italic. Chapter numbers are 36 point Scotch Roman italic and chapter titles are 18 point Scotch Roman. The size of the type page is 27 by 45½ picas.